A Legend
for the Legendary

A Legend for the Legendary: The Origin of the Baseball Hall of Fame

James A. Vlasich

Bowling Green State University Popular Press
Bowling Green, Ohio 43403

For Grace

Contents

Acknowledgments

Long before this book was even an idea, I began to prepare myself for its writing. After finishing my doctorate, I immersed myself in baseball literature. There was no immediate plan to write something on the national pastime. This was merely a form of relaxation following years of intense study. Most of these books were general overviews of the game's history or personal accounts of individuals who played or fans who followed it for years. Then I read Jules Tygiel's work on Jackie Robinson and realized that it was possible to combine my vocation and my love of baseball. This was no minor discovery for a person who couldn't remember a time when box scores, standings, and batting averages weren't the most important statistics on the planet. Suddenly, there was a professional purpose in my reading.

The next thing to consider was, of course, a topic. Historians need documents. They also need to know what kind of work has already been done in their area of interest. Typically they join organizations whose members focus on a particular area of history. For baseball aficionados, this is the Society for American Baseball Research (SABR) and through their publications and newsletters, I became more familiar with the game's history. Naturally I wanted to attend one of their regional meetings, but most of them were held in the east. The long distance and cost of travel ruled out any attempt on my part to make the journey across the country.

About three years ago, the SABR newsletter contained a short item from Don Cleland concerning a regional meeting in Las Vegas, Nevada. Since this was only a three hour drive across the desert, I immediately phoned him to find out the details of the gathering. He said that he was going to display his grandfather's papers. Next question, who was his grandfather? Alexander Cleland, I was told. At the time, the name didn't mean much to me, but Don went on to explain that his forbearer was the first executive secretary of the Baseball Hall of Fame.

When Alexander Cleland left his position in 1941, he took his papers with him and they hadn't been seen since. They had been stored in Don's father's attic and they were about to be thrown away when Don discovered them. As he perused the collection, he found that they gave an insider's view of the origin of the foremost institution of its kind in the world. This was a researcher's dream come true. Later, I wrote to Don and told him that he should have a professional historian look over the papers. And I knew just the right person for the job. Soon after, he gave me the opportunity to utilize the documents for the purpose of writing something on his grandfather's work in the development of the Hall of Fame.

Don's collection of materials extended beyond his grandfather's papers. He also had some rare books, pamphlets, and scrapbooks of newspaper clippings that his grandmother had collected while her husband worked for the Hall of Fame. A treasure had fallen into my hands. When I was in graduate school, I used to hear about situations like this, but I never thought that I could be this fortunate. Don Cleland had fulfilled my dream and I shall always be thankful for the opportunity and friendship that he provided.

It didn't take me long to realize that this was an important story. Very little had been written about Mr. Cleland or the origin of baseball's valhalla. In order to complete my research, a trip to Cooperstown was necessary. In the army, we used to call this good duty. I had always wanted to go there but never had the chance. Now a professional obligation became my excuse or at least that's what I told my friends.

My first action was to contact the Hall of Fame library concerning my visit. What kind of facilities did they have? Did they have any more information that was pertinent to my investigation? I was fortunate to be talking with Tom Heitz. Not only did the hall's librarian have the answers, but he was also of great service to me in furthering my research. Competent, intelligent, and friendly, Tom also understood the historical process. He and his assistant Bill Deane accommodated me in every way possible. Over the next three years, a cross-country friendship developed. I am very thankful for their assistance and comradery.

In the process of learning my craft, I discovered very early that one can't write in a vacuum. Criticism from a colleague can provide some important guidelines. I turned to two former teachers who had remained friends through the years. One was a history professor and fanatical Cub fan. When I took classes from him at Fort Lewis College in Durango, Colorado, I found out that Duane Smith and I had some things in common—the love of the American west and the national pastime. He was just the right person to read my manuscript and I appreciate his suggestions and encouragement. Ken Periman, an English professor, had co-taught a class with Duane that I took as an undergraduate. Ken knew that a big job awaited him, but without complaint, he plunged into the project. He did a yeoman's job in regards to offering criticism of my writing. Both of these men proved to me that the educational process continues long after the class is over. Thanks guys.

Finally, I should recognize my most important support base—my family. My parents, Hank and Emma Vlasich, have given me every means of support in pursuing my career. Without their unwavering encouragement through the years, this book wouldn't even be an idea. My two daughters, Brooke Thieu and Ming Lyn (who were named after my favorite team, the Brooklyn Dodgers), were good girls while dad baby-sat them and wrote this book. My wife Grace decided a long time ago that she wasn't going to be a baseball widow. While she isn't on the fanatical finge, like her husband, she appreciates the nuances of the game and never balks about driving 500 miles to see a meaningless spring training contest. She may not enjoy it as much as I do, but she knows how important it is to me. Moreover, she dutifully typed this manuscript and comforted me during the low points of the project. Nobody could ask for more.

To all of the above-mentioned people, I give my heartfelt gratitude. They represent something that I shall treasure for the rest of my life. Because of their assistance, I was able to give back something to the game that has given so much to me.

Preface

Anyone delving into the history of major league baseball must perforce chip away at the various myths and legends that cling to the game and its principals with all the tenacity of barnacles on a frigate's bottom. Among the oldest and most encrusted of such myths is the myth that baseball is our "national game," or that professional baseball began in 1869 with the all conquering Cincinnati Red Stockings, or that major league baseball began with the 1876 National League coup, or that enlightened National League owners attained competitive balance in that circuit by invoking the reserve clause in 1879.

Other myths of more recent derivation include the myth of baseball's single sin and the accompanying myth of the purifying presence of Judge K.M. Landis which saved the game in the wake of the besmirching Black Sox Scandal of 1919.

More recently there is the myth that all records of seasonal performances and individual achievements can be unified in the light of present day standards of record keeping. This wrongheaded myth has been spawned by recent statisticians whose sense of logic runs roughshod over the most basic rules of historical objectivity. For such excesses one can only rebuke these modern figure filberts by invoking Emerson's dictum that "A foolish consistency is the hobgoblin of little minds."

Given the many myths that cling to the major league game it is understandable that baseball historians should indulge in free wheeling myth smashing. But all historians need to be reminded that this is a losing battle. For myths are not lies, but rather they are necessary attempts to interpret reality. As Rafael Patai reminds us, "To say myth equals falsehood...*ergo* myth must be combatted" disregards the salient fact that myths are basic needs of man. Indeed, scholars also play the role of mythmakers and their best efforts only replace unwieldy myths with better fitting successors.

Moreover, some myths are so firmly entrenched as to defy displacement. Such is the case with the great canonical tale of baseball that tells of Abner Doubleday inventing the game at Cooperstown, New York in 1839. An enduring myth it dates back only to 1907, yet such was its power that it inspired the construction of the Baseball Hall of Fame complex at Cooperstown, a shrine that has attracted more than 7 million baseball-worshipping pilgrims since its opening in 1939.

Just how this "immaculate conception" myth ran a gauntlet of critical attackers to gain acceptance and was used to promote the construction of the Cooperstown shrine complex is a suspense story in the history of ideas. And it is told in its fascinating details by James A. Vlasich. With admirable objectivity Vlasich relates how the Mills Commission, spurred on by the powerful

1

2   A Legend for the Legendary

manipulator Albert G. Spalding, hatched the myth which later inspired the canny publicist Alexander Cleland's dogged effort to build the Cooperstown shrine.

Uncovering Cleland's decisive role in the building of the baseball mecca was a major coup for Vlasich. A chance encounter with Cleland's grandson at a meeting of the Society for American Baseball Research enabled Vlasich to obtain and utilize the voluminous correspondence and files that the elder Cleland took with him when he retired from his Cooperstown post in 1941. The records show how Cleland, supported by his millionaire friend Stephen Clark, masterminded the Cooperstown Hall of Fame project from a forlorn hope in 1934 until its completion in 1939. A brilliant promoter, Cleland pushed the idea of electing star players to the Hall of Fame, cajoled collectors of baseball artifacts into donating them to the shrine, and obtained funds to build a museum to house such fetishes.

Bringing it all together was no easy task, but Cleland used the seductive Doubleday myth to full advantage, enlisting sportwriters, baseball notables, and even President Roosevelt to rally the people to the cause. And in a triumph of promotional orchestration the Cooperstown complex opened in 1939 as part of a simultaneous nationwide celebration of baseball's centennial birthday.

This is a fine account of how the power of a myth can be used to shape popular notions of reality. Carping historians might begrudge the outcome, but Vlasich opts for the morale boosting functions of the 1939 triumph of the mythical baseball birthday celebrations for a nation still reeling from the Depression's impact and so soon to be confronted by total war. Certainly the "national game" was boosted by all the hoopla. Thus, it could be argued that the Doubleday myth, like the myth about George Washington and the cherry tree, should be viewed as a "saving myth" rather than as an affront to the muse of history.

David Q. Voigt

Introduction

Sports have held a unique position in the development of the American nation. No modern country so deifies its athletes. Their actions on and off the playing areas hold a special fascination for the vast majority of people. In the modern era, the proliferation of sporting events and their associated heroes overwhelms the cultural scene. Television is, of course, the major reason why so many people in the United States have become aware of the wide array of athletic activity. Before its invention, however, one game in particular captured the fancy of the sports-minded public and became known as the national pastime. In fact, the game of baseball is recognized by outsiders as the sporting activity that is inherently American. That perception can only lead one to conclude that it must have been invented in this country. To deem otherwise would seem incongruous. But when, where, and (most importantly) by whom was baseball invented? Was it really created by a particular individual in this country or did it merely evolve from other games that came from foreign nations?

The first official attempt to answer these questions resulted from a friendly debate between two men who were intimately involved in 19th century baseball— Henry Chadwick and Albert G. Spalding. Their disagreement was baseball's version of the Scopes monkey trial. Spalding represented William Jennings Bryan and Chadwick took the role of Clarence Darrow. In this classic contest between evolutionists and creationists, Spalding was the protagonist. Rather than allowing Chadwick to express his opinion, that baseball derived from rounders, the sportings good magnate saw an opportunity to enhance his revenue and reputation at the same time. As the editor of the *Spalding Base Ball Guide*, Chadwick had used the yearly publication as his forum. Spalding felt that by keeping the argument alive in his own magazine, he could reap the financial benefits. His method of solving the origin question was a typically American one—form a committee. To an outsider, this may have seemed a bit risky. What if the group thought that Chadwick was correct after all? Wouldn't Spalding look a little silly if his own publication disagreed with him? As usual, Spalding was in control. He was much more active in the decision-making process than anyone on the committee.

On paper the Mills Commission certainly appeared to be authoritative. If they had taken their work more seriously, Abner Doubleday might only have been recognized as a Union general during the Civil War. But Spalding couldn't let that happen and neither could Abner Graves—who claimed that Doubleday invented the national pastime. If the Mills Commission had done their work properly, the Colorado mining engineer's testimony should have been scrutinized. But of course they didn't, and Spalding had his way. Like other Robber Barons, he determined the course of events in his own business.

3

4   A Legend for the Legendary

At the time, few people dreamed that the findings of the Mills Commission would be taken seriously by future generations. However, Graves had not only stated that Doubleday invented baseball; he also claimed that Cooperstown was the place where he did it. Graves couldn't remember the exact year, but that was no problem. Spalding could supply that. With the foundation poured, it was now possible to build on it. But what would the structure be and what purpose would it have?

Enter Alexander Cleland—a Scottish immigrant. He proposed a museum in the small village in upstate New York. More importantly, he also suggested a shrine for the greatest stars of the game. Ford Frick enhanced this concept, and Stephen Clark, Cleland's boss, gave it his blessing and financial support. The result was the Baseball Hall of Fame. Gradually, this organization came to symbolize the highest achievement of the game. Every fan recognizes the connection between greatness in the sport and enshrinement in Cooperstown. Few people, however, have questioned the conclusions of the committee that was set up to trace baseball's origins.

As a youngster growing up in Gillespie, Illinois, in the 1950s, I had no doubt about Doubleday. I also had a source of information to support this conclusion. In an age when only the most important games of the season came into our living room via television, baseball cards supplied the images of our favorite players. Like most youngsters who grew up loving the game, I collected shoe boxes full of them. But the pictures on the front were only half of the story. By turning them over, one could find a wealth of statistical information on each player's card.

I remember that some of the cards also contained questions and answers about baseball history. Typically, the question appeared at the top and the answer was written upside-down at the bottom. In between was a caricature of a situation that was connected with the question. One of the cards dealt with the origin of the game. Who invented baseball, it queried? Turning it over, one could find that it was Abner Doubleday, in Cooperstown, in 1839. As I recall, the drawing in the middle was one of an old-time ball player with a very large moustache. How could I possibly doubt the Doubleday story?

Of course, the idea of doubting it never crossed my mind. At the time, however, I didn't realize that some writers had already cast doubt on the Mills Commission report. Through the years, the claims against Doubleday grew louder. What was once the official story of the beginning of the national pastime gradually became the Doubleday myth. The problem was that Baseball Hall of Fame had been built on this rather shaky foundation. The lack of diligence on the part of Spalding's self-appointed committee had led to a credibility gap for the baseball shrine that continues a half century after its dedication.

Chapter One
The Old Ball Game

Tracing the origin of baseball is risky business. How far back does one go? What exactly constitutes the starting point? Activities involving the striking of a ball-shaped object with some form of stick have been known to be performed by numerous pre-historic civilizations. Ancient Egyptian temples contain drawings of human beings involved in some kind of ball game. Writing for the Egypt Exploration Fund in 1901, H. Edward Naville described a ball game as it was pictured on the wall of a shrine dating back 3,500 years.[1] Indeed, the British Museum in London contains a leather ball from the Nile region that dates back more than 4000 years.

Perhaps the most widely respected authority on the origin of ball games was Robert W. Henderson, who formerly served as the head of the main reading room at the New York Public Library. He spent 35 years researching sports and produced various articles and books on the subject. He concluded that many of these games were derivatives of religious ceremonies. Gradually these activities, he thinks, emerged in Europe in the ninth century and parts of these games eventually became formalized in Christian religious services. As these contests grew more popular, rules were drawn up to govern the proceedings.[2]

Although the Americans were cut off from European experiences in the pre-Columbian era, bat and ball games were a part of the life of its ancient dwellers. Indian societies on both North and South American continents conducted games which became part of their lifestyles. Such was the case of Iroquois-speaking people in the northeastern part of the United States who occupied a camp near Otsego Lake in upstate New York.[3] Although no evidence has been unearthed to verify the playing of Indian ball games in the region, it is not difficult to imagine their existence. Numerous artifacts have been found along the lake's shore indicating that native people of the area utilized it as a fishing and hunting resort. This may have allowed for leisure activities such as ball playing. By the time that the adjacent village of Cooperstown was founded by William Cooper in 1785, a form of the game that would eventually link the village with historic significance may have already been performed there.

In spite of the precedent that may have been set by Mohawks and other Indians of the region, there is no direct link between modern baseball and ancient native games. However, by 1684 the local Iroquois were allied with a country whose citizens would formalize games quite similar to the American national pastime. The English initiated a variety of stick and ball games, some of which were brought to America during the colonial era. Types of these games were played in both Jamestown and the Massachusetts Bay Colony.[4]

One of the games brought over by English colonists to America involved variations on the theme "old-cat" which was borrowed from another game called "tip-cat." The number of players and bases varied. For example, "one-old-cat" involved a batter, pitcher, and two bases. The idea was to hit the ball and run from one base to the other and back. An out was made by catching the ball on a fly or first bounce, or by hitting a runner with the ball as he advanced between the bases. In such a case, the players involved switched positions. This contest also allowed for more players. "Two-old-cat" required four players; "three-old-cat" necessitated six players. As the number of players increased, so did the number of bases.

Another British game called rounders accommodated more players. Sides were chosen and the defensive players simply scattered around the playing area which contained four bases. In addition to the "old-cat" rules, a batter was also out if he missed three pitches or hit a foul ball. In America, rounders became known as town ball; it became popular in the colonies because it was played at town meetings. The rules were not officially established and thus varied from one community to another. Town ball, as it evolved in America, was played on fields of different shape; but it was, in effect, a derivation of the English game of rounders.[5]

Variations of town ball in America included the Massachusetts Game which was played on a square field; the batter stood between the first and fourth base. This contest was eventually overshadowed by the New York Game. The latter was started by Alexander Cartwright and other teammates around 1835 and employed the shape of a diamond field. By 1845 bases were set at forty-five feet apart. His team, the New York Knickerbockers, attracted a large following and started a long-standing tradition of New Yorkers besting their neighboring states in bat and ball games.[6] This evolutionary trend of building one game on another is not without precedent. Rounders may have evolved from the medieval game of stool-ball which was described by Joseph Strutt in 1801. Here, stools were used for bases and the batter was required to strike a ball with his hand before it hit the home stool. Runners could advance from one stool to the next each time the ball was hit. The fielders could hit the runners with the ball as they advanced between the stools and take the place of the runner they struck.

The variety of the names of bat and ball games was virtually endless. Whether it was known as town ball, rounders, old cat, poisoned ball, round ball or even base-ball, the rules were similar. (In 1744 the term "base-ball" first appeared in print in a London publication). Often these likenesses were due to plagiarism. In an age when pirating another's material was not uncommon, the first known description of "Base, or Goal Ball," printed in the United States in 1834, was almost an exact copy of the rules that governed rounders. William Clarke's book, *The Boys Own Book*, appeared in London five years before Robin Carver's *The Book of Sport* was published in Boston, and yet the descriptions are almost exactly word-for-word. (Not surprisingly, Clarke pointed out that rounders was very similar to another English game called feeder.) Henderson first discovered the similarities between these two manuscripts, and the importance of his findings was the documented link between games called baseball and rounders.[7]

In spite of this evolutionary evidence, the early American creation of the modern national game received country-wide support. After all, the game of base ball wasn't exactly baseball. Also few people were aware of any documentary connection which supported the evolutionary theory. The bitterness that had been created by two wars between England and the United States in the late eighteenth and early nineteenth centuries did little to create a British foundation for an American pastime that was palatable to observers in this country. However, evolution as a cause would not go away, and it would be proclaimed by Henry Chadwick, one of the foremost authorities on baseball in the United States. This claim would add insult to injury for fans throughout the country, including the nation's leading promoter of its national pastime.

Albert Goodwill Spalding's life was inextricably interwoven with the early development of baseball in America. Throughout the latter half of the nineteenth century, he utilized various aspects of the game as stepping stones to sports hierarchy. Originally a pitcher and the first major star of the game, Spalding advanced to become manager and owner of the Chicago White Stockings, co-founder of the National League, and the originator of a major sporting goods firm that gained him wealth, notoriety, and influence. Always the entrepreneur, Spalding realized that wealth through sport could only be gained by changing American attitudes towards leisure.

His obstacles in this endeavor were formidable. Imbued with the work ethics of industrial capitalism, the vast majority of Americans accepted the "quasi-religious" value system commonly known as the Protestant work ethic. Linking financial and heavenly rewards with dedication on the job, the concept associated play and recreation with idleness and laziness. Hard work, on the other hand, would reap for the dedicated person all the benefits of life and after-life. Initiated in the early colonial period, this concept had a dramatic impact on the American nation.

Ironically, what resulted from applying this practice was an urban-industrial society that produced the time for leisure through the application of ingenuity, and the need for pleasure to counterbalance the stress produced by vast changes in American society following the Civil War. This paradox was not lost on Spalding, who sought to promote the benefits of sport in terms of social purpose with the hope that the acceptance of this new attitude would reap him financial gain. He was fortunate that his promotional idea paralleled changing American values that were moving away from rural, religious, and Victorian influences and toward rational, scientific, and worldly ones.[8] With the American frontier closing, a new safety valve was needed to vent frustrations of an increasingly complex society and Spalding was at the cutting edge of exploiting this need for profit.

In 1876 Spalding initiated (or helped to initiate) three different institutions connected with baseball that would help to promote his financial betterment. During the centennial year, he aided the founding of the National League and initiated the A. G. Spalding and Brothers sporting goods business. In addition, he requested and received exclusive rights from league officials to publish the official book of the newly formed organization. Utilizing the privilege to promote his business and profit from the sales of the magazine, Spalding added an annual supplement entitled *Spalding's Official Base Ball Guide*. Although it was not an official league publication, he promoted it as such until 1882 when the new league president, A. G. Mills, threatened his publication rights for the book if he continued the practice.

The league's book was not too informative, containing only its rules and constitution. The guide supplement, however, had a wealth of baseball information on the preceding season's activities, individual and club records, instructions on playing the game, and editorials on baseball's development. Gradually, the guide came to be the baseball bible for most American sports fans; and by 1884 some 50,000 copies were being sold, complete with paid advertisements from other baseball related businesses.[9]

Beginning in 1881, Henry Chadwick became the editor of the annual guide. No novice to the writing profession, he had been a pioneer sports writer following his migration to America from England. Through his coverage of games, his compilation of vast statistics and his creation of the box score, he welded baseball to American traditions. Utilizing newspaper coverage, he helped to increase the game's popularity throughout the country. Indeed Chadwick's work had gained him national recognition as the "Father of Baseball." The title was not unearned, for by the time of his death in 1908 at the age of 84 he had devoted fifty years of his life to baseball literature.[10]

Through all of his professional activities, Chadwick became a close personal friend of A. G. Spalding; and this relationship was not based solely on his job as editor of the *Guide*. In 1867 Spalding pitched the Forest City club of Rockford, Illinois, to a victory over the highly regarded Washington Nationals. Chadwick credited the young pitcher's ability for the capitol city team's only loss. In 1876 Chadwick paid A. G. the kind of praise that was uncommon for baseball players at the time. Disdained as a collective group of nere-do-wells by Victorian society, they were generally frowned on. Chadwick, however, praised Spalding as a sober, intelligent, and honorable person who conducted himself in a righteous manner both on and off the field. When A. G. led a global tour of professional players in 1888-89, Chadwick regarded the effort as an unparalleled event in sports history. Spalding realized that those complements were coming from a highly respected source and never challenged his opinions in those early days. Even when Chadwick stated in his first year as editor of the *Guide* that baseball originated from rounders, Spalding acquiesced. His agreement was not surprising since an earlier addition of the *Guide* made the same claim.[11]

However, what Spalding found agreeable then was not something he would concur with about a quarter of a century later. The *Spalding Guide* of 1903 contained an article that would have a dramatic impact on events that would unfold over the next 36 years. The *Guide's* preface promised that the edition's most "readable" chapters contained a history of baseball from its inception to the present. It was more than a history, for Chadwick praised the game as the "sport of sports for Americans, alike for men as for boys." He saw the game as significant in raising the consciousness of Americans concerning the social value of sport and recognized that its popularity was not induced by gambling activities as racing had.

More importantly, Chadwick chose to recognize the seventieth birthday of the game as he saw it. He set the date and place according to available records: The first organized "baseball" club originated in 1833 in Philadelphia where the Olympic Town Ball Club was formed. Although the game that they played was not baseball, Chadwick linked the group with the game's development because theirs was the first organized effort of a sport that he felt evolved into the modern game. To Chadwick the evolutionary process was quite simple: Town ball was an Americanized version of the old English game of rounders which dated back to the seventeenth century, and baseball was town ball with American modifications. Town ball, then known as the Massachusetts game, had been played in New England for at least a decade before it was adopted in Philadelphia. Baseball, which came into its own in the 1850s, was known as the New York game; but it originally contained certain aspects peculiar to his predecessors. All three games were played with a bat and ball and required a four-sided field with a base at each corner. In addition, a runner was out if he was struck by a thrown ball and this rule even applied to baseball until the National Base Ball Association was formed in 1858.

Chadwick's conviction on the matter was rigid. He stated unequivocally that "there is no doubt whatever as to baseball having originated from the two-centuries-old English game of rounders." However, the famous sports writer was not really denying that baseball was an American game. Instead, he was simply emphasizing its British origin. Recognizing that only Native American games were of purely North American derivation, Chadwick claimed that the ancient Indian game of lacrosse was the only sport known by the contemporary populace that originated on this continent. Baseball, he felt, couldn't have come from this practice because the only thing they had in common was the use of a bat and ball.

The organization of the American game of baseball, as Chadwick saw it, was the formation of the National Association of Base Ball players in 1858. Resisting the urge to cite the Knickerbocker club of New York as the innovators, he noted that on March 10th of that year, "the first regular printed code of playing rules of the game was adopted by a base ball association." The New York club had played under their own rules whereas the new Association adopted the laws of a "regularly appointed" national committee. His feeling was that the national game could only adopt that title after it conformed to standardized rules. Although he agreed that the original code had been altered in many ways to fit the contemporary game, he felt that the codification was a bench-mark in the organization and professionalization of the national pastime.[12]

When Chadwick first stated similar contentions about a quarter of a century earlier, Spalding was a young business man in his late twenties who was more concerned with promoting sport than documenting its origin. The contentions of a man in his mid-fifties who was nationally recognized as the country's leading authority on baseball were not to be questioned. However, by the turn of the century Spalding had surpassed his long-time friend in national recognition. Now, his word carried more weight and he chose to exercise it in a debate on the game's origin.

His arguments were not an attack on Chadwick's character or his national origin. His editor was no Anglophile; he merely stated his evolutionary case based on documentation and observation. Chadwick had witnessed the game of rounders in England as a youth and saw all three games played in America as a young man. Also, A. G.'s relationship with his old friend was not challenged by this academic debate. Indeed, Chadwick bequeathed his entire baseball library to Spalding following his death, with the hope that he would write a history on the subject.

Spalding rejected his editor's evolutionary theory and adopted the creation or immaculate conception theme instead. Spalding's reasons for contention were two-fold. First, A. G. had promoted baseball for years on the basis of its contributions to national character. He had long ago adopted the ideology that the game encouraged competition and fair play and that these attributes fit well into the national plan of democracy and capitalism. (Evidently Spalding saw no conflict with the heavyhanded methods of the Robber Barons of this age, probably because he fit well into their mold). If, in fact, baseball was at least partially responsible for developing traditional American characteristics, then the game must be a purely national concept.

It should be remembered that Spalding was making his pronouncements at a time when America was growing as an industrial force and an imperialistic power. Manifest destiny was expanding overseas, and the country's role as an international leader coalesced with the growing rise of nationalism. To deny the native roots of America's foremost game was equivalent in the minds of many to ideological blasphemy. Secondly, Spalding realized the promotional possibilities of encouraging a nationwide publicized debate. Whether Americans would agree with him or not, his notoriety and wealth could only be enhanced in a nationally publicized argument.[13]

In 1905 Spalding presented his retort to Chadwick's argument. Utilizing his annual guide as a national platform for the debate, he challenged his editor's remarks. He contended that the current year marked the 60th anniversary of the game which initiated with the Knickerbockers. A. G. felt that the original members of that team "should be honored and remembered as the founders of our national game." To attribute the development of one country's game to a foreign power would injure national pride. Wouldn't other nations be offended if someone said that their national sports had actually originated in another land? Given the anti-British feelings in the early nineteenth century, would America adopt a game from its former colonial ruler so willingly? If baseball evolved from any game, Spalding concluded, it was the colonial one known as old cat.

Not satisfied with his formal proclamation, Spalding decided to establish a self-appointed committee to verify or renounce his convictions. They would, he promised, collect all of the evidence they could in order to come to an impartial conclusion concerning the origin of baseball. Spalding felt sure that their definitive decision would "be accepted by everyone as final and conclusive." The committee chairman was Abraham G. Mills of New York, a former ball player during the Civil War era, president of the National League (1882-84), lawyer, and current vice-president of the Otis Elevator Company. Mills was hardly an unbiased judge since he had publicly supported the American origin theory of baseball in 1889. Another veteran ball player who had also served as league president following Mills, Nicholas E. Young of Washington, D. C., was added. Two U. S. senators, Arthur P. Gorman of Maryland and Morgan G. Bulkeley of Connecticut (the National League's first president), also became committee members, but Gorman died before its findings were published. James E. Sullivan of New York, president of the Amateur Athletic Union, served as the commission's secretary. Rounding out the group were two former ball players turned business men. Alfred J. Reach, a former member of the Athletics and rival of Spalding in the sporting goods business who had become the head of the Philadelphia ball club, and George Wright of Boston, another competitor of Spalding, were selected.[14]

As formidable as this group looked on paper, their actual work on the project was minimal. Perhaps they were as unconcerned with the friendly argument as were most Americans of the time. Maybe they were simply too involved with their individual pursuits to dedicate themselves to a project that didn't appear to have much merit. Certainly there was work to do. Spalding had invited anyone in the country who had information on baseball's origin to send it in to the commission for evaluation, and Sullivan received hundreds of pages of testimony, most of which contained un-based folklore. While other members apparently just lent their names to the commission, Mills weighed much of the evidence. In December, 1907, he complained that while Sullivan had been collecting the data for two and a half years, he had not issued it to other members until the previous fall, at which time Mills was in Europe.

Mills' task was made lighter by Spalding, who passed him some material in July, 1907, with a cover note requesting the chairman to give "special attention" to its contents. The information concerned one Abner Doubleday, a former general in the United States Army. He was no stranger to Mills, who was a fellow member in the same New York veterans' organization. So close was their relationship that Mills served on Doubleday's funeral honor guard in 1893. The material on Doubleday was written by Abner Graves, a former resident of Cooperstown, New York, and retired mining engineer from Denver, Colorado.

On April 3, 1905, Graves had written Spalding claiming that Doubleday had invented the modern game of baseball in Cooperstown. As boyhood friends in the village, they were active participants in the game of town ball, but Graves stated that Doubleday made improvements to the old game. First, he limited the number of players on a side to avoid collisions in the field. He called the game baseball because it utilized four bases, three of which runners could use a free zone and therefore could not be put out. A runner could tally a score if he could touch home base before being hit by the ball. Doubleday also designed a six-foot ring for the pitcher to stand in while he pitched under-handed to the batter. Besides the pitcher and catcher, who was stationed behind home plate, he also placed two infielders between the other three bases. Graves described the ball as having a rubber center wound with yarn so that it grew to a "size some larger than the present regulation ball." The ball was then covered with "leather or buckskin" which resulted in "wonderful high flies."

The following November 17th he wrote again, apparently answering questions posed by Spalding, who wanted to know the exact year of Doubleday's invention. Graves said he wasn't exactly sure but thought that "it was either 1839, 1840, or 1841 and in the spring of the year." As he recalled the incident, he remembered Doubleday explaining the game to a number of youths who were playing marbles in front of a local tailor shop. He said that Doubleday drew a "diamond" in the dirt and marked the position of the bases and the players with a series of punch marks. Graves lamented that there was no way of documenting this event because nobody thought to preserve baseball memorabilia at that time.

In another letter Graves gave more detail on Doubleday and the locations where they played the game. Acknowledging that he was several years younger than Doubleday, who was about twenty years old when the alleged incident took place, Graves stated that they were attending different schools in the area at that time. In terms of where the first game was actually played, he couldn't recall and felt that it was not "possible for anyone to know, on what spot the first game of Base Ball was played according to Doubleday's plan." Since the alleged creator encouraged boys from around the area to play the game, it was conducted on a number of places in the vicinity of Cooperstown. He cited three specific locations of the games including an "old militia muster lot, or training ground, a couple of hundred yards southeasterly from the Court House, where County Fairs were occasionally held." This location was identified by Ralph Birdsall, author of a book on Cooperstown in 1917 and local rector of Christ Church, as an area opposite the Village Hall "which extended east and south to the rear of the buildings on Main Street, and included part of the Phinney lot." The other locations he cited were that of the Otsego Academy (later the clergy house of St. Mary's Church) and the grounds of the Country Club.[15]

Although the Phinney lot was only part of one area where Graves claimed the game was played, its role in the village's history would be more significant than the others. Beginning with the writings of James Fenimore Cooper, son of the community's founder, a tradition of literature became associated with Cooperstown. Elihu Phinney, who owned the property, started a publishing house there in 1795 and began to produce "The Phinney Almanac" for the reading public to consume. His firm published voluminous works including almanacs, Bibles, and assorted reading materials and outfitted wagons as traveling bookstores to spread the written word to outlying farms and villages. Following the construction of the Erie Canal, Elihu ran floating bookstores between Albany and Buffalo. All of this activity helped to establish the village as a cultural center in the region.[16]

There was but one brief attempt by Mills to corroborate the claims of Abner Graves. Attempting to link Doubleday with the famous Knickerbocker club of New York that he had heretofore connected with baseball's beginnings, Mills wrote to the city's customs collector, Colonel Edward Fowler, on December 20th, 1907. He wondered whether a former employee, a Mr. Wadsworth, had been raised in Cooperstown about the same time as Doubleday. Mills' interest stemmed from a statement by a Mr. Curry of the original Knickerbockers and confirmed by a Mr. Tassie of the old Brooklyn Athletic club that Wadsworth had brought a diagram "showing the ballfield laid out substantially as it is today" to the New Yorker's playing field in 1845. If this drawing was originated by Doubleday, a connecting link could be established between his game plan and the one played by the first professional team. Proving this conjecture would definitely establish the former general as baseball's originator. However, Mills never waited for a reply. He promised to relay any significant data concerning Wadsworth, but no proof of the connection ever surfaced.[17]

The arguments of Chadwick and Spalding and the final findings of the committee were published in the *Guide* of 1908. Chadwick's letter, dated August 1, 1907, contained facts that he thought were "incontrovertible." He felt that the argument centered first around "the use of a ball, a bat, and of bases, in the playing of the game of ball" and secondly around the date "when this self-same basic principle was carried into practical effect on the field of play." He stated quite clearly "on behalf of my English clients that the established American national game of Base Ball had for its origin the old English school-boy game of 'Rounders'." Some people in England at the time believed that cricket came from the same old game. Chadwick noted the similarities between rounders and baseball including two opposing sides, a special playing field, the use of a pitcher and batter and a common way of making points and winning the game. He brushed aside the deviations in the exact methods of play because "that matter in no way affects the question of the origin of the American game of Base Ball." Countering Spalding's claim that the game came from the colonial one of old cat, Chadwick felt that the Canadian and Indian game of lacrosse and the British one of cricket were the only types of ball games that were played in America during the revolutionary period.

Spalding's arguments, which were much more extensive, were written on July 28, 1907. He not only claimed that baseball was of American origin but unequivocally stated that it "has no relation to or connection with any game of any other country, except in so far as all games of ball have a certain similarity and family relationship." The very heart of the controversy lay in this statement because one side believed that any game of a slightly similar nature served as a baseball beginning, while the other side looked for the origin of the game as played by the modern rules. The word evolution implied gradual development while birth signified a suddenness of action, and around this different connotation lay the argument.

While Spalding felt that "the beginning of Base Ball is more or less shrouded in mystery," the committee had received enough evidence to "convince the most skeptical that Base Ball is entirely of American origin, and had its birth and evolution in the United States." Evidently the baseball magnate felt that evolution took place after birth and not before. Emphasizing the correlation between the country's "characteristics and temperament" and that of baseball, Spalding expressed his firm belief that baseball was "of purely American origin, and no other game or country has any right to claim its parentage."

Spalding cited his own experiences as additional proof of the American origin theory. A. G. had led a barn storming group of all-star baseball players on a world-wide tour in 1888-89. During their trip, people of various countries claimed some similarities between local games and that of baseball, but the Americans disagreed. Whenever they requested a rule book of the foreign games, none could be provided. The American party particularly resented the parallels that British observers around the world had drawn with rounders. When the Americans arrived in England, they challenged any club in the country to a game of rounders. The contest which resulted involved a game with the Champion Rounders Club and only served to confirm Spalding's American origin belief.

A book of rules for each game was exchanged and A. G.'s comparison "revealed very little similarity between the two games." The field for rounders was square (not diamond shaped) with the corners some 50 to 60 feet apart (not 90 feet) and marked by three foot high sticks with flags on the top (instead of bases). Rounders required eleven men and two innings constituted a game, and all players had to be retired to end a frame. Those differences indicated to Spalding that rounders had a closer affiliation with cricket than it did with baseball. The ball for rounders was much smaller than a baseball and (although the cricket ball was about the same size and weight) the latter was constructed differently. The bats for the English games were flat and both contests had a similar method of counting a tally that involved a run scored for every base the runner touched. Spalding concluded that not only was cricket more like rounders than baseball, but also that "any comparison with Rounders only tends to belittle both games." In this manner he could tout the American game without creating an affront to the British character.

Recognizing his long-time friendship with Chadwick and the contributions that the famous sports writer had made to baseball in its early struggling days, Spalding confessed a reluctance to disagree with him on any subject concerning the game. However, he felt that his editor had been mainly responsible for promulgating the unsubstantiated notion of the rounder's origin for forty years, and Spalding's "American birth and love of the game" wouldn't let this "absurd" claim go unchallenged. Continuing this emphasis on nationalism, A. G. claimed that if Chadwick had been born in the United States, he wouldn't have any more knowledge of rounders than an American fan. The implication was that if Chadwick hadn't come from England, he might never had made the rounders claim in the first place. Spalding felt that before he came to America at the age of ten (he was actually in his mid-twenties), Chadwick may have seen or played rounders, but A. G. could not recall that he had claimed to have done the same after his arrival. More importantly, Spalding had never "seen or heard of his producing any convincing proof in support of his contention." Also he wouldn't accept the rounders theory "until more satisfactory evidence" was produced and accepted by the Mills' commission.

Spalding had good reason for disclaiming Chadwick's participation in rounders after his arrival in the United States. The game had changed quite a bit since baseball began, and it was obvious to A. G. that its modern version had "appropriated bodily many of the Base Ball rules." Perhaps Spalding felt the sports writer was too young when he left England to remember the ancient rounders game and never realized how its modern derivative had come to copy baseball. It was understandable to Spalding how observers could see the similarities of the modern version of both games. However, he felt that any likeness shared by ancient rounders and early baseball as evidence of evolution was "a coincidence and not...an established fact." He emphasized his belief that no evidence had been uncovered even to prove that rounders was ever played in the United States, and this lack of proof confirmed his belief in the American origin of baseball.

Recognizing that the evidence that had so far reached the Mills Committee was inconclusive, Spalding still felt that it was substantial enough to conclude "that Base Ball is of American origin and in no way connected with Rounders or any game of any other country." To prove this rather grandiose claim, he noted that America would have never adopted a British game at a time so shortly removed from the American revolution and the War of 1812. Nationalism aside, he began to trace the American origin of baseball in order to assure the commission that his contentions were bonafide. According to his "rather exhaustive research," baseball came from the colonial game of old cat which corresponded with "the present day so-called 'Scrub Games' of Base Ball." At some unspecified date, the game of town ball evolved from old cat in order to accommodate more players. Even after baseball "was established by the Knickerbocker Club in 1845," Americans continued to play town ball. Here, Spalding was confusing his own arguments because he was implying an evolutionary process. For him there was no contradiction because his emphasis was still the American origin-evolutionary or not.

To further his contentions, Spalding quoted his life-long friend, Hiram H. Waldo of Rockford, Illinois, who was the president of the first baseball club for which A. G. had played in 1865. Waldo said he had come west in 1846 and recognized the popularity of town ball at that time. He always regarded baseball as a modification of that game. Waldo had never heard of rounders and felt that "We had too much national pride in those days to adopt anything that was English in our sporting life."

Spalding pointed out that, without any printed rules, the playing of town ball varied from one place to another and even the name of the game was different in various parts of the country. New Englanders adopted the title of round ball, but Spalding was "unable to find any evidence where it was ever called 'Rounders'." In the early 1850s they changed the name of town ball to the "Massachusetts game of Base Ball" which was different from the "New York game of Base Ball" that was really American baseball. While other games died out in the early 1860s, the New York one became "thoroughly nationalized, and at present is the only game of 'Base Ball' now played anywhere in the world."

Next, Spalding called the committee's attention to the letters that he had received from Abner Graves who claimed that Doubleday originated the game in Cooperstown "during the Harrison Presidential campaign of 1839." A. G. pointed out that the date of origin claimed by the Colorado mining engineer preceded the organization of the Knickerbockers by six years and the first games conducted by young New York City businessmen by three years. Spalding traced Doubleday's history from his graduation at West Point in 1842 to his Civil War activities and retirement from the service in 1873. He restated Graves' claim that he had witnessed Doubleday drawing "the present diamond-shaped Base Ball field" first in the dirt and added that he also put it on paper. He also saw him write up a "memorandum of the rules for his new game, which he named 'Base Ball'."

Recognizing the "apparently accurate manner" of Graves' narrative and "the circumstantial evidence with which he surrounds it," Spalding stated his inclination to believe the account and felt that the committee should give it serious consideration. Striking a nationalistic tone, the sports magnate felt that it would appeal "to an American's pride to have had the great national game of Base Ball created and named by a Major General in the United States Army." Adding to the military's role in promoting baseball, he recognized how Civil

War soldiers, who having played the game in camp, later spread it around the country and how in recent times the Navy had disseminated baseball information around the world.

Spalding ended his argument by calling the committee's attention to an enclosed copy of the original Knickerbockers rule book. Compared to the modern laws governing the sport, it showed "practically no change in the underlying principles of the rules of the game." However, he pointed out, the rules of rounders were totally dissimilar to the New York game and that "should convince the most skeptical that there is absolutely no resemblance between the two games." Typically confident of his own conclusions, Spalding rested his case for the American origin of baseball.

Although Spalding's arguments were unequivocal and resolute in his own mind, he enclosed further confirmation to his American claim in the form of a letter from John Montgomery Ward, a nineteenth century baseball star and a prominent New York City lawyer. According to A. G., Ward had "made an extended research and study into the origin of the game" and agreed with his American birth theory. Writing to Spalding on June 19, 1907, Ward recognized the materials that A. G. had sent him concerning baseball's beginnings, but he lamented that his efforts would probably end in failure in spite of the light that they might shed on the subject. He contended that the game originated "so many years ago that the living witnesses have long since passed off" and that in the beginning "no written records or memoranda of any kind were ever made."

Ward claimed that baseball was first a boy's game that was adopted by some prominent professional men from New York City "in about the year 1842, or earlier." These people, including Alexander J. Cartwright, Colonel James Lee and William F. Ladd, testified that they "formulated its rules for the purpose of making it a manly pastime" since no code of playing the game then existed. This group relied on their boyhood recollections of how the game was played and whatever rules had been passed down to them "like folklore, from generation to generation of boys." This code of conducting a baseball game was not put into writing until the Knickerbocker club was formed in 1845. Twenty years later, Ward began to investigate the matter by talking with some of the original members of the team. Ladd, an 84 year-old Wall Street jeweler, clearly remembered Lee as one of the main motivators behind the organization. The colonel said he played the game as a boy (which would have been before the turn of the century) and the rules that were formulated were based on his and other old-timers' recollections. The Knickerbockers chose baseball, Ladd claimed, because they regarded it "as a purely American game" and there apparently was "some considerable prejudice against adopting any game of foreign invention."

Ward felt that the original code of baseball was marked by its simplicity and so nobody should confuse its rules with those of any other game. It was clear to him then that those who adopted the rounders origin of baseball were ignoring a major difference between "the original central and controlling ideas of the two games." Rounders adopted its name from a term identified with rounding the bases after a hit (a home run in baseball terms) which wiped out all outs and necessitated another turn at bat for the entire team. No detractor ever claimed that baseball had ever had this unique aspect and, given the simple nature of the game, there was no confusion on this point. Certainly, Ward contended, it was only reasonable to assume that if in fact baseball had come from rounders, it would contain this unique feature. After all of his investigations, Ward could only concur with Spalding "that Base Ball was a purely American game."

A G. Mills wrote the final decision of the special investigating committee on December 30, 1907, after he had reviewed the testimony that Sullivan had received. Dismissing any prejudice based on nationalism, he could not reject the claims of Chadwick simply on patriotic grounds. In fact, he condemned America for being slow to follow the British example of "fostering healthful field sports generally." If anyone could prove a British antecedent to the American game, he didn't feel that this would detract in any way from the national pastime. Before perusing the documentation received by the committee, Mills had held the belief that baseball originated with the Knickerbockers. Although he had not always agreed with "Father" Chadwick on other issues in the past, he gave full consideration to his contention.

Mills felt that the sports writer's claim was based "chiefly upon the fact that, substantially, the same kind of implements were employed" in both rounders and baseball. Rejecting this notion, Mills argued that "if the mere tossing or handling of some kind of ball, or striking it with some kind of stick, could be accepted as the origin of our game," then Chadwick would have to extend his research beyond the beginnings of the Anglo-Saxon civilization. He recognized that inventors like Thomas Edison and Frank Sprague had been pioneers in the electrical field who created practical devices to harness electricity for useful purposes, but they didn't "invent" it, nor did anybody even understand the phenomenon. According to Mills' understanding, "the invention or the origination of anything practical or useful...is the creation of the device or the process from pre-existing materials or elements."

Here, Mills was getting at the heart of the matter of evolution versus creation. Rejecting the concept that the use of similar tools to perform both games implied evolution, he felt that the birth (the creation of something from original materials) of baseball was marked by the beginning of the game as currently played in America. Therefore it could never have come from England because "It certainly had never been played, in however crude a form" in that country. To emphasize his point, he reminded the commission that baseball "was strange and unfamiliar when an American ball team first played it there."

In spite of his early convictions concerning the Knickerbocker origin of baseball, Mills acknowledged the Graves testimony which contained "a circumstantial statement by a reputable gentleman" concerning his witnessing of the Doubleday drawing of the baseball diamond in Cooperstown in 1839. Then Mills went on to give a brief description of Doubleday's military background so that the committee would have some idea about his character. Due to the haphazard nature of the game that the boys of Cooperstown played, Mills pointed out a number of injuries resulted. He could "well understand how the orderly mind of the embryo West Pointer would devise a scheme for limiting the contestants...allotting them to field positions...and substituting the existing method of putting out the base runner for" plugging him with the ball. While

Mills recognized that Doubleday's game involved eleven players instead of the normal nine, he dismissed this difference as a minor detail.

Finally, Mills brought up the statement made by Curry, the pioneer Knickerbocker, that a Mr. Wadsworth had brought a diagram, similar to the modern playing field, to the team's practice one afternoon. While Curry admitted that they tried the new game, he never declared that they adopted it. Mills, however, felt that he did, for "the scheme of the game described by Mr. Curry has been continued with only slight variations in detail." Mills also pointed out the importance of Curry's role in baseball development as he was the club's first president and a participant in drafting the game's first published rules. Mills had not received any confirmation on the connecting link between Doubleday's diagram and the one that Wadsworth already brought to the field (and never would), but he promised to deliver it whenever it arrived.

It appears that, even though this important link could not be verified, Mills simply glossed over the facts. Nobody else seemed to know what game Curry described nor how close it was to modern baseball; nor was the identity of Wadsworth ever revealed. Mills was making some weighty assumptions, and his promise to reveal future information appeared to be shallow. There was no real due date for the findings of the committee. Why not wait until this rather significant issue could be cleared up before allowing any assumptions to appear in print?

The significance of Mills' letter to the investigating committee cannot be understated. He boldly stated his deductions from the testimony that he had received. His first conclusion was "that Base Ball had its origin in the United States." Secondly, he affirmed "that the first scheme for playing it, according to the best evidence obtainable to date, was devised by Abner Doubleday at Cooperstown, N.Y. in 1839."

The first judgement, while still not absolute in conviction, could be attributed to an exercise in semantics. What did the word origin really mean? Mills was assuming that it meant the creation of something totally original and to him baseball fit that description. The second, and perhaps the more significant opinion, relied solely on the information supplied by one man—Abner Graves. Mills attempted to satisfy second-guessers by acknowledging that it was based on the best information available at that time, but no further reports based on new evidence were ever written by him. Other papers on the origin of baseball had been received by Sullivan, but they were generally labeled as folklore. The significance of Graves' testimony, of course, was that he claimed to be an eye witness to the creation. For a decision of this magnitude, the committee should have sent out a personal representative to interview the retired mining engineer (he may have been too old to travel that far). Their lack of diligence in this matter would later lead to a great dilemma over the confirmation of Cooperstown's historical significance and the right to capitalize on this theme.

While Mills wrote this summation independently, other members of the commission, except Sullivan, co-signed his statement and totally agreed with its conclusions. The secretary wrote a letter of introduction concerning the controversy in the *Guide* of 1908, describing the nature of the debate, the membership of the special investigating committee, their work and the decisions that they formulated.

Deluged with a wealth of information received from around the country, Sullivan revealed that the well-publicized arguments of Chadwick and Spalding had created considerable public interest, especially among those who had followed the game for a long time. For three years Sullivan conducted extensive correspondence in order to collect information and to follow up on a variety of suggestions dealing with baseball's beginnings. He compiled this information and forwarded it to the committee for its scrutiny. After spending several months perusing the documentation, Sullivan stated, they unanimously concluded "that Base Ball is of American origin, and has no traceable connection whatever with 'Rounders,' or any other foreign game." This conclusion was right out of Spalding and only partially agreed with the Mills report. There was absolutely no mention of the second commission finding that labeled the time, place, or any person responsible for the creation of the national pastime.

Sullivan had only recently received the committee's decision before it was published in the *Guide*. Although there was not enough space in the Spalding publication to include all of the information that had been received concerning baseball's origin, the secretary stated that the publisher would produce a special book on the game's beginnings that would detail the investigation. Sullivan concluded his introductory remarks by thanking the commissioners for their effort and claiming that "their decision should forever set at rest the question as to the Origin of Base Ball."[18] The irony of his final statement would not be lost on those who would review the committee's findings in the future.

In spite of the fact that Spalding had "won" the argument, Chadwick demurred. On March 20th, following the publication of the conclusions, he wrote to Mills complaining that the decision was reached by "a masterly piece of special pleading which lets my dear old friend Albert escape a bad defeat." He continued that the entire affair was simply a joke between the two men. What may have been a source of humor to two of baseball's most significant personages would be taken very seriously in future decades. Even at the time of its publication, the committee's decision and the arguments of A. G. Spalding gained nation-wide acceptance among those who were concerned.[19]

With the findings of the Mills Commission, the lives of two men named Abner had become firmly united in the minds of baseball authorities. Graves, who was born on February 27, 1834, in Cooperstown, was almost fifteen years younger than his military counterpart. It doesn't seem likely that they could have been boyhood playmates since they were approximately five and twenty years old respectively in 1839. However, the younger Abner must have been curious, adventuresome and advanced beyond his age. According to newspaper accounts of his life, which must have come from his only son, he was a participant in the first baseball game which took place in the village in 1840. In the contest, which allegedly took place while he was attending Green school, he played one of the two shortstop positions. Always willing to take the leadership role, young Abner organized his own team a few years later and they engaged in a number of contests.

The name Abner Graves was not unique in Cooperstown. The United States census for 1840 listed two men by that name—one in his 70s and another head of a household in his 30s who carried the title of junior. The older family was quite large and may have contained eight children. The youngest was a boy under five years of age, and he may have been the future writer to the Mills commission. If the census was taken after his fifth birthday, he was one of two boys listed between the ages of five and ten. Since the family also contained a man and a woman in their 30s, the older couple may have been his grandparents.

Intrigued by the lure of California, Graves left his native New York in 1848 at the age of 14 and never returned. He took passage on a sailing vessel and made the arduous journey around Cape Horn. Thus he was a part of the first group of pioneers to participate in the famous gold rush of 1849. While this experience served as a basis for his later work in the mining area, Abner took up a number of other occupations. In 1852 he became a pony express rider and for a number of years he braved the dangers of Indian attacks while helping to get the mail through to the Pacific coast. Before the completion of the first transcontinental railroad, he also served as a rider for the Wells Fargo and Adams Express companies.

Following the Civil War he became involved in the cattle and farming business near Cedar Rapids, Iowa. He married his first wife, Chloe Alma Dow, on May 28, 1868. At age 34, Abner had finally added some stability to his life. His father-in-law, S. E. Dow, was the founder of Dowville which was later named Dow City. Mr. Dow was born in New Hampshire in 1821 and married his wife in the state of New York twenty-five years later. On their way to California in 1854, the couple and their young daughter stopped in Iowa in Crawford county and began the settlement that bears his name. As founder of the community, he was elected to the positions of county judge, county treasurer, and various minor local offices.

Therefore, Abner Graves had married into a prominent family. S. E. Dow was a relatively wealthy man when he arrived and was highly recognized by his peers. Since he came to Iowa with a fine herd of thoroughbred short horn cattle, it was only natural that his son-in-law would enter this business. However, the two men would soon join forces in a new partnership after the Northwestern Railway established a station in the community. The firm of Dow and Graves built an elevator to serve the nearby farmers, and gradually theirs became the leading business concern in the western part of the county. Industrious, energetic and friendly, Dow had all of the attributes of a successful business man and Abner, always innovative in the business world, seemed to fit well into this scheme.

Abner had come a long way since he fled from his home in Cooperstown as a young teenager. Successful in business, well married and a home owner, he also became a father when the couple's first and only son, Nelson, was born about 1882. By then they had been together for some 14 years and may have lost other children at birth. What seemed like a happy family life was about to change in a rather drastic manner. The prosperous years ended when financial reverses hit the business and caused it to close. This failure not only reduced Dow from affluence to relative poverty but also caused economic duress throughout Crawford county.

The hardships that followed must have put a great deal of stress on both families and may have caused a split in Abner's relationship with his wife. In the mid-1890s he moved to Denver and apparently left his wife and child in the process. By 1900 he was still on shaky financial ground and lived as a lodger in a house on 17th Street. Chloe Graves died in 1902, and his son may have moved to Colorado shortly afterwards since they became full-time business partners the next year. Like many of his western counterparts, Abner had previously tried his hand at a number of jobs and gradually got involved in several mining ventures. Evidently, he was quite the entrepreneur as he generally served as an engineer and organizer of these operations. His mining activities led him to work in a number of western states and he also served as a mine manager in Mexico where his son became involved. Graves never lost interest in mining, and as late as 1922 he purchased extensive coal properties just across the border in Medicine Bow, Wyoming, and built a shortline railroad to the area. It was quite an experiment for a man who was nearly ninety years old.

Nelson's mother had left him some property in Iowa, and his grandmother also willed him a farm there. Perhaps Abner was left out of these estates because of a strained relationship with his spouse. His mining adventures may have caused them to live apart at various times and this may have added to the problem. However, the older Graves wasn't shy about spending his son's inheritance as he invested $8,000 acquired from the sale of his mother-in-law's farm into their business. Known as the Graves Investment Company, it was located in downtown Denver and specialized in real estate, stocks and bonds.

A year after the Mills commission report came out, Abner (who was then 75) married Minnie L. Graves (only 33 years old). In spite of the vast age difference, their marriage appeared to go well, and in 1921 he included her in his will. Graves drew up the testament because he had become fearful of dying in an automobile accident. Evidently he had made several extensive trips into outlying areas possibly to look at potential mining sites. He made sure that his son was paid back the sum that he had previously borrowed from him for the business and split most of the rest between Nelson and Minnie.

Three years later tragedy struck. On June 16th, the ninety-year-old Graves requested rather strongly that his wife should sign a bill of sale for their home. Perhaps he wanted to use the money for investment purposes, but Minnie refused to go along with it. Always quick-tempered and frequently in conflict with his wife, Graves became quarrelsome over the issue. Crippled and unable to walk without the aid of crutches, he requested that she bring him a drink. When his wife returned to the room, he accused her of putting poison in it. Abner became abusive when she attempted to quiet him, and he pulled out a gun and fired four shots into Minnie's body at point-blank range.

Upon hearing the shots some neighbors notified authorities. The Denver police had to break into the house where they found Abner and saw his weapon on the bed. When questioned about his motive, he claimed that he had to protect himself. Then he flew into a rage and tried to attack one of the authorities. Later he claimed that "one of us had to go." He explained this by stating that she had tried to poison his coffee, but following a hospital examination, no traces of the substance were found in his stomach. Before she lapsed into a coma she said to "tell Abner I forgive him." However, she left him out of her will. By this time Graves was "a physical and mental wreck" and in no mood to reconcile. He simply muttered "I hope she dies."

Following a jury trial, the court found Abner to be mentally unbalanced and committed him to the Colorado State Insane Asylum at Pueblo. He caused little trouble after that and was considered to be a model patient. Graves remained there until his death of heart disease on October 4, 1926 just two years after his wife's murder. At the direction of his son, his body was sent to Dow City for burial. So little had been heard about the 92 year old Graves that his death was not reported in the Denver papers for four months. His passing marked a tragic end to an eventful life.[20]

The other Abner was more highly recognized because of his significant contributions to the northern forces in the Civil War, but he was not a national hero on the scale of Grant or Lincoln. Those people interested in the history of the North-South conflict would have been familiar with his name and exploits, but by the turn of the century few people were alive who knew him personally. Soon he would gain the national recognition that had eluded him following the war, but this adulation had little to do with his military exploits.

Born in Ballston Spa, Saratoga county, New York on June 26, 1819, to Ulysses Freeman and Hester Doubleday, Abner was thus a descendant of an old Otsego county family. Following his private education in Cooperstown, he entered the United States Military Academy from which he graduated in 1842. During the Mexican War of 1846, he was in the First Cavalry and was engaged in battle at Monterrey and in Rinconada Pass during the Battle of Buena Vista that catapulted Zach Taylor into the presidency. He was promoted to first lieutenant the next year and advanced to the rank of captain in 1855. For the next three years he fought against the Seminole Indians of Florida.

In 1860 he was stationed at Fort Moultrie until his garrison moved to Fort Sumter at the end of the year. As an artillery captain he commanded the first gun to be fired on the Union side of the Civil War on April 12, 1861. The following month he was promoted to Major of the Seventeenth United States infantry, and during the summer he served under General Patterson in the Shenandoah Valley. Following this assignment, Doubleday helped to lead the defense of the nation's capital by commanding forts and batteries along the Potomac River from September, 1862, to July, 1863. Because of this bravery in action he was promoted to Brevet Lieutenant-Colonel of the regular army. Then he left his post for an assignment at Gettysburg. His battle involvement had been extensive and included participation at the second Battle of Bull Run and the bloody conflict at Antietam. In this latter battle his division led the charge and accrued numerous casualties, but they also scored heavily against the opposition. In November of 1862, he became Major-General of volunteers and he was also active in the battles of Fredericksburg and Chancellorsville.

Doubleday's heroics were an important factor in the most celebrated battle of the war, which took place at Gettysburg. In July, 1863, General John F. Reynolds, under whom Abner had previously served, assigned him to reinforce the cavalry that was defending a ridge west of town. His troops fought the Confederates for five hours and inflicted heavy damages before their retreat to Cemetery Ridge. Doubleday continued to harass the opposition the next day, and in the last phase of the conflict, his forces were gallant in their effort to repulse Pickett's charge.

Doubleday was promoted to the rank of Major-General for his war-time bravery and, following the conflict, he served as assistant commissioner of the Freedman's Bureau of Galveston, Texas. In 1868 he was a member of the Retiring Board in New York City. For the next three years he superintended the San Francisco recruiting service and, while living in that city, he suggested and received a charter for the first cable car system in the country.

In 1853 Abner had married the daughter of a Baltimore attorney, Mary Hewitt. Following his military career, which officially ended with his retirement from active duty in December, 1873, he authored numerous articles on subjects ranging from military matters to the water supplies for cities. On January 26, 1893, Doubleday died at his home in Morristown, New Jersey, and he was supposedly buried in Mendham. A monument recognizing his bravery was later erected at the Gettysburg battlefield.[21]

If Doubleday had lived to the age of his Colorado counterpart, he would have been alive when the Mills commission report was published. He may have been somewhat dismayed to learn that his newly found glory had little connection with his heroic endeavors on the battlefield. On the other hand, he may have been surprised to find himself focused in the national spotlight because of his alleged connection with an old Colorado mining engineer who he probably hadn't seen since his boyhood days in Cooperstown. Still, the link had been made; and in the process, the story of baseball's beginning moved from a foggy question in the minds of most fans to a clear understanding of historical fact. The reality of the Mills Commission report mattered little at the time, but it would have a dramatic impact on future generations of the game's followers.

Chapter Two
The Ball Gets Rolling

Since the Chadwick-Spalding controversy appeared to be nothing more than a good-natured debate over a matter that some fans considered superfluous, no action of any consequence resulted in the immediate aftermath of the Mills Committee decision. Doubtless, few people were surprised at the conclusion that baseball was American and many fans simply viewed the decision as being more intuitively based than scientifically formulated. However, the committee's second major finding concerning the Doubleday-Cooperstown connection could either be viewed with skepticism, curiosity, or surprise. Because there was no link between the upstate New York village and the Mills Commission, the people of Cooperstown didn't make any plans to develop their newly discovered national claim to fame. The Phinney lot, which Graves cited as one of the places where Doubleday's new game was played, had not yet become sacrosanct ground. In order to recognize the plot's significance, concerned villagers and outsiders needed to combine their efforts.

The initial work to recognize Cooperstown began with the efforts of Sam Crane, a former major league player in the late nineteenth century. He took up sports writing when his playing career ended; and, although he was never considered one of the greats in the journalistic profession, he was forthright in his writing and his love of the game. According to Ford Frick, himself a writer turned commissioner, Crane was the first person connected with baseball who publicly encouraged major league owners to recognize the game's great players through some kind of memorial. Following the Mills report, he began to focus on Cooperstown as the place for this tribute. Indeed, from 1917 to 1925, he made numerous trips to the village to encourage support.[1]

Local activity commenced in 1917 when five men from nearby Ilion, New York, began the Doubleday Memorial Fund with the modest contribution of a quarter each. The group included two former major leaguers, Arthur H. Richardson and George (Deke) White, and three fans of the game, Michael Fogarty, George Oliver and Patrick Fitzpatrick. They enlisted Crane's support because of his endless efforts to gain recognition for Cooperstown. In addition to a "national" baseball field for the village, the New York baseball writer also planned a home for retired players to be financed by nation-wide contributions and deductions from major leaguers' salaries.

The Phinney property was still being used by youths as a playground when a local dentist by the name of Dr. Ernest L. Pitcher organized, in the same year, a fund-raising group governed by the Cooperstown Chamber of Commerce. Their purpose was to solicit subscriptions to be used for the purchase of the old pasture which would be turned into a permanent baseball field for the village.

Members of this fund-raising drive included Dr. Harry L. Cruttenden, George H. Carley, a prominent Rotarian, Monroe F. Augur, who ran the Corner Book Store, and Loren J. Gross, the manager of the Leather Stocking Garage. Through their efforts they raised $3,772; and on June 2, 1919, village officials obtained a two year lease of the lot from Alexander Phinney, a descendant of Elihu Phinney. Swampy portions of the pasture were filled in with dirt and ashes with the idea of simply creating a public playground.

Sam Crane wanted more than this, and he continued to stir up interest in the project. Inspired by his earlier writings on the subject, Harry N. Hempstead, former New York Giants owner, and John K. Tener, recently resigned president of the National League, visited the village a few years earlier in order to observe baseball's birthplace. Then, in 1919, Cruttenden and Gross met with Tener, who suggested that they talk with his successor, John Heydler. They couldn't have found a more sympathetic listener. The new president became an immediate convert to the Cooperstown cause. Years later he recalled that the field was not much more than a cow pasture when he first viewed it. He remembered an old barn on one corner of the field that "looked as though it had been there when Abner Doubleday laid out his first ball field." Heydler wasn't simply overcome by nostalgia. He was equally impressed with the enthusiasm of the local village people, especially Dr. Pitcher.[2]

If Heydler was the leading supporter of Cooperstown from baseball's hierarchy, then Pitcher served that role at the local level. When the original lease expired on the Phinney property, the doctor determined to undertake another fund raising, and he devoted a great deal of his time to promoting his plan. His fellow committee members joined him in signing a note from the First National Bank for an $1,800 loan to pay for excursions to New York designed to encourage national support. For the first time, the people of the village encouraged outside assistance in gaining recognition for their role in baseball history. This theme would be repeated in future years.

A game was organized to raise money for the project; and, at Tener's suggestions, Heydler was asked to officiate the proceeding. When Doubleday Field was officially opened on September 6, 1920, a game between two local teams, Milford and Cooperstown, was held. Not only was Heydler there to oversee the contest, he even agreed to act as umpire for the first inning. This action was hardly inappropriate; for the former player, writer, statistician and big league boss was also a previous major league umpire. The game was accompanied by a local street fair and together these activities netted $450, which was added to the money already raised.

Heydler's role in the rise of Cooperstown's prominence should not be underestimated. Of course he was an important national baseball figure. In addition to being league president (a position he held until 1934 when failing health forced him to retire), he was also one of the members of the National Commission which governed the sport before the commissioner system was set up following the infamous Black Sox scandal of 1919. Previously (1903-09) he had served as secretary for the National League president, Harry C. Pulliam. During his time as a sports writer, Heydler compiled statistics for batting and fielding averages and sold this information to newspapers. All of this background had established Heydler as one of the major baseball figures of his day, and Cooperstown needed a man of his caliber to gain recognition for their promotion.[3]

Following the opening of the field, no more action on the Phinney lot took place until March 12, 1923, when village taxpayers voted on an appropriation of $1,238 to be added to funds already collected for the purchase of the property. The idea was rejected; but in another special election on July 19, voters approved the money. Abraham Lincoln Kellogg, New York Supreme Court judge, officially transferred the property to the village as a ball park and playground on September 29th. After the addition of a wooden grandstand in the spring of the next year, another appropriation was approved by the taxpayers in March, 1926, for a sizeable increase to the original plot. The ground between the lot and Main Street, which would later become the entrance to the field, was acquired by exchange on June 7, 1927. Construction was halted for six years, but in the fall of 1933 it was resumed under a New Deal program. Additional parcels of land were purchased in order to expand the left field area which was short of regulation size. Under the Work Relief Program, the entire field was graded, a new diamond was constructed, the area was fenced and the entrance was landscaped. When the work was completed in the following summer, Lt. Governor M. William Bray of New York formally re-opened Doubleday Field on August 3, 1934.[4]

The ideas of the original planners had been realized, and perhaps everyone felt that the dream of recognizing the village's contribution to baseball and American history had also become a reality. However, it would soon become quite apparent that Cooperstown's celebrity status was just beginning to be understood. In order to gain further recognition for the village's role in the national sport, two important items were necessary—financial support on a large scale and a grand idea on which promoters could capitalize. Both of these necessities were about to come into focus.

Originally the leading family of Cooperstown was that of the village's founder, Judge William Cooper. His son, James Fenimore, later became a famous novelist; and this added considerable fame to the community's namesake. The renowned writer died in 1851, and three years later the next dynamic group moved in to begin a dominance of the area that has lasted until modern times. This was the Clark family, and their association with Cooperstown and its development dates back to the latter half of the nineteenth century.

The family began to accumulate its fortune due to the business acumen of its patriarch, Edward S. Clark, who was born in Greone County in 1811. Following his graduation from Williams College in 1830, he began to study law at Ambrose L. Jordan's office in Hudson, New York. Intelligent and industrious, he became Jordan's law partner in 1837, two years after marrying Jordan's daughter Caroline. Here began the Clark affiliation with Cooperstown because the new bride introduced Edward to the village. Her father had practiced law there from 1813 to 1820 and had become a leading political figure. Like other families who could afford it, they spent their summer vacations there. Caroline was born in Cooperstown, and by 1854 she and Edward purchased a summer home in her native village.

The law partnership eventually moved to New York City, and in 1848 Clark began his association with the man who formed the basis of his fortune—Isaac M. Singer. Originally from Oswego, he ran away from home in 1823 at the age of twelve. Although he generally served as an itinerant laborer, Singer was also a member of a Shakespearean acting troupe. Creative by nature, Isaac invented a wood carving machine in 1839 and sought Clark's help in clearing up its title. Failing in this effort, Singer remained undeterred and struck out on a new venture that would make him famous. Instead of a totally new device, he sought to improve an early version of the sewing machine, patented by Elias Howe and others just a few years earlier. Although his invention eventually became the first practical model to be marketed, Singer had combined parts from earlier machines that resulted in his own production.

By 1850 patent-infringement suits had forced Isaac to the edge of bankruptcy. Court cases were not his only source of financial drain. At the same time the mercurial inventor was living with three different women and trying to support each household and the fourteen children these relationships had produced. To confuse matters even more, he also had a legal spouse and two legitimate children. He hoped that his invention of a single-thread chain-stitch sewing machine could end his financial woes, but court battles were too costly to allow any marketing progress. In the court settlement which followed, Clark arranged an equitable solution whereby he, Singer and another associate were allowed to form a company for the mass production of the machines while other patent holders were allowed to receive royalties. I. M. Singer & Company was formed, but while it was still in its initial struggling stages, the third man's interests were bought out for $6000—a paltry sum compared to the fortune that the remaining owners were soon to amass. Clark had wisely refused a cash settlement for his services. Instead, he arranged for a 50 percent share of the profits of what became the Singer Manufacturing Company in 1863.

Edward Clark was not merely a silent partner in the growing corporation. Possessing a good sense of business and a crafty legal mind, he guided the organization through legal battles, acquired financing for the company, and got it into a productive state. As a dynamic businessman, he was able to expand the organization into world-wide production. Although the business end of the Singer-Clark relationship worked out well, the personal aspect did not. The two men despised each other; and in 1867, their working relationship beyond repair, Singer completely withdrew from company operations. He did, however, continue to share in its profits; and they were considerable, as Clark accumulated one of the great American fortunes of his day. The wealth was understandable because their product was one of the first mass-produced items of the industrial revolution.

As the wealth of the Clark family grew, so did its holdings in Cooperstown. Following the Civil War, Edward built his own summer home in the village known as Fernleigh, and gradually he acquired numerous properties in the area. The dominance of a single region by one particular family could prove to be detrimental if they simply wanted to accrue vast holdings of property. But according to Cooperstown historian Louis C. Jones, the Clark family members "were blessed with a sure sense of civic responsibility so that many institutions which today set the village apart have stemmed from their imaginative leadership." Gradually, the Clarks became solely responsible for many important community projects.

In 1882 Edward died and bequeathed his fortune of some $35 to $40 million to his sole surviving son, Alfred Corning Clark. Ably assisted by a former library clerk named Frederick Gilbert Bourne, the family's wealth continued to grow. By the time Alfred died in 1896, the Clarks had amassed finances amounting to some $120 million. This fortune was equally divided among his four sons— Stephen Carlton, Edward Severin, Frederick Ambrose (generally known as Brose) and Robert Sterling Clark.

Both in personality and physical appearance, the brothers had little in common. Edward Severin, known as the Squire in Cooperstown, was no physical specimen; but he had a passion for building imposing structures. Although he had inherited the stately Dakota apartments, constructed by his grandfather on Central Park West in New York City, he also built a mansion in Cooperstown, known as Fenimore House, in the early 1930s. (After he died, his brother Stephen arranged to have it transferred to the New York State Historical Association in 1944 as a method of coaxing the institution into the village). Edward had also built the imposing Otesaga Hotel (1909) and, in memory of his father, the Alfred Corning Clark Gymnasium (1930), which served as the village recreation center.

Although he never married, Edward greatly admired Mary Imogene Bassett, a local physician. With ample support from the Clark family, a hospital was constructed in 1922 in the village and named for her. Edward, who took great pride in his prize herd of Guernsey cattle, built an imposing stone barn for them in 1918 on Fenimore Farm where he lived in a house previously occupied by James Fenimore Cooper. Eventually, this "cow palace" became a tourist attraction known as the Farmers Museum, which depicts pioneer agricultural life.

Two of the other brothers, F. Ambrose and Robert Sterling, shared a common love for horses; but neither contributed as much to Cooperstown's development as did their siblings. Brose became internationally known as an owner of famous thoroughbreds; and, in addition to his 500 acre estate in Westbury, Long Island, he also owned a 2,500 acre spread at Cooperstown known as Iroquois Farm. Never much of a money manager, Ambrose was more interested in the animals he raised and the people in the horse racing business. Robert shared a love for these animals, but he also enjoyed good bourbon and lovely women. A former military man, he served in the Phillipines and in China around the turn of the century. Although he bred and raised thoroughbreds on his Virginia Farm according to his own experimental principles, he loved Paris, French cooking, and collecting rare and expensive works of art. He began his collection following a trip to Europe in 1912 and, along with his wife, helped to establish one of the significant legacies of the Clark family—the Sterling and Francine Clark Art Institute, which was established in Williamstown, Massachusetts, in 1955.

Concerning the economic development of Cooperstown, none of the offsprings of Alfred Corning Clark was more important than his son Stephen Carlton. Although he shared Robert's interest in art, he was involved in a diverse number of activities. Following his graduation from Yale and Columbia law schools, he served in the New York State Assembly in 1910. Later he was a vice-president for the Safe Deposit Company of New York and a director of the Singer company. During World War I he achieved the rank of lieutenant colonel and received the Distinguished Service Medal. Assisting his brother during their first art collection trip to Europe, Stephen became an enthusiastic and well-informed collector. From 1940 to 1946 he was board chairman for the Museum of Modern Art in New York City, and he was also a trustee of the Metropolitan Museum of Art. In addition to his involvement in the art world, he was a trustee of Roosevelt Hospital, chairman of the board of the New York State Historical Society, director of the Scriven Foundation, and owner and publisher of a newspaper in Albany, New York, in the 1920s.

As a nationally known philanthropist, Stephen Clark was ideally suited for becoming the leading developer of Cooperstown. His creation of the Clark Foundation led to the financing of the hospital, recreation center, and college scholarships for local high school graduates. He became worried about the village's economy shortly after the First World War when a hops blight began to kill off the major crop of the area. Previously, the hops had been exported to Germany for beer production; but after the infestation, the crop could no longer be grown. Concerned about the economic self-sufficiency of the region, Clark began to focus on the promotion of tourism as a means of attracting money to the village while preserving its charm and unspoiled character. Eventually his plan led to the development of six museums and a legacy of tourism for the upstate New York village.[5] None of these visitor attractions was more important in elevating Cooperstown into international recognition than the National Baseball Hall of Fame and Museum.

While Stephen Clark would eventually become the financial backer of this renowned sports institution, the idea for its inception belonged to one of his employees—Alexander Cleland. Like Clark, Cleland was no fan of the sport of baseball. In fact, he didn't even move to the United States until he was 26 years old. Leaving his native Scotland where he was a coal salesman in Glasgow, he moved to England for about a year and worked as a chimney sweep. Following his father's death, Alexander came to America in the same year (1903) that Chadwick's controversial editorial was published. He never became an avid fan of the game; but through his years of association with it, he gradually came to enjoy it. His real calling came in the area of social work and his first job (1904-06) in Chicago involved work as industrial secretary for the central Y.M.C.A. Then, being an immigrant himself, he got involved in work concerned with new arrivals to the country.

From 1906 to 1913, Cleland served as investigator for the Dillingham Federal Immigration Commission, the North American Civic League, and the State Immigration Commission in New York. He was also employed as superintendent of Emergency Lodging House in Chicago and executive secretary of the New Jersey Immigration Commission. Following this job, he served as executive secretary of the New York Joint Committee on Prison Reform (1913-1917); and, during World War I, he was chief of the Operating Division of the War Camp Community Service in New York. From 1921 to 1931 he continued to work in the Empire State as financial agent and assistant superintendent of the Broad Street Hospital and secretary of the Bowling Green Neighborhood Association.

Although Cleland's work record was laudable both in his effort and his service to mankind, it hardly seemed to be a background that would qualify him for a position connected with the national pastime. When Governor Charles

Evans Hughes of New York appointed him as investigator in 1908, Alexander looked into the exploitation and abuse of immigrants; and, three years later, New Jersey governor Woodrow Wilson assigned him to a similar position. During the war the organization he headed attempted to supply food, lodging, and entertainment for soldiers in New York's metropolitan area. Given this work record, however, Cleland became acquainted with people in high places and demonstrated a sincere concern for the welfare of others. Both of these characteristics would prove to be helpful when he encountered his new employer in 1931.

Cleland's association with Stephen Clark began that year when he became director of the Clark House in New York City, which was founded by the Clark Foundation. Like similar organizations throughout the country at this time, this settlement house was designed to provide services for immigrants such as temporary housing and aid in obtaining employment. Located on the lower East Side of New York, this institution introduced Cleland to a wide variety of people and served as an outlet for his humanitarian zeal. He established a personal reputation for efficiency, fairness, and ethical principles.[6] In many ways Clark was the same kind of man, and it was not surprising that a mutual admiration developed between the two.

The WPA project designed to expand and improve Doubleday Field was in full swing in the spring of 1934, activities having commenced the previous fall. On Saturday, May 6th, Cleland and Clark met at Cooperstown to discuss some Clark House matters. Finishing the affairs of business, the 57 year-old director decided to take a walk through the pleasant environment of the village. As he passed the field of construction, a number of men were grading and filling in the property. Cleland was greeted by a young, enthusiastic worker who asked what he thought of the construction work. He also mentioned that the village was becoming very excited about plans for celebrating baseball's 100th anniversary in five more years.

Taking the train back to New York City, Cleland began to ponder the young man's remarks. Always capable of recognizing the business side of things, he wondered if a large number of people might be enticed to visit the village before the celebration took place. Alexander began to develop a plan which would attract a great deal of publicity for the project and wrote a memorandum to Clark concerning the subject. He carefully edited his remarks before sending his plan to his boss. When he returned to New York City the following Monday, his secretary typed up a formal memorandum and he submitted it. This was not a mundane proposal, and Cleland knew that the idea had great potential.

Cleland's idea centered around the construction of "a building on Doubleday Field where a collection of all past, present, and future historical data of the game could be shown." He felt that there must be a large selection of baseball memorabilia throughout the country "that would make an interesting museum." In addition to pictures and "funny old uniforms," he also suggested that baseballs thrown out and autographed by presidents and the bats of baseball's greatest players would fit well in this theme. He suggested that he could present this idea to the Baseball Writers Association, who he hoped would promote the building. Addressing the issue of financing the project, he explained that the cost of construction and maintenance could be paid by the governing bodies of both leagues. He also suggested that some of the profits from the World Series or perhaps a special game played by representatives of the National and the American Leagues could help to finance the proposed museum. This latter suggestion may have evolved from the All-Star game that had been initiated the previous summer. Finally, he believed that the village of Cooperstown would simply donate the site for the project.

Cleland appealed to the intrinsic historical nature of his venture. He stressed that numerous fathers "would be interested to stop at Cooperstown and show the building to their sons and perhaps throw a baseball or two on the Field." Recognizing the busy schedule of his boss, he was reluctant to develop the idea further if Clark did not find it appealing. However, he was adamant in his belief that if the concept he visualized could receive proper publicity then "hundreds of visitors would be attracted to the shopping district right in the heart of Cooperstown." Alexander had struck all the right notes-nostalgia plus publicity equals profit. Not only would the village benefit, but baseball clubs would profit "from a publicity point of view." Therefore, he concluded, they should be willing to finance the scheme.[7]

If Cleland was doubtful that his boss would find any merit in his plan, he shouldn't have been. Clark was quite the entrepreneur himself, and he quickly recognized the possibilities of his employee's idea. After all, the concept was simple, straight-forward, and appealed to the business instincts of both men. About two months later, Cleland again wrote to Clark with some more suggestions for him to consider concerning the project. Realizing the limitations of a one-man plan, he proposed the formation of a committee "to formulate a policy and plan of action for the furthering of the Memorial plan." Prior to its formation, he hoped that interested persons could draw up a tentative program for the group to follow. This included a drawing of the proposed building and an estimate of its cost, which Cleland projected at $100,000 for construction and twice that much for maintenance. Other preliminary things to consider were additional committees to advance the idea and the person who would handle the funds.

By this time an architect named Ken Root had made some preliminary sketches of the building and Cleland had contacted Walter F. "Dutch" Carter, a Yale graduate of 1895, who was a lawyer for a long-established firm in New York City. Carter, who had pitched on the school's baseball team, was considered one of its greatest players. Although he shunned the game following graduation from Columbia law school, he became a member of the board of directors of the Brooklyn Dodgers in 1930 and served there for three years. A member of the Clark Foundation had informed Cleland of Carter's background and knew another member of his firm who could be persuasive in obtaining assistance. Cleland suggested to Clark that the two men meet in Cooperstown to observe the ground and confer with the architect, the president of the local Chamber of Commerce, and a village banker. Following this discussion, he planned to outline his ideas for the inspection by Carter. After Clark approved the concept, Cleland suggested a meeting with baseball authorities which Carter had already promised to arrange.[8]

Clark's interest in the project was growing, and he began to discuss the concept with village elders concerning the field's development and a site for the museum. Townspeople wanted to enhance the project by planting an avenue of trees from the main street to the ball grounds. The local head of a New Deal agency know as Temporary Emergency Relief Administration (TERA) had informally approved the idea and, according to their rules, they would cover 75% of the cost. However, Clark had been confidentially informed that their regulations would soon be altered so that the agency would bear the complete cost of such improvements. Village authorities decided to wait until this happened before initiating the work.

Concerning baseball's officialdom, Clark encouraged his employee to follow through on the idea of encouraging Dutch Carter, who he hoped would contact baseball's commissioner, Judge Kenesaw Mountain Landis. Carter was a brother-in-law of Supreme Court Justice Charles Evans Hughes and very influential in baseball circles. If making a connection with the game's czar wasn't possible, perhaps Carter could write to a member of a committee that had already been set up by baseball to celebrate the game's anniversary. Clark was even willing to travel to New York City to meet with Carter if his presence were necessary.[9]

The Carter connection proved to be the necessary link between the forces of Cooperstown and major league baseball. The New York lawyer sent a letter to the New York *Evening Post* concerning a recent column they had written on Cooperstown as the birthplace of baseball. He acknowledged that on a trip to the village about ten years before, he was saddened by his visit to the field because it contained no fitting memorial for this sacrosanct ground. Recognizing that baseball had become the national game, Carter hoped that someone had contacted baseball's administration about this oversight so that a monument could be initiated to correct it. He added "that the powers of baseball should be not only willing but anxious to make this cradle of our greatest game a shrine."[10]

By October, 1934, the trustees of Cooperstown had officially appointed Cleland as their representative in New York City for the promotion of a memorial at Doubleday Field that would become a national shrine for the game. The next month, he and Carter collaborated on a memorandum concerning their position and forwarded it to league president Heydler. He, in turn, sent copies of it to Landis and William Harridge, the American League president. Heydler apparently agreed with Cleland's plan and only opposed the idea of an inter-league game at Cooperstown. Instead, he proposed that, with the player's consent, a small portion of the annual All-Star game's revenues could be used to finance the memorial.[11]

Cleland's plan progressed slowly during the winter, but he hoped that some action on the matter might be taken during the baseball owners meetings in December. Anxious to hear the reaction of the game's leaders, he contacted Carter in January. Acting on Carter's suggestion, Alexander wrote to Ford Frick, who had recently become president of the National League following an illness of Heydler. Reiterating his earlier correspondence with the former president, Cleland pointed out that concerning the museum (which would show the growth of the game since 1839) the planners were not actually seeking any financial assistance from the league. Rather, they sought only "the approval of the project in order to give it standing and dignity in the eyes of the baseball public."[12]

Evidently Cleland was fearful that his original request for financial aid, made during a time of economic hardship, would cool baseball's leaders on the project, and he was simply seeking their moral backing. He would have been more confident if he knew what a strong supporter he had in the new league president. Frick wrote to him a week later, and he assured the project's director that his plan had not been forgotten. Moreover, Frick revealed that both leagues wanted to help "in perpetuating the birthplace of baseball." The president emphatically stated that Cleland had not only the league's approval but also their "fullest cooperation in any project you may evolve."[13]

Cleland anxiously forwarded Frick's reply to Carter and asked him for some assistance in contacting two baseball writers who could help to advertise the plan. The lawyer proceeded to contact Hugh Bradley of the New York *Post*, Rud Rennie of the *Herald Tribune*, and Frank Graham of *The Sun* concerning the director's proposition and encouraged Cleland to write to them. In contacting these writers, the director sought their advice on promotion and assured them that his organization was voluntary and desired only contributions of historic memorabilia. Graham suggested that Cleland contact William Brandt, who was the manager of the National League Service Bureau, and seek his assistance in developing the museum. Brandt offered his complete cooperation with the project. The association with the press continued to pay dividends as John Minnoch of the Associated Press wrote a story on the proposed museum and the appointment of Cleland as its director. He also requested information on future developments that would be of interest to his readers.[14]

In Cooperstown, plans for future developments were taking shape. In late February the Board of Village Trustees, the Chamber of Commerce and the Otsego County Historical Society appointed Cleland as secretary of the museum. By this time these three organizations had become the sponsors of the secretary's original plan and they hoped that more progress could be made by placing all local activities under his direction. About a month later a group of citizens met to discuss the formation of a local organization to promote baseball development in the village. Their purpose was to solicit the cooperation of major league officials and to set up a program for the centennial celebration. The only action taken at this initial meeting was to set the annual dues at one dollar and to encourage other people in the area to join. It was a modest start but important for the future of the village.

As Cleland had predicted in the initial plan for the museum, one man was simply not enough to promote such a formidable scheme. Consequently, on April 10, 1935, the first meeting of the Doubleday Field Association was held at the Alfred Corning Clark Gymnasium. B. G. Johnson, the local postmaster, was selected as temporary chairman; and Walter R. Littell, editor of the local newspaper, was nominated as temporary secretary. Johnson appointed Alton G. Dunn, a local insurance agent, Justice of the Peace Russell Warren, and Ralph W. Perry to a committee which would nominate nine directors to be approved by the association. They in turn recommended Steven C. Clark, Dr. H. L. Cruttenden, and Ken R. Root for three year appointments, William C. Smalley, C. L. Shearer, and Rowan D. Spraker for two years and Lester J. Clark,

M. F. Augur, and Dr. LeRoy Pitcher for one. Cruttenden, Augur, and Pitcher were no strangers to the promotion of Doubleday Field as they were members of the first fundraising group in 1917. The local county historical society was represented by Littell, its secretary, along with Clark and Spraker, two of its vice presidents. Evidently, the group planned to conduct games on the field that summer as a means of raising money. William Beattie, director of the Clark gym, offered the building's bathing facilities to teams in Cooperstown and all visiting white ball clubs for the entire summer.

The local newspaper coverage helped to inform Cooperstown of the museum's progress while its editor kept Clark abreast of the recent developments. Littell immediately wrote to Clark in New York City to inform him of the progress to date. He mentioned an article that he wrote for the local newspaper in which he described the proposed museum and the association's meeting. He also revealed that officers for the group had been chosen including Johnson (president), Clark (vice-president), Warren (secretary), Cleland (executive secretary) and Beattie (treasurer). Littell made a clear distinction of Cleland's role, which would be much more authoritative than Warren's. He also requested Cleland's presence in Cooperstown as soon as possible to confer with the other officers and give them the reassurance of outside support. Littell assured Clark that the committee would give its complete cooperation to both himself and Cleland.[15]

Littell had begun a working association with Clark and his assistant that was bound to produce good fortune for the museum project. His dedication to the advancement of Cooperstown's recognition should come as no surprise. Although he was born at Oquaga Lake, New York, on October 23, 1880, his family had moved to the village in 1902 when his father became the pastor of the Methodist Episcopal Church. At various times he lived away from the area to attend the college at Wesleyan University in Middletown, Connecticut, where he received his degree in 1905. On his return he began an affiliation with the local newspaper, *The Otsego Farmer*, which was to last for a half century. When that publication merged with another local tabloid, the *Freeman's Journal*, in 1924, he became the editor of the former and managing editor of the latter. Littell was also quite knowledgeable of Cooperstown's history, having written a valuable manuscript on the village in 1929. He also married a local girl, Sara E. Lippitt, in 1912.[16] Like most small town newspaper editors, he was a constant booster of the community; and he also served as Cleland's link with the village in the early years of the Hall of Fame development. As a long-time resident of Cooperstown and a knowledgeable source on all of the village's activities and the people within, he was ideally suited for this job. He would also be in direct contact with Clark who was often away on business.

Clark possessed a historian's interest in antiquated objects, and this fascination for collecting ancient artifacts led him to an important discovery that took place in a nearby area known as Fly Creek. Allegedly a farmer there opened a trunk that had been put away in the attic and remained untouched for generations, and in it he found the belongings of Abner Graves. Among the contents of the trunk was a homemade, undersized baseball that was misshaped and stuffed with cloth. The farmer told Littell who mentioned it to Clark.

In the minds of many residents, the discovery of the ancient spheroid strengthened the belief that there was a direct connection between the old ball and Abner Doubleday. Previously, numerous doubters had cast a dim view on the Doubleday connection, but here was proof positive-or so it seemed. There was no doubt in the mind of Stephen Clark that Littell had discovered the missing link. Probably not wishing to attract attention to his find, he offered only five dollars for its purchase. This was a conservative sum for an object that was soon to become the centerpiece of the most famous museum in Cooperstown and one of the most recognized sports establishments in the world. At the time, however, even Clark may not have realized what a vast potential the old baseball held.

When the ball was first reported in the local newspaper in April 1935, Littell labeled it the Doubleday baseball. The editor pointed out, however, that it was really the property of Abner Graves. He also stated that the fellow students used the home-made item after Doubleday taught Graves how to play the game. Although he never mentioned the basis of this claim, he did reveal that it was discovered in an old house in Fly Creek that was being torn down by a local contractor. In spite of the story that the ball was originally the property of Graves, it has always been referred to as belonging to Doubleday.[17]

Shortly thereafter, Littell wrote another piece for the *Otsego Farmer* which detailed the progress that had been made in connection with Doubleday Field and the success that Cleland was having in attracting the support of organized baseball for the centennial. He anticipated a large number of tourists for the village that summer and mentioned the collection of materials that could be on display at the village club, which would serve as a temporary museum. To emphasize how the memorabilia might attract visitors, he added a picture of a china plate that contained the drawings of the 1889 championship team from New York. In his previous article, Littell had also included a picture of the field and another of what he labeled the Doubleday baseball.[18] These articles helped to garner local support at a time when some people were still uncertain about the project's possibilities.

The connections that Clark and Cleland had made with Frick and Littell would prove to be significant relationships in the early development of baseball promotion in Cooperstown. While the editor served as the most important communications link with the village, the new league president helped to attract the interest of baseball's highest authorities. Cleland was concerned about the lack of progress on the museum idea and realized the necessity of attracting the support of influential people. He began a committee in New York City to fill this void and chose Dutch Carter as chairman. At the same time, he also hoped to attract Julian Curtis, chairman of the board of A. G. Spalding & Company, who had expressed a great deal of interest in the project. Although he had already met with Heydler and Brandt, the National League's board chairman and publicity promoter respectively, he had not conferred with Frick. Typically, the new president was inundated with the details of the league's everyday operations, and Cleland waited patiently for a meeting with him before he began the Cooperstown publicity campaign.[19]

While Littell encouraged local organizations to support the centennial cause, Cleland sought the backing of major league baseball. In May, 1935, he contacted the venerable commissioner of the game, Judge Landis. Dogmatic and dictatorial, baseball's first individual overseer had exerted considerable influence on the game since he took over control of its operations following the Black Sox scandal of 1919. His support was essential if the Cooperstown activities were to be a success. In order to familiarize the commissioner with his project, Cleland enclosed a folder which described the beginning of the museum that he hoped would be a major part of the 1939 celebration. He made no mention of the yet unannounced Hall of Fame and instead concentrated on garnering administrative support for the museum project.

Alexander pointed out that the Board of Trustees and the Chamber of Commerce in Cooperstown had joined with the Otsego County Historical Society to form a local committee to further the centennial cause. He felt that it was essential for the project's success that a national committee be formed to cooperate with these village forces, and he wanted Landis to act as its chairman. Cleland felt that the prestige of the commissioner's name would add a certain dignity to the museum and reveal to the baseball public that the project had the endorsement of the high councils of the game's organization. He pointed out that the committee's work would be voluntary, that no money would be solicited from its members, and that its expenses would be taken care of by the local organization. The only solicitation to be made of the national group would deal with the collection of historical data and relics.

Cleland had already consulted with some influential people in New York who made some suggestions for committee appointees. Included in the list of possible members were Clark, Cleland, Frick, Heydler, minor league president W. G. Bramham, Judge F. E. Crane, sportswriters Dan Daniel and Frank Graham, editor of the *Spalding Guide* John B. Foster, the commissioners' secretary Leslie M. O'Connor, American League president William Harridge, Chairman of Spalding Brothers J. W. Curtis, John Doyle of the American Sports Publishing Company and William J. Manlay. While the list was formidable, Cleland assured the commissioner that its makeup would be subject to his approval and that he would be free to add people to the committee as he saw fit. Since Landis was already the chairman of the major league Centennial Celebration committee, Cleland felt that his appointment as head of the museum group was necessary in order to concentrate the management of the 100th anniversary under the commissioner. The secretary, recognizing the Landis' typical desire for authoritarian control, was appealing to these instincts in order to garner support for his museum idea from baseball's highest authority.

Cleland waited patiently for a month and received no reply from the commissioner's office. Anxious for a response, he contacted O'Connor and asked him to forward his letter to Landis if in fact it had not been received by him. When the commissioner replied, he was noncommittal on the museum subject. Recognizing that the centennial celebration was four years away, he deferred the matter until it would be taken up in December at the baseball winter meetings.[20] Alexander had to be disappointed with this lack of commitment from the game's front office, but he would eventually discover that Landis would never match the enthusiasm of Frick in the Cooperstown extravaganza.

It is no small wonder that Frick was such an important factor in furthering Cleland's idea of a baseball museum because he was eminently qualified to accomplish this task. Born in Wawak, Indiana, in 1894, he graduated from Depauw University in that state in 1915 after playing four years on the school's baseball team. The next year he played semi-pro ball in Walsenburg, Colorado, where he also taught at the high school. He then moved on to the college level at Colorado College in Colorado Springs, where be became an assistant professor of English. Following his work with the War Department's rehabilitation division in the Rocky Mountain area during the First World War, Frick became a sports writer for the *Rocky Mountain News* in Denver. Earlier he had worked for newspapers in Colorado Springs and Fort Wayne, Indiana, and this served as an adequate foundation for building a new career. Apparently he was interested in the business of promotion, as he returned to Colorado Springs in 1919 to start an advertising agency while he wrote editorials for the local newspaper.

Frick always seemed to be the right man in the best place at the most opportune time. In 1921, one of his articles was read by Arthur Brisbane, editor for the Hearst newspapers in New York, and he was so impressed with the work that he offered the writer a job on the sports staff of the New York *American*. Thus Frick's career had turned a new corner that would later lead him to be the National League president for 17 years and the third commissioner of baseball from 1951 to 1965. For the time, however, he was content to be a sports writer; and he covered the Giants for his new paper until he switched to the New York *Journal* for whom he wrote about the Yankees. In addition to writing a column for thirteen years, he also did two daily radio sport shows. His ties with baseball and the mass media were thus well established by the time he took over for Heydler in 1934.

In addition to his other established abilities, Frick would also need to be a competent business manager when he took the reins of the National League. America was in the grips of its worst economic crisis and baseball attendance was suffering because of this decline. Especially hard hit in the baseball world were the franchises in Boston, Philadelphia, and Brooklyn. Salvaging these organizations required adroit business practices. At first he was not very concerned because his original job with the National League was that of public relations director. However, with Heydler's health failing, he became its president and immediately sought to cure the economic vexations that plagued these franchises. He managed to find financial backing for the three cities and developed ways for them to pay for their league obligations without folding.[21]

While these financial dealings were significant, Frick's role in combating the forces of the depression that plagued baseball's revenues took a new turn during the 1935 season. At some time in the spring of that year, Clark decided to send Cleland to visit the league president. As a former sports writer, Frick had previously visited Cooperstown and wrote an article concerning the village; and Clark was therefore aware of his abilities in public relations. Cleland informed him that the village wanted publicity for their baseball celebration, and he suggested an All-Star game for Cooperstown to attract newspapermen. However, Frick had a more expansive idea that went far beyond a museum display. As he later recalled, he suggested a grandiose plan whereby the superstars of the game could be enshrined in a Hall of Fame that would be part of the museum complex.

Frick's proposal was monumental in terms of baseball history, but it was also significant in that it embraced the concept of honoring those who had excelled in a particular field of endeavor. His plan was actually based on the Hall of Fame for Great Americans that had been initiated by New York University in 1901. Since the league president had resided in that city for 14 years, he may have been aware of this original shrine and just adapted the concept to baseball. As simple as this explanation may seem, it should not diminish the genius behind the idea. More than a promotional scheme, Frick believed that it would keep the continuity of baseball flowing from one generation to the next and allow fans to compare old stars with new ones. Recognizing the importance of history to the game, he wanted to make a permanent record of what had happened in the past. Years later, after his retirement from baseball, Frick stated that "in the beginning the Hall of Fame was a vision-and it came to pass."[22]

By early May, Frick had joined Cleland's committee to help with the museum plan, and during its first meeting he donated the only known National League cup, which was won by the Giants in 1889. With the initial contact complete, Frick was ready to play a more significant part. Previously, the centennial celebration had focused on Cleland's concept of a museum. The discovery of the Doubleday baseball, recently purchased by Stephen Clark, encouraged other people to contribute memorabilia for display. The Doubleday Field organization had elected Cleland as their executive secretary and as such he had complete control over the baseball organization in Cooperstown. The local club had been cleared out, and the museum complex was about to begin its operations. While Frick assisted Cleland in tracking down items that might be put on display, Alexander had made little progress on enticing league officials to the museum project. However, Frick promised to take the matter up at the summer meeting on July 7.[23]

Although the Hall of Fame plan was not revealed to the general public until mid-August, Cleland met with members of the Otsego County Historical Society and the Doubleday Field Association in early July. Frick had evidently talked with him about the idea by this time, for the secretary explained the details of the plan during this meeting. Even though the concept received the whole-hearted support in the village, no one expected it to be launched on a national scale until after the season was over. However, the plan was so appealing that Frick commenced its implementation. On August 15, 1935, he invited Cleland to his office to meet with baseball officials concerning the hall. The next day the village of Cooperstown was advertised across the country as the Associated Press announced the plan to create the Hall of Fame within the National Baseball Museum. The secretary had already collected a number of valuable items and had the "Doubleday ball" on display in the village club, but these were minor accomplishments next to the AP's startling revelation. Museums were fairly common, but the hall of fame concept, while not original, had never been applied to a particular field before this time and had only been utilized once previously. Nobody, not even Frick, could have predicted the impact that this idea would eventually have on baseball and other areas of work and play throughout the country.

In addition to implementing the hall of fame concept, the organizers also established a plan by which they could elect people into enshrinement. They desired ten members for the hall's initial induction—five from the 19th century and an equal number from the modern period. Gradually new members would be added on a yearly basis so that by the centennial year they hoped to have 50 people in the shrine. While the major leagues would cooperate with village officials on the hall's development, a nation-wide vote would be taken among writers and editors. The final determination of its exclusive membership would be left to the Baseball Writer's Association of America—an organization that was formed in 1908 consisting of baseball scribes from every major newspaper. They wanted to have the Hall of Fame firmly in place before the observation of the centennial took place in Cooperstown.

While Frick could never have envisioned the dramatic and significant impact of his idea, he understood history and the importance of baseball in American society. No longer just a school boy's game, it had become the national pastime. In the minds of many fans, years were measured by championships and individual performances. The game had also become a big business and, lamenting this development, Frick felt that it needed more sentiment. When he was ultimately elected to the shrine in 1970, he stated that "we need a little memory of what has gone on in the past if we are to have hope in the future and intelligent planning today...Baseball helps to supply a continuity in this age of chaos."[24]

Since Frick's announcement came out during the middle of the 1935 season, little more attention was focused on Cooperstown during the rest of the summer. The league president had merely planted the seed for the Hall of Fame development and it was up to Cleland, Clark, and Littell to follow up on its growth and promotion. Other aspects also had to be considered—including the selection of a building for the expanding museum, the gathering of historical items, and the selection of a process for choosing the hall's members. Progress on the museum slowed to a halt during the fall, but Cleland was not discouraged. Following the Cubs-Tigers World Series, he made an appointment with Frick to make concrete plans for future developments in Cooperstown.[25]

Littell remained a source of inspiration for Cleland during the early months of the development of the Hall of Fame. In February, 1936, he praised the secretary for a recent article on Cooperstown that appeared in the *New York Sun* and promised to reprint it in the local newspaper. Cleland apparently wanted to know more about the people of the village for his next publication, and Littell dutifully sent him a wealth of information concerning the mayor, the Board of Trustees, the Chamber of Commerce, the officers of the Otsego County Historical Society, and the Doubleday Field Association. The latter had grown to a membership of 300 people. While it continued to promote baseball locally, the organization still had much to do in trying to coordinate arrangements for the 100 year celebration. However, Littell promised that they would be ready to support Cleland when the time arrived. The editor and his cohorts were anxious to do everything they could to raise the nation's consciousness concerning the village and the baseball projects of the future.[26] The completion of this task would be no small venture.

Although there was much to be accomplished before the 1939 centennial, the progress to date should not be overlooked. Encouraged by the promotions of Sam Crane and the backing of John Heydler, the people of Cooperstown worked hard to develop and dedicate Doubleday Field. The Clark family, long devoted to the village's development, had become a central focus in the centennial celebration. Indeed, Stephen Clark's purchase of the ancient ball that had allegedly belonged to Abner Graves served as an important link between baseball's beginnings and the construction of its shrine. But most important for the village's future were two very significant plans whose implementation would unite Cooperstown and the national pastime in the minds of fans and players throughout the country and eventually around the world. This small upstate New York location was soon to become synonymous with greatness in the sport as the ideas of Cleland and Frick came to fruition.

Chapter Three
Greats of the Game

Although the momentum was now gathering for future developments in Cooperstown, there was still a great deal of work to be done. It may have appeared to many that the ideas of Cleland and Frick initiated a publicity man's dream. However, the centennial celebration was less than four years away; and the workers in the village had neither established a building for displaying memorabilia nor had they collected many items for the museum. Even though a method for choosing Hall of Fame members had been selected, originators would soon encounter stiff opposition to their plan.

Cleland realized early that the selection process for enshrinement required immediate attention. After all, a Hall of Fame without members would attract little notice. Recognizing the importance of this issue, Cleland contacted the National Broadcasting Company, the Columbia Broadcasting Company, and radio station WOR in May of 1935. His letter to Roy Witmer of NBC, dated the 13th of the month, is the first mention of the Hall of Fame and predates the official announcement by three months. (Since he had been in contact with Frick since January, the league president may have discussed it with him sometime during the interim.)

Cleland saw no problem in selecting baseball relics for display in the museum, but he recognized a more crucial situation in choosing members for the hall. The museum committee felt that those chosen should reflect the feelings of baseball fans in general. Since the Cooperstown connection with baseball centered on Abner Doubleday, Cleland naturally felt that he should be the first choice. But who would be next? The committee members felt that the best way to solicit the opinions of fans throughout the country was to attract a radio sponsor to their cause. A limit of fifty players was set for selection and a national contest would be conducted to fill the roles—a plan that was similar to the current method of voting for yearly All Star teams. Cleland felt that the ultimate decision for enshrinement, however, should rest with the Baseball Writers. The committee's plan would not only allow the average fan some voice in the selection process, but it would also start a national controversy over who should be chosen. This, in turn, would be of great advertising value for the entire program.[1]

Nothing more was mentioned about the selection process until the official announcement of the Hall of Fame was made in August. By that time, the secretary had decided to limit the number of selectees to ten, and Cleland had also gone against the original plan of including the fans in the process. Deciding who would be in this select group was the problem facing the baseball writers, and the whole affair promised to keep the Hot Stove League warm all winter. On the day before Christmas, a list of 33 modern era players nominated for the hall was released to the press by Henry P. Edwards, secretary of the American League Service Bureau and the Baseball Writer's Association of America. These candidates were selected from the era beginning in 1900 and continuing through 1935. They included ten pitchers, eight outfielders, three each of catchers, first and third basemen and only one shortstop. Edwards emphasized that the number of players selected from a particular position didn't matter; the players selected did, however, have to get 75% of the votes. The writers were supposed to select ten inductees from this list, and then a committee of veteran baseball men would choose five players from the pre-1900 era. Following this selection, five additional men would be added to the hall each year.

Naturally, the initial list contained the names of some of the game's most formidable stars. Of the moderns, all but four (Lew Criger, William Bradley, Ross Youngs and Ed Roush) were eventually elected into the Hall of Fame. One wonders why two of them were even nominated, especially Criger who fashioned a .221 lifetime batting average with a grand total of eleven home runs. Bradley, who spent most of his career with Cleveland as a third baseman, hit for a .271 average. Although many fans found agreement with those who made the cut, there were complaints concerning those who didn't. Some of the names mentioned that were missing included Ray Schalk, Frank Chance, Joe Tinker, Ed Plank, Joe McGinnity and Sam Crawford—all of whom were eventually added to the shrine.

The need for two separate lists was understandable. Although modern fans were quite familiar with the 33 nominees from the list of contemporary players, the names from the previous century may not have been so recognizable. Some of them, such as the curve ball inventor, Arthur Cummings, were included as much for their innovations as for their skills. Although the list included A. G. Spalding and John M. Ward, who were instrumental in the Mills Committee's decision, it surprisingly excluded two prominent names often associated with baseball's early development—Alexander Cartwright and Abner Doubleday.

The old-timers list appeared to be more padded and contained the names of twenty-six former players and included seven pitchers, five catchers, two first basemen, second basemen and third basemen, five shortstops and only three outfielders. Of this group all but nine would eventually be elected to the Hall of Fame. The ones not chosen included Lee Richmond, whose claim to fame was based on pitching the game's first perfect game, Matt Kilroy who hit for a .222 lifetime average, and Silver Flint, who batted .239. In addition to playing outfield, Kilroy was a successful pitcher who won 46 games in 1887, but was barely over .500 lifetime and once lost 34 contests. During his career, Richmond lost 13 more games than he won and Flint committed more errors than games played in two different seasons. Others with just average statistics were Charles Bennett, Ross Barnes (who only played for four years), Jerry Denny and Herman Long. Only Fred Dunlap who averaged .292, was a serious contender. With so many short careers in the nineteenth century, it may have been difficult to find some worthy names.

The publication of the original list was not done without controversy. Two days after its release, Dan Daniel of the *New York Evening Telegram* published his choice of ten (selected by position) and complained about what he thought were glaring omissions. Daniel lamented the failure of Hal Chase, Buck Weaver, and Schalk to make the list. The latter two were members of the Chicago team that was involved in the infamous Black Sox scandal of 1919 that centered around throwing games during the World Series. Chase became a central focus in the investigations following the scandal when it was revealed that he had profited by betting on the Cincinnati team in the Series. In 1920 Judge Landis, in a move designed to clean up baseball's tarnished image, ousted Chase and others from the big leagues. Daniel felt that the achievements these players accomplished on the diamond were being ignored because of their past association with gambling and the fact that Landis was still commissioner.[2] A player's personal conduct off the field was, evidently, a factor in his selection possibility from the first election.

A week after the list of nominees was published, nation-wide protests by fans and writers against the selections were causing baseball's authorities to reconsider their choices. Frick announced that the original selections would be voided and that a new group, more acceptable and logical according to the league president, would be established. Two of the major complaints against the original system were the restrictions placed on voters by limiting the number of players to be voted on and by restricting the number of 19th century choices to half of those from the modern era. Baseball's leaders claimed that the first list was provided to aid the memories of the voters and not to restrict any individual. But because of the rather adamant protest over the omission or inclusion of certain players, Frick and his associates considered a new vote. Rather than restricting the writers in their choice, the new plan simply called for an inductee to receive three-quarters of the ballots cast. This, of course, would mean that baseball's hierarchy could not omit players whom they felt had violated a code of ethics. Frick also felt that the new system would make it as difficult as possible to gain entry. He didn't want to "provide any automatic system for piling up additions."[3]

Another major concern over the Hall of Fame choices had to do with the restrictions placed on the early developers of the sport. Thomas S. Shibe, president of the Philadelphia Athletics, wrote to American League president William Harridge concerning this matter following a conversation with Cleland. He regretted that the selection of possible inductees started with the formation of the National League in 1876. Shibe pointed out that this did not coincide with the centennial celebration, which was to honor people connected with the game since Doubleday invented it in 1839. Frick felt the same way, and he also believed that those who had helped to build the game (including Spalding and Chadwick) should receive equal consideration with modern players.[4]

The controversy over the selection process was not restricted to fans and administrators. Two of baseball's major publications, *Spalding Guide* and *The Sporting News*, also entered into the argument. The former had deteriorated as a yearly source of information since the First World War, but its very name still carried considerable weight in baseball circles. While praising the Hall of Fame concept as a form of recognition long over-due, editor John B. Foster reminded his readers that another Spalding publication, *Baseball Record*, had previously listed a yearly selection of the most famous players before it became defunct. Given the long association between the *Guide* and the game, he felt eminently qualified to make suggestions for enshrinement. Early returns from the initial balloting revealed that Babe Ruth, Walter Johnson, Ty Cobb, Honus Wagner, and Christy Mathewson were leading the field of contenders. Foster could see no reason why all of them shouldn't be included. However, he felt that the 19th century figures were being slighted and deserved further consideration. In addition to former players such as Spalding, Cummings, Al Reach and the famous Wright brothers, he included other names such as Chadwick, Mills, and Benjamin Shibe—who invented the modern ball. Most importantly, Foster wondered why nobody had thought to include the game's professed inventor—Abner Doubleday.[5]

By the 1930s, *The Sporting News* had long surpassed all other baseball publications and righteously proclaimed itself as the sport's bible. Its word, therefore, influenced a large portion of baseball's fandom. While recognizing that disagreement in the selections was only natural, a majority verdict was the only method deemed feasible. However, the St. Louis based publication endorsed the general method of separating players into modern and previous century categories, allowing experts in both phases to make the individual choices. Having considered several constructive suggestions advanced by critics of the original plan, the publication reviewed their merits.

These proposals included one idea that would eliminate all active players from consideration until their retirement. Those still playing would eventually get a chance to be enshrined when their careers were finished, and they wouldn't block the selection of viable candidates who could no longer prove their worth after the election was over. Under the proposed plan, rejectees would not be given another opportunity. Bob Quinn, head of the Boston Braves and considered an expert on both time periods, suggested that the list of early day players be expanded from five because they would never have another chance to make the honor roll. Quinn felt that the small number of possibilities was an arbitrary limitation that restricted the inclusion number for no apparent reason. The American League PR man, Henry Edwards, urged the inclusion of an extra classification for those figures who had made significant contributions outside of the playing field—such as Spalding, Connie Mack and George Wright.

Recognizing the afore-mentioned problems in the selection process, *The Sporting News* made some suggestions of its own. They realized that including too many people in the hall would only decrease the value of being chosen, and they decided to strike a happy medium by increasing the 19th century selection list to ten (which for some reason didn't seem as arbitrary as five), restricting active players, and selecting a certain number of players each year regardless of the time in which they played. Realizing the permanence of the memorial and the resulting need for fairness, the weekly magazine encouraged baseball's executives to consider those suggestions so that the hall "would be genuinely representative of the game's greatest figures of all time."[6]

Because of the controversy surrounding the selection process, the time limit for choosing the inductees had to be extended. A committee made up of Cleland, Edwards, and Bill Brandt, the National League publicity man, decided to expand the cut-off date to January 25th. Beside the controversy over the means of choosing players, many members of the Writer's Association misread their instructions and voted for an All-Star team instead. Voters were informed that they could change their ballot, if they desired, to include as many players in any one position that they felt were necessary. They could also vote again if they felt that a deserving player had been omitted from the original list. The restriction requiring a 75% quota for eligibility was also established for all inductees.[7]

If the first ballot caused general confusion, the second vote resulted in disappointment. The initial polling, which only dealt with the pre-1900 period, revealed that nobody had received the necessary three-quarter-percent required for induction. The leading vote getters were Buck Ewing and Cap Anson, who tied for first place with a little more than half of the 78 votes cast. They were followed by Willie Keeler and Cy Young; the latter of which had received only 32 1/2 votes in spite of his more than 500 victories on the mound. Others who garnered support among the voters included Ed Delehanty (who led the others in the first poll), John McGraw, Charles Radbourne, Herman Long, Mike Kelly, Amos Rusie, Hugh Jennings and Fred Clark. Spalding received just four votes and Ward only three. Because of the vote's failure to produce a viable candidate, the names of the top ten players were resubmitted for another tally.[8]

The results of the vote on modern players were far more satisfying. The selectors were obviously more familiar with the recent greats of the game as five of them received the required percent of ballots. They were led by the fiery Ty Cobb, who lacked only four votes of being a unanimous choice. Seven votes behind the Tiger great were Babe Ruth and Honus Wagner, with Christy Mathewson and Walter Johnson completing the list of original selections. Some of the players who received consideration in the 19th century poll were also listed—including Young, Delehanty, and McGraw. This confusion pointed out the need for a list of early day players who might not have received the required percentage because they fell into two different categories. Since the planners had established a limit of ten for the modern vote, they decided to hold another election during the next year. It was expected that Napoleon Lajoie, Tris Speaker, Cy Young, Rogers Hornsby and Mickey Cochrane, who rounded out the top ten, would ultimately be chosen in the next poll.

Cobb, who had never endeared himself to his baseball contemporaries because of his irascible personality, was a popular choice among the writers and fans. They admired his tenacity and daring on the field and, above all, his uncanny knack for thinking one step ahead of everyone else. Never a person to accept criticism, he may have resented the four judges who left him off the ballot, but he never admitted it. As was true of others who would follow him into baseball's Valhalla, he considered his induction as his greatest accomplishment.

Ruth was the most highly recognized player in the history of the game. His appearance at a ball park would ensure a large audience, and virtually every action he took was a headline news story. His dramatic rise to national acclaim made many fans forget the tragedy of the Black Sox Scandal, and he was credited with saving the game at its darkest hour. His feats in and out of the game made him, perhaps, the most recognized American in the world. If there were any surprises in this election, it was only that he didn't finish first in the voting. However, a man of such excesses may have annoyed some of the more conservative voters.

The other three may have been the best players ever at their respective positions. Even modern-day shortstops would fall short in comparison with Wagner, the Pirate great who had won eight batting titles and led his club to four pennants. Of course he hit many pitchers well, and one of them was Mathewson, against whom he batted over .300. This was quite an honor because many people considered Christy the greatest pitcher of all times. Certainly the National League players would have been overwhelmingly in agreement since nobody ever won more games in the senior circuit. His performances on the field of play and the battlefield endeared him to Americans young and old. Johnson's tremendous fast ball earned him the nickname "Big Train" and he was certainly Mathewson's equal in American League history. Nobody won more games against opponents of the junior division.[9]

With the initial ballot now official, the hall's promoters could begin to focus on other tasks; but for those who barely missed election, the wait for the next vote must have been an anxious one. However, for Cleland and his associates, this only meant a period of controversy in which the debate over selections would continue. Naturally, this would enhance the importance of the hall of fame concept and create additional interest for the centennial celebration. By October of 1936, Edwards, Cleland, and Brandt began to prepare for the upcoming election. The National League's PR man wanted to start the operation as soon as possible and suggested that voters should also include managers, presidents, and umpires in their considerations. Cleland contacted Littell about this possible change in the voting procedure and promised to inform him about the league's decision. Even though he planned to visit Cooperstown in the near future, the secretary was delaying his trip until the first five bronze plaques commemorating the initial inductees were completed. He hoped that his trip to the village would stir more interest if he brought them with him. After the first plaques were installed, Littell contacted Cleland in May, 1937, to praise their appearance; and he added that they were a great addition to the museum.[10]

As was true with other aspects of the museum, there was more than one firm wanting to supply plaques. The Medallic Art Company of New York City expressed an interest in their construction. Although the company specialized in designing and preparing bas-reliefs in bronze, the league officials had already chosen Lambert Brothers of the city to make the plaques. Evidently the quality of the finished product did not meet with the museum official's standards. They contacted Cleland in New York and complained about the patina that had formed on the surface. The secretary requested that Beattie ship him one of the plaques for his inspection. He hoped to work out some arrangement with the Lambert firm to improve them .

Brandt contacted Henry Lambert in the spring of 1938 concerning this problem, but his response was somewhat disheartening. Cleland requested a brown color scheme which would require a French bronze in order to harmonize the colors. This change in color required additional hand work and tooling which would increase the price of each plaque by thirty dollars. Evidently the original plaques were never changed because a number of guests to the museum noted the differences between them and the newer ones. However the problem of a green finish continued. Twelve of them were so bad that they had to be removed for inspection following the centennial celebration.[11]

By the time the results of the second election were announced in January of 1937, new procedures had been established. First, only 20th century players were to be considered by the writers since the hall's leaders would soon announce those selected from the early days. Each of the writers who cast his ballot voted for his top ten selections, which could not include any players who were considered active in the 1936 season. The 75% limit meant that 151 votes were required for induction and only three people surpassed that number—Lajoie, Speaker, and Young. While each man was undoubtedly qualified for induction, some people were shocked that baseball's most durable pitcher and all-time leading winner on the mound had only made it by two votes. Previously, Young had fallen 58 votes short of election and finished eighth in the voting. But with five players inducted in the previous election, he and the two others who finished ahead of him had the way cleared to make it.

Even though few would doubt the credibility of the new choices, there was some surprise about those who fell short. Bill Slocum of the New York *American* questioned the omission of Ed Delehanty, John McGraw, Frank Chance and Ross Young. He was more surprised about the exclusion of Willie Keeler, who finished in a tie with Eddie Collins for fifth place behind Grover Cleveland Alexander. The diminutive outfielder had averaged over .300 from 1892 to 1906 and collected more than 200 hits in a record eight straight seasons. In addition to leading the league in hitting twice, his .432 batting average in 1897 had never been surpassed. In a final observation on the election results, Slocum noticed that Joe Jackson had not overcome the Black Sox scandal since he received only two votes. Even Hal Chase, with a total of 18 ballots, had surpassed that count.[12]

Now that the election process had become a yearly event, the news of its results were receiving far more print than the first poll. Naturally, a number of writers expressed their concerns for those who did not qualify, and nobody received more support among the losers than McGraw. If one of your favorites came close in the recent election, you could hope that he would make it the next year since those elected wouldn't be in competition. However, there was concern about the former Giant leader since he received only 35 of the necessary 151 votes for enshrinement. George Daley of the New York *Tribune* felt that McGraw had to overcome two major obstacles. First, he had gained fame mostly as a manager rather than a player. In addition, he was widely known for his fiery and aggressive manner and this type of behavior had left him with many enemies. Still, Cobb had overcome this handicap and the Little Napoleon's supporters would soon be rewarded.

Shortly after the tabulations were revealed, Littell gave his support for the election process in a Cooperstown editorial. He quoted a recently received bulletin from National League officials which praised the efforts of writers around the country for their excellent judgement. The fact that the three recent inductees had ranked directly behind the winners in the previous poll proved the consistency and research ability of the writers. However, the league officials warned that this did not necessitate similar results in the next election. Each year was a new contest with a different deck of cards, and the results could change dramatically. The electors had cast ballots for 111 different players, a number of whom could move up in the next count. Two men who stood to rank high in the next poll were Roger Hornsby and Pie Traynor, who were close to retirement but had been listed as active players during the 1936 season.[13]

Aside from the controversy that accompanied the election, there was also some levity to be found by Dan Daniel. In a *Sporting News* article in late February he poked fun at those who lamented the exclusion of their favorite player. He joked that the player who was the first hold-out in contract disputes should be included because his eventual pay increase would also mean more money for the other players in addition to more independence. Another inductee, according to the sports writer, should be the inventor of the alibi who originated excuses for muffed plays, missed signs, and broken curfews. He would also include the man who invented spring training because this innovation allowed writers a yearly vacation in a warm climate. Club owners, according to Daniel, wanted to include the inventor of the turnstile which regulated entry to the park, insured an accurate head count, and signaled higher profits. Still kidding but on a more serious note, Daniels lamented the exclusion of umpires without whom the game could not be played. Finally, he felt that baseball games without concessions were unnatural. He also included in his list the inventor of the hot dog and the peanut.[14]

While Daniel's article may have smoothed some ruffled feathers with its humor, it was obvious from the overwhelming response to the election that the interest of baseball fans around the country had been stimulated. Littell expressed his surprise to the extent of curiosity in activities surrounding the centennial celebration. In an article for the village newspaper, he praised the work of Cleland in advancing the national concern in the museum and acknowledged Frick as the initiator of the Hall of Fame. The editor was convinced that the instant appeal of the league president's innovation had captured the imagination of the fans and writers, thereby assuring the success of the plans for Cooperstown. Indeed, Cleland had already begun to receive correspondence that reflected the fan's desires for more information on the players selected for induction.

Littell also praised organized baseball for its moral and practical support and recognized their adamant resolve to see the project through to its conclusion. While their efforts had been formidable in popularizing the baseball shrine, they had also interested fans of other sports in developing similar institutions. For example, Damon Runyon, the renowned New York sports writer, had recently suggested the construction of a football hall of fame in New Brunswick, New Jersey (which he considered as the birthplace), and his idea had already received a positive response. While Littell wished the home of Rutgers success in their project, he admonished the residents of Cooperstown to continue their vigilance lest the home of football might outstrip them in the race to recognize their game's outstanding contributors. Realizing that the centennial celebration was only two years away, he wanted the entire community to become involved in a united effort that would insure its success.[15]

Although the election controversies aided the need for publicity and debate, they had not satisfied fans of the early figures in the national pastime. Horace J. Bradley of Ephrata, Pennsylvania, contacted Cleland in December, 1936, to inquire into the delay concerning nineteenth century choices. The secretary informed him that a committee of former managers and players had been established to nominate players from the early period. Evidently, the disappointing results of the initial vote on the old-timers had inspired this decision. Bradley was anxious for the results of this poll because he was concerned about his father's chances for consideration. George Washington Bradley played at a number of positions for several teams from 1876 to 1888, but he was primarily a pitcher. His main claim to fame was that he pitched the first no-hit, no-run game in the National League in 1876. Horace would have to wait for awhile for the decision on his father since the hall's originators were still working on the proposition.[16]

Others raised stronger contentions concerning the omission of the early generation of baseball figures. *The Sporting News* lamented the exclusion of Anson, Young, and others who failed to gain support in the first vote and complained that the balloting process reflected "that great diamond figures of the past soon lose their luster as new generations come upon the scene." After the second election, the *Spalding Guide* expressed similar concerns. Editor John Foster pointed out that those who were voting were contemporary writers, and the *Guide* chastised them for forgetting the deserving members of the first generation of baseball. He felt that this group would "always live in the memory as the great men of base ball who lived many years before the present glamorous candidates."[17]

Despite the difficulties that the electors were having with the nineteenth century selections, *The Sporting News* suggested a rather novel idea for overcoming these problems. Realizing that many long-time fans were avid readers of their publication, they called for them to express their opinions on the matter. They invited "anyone who has seen or played with these early-day performers" to send in a list of names for consideration. The magazine asked those who wrote in to identify themselves so that they could prove that they had "first-hand knowledge of the players." They also asked these subscribers to include their reasons for supporting the players of their choice. In the process, the older fans would be helping the selection committee to make a wise decision, and at the same time they would be doing a good turn for old, deserving players.[18]

As the weight of the complaints had begun to overwhelm Cleland, a centennial committee was formed in 1937. Its executive leadership consisted of Landis, Frick, Heydler and Harridge representing the majors. William G. Bramham and George M. Trautman, president and chairman respectively of the National Association of Professional Baseball Leagues, participated for the minors. Since these men had long been associated with the sport, they were charged with the responsibility of choosing five of the most important "builders of baseball" who would represent 19th century contributors as members of the Hall of Fame.

The inductees representing baseball's early years were announced by Frick at the baseball convention in Chicago in December, 1937. Given the host of names from which they picked, there were some surprises in their selections. Included in the original list were George Wright, Morgan G. Bulkeley, Ban Johnson, Connie Mack and John J. McGraw. Of these men, perhaps Wright belonged on the list more than any other. As an outstanding shortstop for the Cincinnati Red Stockings as far back as 1869, he was a leader of what many people considered to be the first professional team. Perhaps his brother Harry was even more deserving. Although he couldn't match George's play on the field, his role as manager and founder of the first professional team, league organizer, and promoter led to his title as "the father of the professional game" during the late nineteenth century. Unfortunately, sixteen years would pass before his election to the Hall of Fame.

Still, there was some controversy as to which Wright should be inducted into baseball's shrine. Richards Vidmer of the New York *Herald Tribune* was made aware of the dilemma by Bill Braddock, whom he recognized as a walking encyclopedia of sports history. The latter pointed out that the selectors may have been somewhat confused when they chose George instead of Harry and that in the process they may have given the former some credit he didn't deserve. Braddock felt that baseball's officials had allowed sentimentality to enter into their decision since George had only recently passed away. However, both men had strong credentials; and he thought that an easier solution would be to induct both at the same time.[19]

The other picks from baseball's first century must have caused consternation for the fans of this period. Obviously, Mack and McGraw were deserving of enshrinement, but should they have been selected by this committee or did their names belong to the modern era. While both had been a part of the game's development in the late 19th century, their real success had been achieved during the recent period when they took over the reins of management of the Athletics and the Giants.

The inclusion of Bulkeley and Johnson were even more controversial. As the first presidents of the National and American Leagues, they were certainly important baseball figures; but Bulkeley was better known as a politician. As the first league president, he seemed to be the right choice, but he won the office by a drawing and did little to further baseball. William Hulbert, one of the leading founders of the National League, would have been a better candidate, but he was never enshrined. Johnson, like the two famous managers who were chosen, was probably more recognized for his activities in the more recent past. It may have seemed suspicious to baseball observers that a committee dominated by four league presidents and a commissioner would recommend enshrinement for two of their executive predecessors. In addition, four very significant people were omitted—Spalding, Chadwick, Cartwright, and Doubleday.

The election process continued in 1938 under the guidance of Bill Brandt. He contacted Cleland in January, a week before the polling was to be finished. By this time, newspapers throughout the country were anxious to report the yearly results, and the Service Bureau's manager had already set up a meeting with the press. Two days after the balloting stopped, representatives of the Associated Press, United Press, and the International News Service met in Brandt's office for the counting of the votes.

The results of the election appeared a week after the polls closed, and once again they were surprising. The 262 members of the Baseball Writer's Association could agree on only one candidate out of 119 eligible players—Grover Cleveland Alexander. In the three elections, the number of inductees had declined each year. Although this may have frustrated the fans of individual candidates, it pointed out the degree of selectivity involved and enhanced the prestige of being chosen. The only question concerning the former pitching great's inclusion in the Hall of Fame was not his credentials but rather why he hadn't been selected in the past. Still, fifty voters had rejected Alexander before his election brought the total membership of the shrine to 14. George Sisler fell 18 votes short of election, and he was followed closely by Keeler and Collins.

The inclusion of only one more player to the Hall of Fame was disappointing to fans and scribes alike. Even though "Old Pete" (as Alexander's supporters had dubbed him) had more than sufficient credits for his election, some critics continued to point out that he should have been included in earlier elections. There was a belief by many that he had been bypassed up to this point because of the rugged individualism and hard drinking that had characterized his later career. Similar behavior on the part of Babe Ruth, however, had not kept him from enshrinement. By the time that the news reached him in Springfield, Illinois, a bitter Alexander expressed more concerns about his present state than the honor that had been accorded him. He felt that the "Hall of Fame is fine...but it doesn't mean bread and butter. It's only your picture on the wall." Relegated to a role as "greeter" in a local bar, the famous pitcher was down on his luck and had no financial reserves because borrowers had always taken advantage of his friendly nature. As *The Sporting News* succinctly stated, Alexander "was everybody's friend before he was his own."[20]

Following the announcement of the election results, the debate on the vote continued. *The Sporting News* recognized that a number of baseball fans had expressed dissatisfaction with the slow induction process and wanted to change the system. The weekly publication believed that the hall should include a wider variety of positions in the game including officials and prominent minor league representatives. This was the first mention of the lower echelons of baseball, who had been overlooked in the election plans. Recognizing the important role that the minors had played in the game's development, the tabloid felt that they had made significant enough contributions to warrant inclusion into the shrine. In spite of this contention, the baseball bible did not hold to the theory that the election process should be escalated. The difficulty that the players encountered in achieving the honor made it all the greater, and they discouraged any agitation that would allow for an easier entry.[21]

By the time of the fourth vote, sports writers were beginning to focus more on who they thought might be elected before the selections were announced. Previously, they had reserved their remarks for the post-election period, during which they lamented about a certain player's failure to gain recognition. Perhaps the scribes felt they could persuade others to support their cause. A popular re-election choice was Sisler, who had barely missed in the previous year. One of the game's great hitters and fielders, Sisler had ascended to the position of commissioner of the semi-pros and was well liked in baseball circles. He would not disappoint his supporters in the next election, as he was the leading vote getter.

The election of 1939 was the final selection process for modern-day players before the centennial celebration of that summer. Three names which had been prominent in previous polls had finally risen to the top. In January of that year, Sisler, Keeler, and Collins were elected after three previous flirtations with glory. Since the order of their finish had been mixed in the earlier balloting, the voting process had once again displayed its unpredictability. This time 206 voters were needed to gain enshrinement and Keeler had made it by only one ballot. A brilliant bunter and place hitter, he had hit over .300 for 15 straight years and twice led the league in batting average. He played for four different teams and gained notoriety with the Baltimore Orioles in the late 1890's. He died in Brooklyn in 1923 and was one of only two players (including Mathewson) to be elected from the modern era who had passed away. Collins, a graduate of Columbia University, was a second baseman for Connie Mack's famous $100,000 infield and finished his career with the White Sox. At the time of his election, he was the vice-president and treasurer of the Boston Red Sox.

Although the final roll call of 20th century members of the Hall of Fame had been established, the earlier figures in the sport awaited recognition. Following the original five selections from the previous century in 1937, Chadwick and Cartwright were added the next year. The game's first sportswriter might have been amused at his inclusion since it was his editorial 35 years earlier that had ultimately led to Cooperstown's fame. Complaints about the exclusion of prominent figures in baseball's past continued, however; and in 1939 Landis, Frick, and Harridge collaborated in the selection of Spalding, Charles Comiskey, William Cummings, Buck Ewing, Cap Anson, and Charles "Old Hoss" Radbourne. The commissioner and the two league presidents had worked closely with baseball writers throughout the country on this decision before it was announced to the public just five weeks before the centennial celebration.

Apparently not satisfied with the method of selecting old-timers, Landis continued the search for a proper committee for this purpose. He appointed Sid Mercer, the dean of baseball writers, to serve with three team presidents on an investigating team. Robert Quinn of the Braves, Connie Mack of the Athletics, and Edward Barrow of the Yankees were appointed to join the sports writer in an effort to select great veterans for induction. This was the finest effort to date to fill the 19th century void that had been such a source of complaint. All three executives were former players who were now in their seventies, and Mercer had a solid background in the game's history. As formidable as this group was, their other activities kept them from any concerted action. During Landis' reign as commissioner, the veteran's committee never chose any additional immortals for the Hall of Fame induction.[22]

With the completion of the final poll before the shrine's dedication, *The Sporting News* commented on the method of choosing inductees. Previously fearful that the election process had become too cumbersome and needed revamping, they were thankful that the Baseball Writers Association had made three acceptable choices in 1939. Their initial cause for concern was understandable as only one player had been chosen in the previous year. Since the Hall of Fame had altered its manner of selecting stars in the past, they felt the election procedure should be flexible until an acceptable way was found. After all, the polling system was an experiment and could be changed if it didn't produce the desired results. However, the new election dispelled those fears since it produced a desirable number of players for the shrine.

The baseball magazine reserved the strongest criticism for the committee in charge of choosing important figures from the previous century. They felt it was taking too much time to reach a decision. They also believed that these selectors had picked too many officials as compared to players and had gone too far in their attempt to achieve a balance between the two leagues. However, they were pleased with the choice of Keeler—whose election halted criticism that too many modern-day players were being chosen while the older ones were being left out. Although Collins and Sisler belonged to the recent past, the sports publication was thankful that they were men of high character and lamented that Alexander had not followed in their footsteps.[23]

The final tally of inductees for the centennial was 25, including 13 from the pre-1900 era. This formidable array of stars was indeed impressive. Contemporary fans could look with pride at the selection of people such as Ruth and Cobb, considered to be respectively the games' greatest slugger and the best all-around player. The pitchers included the four biggest winners of all time (Young, Johnson, Mathewson, and Alexander). Sisler and Speaker, in addition to their hitting prowess, were considered to be the finest fielders at their positions while Wagner was felt to be the greatest shortstop of all time. Lajoie and Keeler, who both began their careers in the 1890s, were two of the game's most renowned hitters. Collins, in addition to being a great hitter, was second only to Cobb as a modern base stealer. The only positions not elected were catcher and third base, but Mack and McGraw had filled these roles during their playing days.

The selectees from the early generation were a mixture of players, executives, and innovators. Because of the diversity of the people chosen from this era, the group as a whole may not have seemed as impressive as their modern-day counterparts to the fans of the 1930s. However, they did contain some of the greatest players of the period; including first baseman Anson, who hit over .300 for twenty seasons; Wright, the best shortstop of his day; and Radbourne, who won over 300 games including 60 in the 1884 season. Nineteenth-century executives included Bulkeley, the senior circuit's first president; Comiskey, father of the White Sox organization; and Johnson, the junior league's originator. The two twentieth century managers, Mack and McGraw, may have seemed out of place; but they had both played in the previous era. Innovators included Chadwick, the first sportswriter and inventor of the box score; Cartwright, organizer of the first professional team, Cummings, originator of the curve ball; and Ewing, who utilized the first big catcher's mitt. As a former pitcher, owner, and sporting goods magnate, Spalding was a cross-section of all aspects of the game and remained in a class by himself. Nobody mentioned that he was primarily responsible for Cooperstown's biggest claim to fame.

The election of baseball's elite group attracted tremendous interest among fans, writers and players throughout the country. The yearly announcement of the polling results caused a great deal of anticipation as the time drew closer for the centennial celebration. The response to the election process surpassed all expectations and represented a major coup for the shrine's innovators. The balloting process served as an important promotional device; but it also resulted in filling the Hall of Fame with the famous plaques for each inductee that would eventually become a major drawing card for the museum complex. Still, the museum half of the project needed to be fulfilled; and, since this part of the plan had emerged first, Cleland had begun to collect items for display before the Hall of Fame concept was even announced.

Chapter Four
Trivial Pursuit

When Cleland first purposed the idea of establishing a baseball museum in Cooperstown, he probably didn't realize how difficult it would be to assemble. Of course a building was necessary, but there was already a temporary room in the village that would suffice for a while. The secretary's major problem was how to find significant material and to convince the owners that their items deserved a fitting place in the new museum. When other halls of fame were initiated in future years, their originators would sympathize with the difficulties that Cleland would encounter.

There was nothing novel about the idea of establishing a museum. Generally, their purpose was educational but they were also organized for their entertainment value. Charles W. Peale, the famous painter and naturalist, and showman P. T. Barnum were renowned for their efforts in this area in the eighteenth and nineteenth centuries. The baseball museum was unique, however, in that its focus was sports memorabilia and specifically artifacts connected with baseball. Cleland was correct in assuming that these items would hold a certain fascination for fans young and old. While not a baseball fan himself, he understood how those apparently trivial objects could take on significant meanings. Displaying them in a museum would only tend to increase their value both monetarily and historically.

Shortly after Cleland was appointed as secretary for the museum, local officials announced the acquisition of some valuable materials for the facility. They included two large colored prints which illustrated how a game was played in the early days. One of them, drawn by Major Otto Boetticher during the Civil War, depicted a game involving Union prisoners at Salisbury, North Carolina in 1863. In addition to being the earliest known print on the subject of baseball, it also served as a link between Doubleday, who established a distinguished war record, and the national pastime. It was well known that the playing of the game during the war years was a major impetus in spreading its acceptance after the conflict was over. Certainly many fans were convinced that Abner had a significant role in this development. The other was a Currier and Ives print showing a game in progress at Elysian Fields—the famous playground where the first professional contest took place in Hoboken, New Jersey.[1]

Cleland soon discovered that the pursuit of baseball artifacts could be very frustrating. At the suggestion of Frank Graham of the New York *Evening Sun*, Cleland contacted Jack Ryder of the Cincinnati *Enquirer* in order to obtain the address of the 19th century player Harry Wright. Ryder responded quickly and informed Alexander that although Harry had died, his brother George could be contacted through the Boston address of his famous sporting goods firm. Evidently this was not the first time that someone had inquired about Wright's collection of equipment and literature pertaining to baseball's early days. In the past he had loaned out certain artifacts only to find that they were difficult to retrieve. Since he had spent so many years collecting and caring for the items, he was reluctant to loan them out. However, Wright realized the significance of the Cooperstown museum and promised to forward any duplicates from his collection. Two and a half years later, Cleland was still not able to get a donation from the Wright family. Consequently, he contacted Julian Curtiss of the Spalding Brothers to seek his help in the matter. The secretary hoped that the recent inclusion of George Wright to the Hall of Fame might reduce the family's reluctance to part with some items, but they remained adamant in their resolve.[2]

Although Cleland's first venture into collecting historic items met with failure, he remained determined to acquire donations. He continued to pursue the former greats of the game, often by contacting their closest living relative and sometimes by utilizing intermediaries to overcome the reluctance of possible donors. For example, John T. Doyle contacted Keith Spalding in order to acquire some drawings by Homer Davenport that belonged to his father's collection. Doyle was the head of the American Sports Publishing Company, originally owned by A. G. Spalding, and publisher of the *Guide* and the sporting magnate's famous book on baseball history, *America's National Game*. The drawings, including one hundred full page engravings and sixteen cartoons, made up a major portion of A. G.'s book. They had been given to the New York Public Library by Keith's mother, and Spalding had to contact librarian H. M. Lydenberg to get his approval for their display in the museum. Lydenberg was willing to mail reproductions of the drawings, but he didn't feel that he had the authority to send the originals without the consent of the library's board of trustees. He was also reluctant to break up the original collection. Because of these restrictions, Cleland was willing to accept photostats of eight originals.[3]

The reluctance of collectors to part with memorabilia inspired Cleland to utilize a pamphlet that had been put together concerning the National Baseball Museum. In this brochure, the history of Cooperstown's progress was detailed, complete with photographs of Doubleday Field, a Civil War baseball game, the Currier and Ives print of an 1866 game in Hoboken, New Jersey, the Doubleday baseball and the now famous general himself. It gave a brief account of the Mills Commission, the work that had been done to the field through its 1934 dedication, and the life of the game's alleged inventor. Perhaps inspired by this publication, Samuel Simon of Brooklyn sent Alexander his first major item. His father was the owner of a china dinner plate containing photos of the championship Giants team of 1889. Shortly after this acquisition, Frick donated the same team's winning cup.[4]

Cleland also sent a copy of the museum folder to Frick in June, 1935. Previously, the league president agreed to write various National League clubs to get their cooperation in furnishing materials that might be suitable for display. Because his earlier inquiries had produced a few tangible results, the secretary requested Frick's assistance in acquiring materials and hoped that his correspondence could give a much needed boost to the museum project. Alexander also reminded the league president that he had promised to contact Judge Emil

Fuch, owner of the Boston Braves, concerning the acquisition of a Babe Ruth uniform. The team had recently acquired the great slugger in order to boost its sagging attendance, and he was willing to join because of his desire to be a manager. In early June, Ruth resigned following a dispute with his new owner; and this meant that Frick would have to pursue the elusive Ruth through another channel.[5]

The Doyle connection, which had already produced some pictures for the museum, once again proved to be fruitful. The publisher visited Thomas S. Shibe, Vice President of the A. J. Reach Sporting Goods Company (a Spalding concern) and president of the Athletics, in early May, 1935, and asked him to get in touch with George Reach for the purpose of conducting a tour for himself and Cleland of the company's mitt and glove factory. Doyle, aware that Stephen Clark desired an exhibit demonstrating these products, wanted to arrange this with the company. Due to a variety of business concerns, the meeting did not take place until late November. As brief as their relationship was, Cleland developed a liking for the head of the Athletics. Shortly before his death, Shibe had arranged for an elaborate exhibit to be sent to the museum demonstrating the various stages of development in the manufacturing of a modern baseball. Afterwards, his heirs arranged for the museum to acquire another important collection of artifacts that had originally belonged to Benjamin S. Shibe, Thomas' father and original owner of the Philadelphia club. Originally displayed at the city's centennial celebration of 1876, the noted baseball manufacturer's exhibit consisted of a collection of baseballs showing their evolution from old to modern times. In addition, Reach, whose father had previously been owner of the Phillies, donated another exhibit showing miniature gloves, mitts, a mask and other paraphernalia.[6]

These acquisitions proved to be of considerable interest for the museum, but they weren't delivered until a year after the original search began. Recognizing the futility that Cleland experienced in his early collection plans, Frick suggested that he contact Clark Griffith, the owner of the Washington Senators, to secure from him a loan of materials that would help to maintain interest in the project until the collection became larger. Cleland contacted the club president in June, 1935, and assured him that he needn't be concerned about the safe-keeping of his artifacts since the local historical society had acquired adequate experience in this area through their housing of the permanent James Fenimore Cooper collection. Griffith responded immediately and invited the secretary to Washington in order to discuss the matter of loans or donations to the museum. He also mentioned that a collection of pictures of various presidents and other dignitaries which had been taken at opening day celebrations might be of interest.

Shortly thereafter, Griffith's secretary sent Cleland a box of 17 pictures and a list containing the names of each one and a note as to whether they were a gift or a loan. It was a formidable collection and contained pictures of presidents Wilson, Harding, Coolidge, Hoover, and Roosevelt at the opening games. There were also pictures of old ball clubs, General John J. Pershing and Connie Mack, in addition to photographs of Nap Lajoie and Abner Doubleday. Cleland expressed his appreciation for the delivery and stated that he planned to make reproductions of the loaned items.

For the museum's secretary, it was time to take inventory and pass this information on to his boss. Two days after receiving the correspondence from Griffith, he drew up a list of donations received and mailed it to Clark in Cooperstown. In addition to the Davenport reproductions, the Giants memorabilia of 1889, the Griffith pictures and the Philadelphia baseballs, he had also acquired a 56 year-old Canadian baseball from Doyle. Clark was well aware of the other gifts for he had donated them himself—the Doubleday ball and two prints that had become part of the museum pamphlet.[7]

In addition to these brochures, the press had released stories concerning the museum project, and this advertising helped to increase interest in their holdings in a number of ways. For example, in August, a man from Petersburg, Michigan, informed the secretary that he was willing to donate a picture of the 1884 Toledo baseball team. In some of the inquiries to the secretary, however, collectors wanted to sell their memorabilia. A fan from Milwaukee contacted Cleland about three of the old Spalding baseball rule books, the oldest of which was dated 1883. Cleland replied that the museum had no funds with which to purchase relics or materials and referred him to Doyle, who might make him an offer. Another person from South Bend, Indiana, wanted to sell Cleland a book on the 1888 Stockton, California, baseball club of the California League.

The secretary was also contacted by the library bureau of the Remington Rand corporation for the purpose of selling their metal frame display cases. They had previously read an article about the Cooperstown museum in the New York *Herald Tribune* and, since their Ilion factory was only thirty miles from the village, they hoped to supply these items for housing the baseball exhibits. Others wanted to purchase things from the museum. They included a man from Akron, Ohio, who wanted to buy any baseball literature and another from Binghamton, New York, who wanted miniature paraphernalia after viewing the Reach collection in the museum.[8]

As Cleland struggled to assemble a suitable collection for the Cooperstown memorial, he found that his efforts were not always rewarding. A classic case of frustration involved his pursuance of memorabilia from Roger Connor, a former National League great from the late nineteenth century. W. H. Dunbar of Woodmont, Connecticut, suggested to Cleland in June, 1935, that he might be able to acquire one of Connor's old uniforms from his younger brother Joe, who had also played major league ball. The secretary contacted him and asked about donating the clothing or any other of his brother's relics that might be available. Unfortunately, the younger Connor could find no artifacts but suggested that Cleland get in touch with a local sports promoter, George Mulligan. Evidently, Roger's daughter had sent him all of her father's sports belongings. The secretary dutifully followed this lead, but there was never any reply to his request.[9] Alexander was beginning to discover that his desire to acquire salient items for display was not going to be easily fulfilled.

The first year's attempt to gather artifacts had resulted in little more than frustration for the museum's first secretary. Sickness had slowed the process even further and prevented him from attending the 1936 Baseball Writer's Dinner in January. Adding to his woes were the disappointing results of the pre-1900 Hall of Fame vote, which had turned up only five candidates. Undaunted, Cleland continued to press forward in spite of the complications and frustrations involved.

While he admitted to Littell that he had been pessimistic about the museum's success in the past, he felt that they were beginning to turn things around. He planned a trip to Cooperstown in April to organize the museum and felt that by the summer they would have some interesting items for display.[10]

Cleland's perseverance would eventually pay off. He must have been surprised by the wide variety of artifacts that actually came to be offered to the museum. One of these items was the bat of the Penobscot Indian slugger Lou Sockalexis, whose feats for the Cleveland Spiders in 1897 led to a fan's suggestion that the team change its nickname to the modern designation. Dennis "Dinty" Moore, of New York, a collector of old bottles, contacted the secretary about purchasing such an item. He pointed out that in the previous century many important events were commemorated with a flask that signified them. Among his collection was a bottle that resembled a baseball in size and appearance. Other items acquired by the summer of 1936 included Civil War period baseballs and dinner receipts for the 1846 Knickerbocker club.[11]

One of the more interesting items came from Jesse A. Morrill, who wrote Cleland in December concerning a silver baseball. Having gained an interest in the museum through the pre-1900 election process, he contacted the secretary concerning the 1866 relic. At the age of eleven he had witnessed a game in his hometown, Fulton, New York involving the Hercules Baseball Club, whose members came from a local seminary. The players had their names engraved on the ball and Morrill noted that one of them was W. A. Cummings, who had become famous as the inventor of the curve ball. Since he had preserved the relic and could authenticate it, he asked the secretary to visit him as soon as possible and Cleland complied.[12]

As the museum continued to gather memorabilia, the variety of items offered expanded. They included a small statue of John McGraw (donated by his alma mater, St. Bonaventure College), a sketch of a Civil War game in Salisbury, North Carolina (offered by a woman whose father was a prisoner at the time), a ball similar to the Doubleday type that Clark had purchased and dated to the 1850s, uniforms from 1876 (from Frick), shoulder straps from the army uniform of General Doubleday, old scorecards, and a plethora of historic baseballs. Even though the number of the latter had become overwhelming, Cleland was particularly interested in what he read about the supposedly oldest baseball in existence. An article had appeared in the Des Moines *Register* in December, 1937, which claimed that this item belonged to a local resident, Reverend Kitt Krenmyre. While he sometimes rejected other balls, especially if the owner only wanted to profit from sale, Cleland had an obvious interest in a ball that might predate the one purchased by Clark. However, the minister decided to keep the memento and the secretary let the matter rest.[13]

As time drew near for the centennial celebration, the museum became overwhelmed with artifacts. The interest in the museum was becoming widespread through various promotional campaigns. Even the *Spalding Guide* encouraged its readers to contact Cleland if they had any contribution of historical interest. This activity helped to expand the variety of donations which, by the end of 1938, included various prints and paintings from Clark, a photo of an old Cooperstown baseball team, and a signed Babe Ruth ball. Clark also gave the museum a bust of Christy Mathewson, a wax figure of an old ball player, four plates with various game situations depicted on them, and an old novelty bank showing underhand pitching. The hall also came into possession of the official scorecards from John Vander Meer's consecutive no-hitters in 1938 and the longest game (between Brooklyn and Boston in 1920), framed pictures of an old-timer's day at Boston Braves field in 1930, and the Spalding team on its world tour of 1889. Other items included documents, equipment, pamphlets, scrapbooks, lithographs of old time players, and a display of World Series buttons.

The amount and variety of artifacts expanded, and the hall's promoter continued to request donations from the baseball public. In the beginning of the centennial year, Frick encouraged fans from around the country to become part of the celebration by giving baseball heirlooms to the museum's collection. Since each item received would bear the name of its donor, individual contributors could have their names in the Hall of Fame displays. The league president assured the fans that their items would become part of a prominent and permanent setting in the Cooperstown display.[14]

One man desired to include his gift to the museum in his will so that he could hold on to this treasure item during his lifetime. William M. Earle of Omaha, Nebraska, had been a catcher for the famous Spalding world tour team and later played for professional teams in the National League and the American Association. He also helped to introduce baseball in Cuba, where he managed the Almendarin club to the pennant in 1901. For this feat he was rewarded with a gold watch from France that carried an inscription commemorating the event, and he was willing to donate it. Cleland eventually wanted the heirloom for the museum but recommended that Earle hold onto it until "the Great Umpire finally calls out."[15]

Rounding out the items offered to the museum through 1938 was a ball offered by Elwood C. Smith of Monroe, New York, that formerly belonged to his father, a one time catcher for the Wallkill Academy baseball team. As Smith pointed out, the ball was unusual because the horsehide cover was in one piece (instead of the modern two piece type); and it contained team names and the date of October 6, 1866. The New York *Times* ran his letter concerning the ball in their paper, and this type of published correspondence helped to advertise Cleland's quest for more materials.[16]

The collection continued to swell as the centennial year opened. Fred Lieb, the well-known sports writer from St. Louis, donated yet another baseball. This one was used by a group of major league ball players who journeyed to Japan in 1931 to play a series of games in the Orient. Lieb also included a number of photographs of the American visit including shots of the official welcome by the Japanese government, the crowds greeting the U. S. players, and a visit to the shrine of a former emperor. There were also local newspaper accounts of the game, a Japanese scorecard, and a picture of the American men and their wives being entertained by the premier at his residence.

Of special interest was a painting of the first night game ever conducted in organized baseball. E. L. Robinson offered this item, which depicted the scene as it took place in Des Moines, Iowa, on May 2, 1930. Perhaps more significant was the catcher's mitt offered by 76-year-old major league veteran, Joe Gunson, a catcher in the National League in the 1890s. Included in his donation package was documentation from a number of newspapers (including *The Sporting News*) proving that he came up with this innovation. He also possessed seven affidavits from former players verifying his claim, including one who first used it in the spring of 1888. Gunson stated that there was some confusion over who invented this unique type of glove because he had explained the construction of it to a former catcher named Ted Kennedy while one of the players he coached, Tom Nagle, was trying it out.[17] Evidently, Gunson hoped not only to have his relic enshrined but to offer official proof of his invention in order to gain the recognition of baseball's hierarchy for his role in the game's development.

Cleland sought to recognize more than just players and officials of the game. In the fall of 1935, he contacted Frank Crumit of the Lambs Club in New York City for the purpose of commemorating De Wolf Hooper, who had gained quite a reputation as an entertainer with his stirring rendition of baseball's most renowned poem—"Casey at the Bat." Crumit knew of Hooper's son, John, from a mutual friend; and through his connection, Cleland requested a photograph, drawing, or painting of his famous father with the inscription of the poem's title on the bottom. John, who claimed that his father had performed before more teams than any other artist, was proud to accommodate the secretary. More than two years later a man named Dan Casey visited with Richard Vidmer of the New York *Tribune* and claimed to be the famous victim of the strikeout in the Ernest Thayer verse, and he even corrected some of its alleged inaccuracies.[18] However, the hall made no efforts to recognize his claim.

The need to acquire as many significant artifacts as possible led Cleland to utilize a variety of sources of information concerning these items. Russ Hall, yet another friend of Doyle and the secretary for the National Association of Professional Ball Players of America (the minors) in Los Angeles, responded enthusiastically to the secretary's request for donations. Another important source on the local scene was Hubert S. Mumford, who was employed as a guide for the museum in its early years. Because of the nature of his work, Mumford encountered numerous visitors who in turn made him aware of people who might have artifacts suitable for donation. Shortly after the museum opened in July 1936, an observer of the setting informed him of a woman in Sioux City, Iowa, who still had some of her father's old uniforms. Without contacting Cleland, Mumford wrote directly to the lady for a donation, and he made other requests in a similar manner.

Mumford continued his services for Cleland as the secretary made future arrangements for the museum. Like Doyle on the national level, the guide served Alexander locally by trying to recruit artifacts through the connections he made. Mumford sent him a list of names and addresses of people who might be willing to donate their treasures and even suggested a company that might construct a pair of miniature baseball shoes to add to the Reach equipment display. In addition to this collection work, Mumford typed description cards for various pictures, passed along suggestions from visitors, and notified the secretary of developments related to the museum. For example, he once informed Cleland of a privately owned baseball display in Nashville, Tennessee. He also told him of an Indian named John Carl Fast-Deer of New York City who was born in Cooperstown in 1830. Since he would have been nine years old at the time of Doubleday's alleged invention, perhaps he might have information to verify the claim. Finally, Mumford's efforts even led to the production of a single folder history of baseball that he wrote for interested tourists.[19]

No single item was donated more than the baseball itself, and they continued to be sent in throughout the centennial year. Most of them had a unique historic significance, including three that a man brought to Frick's office that were used in the Civil War era. New York Congressman Bert Lord, who had been on hand at the 1939 opening day festivities in the nation's capitol which inaugurated the anniversary season, offered a ball from that game. Previously, he had made arrangements with Clark Griffith that the first ball of the season would be recovered in order to be placed in the museum. Recognizing baseball's right to be called the national pastime, Lord expressed his pride in representing "the district in which Abner Doubleday put the base in baseball." Other balls received by Cleland included one of many dated 1876 that was used by a New Jersey fan's father and another that was a souvenir of the first game where people paid an admission to view the contest. The latter, a gift from Miss Helen N. DeBost of New York City, was used by her father in a game between her home city and Brooklyn in 1858. (Typically Brooklyn lost 22 to 18). Larger than a modern ball, her antique was made of a single piece of leather that had been cut in four petal shapes and sewn together. Her donation had originally been offered to Doyle who passed it along to Cleland.[20]

Another popular item for the museum was books. Dorothy Putnam was one of the first people to offer one when she contacted the museum in July, 1936. As the manager of an old book and curio shop in Newport, Maine, she acquired the sixteenth annual edition of "Beadles Dime Base Ball Player" edited by Chadwick in 1877. In addition to a wealth of statistical information from the period, it also contained instructions on scoring and the new league rules for that year, and she hoped that the museum would purchase it. F. H. Russell of Jamaica, New York, had an original copy of the constitution and by-laws of the Brooklyn baseball club in 1856 complete with rules and regulations of the National Association of Base Ball Players. Because of its intrinsic historical value, the owner hoped to sell it to the museum or anyone else who might be interested.

Charles W. Mears of Cleveland sent Cleland a catalog of his baseball literature collection along with a letter explaining its uniqueness. Besides box scores, it also contained an index of big league players dating back to 1871. Mears said that he would gladly donate the material if he were a wealthy man; but, that not being the case, he hoped to sell it to a rich collector who might pass it along to the museum as a contribution. His asking price was $10,000. This collection was indeed valuable and of great interest to Cleland. Instead of his typically flat rejection of items for sale, he lamented that the museum could not purchase his documents. Since the construction of the building to house the artifacts was about to start in October, there was simply no money available to invest for exhibits, and museum officials did not have the wherewithal to solicit money for such purposes.

More often than not, the donation of artifacts was encouraged. When W. F. Coyle, an attorney for the Southwestern Bell Telephone company, contacted the museum about their possible interest in an 1868 rule book, Alexander responded that he would be happy to have it as a donational item. The secretary also informed the museum director, William Beattie, that he should disregard any items for sale that might be secured through a gift from someone. Of course, many items were donated (including a portfolio of old photographs) or loaned (such as a copy of *DeWitt's Baseball Umpire's Guide* for 1875).

Perhaps the most unusual story in this regard involved a local farmer named C. E. Van Alstyne who lived in the mountains outside of Cooperstown. He had a complete set of baseball record books from 1894; and, when he advertised them for sale, he received an attractive offer. Beattie sought to find him, and at first the farmer wasn't friendly. However, after he realized that the director worked for the baseball museum, he proudly displayed his collection. During the visit, Van Alstyne changed his mind and decided to give it to the expanding collection in the village. He also made plans to visit the museum to see his valuables dedicated in the library.[21]

The strongest interest in books for the museum came from E. T. Stevenson, who was the owner and publisher of the local newspaper in Titusville, Pennsylvania. He visited the collection immediately after it was opened to the public; and, based on what he saw, he offered his services to its secretary with no charge. Instead of receiving pay for his work, Stevenson's sole concern was to help with the development of a permanent museum for the game that he had followed for over forty years. During his visit, the publisher noticed a feeling of discouragement among those interested in the project because its progress had been slow up to that point. However, he disregarded this disappointment and predicted a great future. He felt that once the movement got some momentum, it would expand so rapidly that those in charge would not be able to keep up with its progress. Having been involved in an oil industry museum in his hometown, he was speaking from experience.

Stevenson had more than words of encouragement; he had an idea. While talking with Littell and Mumford during his visit, he outlined some thoughts he had concerning the museum's development. He felt that a baseball bibliography was in order, and to that end he offered his services. Since his work had led to numerous contacts with libraries, he would be able to compile a list of books from them that should be part of the museum's collection. Following this compilation, he planned to obtain them for the collection and, in order to initiate the progress, he volunteered two small books of his own. He also decided to contribute a recent anniversary edition of *The Sporting News*, which was to be treated with Japanese rice paper before it was bound.

The publisher planned to serve the museum in a number of other ways. First, he thought that a collection of bats depicting their evolution from the early days of the game would be a desirable item and offered to help in its collection. He also hoped to add a number of trophies of famous players and promised to start work on that immediately. Finally, having conversed with Mumford on the Nashville baseball collection, he desired to visit the private collection as soon as possible in order to gain further insight for the Cooperstown museum.

Stevenson's letter, while warmly received by Cleland, did little to ease the secretary's concern of the museum's slow start. He explained his staff's discouragement by noting that in spite of a tremendous publicity campaign the previous winter, the material gained was in no way commensurate with the advertisement. With respect to the publisher's other ideas, Alexander was in complete agreement. He thoroughly believed that a baseball bibliography should be part of the museum, but since the building was still in the embryonic stages of development, the planners were hardly ready to commit themselves to the project. The bat display was another example of frustration for the secretary because his efforts to meet with A. J. Reach had not been successful. Regardless of these frustrations, Cleland hoped to meet with Stevenson in the near future in order to discuss the project that was obviously significant to both men.

The publisher remained true to his word, for early the next year he sent a package to the museum containing the promised materials. In addition to *The Sporting News* anniversary issue and a copy of *Balldom,* a valuable compendium of early day records, he added a local baseball history including the names of stars who later became famous. With a look to the future, Stevenson hoped that the museum would add a library annex to hold its collection of baseball materials.[22]

While Cleland's early frustrations continued, he had no idea how wide an area his advertisements had reached—even outside of the country. The one region of the world that responded the most to the museum's development was Australia. In February, 1937, he received a letter from Tom Rees of New South Wales who informed the secretary that his country's interest in the "World's Best Pastime" was demonstrated by the fact that they had almost five hundred teams playing in the previous season. Rees had read an article on the Doubleday museum in the recent *Base Ball Guide* and this inspired him to send in a picture of the latest Australian team. He hoped that the display would have a section on baseball overseas, but if this weren't possible, at least fans in America would realize that the national pastime had gone international. Indeed, as Rees pointed out, ball games were also being played in England, France, South Africa, Germany and several south sea islands.

In addition to fans from the land down under, Cleland also received correspondence from one of its country's umpires. W. G. Bannerman of Victoria contacted the secretary in regard to the early history of the game. Lacking the resources on this information in his home country, he hoped that Alexander could direct him to sources covering the original layout of the diamond and the rules as they had evolved. The secretary was pleased with the Australian interest in the game and expressed the hope that in the future a team from that area could challenge an American team in a real world's championship. He also forwarded the foreign correspondence to Littell in order that he could work up an article on the theme of baseball interest throughout the world. As Bannerman had pointed out, developments in baseball were progressing well in his country in spite of the competition received from the game of cricket. Because the traditional British game continued to dominate the sports scene in the former colony, baseball was relegated to the winter season (April through August). Still, a training school had been set up about forty miles from Melbourne in order to encourage youthful interest. This special concern by fans in Australia did not go unnoticed in the United States. One of America's major advertising firms was putting together an elaborate calendar for the centennial year and planned to include a picture of the foreign championship team.

Letters from Australia continued to be received by Cleland even after the summer of celebration commenced. Keith W. Tucker, Chairman of the Metropolitan Division of the Victorian Baseball Association in Melbourne, contacted the Hall of Fame in June, 1939. Having heard about the Cooperstown institution through the *Spalding Guide*, he wanted to know if the museum would be interested in a souvenir from his native country. Tucker had become a regular correspondent of John Heydler, and this connection served to keep his interest in the developing complex. Since the city of Melbourne was staging the biggest baseball carnival in its history, the chairman wanted to send Cleland an autographed ball or bat. Later that fall, the secretary forwarded three baseballs from Tucker to Beattie and he put them on display in the museum.[23]

The vast majority of donated items had focused on the early days of the game. Although the memorabilia had obvious historical significance and served as physical reminders of the game's development, they may not have aroused as much curiosity as the planners had hoped. In order to attract the interest of younger or more recent fans of the game, the museum needed to acquire items from more contemporary stars. Especially important in this regard were contributions from those who had already been elected to the hall.

Even before the inductees had been chosen for enshrinement, the secretary began to pursue items associated with some of the game's greatest stars. As early as April, 1935, he contacted the wife of Christy Mathewson, whose husband had died of tuberculosis a decade before at the age of 45 following service in World War I. Enclosing the museum's new pamphlet, he asked the great pitcher's widow if she could cooperate with the Cooperstown effort by contributing any of her husband's materials from his playing days. Trying to express his sincerity in this matter, Cleland stated that a baseball display which lacked items of this nature would simply not have any real historical value. He also wanted to overcome any fears she might have of exploitation by reassuring her of the credentials of the museum and its backers. This direct kind of approach was not really Alexander's style and may have seemed too forward for a woman who had lost her husband at such a young age. Since his inquiry produced nothing tangible, he pursued other items through connections he made and waited to meet someone who knew the former stars.

E. T. Stevenson proved to be the link to the Mathewson family. The Pennsylvania publisher attended Bucknell at the same time as the future Giants star and became acquainted with his wife. Given this relationship, he felt compelled to contact her for a donation without Cleland's approval. Adroit and straightforward in his approach, he also proved to be timely in his request. Mrs. Mathewson had recently returned from a long trip to Europe, and this had delayed her response to the museum's secretary. In her absence she had let her affairs go unattended, but now she was quite willing to cooperate. Although unaware of its location, she was sure that Christy's favorite mitt was in her possession; and although she treasured it greatly, she agreed with Stevenson that it deserved a permanent repository.

Not only did this connection lead to the acquisition of materials from Mathewson, but it also meant cooperation from the McGraw family since the pitcher and his manager had developed a long-time friendship. The wife of the famous manager was visiting Christy's widow for a month at the time of her correspondence with Stevenson, and the latter was sure that she could convince Mrs. McGraw to send something to the museum. Relieved that he had finally received a reply to his initial response to Mrs. Mathewson, Cleland encouraged the publisher to follow through on her response and obtain artifacts from both widows. Following Stevenson's instructions, Mrs. Mathewson had Christy's favorite mitt (which contained his autograph on the flap) delivered to Littell in Cooperstown in mid-September. About a month later she also sent one of her husband's uniforms. The editor conveyed to Cleland the widow's request that all of Mathewson's artifacts should be displayed in one case or section.

The McGraw gift resulted in some confusion and embarrassment for the museum. The Mathewson glove was delivered by a lady who owned a summer home in Cooperstown, and she immediately asked what had become of the cup that Mrs. McGraw had donated. Littell had no idea what she was talking about, but Mrs. Mathewson was able to clear up the matter on her later visit to the museum. McGraw's relics had been donated to his alma mater, St. Bonaventure College; and they had just selected an item, at his widow's request, and forwarded it to her. It wasn't really a cup but actually a small statue of the famous manager, and Mrs. McGraw had simply re-addressed the package and sent it to Littell. The card which accompanied it mentioned nothing about her, and that was the source of confusion. Both the McGraw statue and the Mathewson glove and uniform became the first objects of adoration gathered from modern major leaguers.[24] They were not only admired as gifts but they also served as examples for other stars of the game who may have been hesitant to make a donation to the museum. Naturally, the planners had been concerned over the McGraw piece since it originally appeared to be lost. This was not the kind of embarrassment that the struggling complex needed during its early stages.

Besides these souvenirs, the museum's effort to recruit memorabilia from modern-day baseball figures met with failure in 1936. Cleland began the year by contacting Walter Johnson directly, and this correspondence became a basic form letter that would eventually be sent to other greats of the game. In it, the secretary mentioned the baseball writers' poll that had recently been conducted for Hall of Fame enshrinement. Since Johnson was one of the first players chosen for induction in the recent election, Alexander reminded him that a museum was being developed in conjunction with the shrine. He pointed out that it would contain photographs, relics, and museum pieces that would be of interest to baseball fans around the country. While the centennial was still three years away, the secretary expressed the urgency on the part of museum officials to garner items for display that would demonstrate the historical aspects of the game since Doubleday's invention. Although the major leagues would furnish the plaques for inductees, Cleland expressed the museum's desire to gather mementos from those already elected. He felt that these personal effects would attract a great deal of attention and publicity for the Cooperstown repository. To encourage Johnson even more, he enclosed a recent article from the New York *Sun* concerning relics that had already been secured.

Perhaps the lack of response to this letter convinced Cleland that he should stick to his method of making requests through those people who knew the stars well enough to intercede. In June, again at the suggestion of Doyle, he contacted Edward F. Balinger of the *Post Gazette* in order to obtain some item from the former Pirate shortstop, Honus Wagner. He hoped that the newspaper man could provide a link to acquiring one of his relics, and this quest was significant since he belonged to the first group to be inducted. On the same day, the secretary wrote to Norris O'Neill of the White Sox organization. Doyle thought that he would be a good contact for material from Charles A. Comiskey, who had been one of the forerunners of the American League since he first moved his club from St. Paul in 1900.

Like Doyle, Mumford continued to serve the museum's development by expanding the network of connections. In August he was contacted by Vincent G. Bird, the Assistant District Supervisor of the Federal Historical Records Survey, concerning the acquisition of materials. By this time the supervisor had already begun to negotiate for these items and initiated a publicity campaign to advertise the need for more donations. For Bird, this was a labor of love. And he emphasized that there would be no charges for his services. More importantly, he offered the museum something that it could not do without—a connection with Babe Ruth. As the most recognized player in the game and a member of the original set of inductees, Ruth and any donation he made would be a tremendous boost for the museum project. However, even this action was not enough for Bird, who did not plan to confine his efforts to the former Yankee slugger and instead attempted to contact other stars.[25]

The dismal returns from the museum's initial quest to acquire display items only served to strengthen Cleland's resolve to turn this situation around. He may have been disappointed in the progress to date, but it would have been totally out of character for him to give up. Always ready to answer a challenge with total dedication, Alexander pursued his goal from a different angle. Following the disclosure of the second election results, in January, 1937, he sent similar letters directly to Babe Ruth, Honus Wagner, Napoleon Lajoie, Ty Cobb, Tris Speaker and Cy Young. Since Mathewson and Johnson had already been notified, he concentrated on the other inductees. The letter was similar to the one sent to Johnson the previous year, and since that had produced no response, it may have seemed implausible to try it again, but Cleland pushed on.

This extensive letter writing campaign produced mixed results. Neither Ruth, Cobb, nor Lajoie sent any immediate response to the museum although the latter two would eventually respond during the year. Ruth, who always seemed to live life according to the beat of his own drum, probably never realized that he was threatening the museum's success because of his inaction. Often oblivious of situations surrounding him, the Babe was simply unconcerned with the historical process. Undoubtedly he was pleased with his election to the Hall of Fame, but he may have been disappointed that Cobb (or anyone else for that matter) finished ahead of him in the balloting. More than anything else, Ruth's lack of correspondence could possibly be attributed to the fact that he was hardly a man of letters.

The first of the Hall of Fame members to respond to Cleland's call for memorabilia was Cy Young, who sent a hand-written note to the secretary. Not only was the renowned pitcher in possession of these kinds of items, but he was also quite willing to donate them. The list of his collectibles was quite impressive and included a number of photographs, the ball he used in 1908 to win his 500th game, a collection of valuable cups, and the last uniform he used while playing for the Boston Braves in 1911. Young cautioned Alexander that it would take some time to get his collection packaged and sent off. Since the former pitching great was soon to become a septuagenarian, Cleland never tried to rush the matter. Indeed, this first response to his writing campaign brought to him a tremendous satisfaction.

Excited by the correspondence, Cleland immediately contacted Young in Ohio to express his gratitude. He told the pitching great that the National League president had recently advised him that Young's plaque was in preparation and should be ready within a month. He hoped to have the Ohioan's collection by May so that it would be on display for the summer tourist season. The secretary wanted to make the delivery as easy as possible for the aging pitcher so he offered to visit him in the spring in order to pack and ship the donations. Extending every accommodation possible, Alexander offered to pay for any expense involved. Recognizing Young's generosity, Cleland extended his thanks on behalf of the museum personnel and the baseball public for his contribution towards the completion of the Cooperstown baseball exhibit.

Respecting Cleland's request for a May delivery, Young encouraged the secretary to visit his home and pick up the materials. He gave Alexander instructions on how to reach him and directions on car or train travel to his home in Peoli, Ohio. Without really knowing it, the hall of famer was playing right into the secretary's hand. Frustrated with the disappointing results of the collection process, Cleland decided that a personal touch was needed. His plan consisted of a trip by automobile from New York City to Washington D. C. (to visit John B. Foster), then on to Germantown, Maryland (to see Walter Johnson), and finally to Young's home. Following this visit he desired to continue on to Cleveland in order to visit with Lajoie and Speaker. His schedule was still up in the air in this latter regard because of an accident which had left Speaker in serious condition.[26]

Cleland continued to pursue the newly elected members of the Hall of Fame with mixed results. Following his initial correspondence to Wagner in Pittsburgh, the game's greatest shortstop promised to mail him some relics as soon as he could get around to it. The secretary's response encouraged him to send those items in soon so that they could be displayed with his plaque when it arrived.

Correspondence with Cobb was not immediately fruitful. Lacking any reply to his initial letter, Alexander contacted the "Georgia Peach" at his retirement home in Menlo Park, California. Since the irascible baseball idol was renowned for his mood swings, Cleland proceeded adroitly to coax him to make a contribution. Catering to Ty's ego, the secretary reminded the former outfield great that he was the first choice among the baseball writers in the Hall of Fame poll. Because of his number one ranking, the hall was extremely anxious to receive some personal contribution. The secretary tried to intrigue Cobb by stating that he would view with great interest the reaction of young fans who came to see the items once used by their baseball heroes.

Finally, Alexander made another attempt to contact Walter Johnson. This was the second year in a row that the "Big Train" had failed to respond to the secretary's request, but Cleland persisted. He sent a follow-up note on his February letter and inquired whether the former Senator had ever received his initial message. Again, he encouraged the famous pitcher to contribute some items of interest to the museum.[27]

Anxious for further developments on the museum project, Cleland began to make plans for his automobile trip. In addition to his original stops, he extended his list of sojourns to include the Spalding Brothers company in Chicopee, Massachusetts, and Wagner in Pennsylvania. Before beginning his journey, the secretary contacted Edward Bang, sports editor of the Cleveland *News*, at the suggestion of Bill Brandt. Cleland desired more information concerning the whereabouts of Speaker and Lajoie. Bang responded that the famous second baseman generally returned from Florida in late April but that Speaker had suffered a fractured skull from a bad fall. Because of the injury to the former outfielder, Cleland bypassed him on the trip and waited for two months before sending him another letter. Lamenting his recent accident, the secretary wished him a speedy recovery and then asked him for a contribution. By this time he was able to claim donations from McGraw, Mathewson, and Young; and he used these examples to urge similar action by Speaker.

Before he left on his sweeping travels, Cleland decided to ensure his success by obtaining letters of recommendation from Doyle. He sent notes to M. B. Reach, Vice President of A. G. Spalding Brothers, in Massachusetts; Harry Hull, manager of the company's office in Cleveland; and John B. Foster of the nation's capitol, editor of the *Guide*. The idea was to provide the secretary with any assistance he might require in trying to arrange meetings and collect memorabilia during his trip.[28] Once again the Doyle connection paid off.

By the end of the summer, Alexander's work began to produce results. In late August, for example, Lajoie responded with a promise of forwarding personal items and a note of thanks for the great honor of being selected to the Hall of Fame. Eventually, he sent the complete uniform worn and the ball hit by him when he registered his 3000th hit in 1915 at a game in Griffith Stadium. On receiving this pleasing response, Cleland immediately contacted Beattie in Cooperstown about the Lajoie shipment in order that he would see that the materials were immediately taken care of. The museum director wasted no time in displaying this significant contribution. The ball was placed with others in a baseball case, and the uniform became part of a display of other clothes that had been received. Although Speaker's serious injury had delayed his search for memorabilia, he promised to visit his native state of Texas in September in order to search for some appropriate souvenirs.[29]

Since his requests from other Hall of Fame players were not exceptionally rewarding, Cleland again contacted Mrs. Mathewson. He informed her that one of the museum trustees was interested in a bust of her husband that he thought would be perfect for the building. Although it was not a normal policy of the museum personnel to suggest the purchase of memorabilia, the secretary realized that this item might be too valuable and too much of a treasure for Christy's widow to donate. Therefore, he suggested that if the price wasn't too high, the trustees might consider purchasing it for a donation.

Mathewson's widow was hospitalized, but she responded to the request as soon as she was able. Frankly, she was not too impressed with the bust, which was done by Gertrude Boyle when her husband was still alive. Although she admitted that it was in a rough stage when she viewed it, Mrs. Mathewson felt that the museum should look it over before they made a bid. To her, the work was not a true likeness of her husband. Cleland agreed that the museum desired a real work of art, but he was impressed that Commissioner Landis called it "a speaking likeness of Matty," as the former pitcher was affectionately known. Still, Christy's widow felt that the art work should be seen before any negotiations were conducted with Miss Boyle's executors, and the secretary reassured her that she would be contacted before any final action was taken. Still, Cleland felt obliged to send her three photographs consisting of different views of the bust. He forewarned her that while it was a considerable expense, a great admirer of her late husband would probably secure it for the museum.[30] Eventually, the bust became one of the museum's more prized artifacts, and a picture of it appeared in future brochures advertising the museum.

E. T. Stevenson continued to recruit items for the museum while Cleland tried to gain donations from the recently elected Hall of Famers. In November, 1937, he contacted Charles Young, the sports editor for the Knickerbocker Press in Albany, concerning the turn-of-the-century ball player named Cy Seymour. Initially a pitcher in the 1890s (he was twice a twenty-game winner for the Giants), he switched to the outfield and eventually established himself as a lifetime .300 hitter. His greatest year was 1905 during which he played for Cincinnati and led the league in hits, doubles, triples, rbi's, slugging percentage and batting average.

Stevenson had read an article in *The Sporting News* concerning the death of his mother, in which it was mentioned that she owned the bat with which the late son won the batting crown. While the publisher claimed no official connection with the museum, he acknowledged the fact that he was a great fan of the game. Having visited Cooperstown on a couple of occasions in the past, E. T. recognized the anxiety of the sponsors to receive worthwhile mementos and hoped that Young might be of assistance in obtaining the bat for the museum. The sports editor conveyed his willingness to cooperate in its obtainment and promised to contact the family concerning their willingness to make a donation.

Continuing his efforts to acquire memorabilia, Stevenson wrote to Tony Lazzeri, who scored the winning run for the Yankees in the final game of the 1937 World Series. The publisher read that the second baseman had obtained the last ball in play when the Series ended and hoped that he would be willing to donate this item to the museum. Stevenson realized that the ball had obviously been of sentimental value to the famous Yankee, but he warned him that artifacts were often scattered or lost unless they were placed in an institution which provided permanent care and supervision. If Lazzeri had any doubts concerning the museum, the publisher encouraged him to contact President Harridge of the American League for his opinion on the matter.[31]

In both of these correspondences, Stevenson addressed a problem that had become a major issue in the museum's collection process-the building which would house the mementos. Originally, the display items were kept with exhibits of the Otsego County Historical Society on the second floor of the Village Club and Library Building. Included with the local items of interest was a complete file of the region's newspapers dating back to 1795. Their donor was, incidentally, Alexander S. Phinney, the last private owner of Doubleday Field. The space at the club was restrictive, and the baseball museum officials had no real control over the club building. The primary considerations concerned the club surrendering its lease to the museum which would preserve the functions of the organization and the library. Concomitant with this proposal was the condition that the museum could make appropriate alterations, with consent of the Board of Village Trustees, that were deemed necessary. The club desired to control the operation of the library and to continue to utilize a large room on the top floor for occasional parties and dances.

This decision was being considered at a time when the collection process was still in an embryonic stage. No one could have predicted the widespread interest in the museum and the hall that would develop throughout the country. While the leading citizens of Cooperstown initially viewed their celebrity status in the baseball world as a source of civic pride, the appeal of its Doubleday heritage gradually overwhelmed all expectations. What was first a small gathering place on the club's second floor became a national repository for America's game. At first there was no cause for alarm, but gradually a host of problems necessitated some major alterations concerning how and where these historical artifacts could be stored.

In July, 1937, *The Otsego Farmer* proudly announced the plan to develop a new fire-proof museum specially designed to house the national baseball collection. When initial plans for developing Cooperstown's baseball heritage unfolded, a separate building was discussed; but it was abandoned as a premature suggestion. However, the overwhelming response by organized baseball, sport writers, fans, and the general public caused the originators to reconsider their proposal. Other factors now made this step not only desirable but also imperative.

Of primary importance among the considerations that brought about the change was the need for the museum's directors to guarantee the safety of the priceless donations that were being received. There were, in fact, a number of inquiries concerning this point from people who were considering a valuable contribution to the repository. One man, who desired to donate a collection of old pictures of players, wanted his materials to be guarded constantly. This was the very issue that Stevenson was addressing in his recent letters to possible donors. The organizers had finally come to grips with the fact that they had hit on a scheme that truly captivated the nation. The result was that a number of priceless items had come into their possession; and they required permanent safety for the sake of the donors, the fans, and the museum personnel. A fire-proof building could provide this kind of protection and nothing else could suffice. While it was true that insurance could be purchased for the building, it could never be utilized to replace destroyed treasures since no duplicate materials existed. Moreover, the collection process had not moved along rapidly enough for the museum's secretary, and it was hoped that a secure building could expedite the program's development.

There were other considerations that helped to confirm the museum personnel's conviction that a new facility was necessary. For one thing, the idea of providing an endowment to finance the museum complex was an important consideration. A number of baseball fans around the country had expressed a willingness to contribute to the museum construction, and there was a distinct possibility that a fund could be set up in the future to ensure the permanence of the project. This action would necessitate the legal transference of the museum property to the organization that ran the baseball collection in Cooperstown—the National Baseball Museum. Otherwise, the acceptance of gifts could become legally complicated and might deter other backers. Also, the planners felt that the addition of another attractive building on the village's main street would only help to make a more positive, lasting impression on visitors. Finally, fans of the game would be pleased that a unique building had been specially constructed for the sole purpose of housing baseball artifacts.

Littell praised the work of Cleland in the article announcing the museum construction plans. Through his efforts and those of organized baseball, the preservation program attracted widespread attention and changed Cooperstown from a relatively unknown village to the nationally recognized birthplace of the game. Still, the community was not unfamiliar with notoriety because it was also the birthplace of one of America's most recognized writers—James Fenimore Cooper. Capitalizing on his fame, the village had recently become a storehouse for some of his materials, but many local people regretted that this work had not been taken up a long time ago. In the interim, Cooper's papers were widely dispersed to the point that a number of places around the country and abroad boasted of collections superior to those exhibited in upstate New York. The lesson was clear. If the baseball officials didn't act quickly and adroitly, their legacy might be similarly doomed.

In addition to fulfilling the need for a baseball warehouse, the proposed building satisfied other needs. Although the museum corporation would actually own and finance the building, they would also set aside space on the second floor for artifacts from the Otsego County Historical Society. Therefore, all of their precious items could benefit from the same security measures that applied to baseball artifacts. In addition, the proximity of the new building to the Alfred Corning Clark gymnasium meant that the construction would be economical; the gym was equipped with a heating plant that could serve both buildings and help cut the cost of fuel in the winter (a major consideration in the village).

Frank P. Whiting, a local architect, designed the original plans for the museum which was to be connected to the gym. Whiting's design contained a substantial exterior with the front elevation having an imposing colonial design that would be similar to other buildings along the thoroughfare. The entrance was to be flanked by Ionic columns on each side with a carved emblem in stone above the door that would include a replica of the Doubleday baseball. The interior, which was accessed via fireproof doors with wire glass, was particularly designed to display collections to the public's best advantage. A room to the left of the entrance would serve as Cleland's office while Beattie, who was the director of the gym, would also serve as the museum's curator and have his office located there.[32]

The word of the new museum construction spread rapidly. About two months after the initial announcement, Cleland was contacted by John F. Clark of H. F. Beers, Inc., who were manufacturers of exhibition and storage cases in New York City. Clark's letter was in response to a recent article in *The Museum News*, published just a week before by the American Association of Museums, which described the new building. He hoped to provide the museum with display cases, and to further his cause he included pamphlets with details on the types that were available. Clark's quick response to the announcement was appropriate, for the new building was to be completed by the summer of 1938 and dedicated during the centennial celebration.³³

With the plans for the museum in order, the collection process continued but not without some confusion. Mumford claimed that a man in Albany could provide the collection with a uniform from Johnny Iver. Cleland must have been surprised when he first read that remark, but he corrected the mistake in his next correspondence. It was, he explained, the wrong name. The museum's guide, helpful though he was to the overall project, was hardly a knowledgeable fan of the game. The secretary pointed out that the last name was Evers and that he was part of the famous double play combination for the Chicago Cubs.³⁴

Even though the initial inquiries concerning the collection of memorabilia from Hall of Fame members produced little direct correspondence with those men, Cleland was able to make connection with intermediaries. With respect to Cy Young, this contact had more to do with what the hall could do for the old pitcher. E. R. Reilly of Columbus, Ohio, felt that the organization should hire Young as a custodian. Although the former pitching great was not in dire circumstances, Reilly felt that he would enjoy spending his final years in close association with the game to which he had dedicated so much of his life. The secretary was forced to reject this proposal on two grounds. For one thing, the museum already had a custodian who had been there for awhile. Also, there was no money to pay Cy's salary or to create a pension for the man who already held the position. Cleland lamented the fact that Young could not be employed, as his presence would have been a big drawing card for the museum.

Another connection to a hall of famer involved Mrs. W. L. Johnston of Brooklyn, who contacted Brandt shortly after Willie Keeler's election was announced in 1939. Her mother had two cups that belonged to the great hitter and desired to sell them to the museum. Her father was one of Keeler's boyhood friends, and she would have never offered them if he were still alive. However, since his death, her mother's financial status had suffered; and she hoped to find a buyer for the mementos.³⁵ Both of these contacts demonstrated that the hall's financial backing was not sufficient. Few people had been willing to put up their money for its support.

Since Ty Cobb had ranked first in the initial Hall of Fame poll, Cleland had to be disappointed that he had not contacted the museum. Over a year following the secretary's last letter, the former Detroit great finally responded. Alexander must have been somewhat shocked when the message arrived in August, 1938. Ty claimed that although the museum personnel might think him ungrateful for the honor, he was deeply appreciative of being chosen as the number one ball player. He explained his procrastination by revealing that he had given away any fitting items for the museum to souvenir sellers. Cobb also complained that he had never received an official notification of his election and knew nothing about the general plan of the museum.

The secretary immediately sent the Hall of Famer a booklet concerning the museum and regretted that the major leagues had not followed through with their commitment. He still hoped that Cobb could find an old uniform to add to those of Mathewson, Lajoie, and Young that already had come in. Since

Ty had expressed interest in attending an official dedication ceremony, Cleland promised to inform him when the date was set. At that time league officials were working on a plan whereby those who were already elected would be invited to the ceremony.

About a month after his original correspondence, Cobb had finally discovered some possible items of interest and forwarded them to the museum. Included in the package was a sweater jacket, shirt, pants and stockings from his Detroit days, a pair of shoes from his time with the Philadelphia Athletics, and his old sliding pads. He had hoped to include a bat but since none were available, he suggested obtaining one of his maple models from the Louisville Slugger Company.

More important than the memorabilia was another matter concerning mistakes on Cobb's plaque that had come to the attention of several observers. Henry P. Edwards, manager of the American League Service Bureau, was shocked that his plaque had three mistakes in six lines. Two of them involved the length of his career which had been cited as 1904 to 1930. Cobb reminded the hall that he first went to Detroit in August, 1905, and retired at the end of the 1928 season. More important was the matter of total hits, since Ty had led all major leaguers in that department and would continue to do so for decades to come. The plaque stated that his total was 4025 when it was actually 4191. Had this situation not been cleared up, it might have caused considerable confusion when Pete Rose eventually passed the Georgia Peach in 1985.

Since Cobb was concerned about other mistakes in Hall of Fame plaques, he suggested that Cleland contact Frank Menke of New York, who was the editor of an all sports record book. Cleland, however, knew that this was a major league matter since any data on the plaques was prepared in their offices before they sent them to the museum. The secretary promised to check the others for similar errors and even spoke to Frick about the matter. The league president assured him that he would straighten out the problem as soon as possible and that a new piece of bronze would be attached in the frame that was used before.

There was one final note from Cobb shortly before the dedication took place. In April, 1939, he sent the museum a highly prized bat that he had located on a recent visit to Georgia. In the process of moving to California, it had been misplaced; but he had discovered it in time for the museum opening. Cleland was delighted to inform him that it was received and quickly placed on display. He was even more pleased that Ty was keeping the museum in mind and promised to thank him personally when he came to the June 12th dedication.[36]

This action completed the early efforts by the hall's promoters to encourage donations from players, fans, and officials. Although the museum had not exactly been inundated with memorabilia, it was certainly a sufficient amount to display proudly for Cooperstown's visitors. The display cases were neatly set up and photographed so that they could be used in pamphlets advertising the museum and its holdings. With all of the frustration involved, Cleland and his supporters had to be pleased with their efforts. However, the word of the developments in the village had yet to reach the entire nation. In order to achieve this goal, a national advertising campaign utilizing every aspect of communications had to be initiated. This was the next challenge for Alexander Cleland.

Chapter Five
Now a Word From Our Sponsor

While the Hall of Fame backers gathered artifacts for the museum and elected members for enshrinement, they were helping to bring about another phase of the centennial celebration—national promotion. In their attempt, they were augmenting the entire project with a promotional scheme on the national level. Although these two important projects had different goals, they continued to serve Cleland, Littell and others in terms of an advertising campaign. Still, these were not the only attempts to spread the word of the museum-hall development, for the originators explored every means possible to inform the entire country of their plans. Indeed, they felt that the success of their project was directly tied to advertising.

In the spring of 1935, Cleland began the advertising campaign by contacting the national radio networks along with station WOR in New York City. Utilizing the museum folder that had recently been developed, he enclosed it in his letter in which he proposed a radio-sponsored contest to encourage national participation in the hall's selection process. The secretary felt that such a procedure would generate tremendous interest among the baseball public. The controversy that was bound to result by selecting people for enshrinement, he believed, would have great advertising value for the promoters. He assured the radio executives that the museum committee expected nothing more from the contest other than promoting their project and obtaining public approval of baseball figures to be honored.[1]

Only radio station WOR responded to this initial request and that was indirect. They had forwarded Cleland's letter to the Paris and Peart advertising company in New York City who represented the Christian Feigenspan Brewing Company of Newark, New Jersey. They sponsored a fifteen minute broadcast of baseball and sports news four nights a week. The idea of connecting a contest to select Hall of Fame members with the program's audience was appealing to the advertising company, who thought that it would add considerable interest to the news show.[2] Although the secretary may have been pleased with this response, he had to be disappointed that a national network didn't pick up on the idea. While an informed New York audience was necessary for the centennial's success, the concept was nation-wide in scope, and regional promotion would fall short of the promoter's intent.

Still, Cleland had to start somewhere and hope that, as the word of the centennial affair spread, other areas of the country would embrace it. In the spring of 1935 Lithgow Osborne, Commissioner of the New York State Conservation Department, requested that the Cooperstown Chamber of Commerce forward publications advertising the village to the Bureau of State Publicity.

The bureau hoped to incorporate this information in their national advertising campaign designed to enhance the summer tourist business for the state. When K. R. Thacher, Assistant Director of Publicity, received some interesting folders from the village, he became aware of Cleland's role in advancing the project nationally. Informed that Alexander had already developed an instructive folder for the baseball museum, Thacher desired two copies. He hoped to incorporate the information he received into a booklet which would cover recreation facilities throughout the state. Following this inquiry, the secretary sent them the recently designed museum folders in order to demonstrate how far the program had progressed. He assured them that the museum project had the cooperation of the major and minor leagues and emphasized that it would expand in scope as time went on.[3] This New York connection was extremely important because plans for a world's fair in the nation's largest city that would coincide with the 1939 baseball program were already being formulated.

Following the announcement that New York City would host the 1939 world's fair, W. J. Adams of Cooperstown contacted Mayor Fiorello H. LaGuardia to point out that his village, only two hundred and twenty-five miles away, would be celebrating the 100th anniversary of baseball at the same time. Adams felt that the people of the village had not received enough recognition for their untiring efforts in perpetuating the "Cradle of Baseball." He pointed out that they had given a great deal of their time, effort, and money to modernize Doubleday field, and he went on to describe the work that had been done before the field was dedicated during the previous year.

Given the national significance of the development of baseball, Adams felt that it was only fitting and proper that the Cooperstown-Doubleday connection should warrant a prominent role at the fair. For display, he suggested a replica of the field along with historical relics pertaining to the early days of baseball and its various stages of subsequent development. He felt that the exhibit should emphasize what improvements were done without outside assistance, thereby recognizing what local residents had done. Since the museum represented the culmination of the dreams of local people in developing a national monument to baseball, Adams felt that the world's fair would make a perfect setting for a replica of the proposed building. Because he was convinced that such a display would attract a large number of visitors, Adams hoped that a small part of the receipts from such an exhibit could be set aside for perpetuating the national sport in his hometown. More importantly, he hoped that this exhibit would convince fans throughout the country that the future promotion of the birthplace of baseball required their support.

Originally, Adams had planned to communicate his message through the metropolitan newspapers, but he changed his mind because he knew that LaGuardia was an avid fan of the game. Thus, he felt assured that the mayor would accept his proposal in order to see that baseball was "perpetuated fittingly." He assured the city's leading official that his appeal was earnest and only concerned with a sport that was treasured by both men. Not wanting to seem too forceful, he decided to leave future developments in this matter up to the mayor.

Littell sent a copy of Adams' letter to Cleland, who expressed sincere interest in its imaginative contents. Coincidentally, he had recently talked with Stephen Clark about the possibility of coordinating these two major events. However, he felt that Adams' letter was slightly premature since it didn't seem likely that LaGuardia would continue to be mayor after his current term. Cleland understood that the organization designed to run the fair was just being put together under the guidance of George McAneny. The secretary decided to wait until various committees were formed concerning the fair's activities before any more contacts were made.

Although the secretary felt that the time was inappropriate for seeking approval of the fair's officials, he encouraged the development of some kind of display that could be presented later on. Cleland suggested that the Spalding Company might be interested in constructing an exhibit in connection with baseball's centennial. He had already contacted a Chicago firm who in turn talked with Landis and Harridge regarding the possibility of a diorama as a type of display for the museum. He sent Littell one of the company's circulars so that he would be familiar with their work and promised the Chicago organization that he would contact Frick about their idea. Cleland felt that any real exhibit at the fair should be sponsored by the major leagues and have the input of a firm like Spalding, who would be able to underwrite its expenses.[4] Perhaps he believed that the backing of such formidable organizations would convince fair officials in the future that the museum's efforts were not exploitive in nature and would only help to further the recognition of the national pastime.

Whatever influence Adams' letter might have had in the political circles of New York City, it was sincerely appreciated by Cleland and Littell. Both men recognized the need for village involvement because it would aid their efforts and confirm local support for the project to outsiders. They also hoped that other Cooperstown residents would make suggestions for future consideration. Littell forwarded a copy of the secretary's response to Adams so that he would know that his suggestion was appreciated.[5]

While the centennial—world's fair concept awaited future coalescence, the Cooperstown promotion continued unabated. In August, 1935, Neil O'Brien, editor of *Fan and Family Magazine* in Chicago, wrote Littell concerning developments in Cooperstown. He expressed the publication's interest in a story concerning the game's first days and the future plans for the upcoming centennial. He sent the local editor a recent copy of the magazine to demonstrate their emphasis on the human interest side of the game. Believing that the museum had a wealth of photographs, anecdotes, and materials on early notables of the sport, they hoped that someone could use this information to write a story for future publication. Within a month, Cleland had prepared a piece according to those suggestions and sent it off to Chicago.[6]

While magazine articles would continue to serve the Cooperstown's cause, the organizers were also approached by companies specializing in public relations. The first of these organizations to contact them was one from New York run by Alden Calkins, who got in touch with Cleland in the summer of 1935. Previously, he had made a trip through the village and met with Littell concerning the possible services that his organization could offer. Although Calkins was cognizant of the premature nature of his inquiry, he wanted to assure the secretary that his firm was well qualified to handle publicity on any scale. His appeal was ideally suited for the upstate residence because his organization had a great deal of experience in the area of sports and resort business. Since all of his clients had continued to conduct their affairs with his advertising company, Calkins offered this information as a testimonial to its effectiveness. As an example, he pointed out that his firm annually promoted the Hambletonian Stake at Goshen, New York, which was now a nationally known event. He felt that any investment on the part of the community to promote its historical and resort aspects would pay great dividends in the future. Cleland decided to put off any financing of public relations until a future date, but he was well aware that Calkins could supply connections to sport editors, press associations, and baseball writers throughout the country.[7]

Actually, there was no immediate need for Calkin's services because the news of the election process was beginning to be publicized throughout the country. Since these stories contained information that was, by its very nature, of extreme interest to baseball fans around the country, it needed no hyperbole. Shortly before the announcement of the election results, Cleland contacted Littell to point out the dramatic impact of these stories. The coverage was larger than ever because the Associated Press sent out one story for the morning papers from the offices of the American League in Chicago and another from National League officials in New York for the afternoon editions. Cleland felt certain that this would demonstrate a unified interest on the part of major league baseball in the development of the Hall of Fame and Cooperstown's role in general. Hopefully, this association with the game's highest authorities would eliminate any accusations of local boosterism.

Cleland sent Littell some of the articles that had appeared in the New York newspapers in order to demonstrate how the baseball writers in the nation's largest city were excited over the merits of various Hall of Fame candidates. Even though one of the stories was patently erroneous, he was satisfied that it was still publicity and that was what the organizers desired most at this time. The secretary predicted that future national stories would be concerned with the selection of modern-day ball players, which would be followed up with ones focusing on the old-timers. He also looked forward to articles by feature writers such as Dan Daniels, who had already written on the election controversies. His only regret at this time concerning publicity was that he had no way of gauging the extent of the advertising that these events were producing.[8] However, he had to feel good that his first year of work on the project had produced such dramatic results with such little effort.

The secretary continued to keep Littell informed on the coverage that the Hall of Fame was receiving by sending him newspaper clippings concerning the report of the first election. He also relayed the reaction of Frick to the recent developments and expressed the league president's judgement that the national coverage of these events had been tremendous. The secretary had also met with Frank Graham of the New York *Sun*, who had just written an article for a monthly publication known as *Base Ball Magazine*. In addition, Bill Brandt, National League publicity man, was scheduled to write a story on the museum and Hall of Fame to be incorporated into the next edition of the *Spalding's Base Ball Guide*. Finally, Cleland had made plans to attend the Base Ball Writer's Dinner in New York at the request of Doyle, who continued to serve the secretary as an important connection. The Spalding's editor promised to introduce him to many of the game's foremost writers at the gathering.

Sickness prevented Cleland from attending the dinner, but he sent Charles E. Main of the Clark Estates office to represent him at the function. Of course, a major topic at the event was the recent election results which had revealed the names of the first five selections to the hall. So, even though he had missed out on a chance at making some important connections, Alexander was pleased with the publicity they were receiving. He was especially proud of a picture of the "five immortals" already selected that had been sent throughout the country by the Associated Press. Excited about the widespread attention that the Cooperstown project was receiving, he was in the process of formulating an idea that would add more plaques for display in the museum.

It seems almost inconceivable that the Hall of Fame should have attracted such a large following in such a short period of time. The span of time from its initial announcement in mid-August 1935 to its first election results in the following January was indeed brief. The national controversy created by these developments was so stunning that it caused a complete reversal by Cleland concerning the project's success. Perhaps discouraged by his early failures in gathering items for display, he had become rather pessimistic about the entire project. However, recent developments changed all of this. While he confessed his earlier misgivings to Littell, he now expressed his belief that they were well on their way to making the project a big success.[9]

One of the best of the early articles on developments in Cooperstown appeared in the New York *Sun* about a month after the first election results were disclosed. Will Wedge, author of the piece, did more than simply give an account of recent happenings. For example, Wedge pointed out other events that would take place in the village during the summer, and he also listed various local officials who had become involved in the baseball project. He pointed out that more than 10 percent of the village residents paid membership dues to the Doubleday Field Association, which had recently been organized to promote and make arrangements for the centennial. The writer also noted a significant change in the perception that people had of the village. Previously advertised in travel folders as the place "Where Nature Smiles," it was gradually gaining recognition as the "Birthplace of Baseball."[10]

Another writer to jump on the Cooperstown bandwagon was Fred H. Majewski, sports editor of *Young America*—that was billed as a national news weekly for youths. He wanted to write a major story on the origin of baseball for an upcoming edition and asked for some photographs depicting early baseball games. About the same time, the New York Conservation Department wanted more information on the village, and Cleland felt that the local Chamber of Commerce would best be able to provide it. The Bureau of State Publicity planned to make special mention of Cooperstown as the birthplace of baseball in its summer vacation literature for 1936, and the secretary made sure that they received a museum folder and photographs.[11]

Of all the early literature on the events unfolding in Cooperstown, none was of more concern to Cleland and Littell than Frank Graham's article in *Base Ball Magazine*. In it, the author traced the developments that led to the village's claim as the place where Doubleday started the game. He was surprised that anyone could have questioned the Doubleday origin theory since modern-day fans had held it as an accepted fact for such a long time. He also mentioned the role of local citizens, the voting procedure, and ended the piece with a brief account of the general's life. Although the article offered little in the way of new information, it was a concise and well-written account of events that was aimed at the nation's baseball fans. Graham also revealed possible plans for the centennial such as a game to be held in the village between two major league clubs or stars from each league. Quite possibly, the 1939 All-Star game could be played there as a fitting tribute for the anniversary. Another article concerning the evolution of the ball appeared in the same magazine and traced how its construction had changed through the years. Both of these were partially reprinted in *The Otsego Farmer* so that local residents could be made aware of the national recognition that the village was receiving.[12]

So overwhelming was the response to the Cooperstown story that congressmen from New York introduced a bill in the legislature in 1936 that would provide for the centennial promotion through state funds. Senator Walter W. Stokes of Otsego County and Assemblyman Fran G. Sherman sponsored a motion, which called for a commission to direct the anniversary observance and an appropriation of $5,000 to defray its cost. Realizing that state taxpayers outside the village might balk at such a suggestion, the two men tied in the upcoming 1939 activities in Cooperstown with the World's Fair in New York City. Recognizing some people's fears that the fair might detract from the baseball celebration, Littell belied these feelings by claiming that the two events should work nicely together. Outsiders who were attracted to the exhibitions in New York, he felt, would be glad to observe the Cooperstown activities which were a short distance away. He even went so far as to suggest that if the great metropolis didn't get more involved in its celebration, it would soon be bypassed by the events to take place in the village. Given Littell's conviction that events in 1939 would be highlighted by the baseball celebration, he felt that the proposed bill should receive unanimous approval.

By mid-summer, the legislation was approved; and a committee was authorized to investigate the kinds of publicity that could be conducted and to make recommendations concerning the state's participation in the project. Senator Stokes was chosen to head the committee, which also consisted of two of his colleagues—Edward J. Coughlin of New York and Jacob J. Schwartzwald of Brooklyn. The assemblymen on the committee included Lloyd J. Babcock of Jamestown, William T. Grieve of Yonkers, William R. Williams of Utica, and Edwin L. Kantowski of Buffalo. Although they received only half of the money proposed in the original bill, the state government clearly gave its recognition to Cooperstown as the place where baseball had started.[13]

Even though a variety of writers were capitalizing on the news concerning the village, none of their coverage was as important as the two most significant publications of the day—*The Sporting News* and the *Spalding Guide*. In the 1936 edition of the latter, Bill Brandt wrote an article that he left unsigned so that readers would feel that it was the opinion of all organized baseball and not just the National League. Cleland lamented that it contained a few inaccuracies, but he blamed that on publicity men whom he felt were generally in too much of a hurry to worry about such concerns. In another part of the *Guide*, Editor John B. Foster discussed the Hall of Fame, members who had been selected, and possible selections for the previous century. *The Sporting*

News article, while equally informative, also pointed out museum developments, plans for the 1939 celebration, and a history of events leading to Cooperstown's recognition. Surprisingly, they stated that nobody suddenly invented baseball; it simply evolved from a variety of unorganized games that were popular at the time. The 1839 date, then, was concerned with laying out the diamond and determining how a run would be scored.[14] Both of these publications served the promoters well since the entire museum-hall-centennial plans were laid out together for the first time in the two most important baseball publications in America.

In March, Littell was again contacted by another national magazine desiring information for an article on the museum. The publication, known as *Hobbies*, was a platform for collectors of memorabilia who would certainly be interested in the articles being sought for display. Cleland forwarded pictures that were eventually used in the piece which appeared that summer. Although this article added little in the way of new information, it did point out the function of the museum and may have encouraged later donations that were slow to come in. About the same time that this appeared, F. C. Lane, editor of *Baseball Magazine*, contacted the secretary for more information that he needed to write a column for his publication.[15] It may seem that the repetition of information revealed through these writings was simply redundant, but they did serve to spread information on the Cooperstown activities throughout the country and they were only the beginning.

Recognizing the need for further information on the village regarding tourist activities, the Bureau of State Publicity contacted Cleland in late August concerning information that they needed for an upcoming travel brochure. Although the baseball museum had been mentioned in their 1936 summer vacation booklet, the bureau wanted some statistical information. For example, they requested an estimate of the percentage of increase or decrease of the local travel and resort business over the previous year. The state organization also desired the number of tourists who came to Cooperstown during the summer and the amount of money they spent. The bureau planned to used this data to guide their future activities and promised not to quote any of the figures directly unless the museum personnel requested it. Since it was impossible for Cleland to know this kind of information, he requested Littell's assistance; and the editor forwarded his findings to the state bureau.[16]

The museum's work in public relations was not curtailed at the end of the regular season. Directly before the opening of the World Series featuring two teams from New York City (the Yankees and the Giants), Littell contacted Cleland. Since the encounter involved organizations that were in close proximity to the village, its promoters decided to capitalize on this unique situation. With the baseball spotlight focused on the state of New York, it was a publicity man's dream. Realizing that fans throughout the nation were focusing their attention on the post season activities, Littell suggested to Cleland that he contact Frick or Brandt concerning the promotion of the village. He hoped that these men could encourage writers and broadcasters to make mention of the progress being made with respect to the centennial and the museum.[17]

The promotional work languished during the off season, but it began to pick up during spring training of 1937. By this time, of course, the annual announcement of Hall of Fame selections had provided the promoters with all of the off-season publicity that they needed. With the new season about to commence, the secretary of Cooperstown Chamber of Commerce, H. E. Adamovitch, wrote Cleland concerning a local bowling team that planned to participate in an upcoming tournament in New York City. Each member planned to wear a shirt with the insignia "Birthplace of Baseball." Desiring to promote the centennial celebration, they hoped to obtain a supply of museum folders for distribution in the city. Although Cleland's supply of these brochures was limited, he sent what he could and promised to have an updated version ready in the near future. Adamovitch assured the secretary that this effort was worthwhile because the Chamber of Commerce had received numerous requests during the past few years for a folder of this type. He assured him that his organization would be more than happy to distribute any future pamphlets locally when they were printed.[18]

Contacts made the previous year with the New York state publicity bureau were about to pay dividends. Batten, Barton, Durstine and Osborne, a New York advertising agency, contacted the Chamber of Commerce concerning the production of a new publicity booklet for the state. They sent Littell a copy of the brochure that they were planning to use so that the museum personnel could make any changes they deemed necessary before the final printing took place. The new pamphlet was supposed to contain a list of literature available regarding certain points of interest in the state, and Littell wanted to include the museum booklet. Later, Cleland contacted the editor of the state publication and made some changes to the article on the museum. The secretary was quite pleased with the coverage that the state was giving them, and well he should have been. Not only was the quality of their work good, but it also had a guaranteed audience. Once again, the price of this advertisement was well within the limits imposed by the frugal Scotsman.[19]

As the summer of 1937 progressed, the museum continued to receive inquiries from a variety of fans who either wrote or visited Cooperstown. Most of the letter-writers were concerned people who desired more information on the developments in the village, and their requests reflected how widespread the message had become. The Cleveland public library, for example, wrote to Cleland in order to obtain a copy of the brochure. As museum director, Beattie encountered a number of people who had some contact with the game. Percy Taylor of Franklin, New York, claimed that he was a close friend of Christy Mathewson. Dan O'Connell of Attleboro, Massachusetts, stated that he was a former scout for a big league team and had played professional ball when he was younger. At the present time he was involved with writing old-time baseball stories. Another man from the same state, Frank Beaumont, also claimed to be a former player.

In addition to private individuals, the museum received letters from firms involved in advertising and promotion. In August, Carvel Nelson of the Adolph L. Bloch Advertising Agency of Portland, Oregon, wrote to the museum concerning literature that would describe the purpose, history, and scope of the Hall of Fame and the amount of material that had been collected. With affiliated agencies in San Francisco, Seattle, Los Angeles and Spokane, this organization could well serve the Cooperstown cause by disseminating information throughout the west coast—an area that had not previously received consideration. Not to be outdone, the public relations firm of Alden E. Calkins once again contacted the secretary on the matter of publicity and promotion of the museum and the centennial. Previously, Cleland had asked them to write after some progress had been made on these projects. Given the incredible amount of print that the planners had received, the secretary decided to put off the matter until the anniversary drew nearer.[20]

Following the announcement concerning the 1939 election results, J. Roy Stockton of the St. Louis *Dispatch* contacted Brandt concerning the status of the Hall of Fame. Due to the large number of inquiries on this subject that the newspaper had received, Stockton hoped to accumulate enough information to keep a column going throughout the winter. The reporter wanted to know how it got started, how far construction had advanced, what style of architecture the new building would have, how large it would be, and the estimated date of completion. Stockton also inquired about the actual procedure that would take place when a person was elected for enshrinement. Would there be a plaque, a bust, or an engraving of the person's name installed in the building?

Brandt forwarded this letter to Cleland who provided the required information, First, he enclosed a copy of an article that contained a picture of the building under construction. Although it would be ready for occupancy in about three months, the secretary mentioned that it would not be dedicated until the centennial year. Concerning the enshrinement procedure, Cleland revealed that the major leagues would provide a large bronze plaque with a summary of the player's achievements listed at the bottom. He also pointed out that the *Spalding Guides* for 1936 and 1937 contained complete information on the hall-museum concept. Finally, he assured Stockton that elections would be held each year so that new candidates could be added.[21]

Shortly after this correspondence, Brandt's office once again served as a connection between the hall's officials and the print media of St. Louis. J. G. Taylor Spink, editor and owner of the *The Sporting News*, desired any pictures of the museum, field, or other important aspects of the Cooperstown development. This request was forwarded to Cleland who regretted that they had few pictures of any real value at this time because the promoters were waiting for the grounds to be in better shape before any new photographs could be taken of the building or the field. Cleland assured the famous editor that he would forward any new photos and expressed his heartfelt thanks for all of the publicity that his widely read baseball journal had given to the entire project.[22]

Another major publication to promote the village was *Time Magazine*. They produced an article emphasizing the election of Grover Cleveland Alexander to the Hall of Fame. In addition to recognizing his fabulous career, the piece also focused on how Cooperstown was established as the place where baseball originated. It revealed how the civic pride of the residents had been stirred by the Mills report and the transformation of Doubleday Field that followed. The article went on to describe how the celebration plans had been laid out, the museum had been constructed, and the procedure to elect members had been established. Cleland had to be pleased that one of the nation's major publications had given such a thorough coverage of the activities that had taken place in the village. No doubt Littell was impressed as well, since the *The Otsego Farmer* contained a lengthy article on the coverage given the Hall of Fame by *Time's* sports department.[23]

As the word of the Cooperstown developments began to spread, the number of requests for more information increased dramatically and revealed the success of the early promotion. Sometimes, as had often been the case in the past, these inquiries were from private individuals who merely wanted to satisfy their curiosity concerning events that related to the national pastime. But increasingly the requests arrived from those who were connected with promotion and merchandising. The World's Fair, for example, continued its interest in upstate developments. Cleland received word that a "sports float" had been one of the entries in a recent parade in New York City, but it contained no mention of the baseball centennial. Apparently ignorant of recent developments in the village, fair officials wanted to know exactly when the celebration would open.[24]

Other inquiries came from sources who were new to the museum personnel. A unique one involved the Philadelphia Inter-State Dairy Council who wrote Cleland at the suggestion of Brandt. Robert C. McKinley of the Department of Health Education desired more information on the dedication date and the people who had already been inducted. The secretary sent him the most recent booklet but mentioned that it did not contain the names of Cartwright and Chadwick. Concerning McKinley's request for more detailed information on the inductees, Cleland directed him to each league's service bureau from which he had received such data. However, he warned him that he should avoid telling league officials who had suggested their offices as a source. Since Cleland felt that he had already overburdened both Edwards and Brandt and their staffs, he felt that they might be somewhat resistive to further inquiries. Fortunately, McKinley accrued all of the necessary data and pictures from the Hall of Fame, and any possible conflict was avoided. He made a set of slides from the photographs which he planned to use throughout the public school system in Philadelphia with the hope of stimulating further interest in baseball and furthering the general knowledge of events taking place in Cooperstown.[25]

Another new inquiry came from Donald B. Foresman, Vice President in charge of Sales Promotion for the Strawberry-Hill Press of New York City. Involved in advertising and printing, the company hoped that plans for the centennial celebration had progressed far enough that additional publicity material could be released to them. They were also interested in obtaining a book on the history of the game since, as they understood it, it was invented in Cooperstown. Their rather casual reference in this last regard certainly demonstrated that while baseball insiders might be aware of developments in the village, those unfamiliar with its background were still groping for a better understanding of these events.

One more promotional concern from New York expressing interest in the museum and celebration was the Associated Merchandising Corporation. Dedicated to retail research and promotion, they were truly an international operation with offices in London, Paris, Brussels, Berlin, Vienna, Shanghai, Yokohama, and Hong Kong. They also represented a number of firms throughout the United States. The corporation wanted to obtain the latest information on the Hall of Fame developments since a number of the stores they represented were interested in coordinating their efforts with the Cooperstown officials. Although Cleland was impressed with their interest, he regretted that he couldn't provide them with additional information. Since local plans were now connected with those on a national level, further developments would be under the control of organized baseball, and they did not plan to release any new information until their annual meeting in New York in January, 1939.[26]

The Osborne Company of Clifton, New Jersey, also contacted the secretary concerning future advertisement for the Hall of Fame. Involved in the more artistic side of promotion, the company specialized in calendars, billboards, booklets, and blotters. Having already made contact with Frick, Doyle, and Ernest J. Lanigan of the International League, they had gone ahead with the creation of a baseball centennial poster which they hoped to distribute throughout the country during the anniversary year. They planned to include a reproduction of the new museum building which they hoped to obtain from Cleland. If no print was available, they suggested a photograph of the architect's drawing as a substitute.

The secretary was definitely intrigued by the offer because it came from the largest calendar firm in the country. However, he also recognized a possible conflict of interest in this matter because the Second National Bank of Cooperstown had made plans for distributing their own calendar. Cleland wrote Fred Seely of the Osborne Company that he didn't want to distribute any pictures of the museum that would conflict with the local bank. Not wanting to do anything that might upset village interests in the centennial promotion, he promised Clyde S. Becker, a cashier at the bank, that any posters from the New Jersey firm would only be distributed in New York, its neighboring state, and to a few selected individuals. Cleland preferred a calendar with the bank's picture on it because he wanted to show the outside world that Cooperstown was a small town but still up-to-date when it came to modern banking facilities. When the Osborne calendar eventually came out, the company presented the museum with the original drawing on the calendar to pacify any ill feelings that might have been incurred.[27]

The Osborne Company seemed to be working under the old adage that it is easier to ask forgiveness than to ask permission, and this point was raised with other promoters as well. Beattie received word from a well-known advertising agency from Philadelphia, N. W. Ayer & Son, concerning a baseball feature that they were planning for one of their clients. They wanted to know the names of the players already elected; and, more importantly, they asked if they needed permission from any source to make reference to the Hall of Fame in their advertisement. The museum director contacted Cleland on this matter, and the secretary wrote the firm immediately. He pointed out that the Hall of Fame was an incorporated organization and as such they reserved the right of exclusive use of that name concerning souvenirs and special printed matter. Cleland, however, did not wish to discourage any advertisement that might come from such a reputable firm and so he offered complete cooperation in any endeavor that they might be planning.

The matter of trademarks surfaced in connection with Earl Stalker, president of the Cooperstown Chamber of Commerce, who claimed to have complete control of the hall-related souvenir business. Realizing the possible problems in this regard, Stephen Clark suggested that Littell contact Owen Baker, a lawyer from nearby Oneonta, concerning this matter. Both Cleland and Clark felt that Stalker's copyright was only to the title "Birthplace of Baseball" and that the originators had the right to use the words "Hall of Fame" and "National Baseball Museum" on souvenirs since they were already incorporated under the latter name.

After conferring with Littell on the problem, Becker immediately began to examine laws concerning copyrights and trademarks. In the beginning of the incorporation of the museum, they recorded the articles of this procedure with the patent office in order more fully to protect their name. This action was done in accordance with laws involving trademarks. These were originally passed in 1905 in order to prevent others from using the same name. Becker advised that further protection could be made by registering the name as a trademark. However, this law required that the name be written in a distinctive manner or associated with an individual's portrait. He believed that even if someone tried to appropriate the name, they would lose in a court of law. Becker also felt that since the words "Hall of Fame" were so commonly used that any attempt to register them with trademark authorities would probably he refused. If, however, they were used in connection with the National Baseball Museum and worked into a distinctive design, the planners could be successful in registering them as a trademark.

The copyright concerns were a different matter since laws in this regard were intended to protect authors of music, maps, books, poems and articles. Therefore, the material involved actually had to be published before any application could be made for copyright since it was intended for the protection of an original work. Becker felt that this would be best applied to any souvenir book concerning the centennial that the museum might produce.

Following this response, Littell sent Becker a baseball bat that Stalker had designed and contained the trademark that he had registered. The lawyer pointed out that while he was not a patent lawyer, he was confident that the words "The Birthplace of Baseball" and "Made in Cooperstown, New York" were merely descriptive in nature and thus not entitled to protection. Because of the possible conflict that the museum might encounter, Becker suggested a scenario for its officials to follow. First, he thought that they should determine what the trademark should look like and then put it into active use by having it inscribed on various objects that they expected to offer for sale. Then they could place them on the market in order to have an original claim. Becker warned them that they should conduct a search of other trademarks as soon as possible to determine whether they were infringing on any of those that were already registered.

Becker also pointed out to Cleland some of the legal aspects that he should consider in working out the proposed trademark. First, it had to consist of a single device or form of words which had not been used previously. This would help to distinguish their product from those that were manufactured by others; therefore a generic name would simply be inappropriate. He also emphasized that a geographic name which denoted locality could not be used exclusively as a trademark but that it could be utilized in connection with other words such as "Rome Machinery and Foundry Company." Finally, he added that no trademark could be registered which was already being actively used by someone else since the exclusive right to its use was founded on the principle of prior appropriation. Therefore, Becker reasserted that they conduct an immediate search to determine any possibility of infringement before the appropriate mark was chosen.

Soon after this correspondence, A. E. Lynch of the merchandising department of A. G. Spalding and Brothers sent Cleland three drawings of stamps for balls, bats, and a regular trademark. He asked the secretary to return the sketches along with his comments on their design. The bat drawing contained the label "Birthplace of Baseball," "National Baseball Museum and Hall of Fame," "Cooperstown, N.Y." which was placed at the top. The baseball drawing was similarly labeled, but it also contained the Spalding trademark. The official trademark sketch contained a diamond-shaped figure with similar wording but in the center it read "Doubleday Field" and below this the dates "1639-1939." If baseball fans accepted the starting point on this label, they may have also looked for Doubleday's name on the Mayflower Compact. Perhaps because of the error in the date or the fact that it might not meet up with Becker's conditions, Cleland continued to ignore the company's letters requesting his approval until he received word from his lawyers.

Cleland forwarded a drawing of the proposed trademark and copyright to Becker and pointed out that while the former was for bats and baseballs, the latter was specifically for the planned souvenir program. The secretary requested an immediate search so that the museum could market the aforementioned articles as soon as possible. In this manner they could establish their claim as Becker had suggested. The museum officials decided to eliminate the inscription "Birthplace of Baseball" because they didn't feel that it was significant. Also the omission would avoid any possible conflict with existing trademarks. The process of selecting the proper design was a slow one due to the difficulty of coming up with an emblem that could be applied to both the bat and ball. Becker found the simplicity of the design he received to be very appealing and had little concern that they would have any infringement problems during the search for existing trademarks. He also felt that they could use the new design on any of the museum literature without having to apply for another patent.[28]

Before the copyright matters were cleared up, A. G. Spalding and Company sent a number of baseballs to the museum. With the attendance figures at the Cooperstown display reaching fifty people a day, Cleland felt that it was a good idea to put the baseballs up for sale. He also requested that Hubert Mumford ship a dozen of them to New Jersey so they could be sold there and asked the museum guide to advise Becker that they were going ahead with the plan to sell balls with the copyright stamp as he had suggested. Within a week's time, Mumford had sold two dozen of the baseball's in spite of his feeling that Spaldings had done a poor job on them. One of these was shipped to Becker with the hope that it would aid his efforts to obtain a copyright in the nation's capital.

Cleland agreed with the museum guide that the famous sporting goods company had not done good work on the baseballs. He suggested that they consult another firm in this regard who might produce a more acceptable finished product with greater expediency. While the Spalding Company had promised the secretary for a number of weeks that they would deliver one of the custom bats, none had yet arrived and Alexander, plagued with a variety of problems at this point, was losing his patience. Even when the product did arrive, it was of such inferior quality that Cleland rejected it and requested a more satisfactory one.

In spite of the unsettled relationship between the museum and the Spalding company, business matters between the two groups continued to be conducted. At the suggestion of outside interests, the sporting goods firm proposed a baseball centennial line for 1939 that would include balls, bats, mitts, and gloves. A. E. Lynch of their merchandise department wanted to know if such a concept would fit in to the museum's program. The secretary, however, was more concerned with how Spaldings could aid the Cooperstown venture rather than the reverse. He pointed out that there would be a large number of games played in the village during the next summer by teams from the collegiate ranks, the majors, and the minors. All of this activity, of course, would require a vast quantity of baseballs and Cleland, always frugal in his business proceedings, was attempting to purchase them at the same price that major league clubs would. He assured the company that such a wholesale price existed because he had become aware of this fact through his friendship with Tom Shibe of Philadelphia. Evidently, his trust with the company had worn thin; and he wanted to put them on the spot before they could reject his proposal outright.[29]

The variety of promotional ideas associated with the centennial had expanded since the initiation of the project, but they had hardly reached the maximum potential. Of course the amount of literature on the subject had become rather prolific due to the yearly elections, but the developments in Cooperstown were beginning to be recognized by nonbaseball publications. In the spring of 1938, *Town and Country* magazine produced an article on the museum which Littell found especially intriguing. He commented to Cleland that the story on the Doubleday baseball was excellent. In addition, numerous other publicity items had appeared, and the museum had recently received a call from one of the radio stations in New York concerning details on the new museum.[30]

Often types of promotional ideas expanded beyond all expectations. E. H. Leon, manager of the pottery division of the Robinson Clay Product company of New York City, contacted Cleland concerning a sample of an ivory ash tray that would be delivered at his office. One of them had "Roosevelt Hotel" stamped in the center and also contained a black and white print of "Baseball Centennial." If the museum cared to order a package of 10,000 ashtrays with a center stamp of the museum or a baseball, Leon promised to deliver them within 45 days. Since this proposal would demand an outlay of over $1,200, Cleland decided to put the company off until the centennial officials met and discussed the matter at their next meeting.

Another unique aspect of promoting events in Cooperstown involved the Standard Oil Company. Cleland had conversed with W. G. Alexander of New York City who was directly involved with the company's route maps. The Cooperstown officials wanted their village to be designated on the maps for the following year, and this plan was forwarded to the firm that was entrusted to design them. Realizing the vast promotional potential in such a scheme, the secretary took every opportunity in his correspondence with Alexander to extoll the virtues of the village. Essentially, he gave him a sales talk on the community, Doubleday Field, the museum, Fenimore Cooper, and the 16 pound bass available in Otsego Lake. Never missing a chance to win over an important promoter,

Cleland also emphasized the fact that Cooperstown was an automobile village since no railroad serviced the town. Thus, every visitor was a potential gas user, and the company's advertisement in their map could turn out to be quite profitable for them.[31]

To this point the promotion had depended on the print media and, to a smaller extent, radio broadcasts to spread the word of the celebration plans to readers and listeners throughout the country. However, the decade of the 1930s witnessed a tremendous growth in the motion picture industry which had captivated audiences throughout the country and offered an innocent diversion for Americans during the years of the depression. As the movie business became more popular, its influence on audiences throughout the country grew accordingly. Recognizing the powerful impact of this relatively new media form, baseball's officials decided to capitalize on it.

At the end of the 1938 league meetings, a preview of the film "First Century of Baseball" was held at the Waldorf-Astoria in New York City. This new sound motion picture, the fifth in a series of films that the American League had produced in the past five years, was essentially a pictorial history of the game over the past 100 years and was specially designed for the upcoming centennial. In fact, the film was partially based on the findings of the Mills Commission and thus properly began with Doubleday's creation of the rules for town ball in 1839 which, according to *The Sporting News*, established the foundation for the basic principles of the modern game. The film also credited Cartwright with limiting the contests to nine innings, extending the distance between the bases to the standard 90 feet, and helping to form the first professional club in 1845.

The picture's general theme was to demonstrate the developments in the game which had taken place since its birth. For example, it showed the role of Cummings inventing the curve ball, the 42 inch limitation placed on the length of the bat, the appearance of the glove and catcher's mask, and the initiation of the stolen base. A number of modern day players appeared in the film to demonstrate various aspects of change in the national pastime. Ted Lyons, Lefty Gomez, Monty Stratton, and others showed the advances made in pitching over the past 70 years. (Stratton had lost his leg in a hunting accident about a week before the film was previewed.) Jimmy Fox, Joe DiMaggio, Hank Greenberg, and Lou Gehrig were among those who illustrated techniques in fielding, batting, and base running. Amateur baseball also received recognition, and famous stars who came from the ranks through high school, college, and the sand lots were also shown. In addition, the film contained clips from a recent old-timers game in Cleveland and the All-Star game at Cincinnati.

One of the highlights of the film was a conversation between two men who had witnessed the growth of the American League since its inception-Connie Mack and Clark Griffith. The two longtime owners discussed the differences in spring training over the years in the background while the audience viewed various camps in action. Umpires also had a role as they showed how close plays should be ruled; then the play was rerun in slow motion to satisfy the audience that the call was correct. The film closed with scenes of the 1938 World Series and emphasized the superiority of the Yankee organization which had won the last three of these events. As the film came to an end, there was a fade-out of a picture showing an old man closing a baseball history book that he had been reading to two youngsters.

The movie's historical portions had been filmed in Hollywood so as to take advantage of the highest standards in professional photography that were available at the time. The anniversary was viewed as far too important an event to settle for anything less. Lew Fonseca, director of promotion for the league, acted as liaison between the film industry and baseball officials, and this helped to ensure technical accuracy in the production. The narration was done by radio announcer Ted Husing. E. G. Brands attested to the film's quality in an article for *The Sporting News* in which he judged it as "interesting and well put together." The Hall of Fame representatives had to be pleased with a finished product that emphasized quality in every aspect of its production. The four previous league pictures had been viewed by more than fifteen million people and the new production was to be made available for public viewing at the beginning of the centennial year.[32]

With all of the positive promotional aspects concerning the hall-museum developments, there were moments of frustration for the backers of the project. Ironically, their advertising plans were frustrated by the very game that they were supporting. With the 1938 season drawing to a close, the American public began its annual focus on the climax of the pennant races and the World Series. Even those who were not devout fans during the bulk of the regular season followed the season's finale with unusual interest. Recognizing this trend, Cleland felt that the leagues would not get involved with any advertisement of the upcoming centennial year until the season was over. The secretary was very much aware of the highly commercialized aspect of baseball and was probably more cognizant of this situation than the average fan because of his business nature.

Just before the season ended, Cleland discussed the matter of the major league involvement in the promotion of the centennial with Frick. Although nothing had been firmed up at that time, the league president stated that the plans had been worked out in detail and that Cooperstown would be central to at least one major celebration. Frick felt that the league authorities might open the festivities in the village with all of the officials and electees in attendance. He stated that an unveiling of the plaques could be part of the pageant that followed. The reason that he wanted to limit the role of the village to one ceremony was that he felt Cooperstown was too small to accommodate the many thousands of fans that a longer celebration would entail. The great benefit for the locals, according to Frick, would be the continuous national publicity they would receive as the place where baseball started and the museum was located.

No doubt the Cooperstown promoters had to be disheartened with the relatively minor role that they were being assigned. Granted, one day in the sun was better than nothing and that one 24-hour period was significant; but village elders and the secretary had to feel that they were being relegated to a lesser role by a powerful outside force. It may have seemed odd to some that Frick, who had played an important role in originating the Hall of Fame concept, would allow this to happen. However, as league president he was in the eye of a storm and had many forces with which to contend. Cleland, as a New York City resident, was able to face these considerations more adroitly than the locals—especially given his business acumen and big city background. However, he had to be disappointed with Frick's further revelation that the announcement for the major league plan would not be made until January. More frustrating was that the delay had nothing to do with baseball. While the game's authorities greatly appreciated the publicity they were receiving from the World Series, they also realized that other sports, like football, relied on their yearly advertisement in sport pages throughout the country. Evidently there was a tacit understanding between the authorities of both games that baseball would not infringe on football's publicity; here again, Frick was coping with a consideration not relevant to the villagers, and it is easy to understand both their frustrations and his responsibilities.

Cleland understood Frick's role, but he pointed out to him that the people of the upstate New York residence had a great deal at stake in the following year and therefore desired more time for planning, preparation and promotion. Frick's response to this plea was that the village could go ahead with any plans they might desire for a local celebration and that the league would guarantee to advertise it in time to make it successful. The president's declaration was supportive but still lacked the kind of commitment that the secretary desired. Given Frick's open ended promise, the secretary felt, therefore, that the village should determine its own course of action and simply accept whatever plans that were forthcoming from league officials. He also discouraged local officials from going over Frick's authority by appealing to commissioner Landis because it would lead to more frustration than results. On a more positive note, Cleland conversed with Bill Brandt after his meeting with the National's president; and the league's publicity agent stated that with all of the advertisement that Cooperstown would receive, it "would be the best known village of its size in the United States."[33]

Lacking the cooperation from the major leagues at this time, the Cooperstown forces were inspired by the ever-increasing interest in the museum. The recognition that it had received through advertising had resulted in a large visiting record. Weekly attendance was up to 365 people in October of 1938, and some visitors had come from a long distance to see the new building which housed the relics of the game's history. Two people from Malaga, Spain, and one from Edinburgh, Scotland, visited the displays during the same week. Recognizing the increasing interest in developments in the village, Frank C. Carpenter, head of the publicity committee, continued to emphasize the attention of tourists who planned to attend the World's Fair in New York City.[34]

One of the people who was making plans to visit the fair was Dr. C. Guyer Kelly, a Ph.D. from Johns Hopkins, who was currently residing in Tunis, Tunisia. The importance of his visit was that he had organized some 150 baseball teams from the west coast of Morocco to Tunisia—a distance of about 2000 miles. His promotional work attracted the attention of Dr. E. Prince Danforth of Sidney, New York, who had visited the Mid-East two years before and had met with Kelly. Danforth was impressed that he could have been so successful in promoting a game from a Christian nation because, as he pointed out to Cleland, Arabs usually disdained any customs not traditional to their culture. The secretary, always ready to capitalize on a promotional scheme, planned to obtain some information that would emphasize the international scope of the game. Danforth hoped to fill this desire by obtaining pictures of the Arab nines in action that might be used in the museum.[35]

The advertising campaign had come a long way since its inception in the spring of 1935, and virtually every form of mass media had been used to promote the hall-museum complex and the 1939 centennial plans. Utilizing local boosters, the timely coincidence of the World's Fair, national magazines, radio broadcasts, newspaper articles and a Hollywood movie production, the Cooperstown promoters had definitely achieved their goal of spreading the word about upcoming events. At the same time that they were trying to capitalize on the various media forms, a number of businesses were trying to take advantage of them. Firms involved in public relations, advertising, and promotion made a number of inquiries of museum officials hoping to acquire permission to work on the selling of Cooperstown to a national audience. Given the fact that the entire project was a publicity man's dream, as witnessed by the attention the elections had received, the originators probably weren't too surprised by the number of promoters they were attracting. At the same time, they could never have predicted the wide variety of concerns that eventually contacted them. From the makers of calendars, maps, ash trays and baseball equipment, to the local bowling team, the number of promotional ideas had gone beyond their wildest dreams.

Nothing on this grand scale could be expected to be completely successful; and, indeed, the designers of the Hall of Fame had their frustrations. Considerations of patents and trademarks, heretofore unthought of, had now taken a place of utmost importance. If the hall's administrators hoped to obtain revenue to support their museum complex in the future, they had to investigate all of the legal ramifications involved in manufacturing and selling souvenirs. There was also the matter of partial rejection by the major leagues, who seemed to lack confidence in the ability of a small village in upstate New York to stage the action. Future events would prove that their concerns were unfounded. Cleland, Littell, and local committee chairmen were already organized for a celebration on a grand scale. Long before, they had set up a local organization to handle these affairs. Still, they required the cooperation of professional baseball at all levels in order to bring their dreams to fruition.

Chapter Six
The Bases are Loaded

Since the very beginning of the hall-museum concept, most of the burden involving its evolution centered around its first executive secretary—Alexander Cleland. While he was able to handle many of the intricacies of electing members, gathering memorabilia and promoting the new creation, additional help from three major forces was necessary to make the centennial a complete success. Of course, the entire program might have fallen through if organized baseball had not given some kind of support to the project. In addition to the major leagues, the minor leagues were sought out for their backing and participation. Secondly, the people of Cooperstown, who wanted their village to be recognized for its role in the game's development, gave the secretary their unwavering support as they united at the local level. Finally, an outside organization had to step into the picture. Their job was to come up with a grand promotional idea that would bring baseball and the village together in their efforts to celebrate the 100th anniversary of the national pastime. The degree to which these three groups helped to make the anniversary a success varied; but without some support from each of them, it could have been a dismal failure.

Recognizing the need to garner the complete support of the major leagues, Cleland had initially contacted the commissioner's office, but Landis offered little encouragement. William Harridge, American League president, never wrote to the secretary. Of course, Frick was the major contributor to the budding concept of the hall and museum. He played a significant role in starting the Hall of Fame, and he had recruited some important artifacts for display. However, even though he previously offered the secretary his complete cooperation, his duties as league president restricted any further contributions he might have been able to make. Cleland, therefore, was forced to find another connection. As early as March, 1935, he had contacted William Brandt of the National League Service Bureau; and this link had served him well during the promotion of the yearly election process.

In June he sent Brandt a memorandum concerning the museum with the hope that he would write about its development in a forthcoming *National League Bulletin*. He pointed out that a large room of a main street building in the village had been set aside to house the artifacts that were being collected. As the collection grew, he assured Brandt, additional space could be made available. Cleland then provided a list of items that had been put on display, including the ball formerly owned by Abner Graves. He also pointed out that there were a number of notable relics scattered around the country that the museum authorities hoped to secure. These included private collections and items belonging to major league clubs. Cleland stated that the museum presently wanted pictures of old games along with examples of equipment used by famous ball players. He hoped that those materials would provide a chronological record of the game from its beginnings. In coordination with this effort, the secretary explained that the opinion of the fans would be solicited to select a list of fifty greats of the game. From this group, the Baseball Writers Association would pick the first inductees. He hoped that this procedure, properly advertised through the major league offices, would accelerate the collection process.[1]

In Brandt, Cleland had found a sympathetic and concerned connection with the major leagues. In the fall of 1935 he wrote the secretary concerning a request by *The Sporting News* for a photograph of the museum. Recognizing the importance of baseball's most widely circulated newspaper, the league's public relations executive hoped to capitalize on their interest. He also suggested that the museum officials should keep a supply of pictures on hand for publication purposes. If this could be arranged, the Service Bureau could act as a distribution center for the material. This service, after all, was a major function of Brandt's office.

Evidently the St. Louis based publication wanted more than a photograph. They had selected Brandt to write an article for their publication concerning the plans for the centennial. Although he was not sure when it would be published, he hoped that Cleland could send the picture as soon as possible least *The Sporting News* backed off their intentions and the hall's promoters lost out on an opportunity for nation-wide publicity. After he received the picture, Brandt requested another one of the field which was now beginning to receive country-wide sanction as the place where the national pastime originated.[2]

Although Cleland's correspondence with Brandt had been somewhat limited, the Service Bureau was of great assistance to the museum's rise to prominence in the early years. This was especially true of the election process to which Brandt offered his services in terms of promotion and procedure. Given his knowledge of the game, its fans, and the officials who ran it, his assistance was invaluable. As the yearly election results became a national story and attracted wide-spread fan attention, he proved to be an important connection for the secretary. With very little effort on Cleland's part, the publicity gained from his relationship with the Service Bureau proved to be a great boost to the Hall of Fame.

In addition to his other services, Brandt also forwarded publications from the league offices such as the yearly *Green Book*, sketches of newly elected members to the Hall of Fame, and the *Bulletin*. He also requested the name of the sports editor for the local newspaper in the village. Cleland dutifully recognized Littell as Cooperstown's only editor, and he was immediately added to the Bureau's mailing list.[3] Following this letter, Cleland would receive little correspondence from Brandt's office until the year of the centennial—which was still two years away.

Landis initially gave minimal support to the Hall of Fame, but he evidently had a large sum of money set aside that might be used to support the developments in Cooperstown. Stephen Clark became aware of the Landis fund after Littell forwarded a letter to him from W. T. Sampson Smith of New York City. In the summer of 1934, he had written to Mr. Curtis of the Spalding and Brothers Company, who in turn had corresponded with the National League president,

John Heydler. Although the details were sketchy, Smith was concerned about a memorial fund held by Judge Landis which amounted to $150,000. Heydler may have wanted to use at least some of this money to upgrade Doubleday Field, and he also suggested that an exhibition game involving "two good teams" be scheduled in the village in order to maintain the ballpark.[4]

The fact that major league baseball had contributed little to the museum did not go unnoticed. In November, 1937, Dan Daniel brought this fact to the attention of the readers of his column in the New York *World Telegram*. Recognizing that the new museum building would be completed by the following spring, Daniel pointed out some of the problems that its officials were having. The immediate concern involved the lack of items needed to fill it. He stated that its promoters wanted four life-size bronze statues for each corner of the main exhibition hall—perhaps of Mathewson, Cobb, Ruth, and Wagner. Unfortunately, sculptors wanted $5,000 for each of these figures, and the hall's officials had no means to accrue this sum. Daniel suggested that major league baseball should devise some method to meet this expenditure and that they should also set up a fund to finance other projects that would enhance baseball's new shrine.

Daniel lamented that the only support heretofore supplied by the majors came in the form of the plaques that were made for each of the inductees. He felt that this was obviously not enough and that the league officials should get behind the project in a much bigger way. While the major focus of his article centered on baseball's officialdom, he also called for more active support from the minor leagues and the Baseball Writers Association. Daniel also pointed out that money wasn't the only commodity sought by the forces at Cooperstown. The museum officials also desired the cooperation of old-time ball players. While some of them, notably Cy Young, had come through handsomely, others had overlooked the entire project. He cited Cobb, Johnson, and Ruth as three former greats who had ignored requests for donations. Daniel felt that if the major league officials would approach those inductees they might be more inclined to cooperate. Finally, he suggested that a simple way for them to help finance operations in Cooperstown was to sponsor a benefit game in the village between the Yankees and the Giants.[5] After all, both teams were located within driving distance, and they would certainly attract a large following.

Even before Daniel's article had been published, organized baseball had planned to set up a fund of $100,000 in order to make sure that the centennial was properly observed. Both leagues officially voted in a joint session in Chicago in December, 1937, to appropriate this sum for the nation-wide observation of baseball's 100th anniversary in Cooperstown. The minor leagues had agreed to a similar action in a previous meeting in Milwaukee. In addition, the leagues approved the appointment of a representative, with headquarters in the village, to oversee the local observance. Frick had arranged for this appropriation but there were no specifications concerning its distribution. However, Cleland was extremely pleased with this support because it demonstrated the concern of major and minor league baseball for the upcoming celebration.[6]

The baseball meetings of 1937 and the report of their favorable support for the anniversary marked the beginning of a turn-around in attitudes concerning the cooperation of organized baseball. Previously distant from the developments in the village, they now began to show more support for the entire project. Other important changes took place at the meeting that were favorable for the Cooperstown program. Frick was re-elected for a three year term as league president, and this reassured local residents of continuous support beyond the centennial summer. This was important not only for the anniversary but also for the future of the Hall of Fame. With Landis presiding over the league's meeting when the appropriation was approved, the village had to feel that the commissioner's office was finally lending some support even if the money never reached Cooperstown directly.

In order to demonstrate their backing for the centennial, the major league officials went beyond the financing that was appropriated from the advisory council fund. At the same meeting they set up a committee to cooperate with minor league officials in arranging the program for 1939. This group consisted of Heydler, Harridge, and Landis. They were given the responsibility of selecting a director who would have complete control over conducting the centennial. The choice of Heydler was important in restoring the confidence of village officials, for he had been in touch with the project from the very beginning. He and his wife had visited there twice the previous summer in order to check on local developments. Although nobody knew exactly what action would be taken by organized baseball, Frick had outlined the general plan for the celebration program for Mayor Theodore R. Lettis, Cleland and others concerned with the local organization. However, this plan was not revealed to the press at that time.[7]

Naturally, the people of Cooperstown were excited about the funding that had been set up for the centennial, but they may have been somewhat disappointed that it wasn't being used in the village. Of special interest was Doubleday Field which, according to Mayor Lettis, needed immediate renovation. The village officials hoped that Frick would consider their needs in his future decision, but they didn't want to take any action that would give the impression of being forceful. Still, the mayor felt that the work on the field had to continue, and he outlined the construction details. They included purchasing a piece of property to extend right field, changing the slope of the diamond, erecting a new grandstand in place of the old one and buying additional bleachers. Frick opposed the idea of new grandstands. He thought that it was desirable to preserve the rustic character of the field, but Littell felt that it was neither rustic nor sightly. He pointed out that it had no facilities for dressing rooms or toilets. Also he opposed the purchase of new bleachers for one summer activity and felt that they could be rented locally.

Cleland promised to meet with Frick upon his return from spring training in 1938 and hoped to get a better idea of his plans. He emphasized that the mayor's concepts involved local projects and didn't include him personally. The secretary and his museum committee were strictly concerned with promoting the village as a national baseball shrine. However, he did hope to get a representative from Frick's office to inspect the field and offer advice in terms of grading and surfacing it. He was also adamant in his belief that Stephen Clark would not put up any of the $5000 needed for building the new grandstand.[8] Clark had already donated a considerable sum to the development of Cooperstown's image as the cradle of baseball, and Cleland was trying to focus local attention on other sources of revenue.

It was obvious to Cooperstown's promoters that they needed to form their own committee for the centennial. Although the major league officials had taken strides to promote the 100th anniversary, they obviously had their own ideas as to how it should be carried out. Indeed, the locals had already taken a step in this direction in April, 1935, with the formation of the Doubleday Field Association. However, as the name implied, this group was concerned with raising money to improve the field and to make it a worthy sight for tourists who wanted to visit baseball's most sacrosanct ground. In order to control the regional events for the summer of 1939, another local organization with a broader perspective was necessary.

In May, 1937, Littell contacted Cleland concerning a meeting of various committees in the village that were interested in the centennial observance. Mayor Lettis had arranged for this conference under the prodding of the Chamber of Commerce, who felt that a united effort was necessary. While no action was taken at this time, a committee was formed to make plans for the celebration. It was made up of one member each from the Board of Village Trustees, the Doubleday Field Association, the Chamber of Commerce, and the High School Athletic Association. They planned to confer with Cleland in the future, and their intent was to be the nucleus of a larger committee which would be in charge of local arrangements for the centennial.

The executive committee did not meet with the finance group until a year later, and at that time the latter requested an estimate for the budget concerning the entire celebration. Also, the village trustees appropriated two hundred dollars for the new organization while the old Doubleday Field group agreed to turn over the funds that they had already collected (less than the amount of the trustees). Lester G. Bursey, head of the centennial program, announced that he had already scheduled two college games for May, 1939, and hoped to arrange a game that would involve Doubleday's alma mater—the United States Military Academy.[9]

It was only natural that the Cooperstown Centennial Committee would choose Cleland as their representative to New York City. As secretary and originator of the museum, he was the ideal choice. Because of the recent developments, he decided to visit the village in the first week of June in order to discuss the centennial plans with the executive committee and various chairmen of other committees that had been formed. He was well aware that the arrangements for the summer of 1939 were under two distinct auspices—the program committee headed by Bursey and the major league group under Heydler, Harridge, and Landis. Given the fact that Bursey's organization had only recently been organized, he was surprised at the thorough and comprehensive planning that had already taken place. Cleland was especially pleased with the arrangements which had been made concerning the West Point game, which he felt was an appropriate and intriguing climax to the college program.

The local committee was making surprising progress, but its major league counterpart was lagging behind. Beset with the whims of a vast variety of interests due to the wide-spread nature of their proposals, they could neither construct nor publish their plans at that time. Therefore, it was impossible for local promoters to advertise what the major leagues would do for the village program. Also, the two sides were not really working together. Members of the local organization had previously attended a conference with Frick in New York City, and the president explained the general plans for the centennial. While the league president believed that the proper observance of the anniversary should be national in scope, he felt that Cooperstown and Doubleday Field should be the central focus. The Cooperstown group came away from that meeting confident that they would play a major role in the celebration. They anxiously awaited the final announcement of the big league project so that it could be unified with the local effort into a continuous program for the entire summer. Cleland, as liaison between the two groups, was prepared to service both in order to bring the summer's plans together.

Cleland spent almost a week in the village, during which time he made preparations for the opening of the new museum and attended two meetings of the executive committee which focused on the plans for alterations to Doubleday Field. Although the area around the old Phinney lot was adequate for local games, it was not of professional proportions. Left field was only 248 feet, and the opposite foul line was only a foot longer. This meant that games involving major league players were out of the question. The condition of the playing area led the executive committee to form a group whose only concern was the upgrading of Doubleday Field. The head of the grounds committee was O. G. Clark, and Professor Ralph W. Perry had recently been added. Eleven other local residents formed the rest of the group, and they appropriately included A. S. Phinney.

During Cleland's stay in Cooperstown, he met with the grounds committee, Lettis, contractor Mathew T. Chapman and surveyors W. Carter Burnett and Lynn G. Parshall at the field to go over the various possibilities for reconstruction. The two surveyors drew up a map of the area to be submitted to baseball authorities in the village. It was hoped that it would help them to arrive at an agreeable decision as to which plan to adopt for a new layout of the diamond that would allow for an extension of the outfield. Local officials requested that Cleland take back to New York City complete information regarding the Cooperstown program so that it could be given special consideration by the major league committee in charge of the national celebration. Just what the officials of professional baseball had in mind was still a mystery. Cleland told village officials that, as he promised earlier, he had met with Frick before his trip to Cooperstown to discuss these plans. The league president stated that a number of tentative programs were still under consideration. Even though a final decision on these matters had not yet been reached, Frick hoped that they would be ready for publication in the near future.

Cleland left the village with the satisfaction that the centennial plans were in good hands. Local officials had moved swiftly and professionally to arrange every aspect of the centennial celebration. Eleven different committees had been established to cover everything from decoration and lighting to legal advice. Each committee was made up of five to thirteen people and included some formidable names from local circles. Lettis was the chairman of the executive committee of which Beattie, Rowan D. Spraker, Perry and B. G. Johnson were members. Littell was chosen as the vice-chairman of the advertising and publicity committee, and Clark was part of the entertainment committee. Senator Walter W. Stokes was made chairman of the finance committee, which included William C. Smalley. Waldo C. Johnston was a member of the grounds committee, and

Ken Root was a member of Bursey's program committee along with Drs. H. L. Cruttenden and L. E. Pitcher.[10] All of these men had been connected with the early developments of Doubleday Field.

The forces of Cooperstown had good reason to feel that they should be a central focus of the centennial celebration. By mid-summer, 1938, attendance figures at the museum had surpassed all expectations. Evidently, the advertising campaign had worked well since visitors were attracted from all parts of the country and their numbers had already exceeded the total from the previous year. The activity concerning the museum had also filtered through the rest of the community, and the resort village was experiencing one of its best years. Not only was the demand for tourist accommodations exceptionally large, it was also on the rise.

A major part of the reason for this increase was the new museum building, which had only recently been officially opened. The grounds surrounding it had been beautifully landscaped, and the building itself was an attractive addition to the other edifices on main street. The entire project had enhanced the beauty of an already charming village. It also contained a sign at the entrance which recognized the museum as being officially sanctioned by organized baseball and a memorial to the game's inventor—Abner Doubleday. Inside the building, new display cases had been purchased for the exhibits; and rugs and furniture had been added to provide a cordial and homelike atmosphere. Although the size of the collection on exhibit was still relatively small, it was put together with the highest professional standards; and promoters had every reason to believe that it would contain a vast array of items in the future.[11]

With the museum attracting customers at a record pace, the alterations to Doubleday Field now took top priority, and the major leagues lent their attention to the project. In mid-summer, 1938, Henry Fabian, veteran grounds keeper for the New York Giants, visited the village at the request of Frick. The league president had received word from Cleland that property adjacent to Doubleday Field had recently been acquired in order to expand the outfield, and the local plans were now ready for inspection by a major league expert. Frick contacted Horace C. Stoneman, president of the Giants organization, and asked him to allow Fabian to visit Cooperstown and lend his considerable expertise to the field renovation plans. Stoneman was more than pleased to offer his employee's services to the field project.

At first glance, Fabian appeared to be old enough to vote on pre-1900 Hall of Fame selection. However, he was still slim and hearty at the age of seventy-three. Local promoters could not have asked for a better authority on playing fields as he was widely recognized in baseball circles as the leading grounds keeper of his era. Fabian had been in charge of the Giants' playing area for a quarter of a century. Recognizing his abilities, most of the clubs in the major leagues had adopted his ideas and even authorities in England turned to him for advice when they began to construct their first diamonds.

Shortly after his arrival in the village, he paid a visit to the historic field with Mayor Lettis, Cleland, and a committee of village trustees. Following his preliminary inspection, the local group asked his opinion on their expansion plans, and the veteran grounds expert stated that while the field was relatively small, it was still adequate for a major league performance. After all, the left and right field foul lines in the Polo Grounds were only 287 feet and 257 feet respectively, and Doubleday Field was larger than those proportions. Fabian was equally impressed with the beautiful setting of the ball park, but he was surprised that the diamond had been constructed with no grass on the infield. He pointed out that all of the big league fields were currently sodded and this had proved to be far more satisfactory than the "skinned" infield.

During his two-day visit to Cooperstown, the famed field expert consulted with the local officials at the Cooper Inn. He suggested that the plans for enlarging the field be perfected during the summer so that he could return to the village in September following the Giants' last home stand to supervise personally the construction work. He was completely confident that the entire renovation project would be finished in time for the anniversary. Fabian also visited the field again in order to lay out the proposed diamond, go over the plans to extend the outfield dimensions and make other suggestions to the grounds committee. He was satisfied that the new playing facilities would be larger than the Polo Grounds and would offer a challenge to major league hitters. The proposed alterations also included the erection of new grandstands which had previously been under consideration. They were to be crescent shaped, drawn up in three sections, and designed to hold about 800 people.

While Fabian stayed in the village, Mayor Lettis and grounds committee chairman Owen G. Clark met with George Von Maur, regional director of the Public Works Administration (PWA) and Kenneth Wick, local representative of the Work Progress Administration (WPA), regarding the completion of the Doubleday Field alterations. Since a New Deal agency had been utilized in previous work on the field in 1933-34, it was only natural for them to investigate which of the two federal units was best able to handle the work. With this accomplished, Fabian and Cleland left the village with the satisfaction that their visit would result in a professional setting for fans to view regulation baseball games.[12]

The construction costs would be formidable; and for many Americans, caught up in the economic crisis of the depression, it may have seemed frivolous and even wasteful. However, the historic significance could not be denied. Also, promoters could assuage the attitudes of detractors by pointing out the jobs that could be provided and the encouragement of nationalism that would come from promoting America's foremost game. Still, the money had to be raised; and before it was appropriated villagers naturally turned to Frick for help; but the league president was too involved with the end of the baseball season. Cleland realized that until the World Series was over no further action could be expected from major league baseball. Therefore he suggested that the grounds committee continue with a minimum extension of the field which would cost the village trustees about $1,500. The secretary had not given up on a total renovation, but he felt that the league would have to cooperate and the community would have to approve a bond in order to meet construction costs. While Cleland had not consulted Stephen Clark on these ideas, he felt sure that his boss would support any reasonable plan.

The major reason why the Cooperstown leaders desired financial assistance from Frick was that organized baseball had already appropriated $100,000 for the centennial and they hoped that some of it could be earmarked for the renovation of Doubleday Field. However, the league president flatly refused to allocate the funds to them. He contended that if the league agreed to finance the field construction in Cooperstown, they would probably receive a similar application for Elysian Field in Hoboken, New Jersey, where the first organized game was played. While some people in the village felt that Cleland should appeal this decision to a higher authority, the secretary believed it was a useless endeavor and refused to have any part of it.[13]

Gradually, the WPA undertook the improvements to Doubleday Field. The work relief project included the construction of a steel-covered grandstand and some wooden bleachers. It also entailed seeding the field, establishing the proper drainage system, building a new board fence for the outfield and constructing a stone masonry wall for the rest of the facility. Fabian approved all of this activity, and the promoters were confident that they would have a first-class facility when the field was opened in the spring of 1939. Lester W. Herzog, WPA Administrator of the state of New York, approved the federal allocation of $23,401.90 for the expected labor costs and the village of Cooperstown provided $17,300 for the cost of materials and equipment rentals.

In December, 1938, work began on the renovation project. The WPA supplied twenty-eight workers, and they began tearing down the steel grandstand that was adjacent to the local fairgrounds. As a cost-cutting measure, the village authorities had decided against an all new facility and opted instead to utilize local materials. The plan was to reassemble the structural material in the shape of a horseshoe along the base lines of the field. The workers began erecting forms for the grandstand's concrete piers and they also engaged in spreading top soil on the outfield as the weather permitted. This work was done under the supervision of Edward Conklin, a WPA engineer for the county.[14] One would have to admire the efforts of these workers because December in Cooperstown is not an ideal season for outside construction work. But time was growing short and there was much to be done before the festivities commenced.

Before any of this construction started, however, the authorities in the village had received word from Cleland that Frick had relegated them to a smaller role in the centennial than they had anticipated. Faced with the possibility of a secondary role in the upcoming celebration, the promoters in the village might have lessened their efforts to boost the centennial. Certainly a less tenacious group of people might have wilted because of frustrations they were facing. In fact, some detractors were beginning to cast doubt about the capability of locals to follow through with plans for the celebration.

However, the Cooperstown forces took Frick's advice of going ahead with any plans the village might want to set up. Following the president's disappointing statements, the local newspaper addressed the issue of stress that museum officials were facing in the present crisis. *The Otsego Farmer* stated that this in no way meant that the preparations for 1939 had been discontinued. Quite the opposite was happening. Lester G. Bursey, the local chairman for the centennial program, intrigued the readers of the paper with a statement that he would release a story in the near future which would be a sensation in the community. Although he refused to divulge the nature of his surprise at the present time, he did reveal that a complete program involving collegiate and scholastic games during the month of May had been completed.

The program for the opening month of activities was impressive. The first of many games to be held in Cooperstown that summer was scheduled for the first week of the month and involved Manlius school and Albany Academy (two military preparatory schools). A large crowd was assured since the latter institution promised to bring the entire corps of cadets to the village. The schedule for the next week involved a game between Williams and Amherst Colleges. The significance of this contest was that these two schools were involved in the first college baseball game ever played in 1859. The third week featured a game between Union College and Rensselaer Polytechnic Institute that was scheduled in conjunction with the annual Otsego county music festival. The 27th of May was set aside for Christy Mathewson day, and his widow would be in attendance to unveil the bronze bust of her husband that had become a part of the museum collection. A game between the famous pitcher's alma mater, Bucknell and St. Lawrence University was set up for that date. The college games would be brought to a close on Memorial Day when the United States Military Academy and Colgate were scheduled to meet on the playing field. Certainly, the planners felt that this would be a fitting tribute to Doubleday.

Bursey's announcement of this schedule may have helped to ease some doubtful minds, but his secrecy might have convinced others that the local centennial program was in trouble. Still, it was significant that a firm commitment had been made to initiate part of the summer's activities. This was a fulfillment of the planning committee's policy of providing a continuing series of events with weekend features that would help to attract a steady flow of tourists in the village throughout the summer. They felt that a single gigantic feature would over-crowd the community for a short period of time and tend to diminish the remainder of the season.

The fact that the forces in Cooperstown continued their original plans with such diligence was a tribute to their tenacity in the face of outside pressures. Actually, the planning within the village had continued unabated. For one thing, Cleland, who had acted as liaison between the village and his home in New York City, opened up an office in the community room of the Second National Bank building. This would serve as centennial headquarters until the celebration commenced in the spring. In addition, the planners had also set up a variety of committees to handle all of the details for the celebration. Theodore R. Lettis was the chairman of the executive committee which governed the activities of others including advertising and publicity, concessions, decorations and lighting, entertainment, finance, grounds keeping, housing, transportation, legal advisement and programs.[15]

Even these developments did little to boost spirits in the village. Frustrations in Cooperstown had reached a peak in September when the president announced that no new plans by major league officials would be revealed until January. Evidently, Cleland knew nothing about their conceptions for the following summer, and there was every reason for Cooperstown officials to feel that they were being ignored. If they did feel this way, they shouldn't have because the foundations for the future were soon to be laid out by the newly organized National Baseball Centennial Commission.

The first meeting of this group convened in Chicago on October 24, 1938, at the Hotel Roosevelt. In attendance at this meeting were Landis, Frick, Heydler, Harridge, and L. C. McEvoy, radio director for the junior circuit. Others at the organization gathering included Leslie O'Connor, Landis' long-time friend and his secretary-treasurer, Larry Smits, Stuart Cameron, Steve Hannagan and Al Stoughton. The latter group consisted of public relations men who had recently been hired to promote the centennial plans.

The first action of this group was to set up an executive committee consisting of the commissioner, the league presidents (including Heydler), McEvoy, Judge William J. Bramham, president of the minor leagues, and George Trautman, Chairman of the National Association's Executive Committee. O'Connor was a natural choice as treasurer of the group, and he was assigned the responsibility for incorporating the commission under the Illinois State laws. Stoughton was selected as the group's secretary, and an additional list of prospective members was drawn up. They were a formidable group and represented people involved in a wide variety of occupations. Given Doubleday's military background, it was only natural that General John J. "Blackjack" Pershing, the leader of American military forces in World War I, Major General Thomas Holcomb, Commandant of the United States Marine Corps, and Scott P. Squyres, Commander-in-Chief of the Veterans of Foreign Wars, were invited to become members of the organization. Other military men who were asked to join were General Malin Craig, U.S. Army Chief of Staff, and Admiral William D. Leahy, Chief of Naval Operations.

Although these people made the list of invitees seem top-heavy with military personnel, a wide variety of civilians were also asked to join. This group included John W. Studebaker, United States Commissioner of Education, Stephen F. Chadwick, National Commander of the American Legion, George H. Davis, Chairman of the United States Chamber of Commerce, Stanford Bates, Director of the Boys' Clubs of America, Paul Shannon, President of the Baseball Writers Association, Neville Miller, Chairman of the Association of Broadcasters, George M. Cohan, famous actor and song writer, C. O. Brown of the American Baseball Congress (amateurs) and Mrs. Sadie Orr Dunbar, President of the General Federation of Women's Clubs. The group also planned to pick a representative from the Semi-Pro Congress and the President of the Inter-Collegiate Athletic Association. The final person to be requested to join was none other than Alexander Cleland, although it would be almost two months before he was officially asked.

The first order of business during the organization meeting was concerned with the selection of an insignia for the centennial. The design, presented by Hannagan, was approved by the group and set up for copyrighting. The official logo was to be furnished to the manufacturers of baseball uniforms (Spalding, Wilson, and Goldsmith) for reproduction on all 1939 team clothing. It appears that this rather mundane task had been discussed previously and reflects a concern for the upcoming celebration that Cleland and his associates had not known.

Getting down to the more significant aspects of the events for the following year, the group discussed league schedules for the purpose of setting aside a time for the anniversary plans. They agreed to a theme entitled CAVALCADE OF BASEBALL. A program designed around this central idea was to be presented at Cooperstown in connection with the dedication of the Hall of Fame. The idea that they had in mind was to demonstrate the evolution of the game from "four-old-cat" to modern baseball. It seems rather ironic that they chose to emphasize evolution over birth since the foundation of the Doubleday story, and thus Cooperstown's claim to fame, was based on the so-call "immaculate conception" of baseball as promulgated by the Mills Commission. The pageant's setting was to be organized by various college teams in the vicinity of the village, and the plan was to have leading players from each league play several innings of the modern game. The group decided to limit the Cooperstown celebration to not more than three hours; and this included both the formal dedication and the cavalcade. The precise date for this ceremony was to be determined later by Harridge and Frick, but the target time was for early June.

Frick, who was probably more aware of the organizational effort taking place in the village than anyone else, suggested that Smits and Stoughton go to Cooperstown as soon as possible in order to survey the situation and make recommendations for future action. In order to facilitate their investigation, he asked that they contact Cleland concerning the integration of the village into the program plans. This was the only mention of the area which had become linked in the minds of many fans as the birthplace of baseball. Either the organizers were unaware of the plethora of committees that had already been set up in the village or they didn't think that a small, remote town in upstate New York had the wherewithal to pull off a major celebration.

The highest concern in the organization meeting was the matter of publicity. Representing the business aspect of the game, this group understood the need for utilizing the media in order to garner national interest and support for their project. The first consideration was when to initiate the big publicity campaign for the summer's activities. They decided to make a general announcement of the forming of the centennial commission and its goals at the minor league meetings in December. However, the group rejected the notion of continuing the publicity campaign throughout the winter and agreed that the real fanfare of advertisement should start around the beginning of spring training.

Rather than taking the time during the first meeting to discuss the basic publicity ideas, the public relations people would simply outline these concepts and include them in a future report that would be distributed to all those in attendance. According to the plan, the initial steps would involve enlisting the support of the motion picture industry (which had already taken place) and the print media. Hannagan had already pointed out to Sam Goldwyn that the history of baseball was replete with drama and the famous movie producer, already very interested in the project, requested a detailed outline of the highlights in its history. He wanted to include a few dramatic incidents that would be suitable for motion pictures.

Even though the committee's promoters concentrated their efforts on a single movie producer, they recognized that the magazine field offered virtually unlimited possibilities and they hoped to explore them to the fullest extent. At Hannagan's suggestion, letters were written to all of the leading literary agents, and they pointed out how baseball's centennial could be written up in serial fiction, feature articles, historical reviews and character sketches. *Collier's Magazine* had already expressed an interest in an article on "Ladies Day" that Cameron had been writing, and Quentin Reynolds of that same publication desired to write a piece on the first century of the game that was to appear at the start of the season. *Look Magazine* wanted to do a pictorial history of baseball over its first century. The *New Yorker Magazine* wanted to focus on an individual for a profile study, and the promoters felt that Judge Landis would be an excellent choice. Ripley and Hix desired material on baseball oddities that would contain a centennial angle.

Another idea focusing on the print media concerned a series of articles on a particular theme. Promoters hoped to entice a Newspaper Enterprise Association series complete with Ding-Bat illustrations or other cartoons with each story. Here they wanted to feature the evolution of the game's rules over the past century. Another series suggested at this time would deal with batting championships in both leagues since their beginnings. Because articles on boxing greats had already been written, writers had a blueprint to follow.

The suggestions by publicity men to promote the anniversary touched every conceivable base. They felt that Jim Farley, Postmaster General of the United States, would be interested in issuing a special commemorative stamp for the centennial. Recognizing that the Sunshine biscuits and the National Biscuit Company had produced new boxes of cookies in the past, the promoters hoped they would do the same for baseball. Previously they had done this, featuring Popeye and Snow White and the Seven Dwarfs; and the baseball officials desired to produce an anniversary cookie box featuring bats, balls, gloves and players. They also wanted to put out a centennial pin for children to wear that would contain the centennial logo.

While most of these suggestions were fairly novel, the idea of having a special stamp for the centennial was not. It was initially proposed by the Board of Directors of the Cooperstown Chamber of Commerce on April 19, 1937. They adopted a resolution on that date to encourage the federal government to issue a commemorative stamp in connection with the centennial, and this proposal was endorsed by the local Leatherstocking Stamp Club. Littell informed Cleland of this concept and suggested that he mention it to Frick, who could assign Brandt to push it through. Evidently the major league authorities like the idea because they talked with Farley regarding its issuance. The postmaster general felt that it would be a natural and began working on the proposition.

The National Baseball Centennial Commission had additional ideas for magazine and newspaper coverage. They felt that a good story would be one comparing the conditions of traveling, clubhouse accommodations and the general care of players in the early days and at the present time. In addition to this kind of special feature, they also wanted to supply complete coverage of the diverse centennial stories to all of the large daily newspapers. They hoped to utilize the Newspaper Enterprise Association, Central Press, Associated Press, and the International News Service to provide sports editors of cities of less than 30,000 people with packets of information on the centennial. Each packet would contain a series on the history of the game, baseball oddities, the inductees to the Hall of Fame, and a glossary of terms that had evolved throughout the first century. This was simply a general outline of ideas, and the commission planned to expand on them as the celebration drew near.[16]

The commission wrote up a charter which described the purpose of the organization, the personnel involved, a list of planned events and promotional ideas and plans for contests that they hoped would attract nation-wide attention. Accordingly, the commission was formed to commemorate the one hundredth birthday of the national pastime. It was composed of representatives from professional, semi-pro, and amateur baseball. The organizers hoped to attract people of such a high caliber that they could easily gain respect and national attention. Thus, every state, city, and village in the nation, it was hoped, would adopt their plans and turn their attention to baseball during 1939.

The focus of their attention was not the typical baseball fan because their interest in upcoming events was virtually assured. Rather, they hoped to attract people who were not generally associated with the sport and didn't follow it in the daily sport pages. The commission felt that baseball could effectively teach "the lessons of democracy, sportsmanship, clean living, physical perfection, the will to win, honesty, and in essence Americanism." They hoped that this educational process would affect "every man, woman and child in the nation, regardless of race, creed or color." The organizers felt that the greatest contribution of the game was the "building of a national spirit of fair play." They hoped that "the building of American ideals and character could be carried into every walk of life" during the centennial celebration. Baseball, they felt, had "taught America lessons never learned in other nations" and was "one of the greatest single contributors to the making of what is known as 'The American Spirit'."

The commission then drew up a list of personnel that included representatives from organized baseball, the amateur game, and the general public. Their function was to integrate Americans of all walks of life into the centennial plans. Their executive committee contained honorary chairmen and vice chairmen from organized baseball and the public sector. As originally set up, they included the commissioners of major league and semi-pro ball and the president of the United States for the chairmen positions. The vice chairmen from baseball were assigned to the presidents of the minors, semi-pro (Raymond Dumont) and amateur leagues (C. O. Brown) along with the editor of the official baseball guide. The members at large included all of the presidents of each of the 37 minor leagues.

The honorary chairman from the public sector was the President of the United States and honorary vice-chairmen included John W. Studebaker, commissioner of education, Rabbi Stephen Wise, Cardinal Dougherty, Dr. Harry Emerson Fosdick, and the National Commander of the American Legion. The Public members at large included the Army Chief of Staff, the Commanding General of the Marine Corps, the presidents of the League of Women Voters, the League of Business and Professional Women, the National Chamber of Commerce and the National Grange. Also included in this group were top executives of the Red Cross, Boy and Girl Scouts, YMCA and YWCA, the National Recreation Association, the Playgrounds Association and the National Social Work Congress.

The commission also laid the plans to set up organizations at the state, area, and local level with chairmen to be selected at a later date. Included in the membership was a vast array of professionals such as Walt Disney, J. Edgar Hoover, Eddie Rickenbacker, Jack Benny, Paul Whiteman, Joe E. Brown, Helen

Hayes, Lowell Thomas, Damon Runyon, Howard Hughes and Fred Astaire. Although most of the people selected for the various committees were only lending their names to a list and would offer little tangible support for the centennial, they reflected the national scope of the program. The committee hoped that the educational aspect of their plans would affect all Americans, but minority representation was woefully lacking.

The National Baseball Centennial Commission also outlined certain details to be taken care of which were included in their charter. First, the official insignia was adopted and contained the figure "100," the years "1839-1939" and the words "Base Ball" in national colors. It was to be used on uniforms, posters, flags and banners. The group also decided to begin the 100th anniversary with the reading of a presidential proclamation in January at the Annual Base Ball Writer's Dinner and to terminate the festivities at the first game of the World Series. The major focus in between these two dates was the dedication of the Hall of Fame in Cooperstown that was tentatively scheduled for June.

Another consideration at this time was the *National Centennial Handbook* which was to be designed and edited as a work book for the leagues, area groups, state committees and local celebrations. The handbook would detail how a baseball centennial observance could be staged in communities throughout the country. Complete with illustrations, the booklet would be the first step in disseminating information locally and integrating local programs into the national celebration. The commission still hadn't decided whether to distribute them free or sell them at a minimum price. They also had to set up a proper time schedule for proclamations by mayors and governors to tie in with local and state-wide festivities.

In addition, the commission outlined the duties of its director. Recognizing the necessity of attracting the active enthusiasm of all aspects of organized baseball to ensure success for their program, they felt that the most effective way to accomplish this was through the director. They planned for him to make personal visits to the baseball winter meetings, association gatherings, and club dinners. Here he could meet with leaders who formed baseball policy and opinion and explain to them the purpose of the centennial and the plans for its implementation. They also wanted him to make other public appearances and to make speeches to a wide variety of groups.

The creation of the national commission along with state, area, and local committees was actually the first step in organizing a national office. Its specific purpose was to promote local celebrations throughout the baseball season. These local events did not necessarily have to take place in conjunction with ball games, however; and they could take on a variety of forms. This would include parades organized by civic associations, dedications of local memorials to baseball heroes, exhibition games by visiting teams, personal appearances by sports and entertainment personalities, public awards to contest winners in different promotions organized by the national office, dedication of new or improved "centennial" baseball diamonds, public meetings addressed by baseball speakers, and service club luncheons and dinners devoted to a baseball topic.

While the commission worked with organized baseball, one of its major functions continued to be the promotion of local events designed to attract the interest in the sport itself in terms of its contribution to American life. A major aspect of this promotion involved contests which would be outlined in the handbook for local implementation and national ones to be handled by large advertisers. One idea involved an essay contest for school children on the subject of baseball's contribution to the development of American life. The awards to the winners could be a trip to the Worlds Fair or Cooperstown or both. Another scheme involved a fan's contest whereby people would vote on the all-time most valuable player on local teams. The names of these players throughout the nation would then be inscribed on a national scroll that would be permanently housed in the Hall of Fame. The commission also hoped to promote local games in addition to the regular league games. These would involve, for example, games between service clubs (Lions vs. Rotary), business departments (banks vs. newspapers), and company units of branches of the armed services. Another local promotional idea centered around art contests in schools for the design of centennial posters. It was even suggested that the National Amateur Championships be moved from Wichita to the Worlds Fair or Cooperstown.

In order to attract the attention of people who were not normally interested in the national pastime, the commission developed a list of ideas that might be employed to suit that purpose. They felt that clothes designers could create a "Centennial Design" for ladies' dresses and hats. They also hoped that playing card manufacturers would issue decks with the centennial logo and that the makers of school supplies would use the design on pencil boxes and book bags. Another plan involved encouraging a leading botanist to patent a new centennial or Cooperstown flower (football had already adopted the chrysanthemum). Perhaps some food manufacturer could come up with a baseball centennial dish. Maybe a sporting goods firm would feature the anniversary in their advertising and window displays. Department stores in large cities might create historical exhibits showing the evolution of uniforms and equipment. The commission might be able to influence beer companies to print the centennial insignia on their coasters. The ideas went on and on.

Outside of these promotional schemes, the commission continued to develop publicity ideas. They hoped to make up a package of information to reach all local committees that would contain stories, features, and pictures. They wanted to cover all avenues of communication including motion pictures, radio, newspapers and even television! While the idea of attracting the interest of Hollywood had already been considered, they hoped that some producer could be inspired to make a feature length film with baseball as the theme. They also hoped for some kind of March of Time newsreel coverage of events in Cooperstown during the summer. This monthly-screen magazine was initiated in 1935 and combined film and documentary techniques to produce programs running from 15 to 25 minutes. Given its tremendous impact on the movie going public, its integration into the commission's publicity program would have a tremendous national impact. Finally, they wanted to induce the National Library Association to produce a baseball bibliography and circulate this compilation to every library in the world.

How much of the commission's plans might eventually come to fruition didn't really matter at this point. The idea was to think, and more importantly, to think big. Since baseball was the national pastime, shouldn't its 100th anniversary be conducted on a grand scale? Certainly the commission felt this way, and they established budget estimates for office expenses, printing, salaries for a director, secretary and a clerk, travel, entertainment, and extra expenses at $36,800.00.[17]

The plans for the observance of baseball's 100th anniversary had been organized on a grandiose scale. Every promotional scheme conceived had been explored by the newly organized National Baseball Centennial Commission. Advertising, contests, organization development, handbooks, and clothes had been proposed as methods of attracting national attention. But who was behind these plans? Frick, Landis and other baseball magnates were certainly attracted to these new developments, but someone else with expertise in promotion and advertising had obviously entered the scene.

Steve Hannagan had run a public relations firm in New York City since 1925, and in the process he had developed a reputation as a flamboyant businessman. Originally from Lafayette, Indiana, he began working as a reporter in that city at the age of 14 and after for the *Indianapolis Star*. Innovative and dynamic, he became a promoter for vacation resorts (such as Miami Beach and Sun Valley), industry, and sports events. His meteoric rise to success would lead him to become one of the country's leading publicists. Given this background, he was very appealing to Landis who needed a professional firm to promote the 100th anniversary.

In May, 1938, Al Stoughton, publicity director for the New York City YMCA, contacted Hannagan. Stoughton hoped that because of his past experience and education he might bring new ideas and contacts to Hannagan's young and growing organization that would prove to be profitable. The thirty-five year old Stoughton had graduated from Bucknell University in 1924 and worked as a reporter for the Jeannette, Pennsylvania, *News Dispatch*. During the late twenties he had served as the AP, UP and INS correspondent for the central part of the state and also worked as alumni secretary and publicity director for his alma mater until 1936. Stoughton had created these two positions at the university, and he had also organized alumni clubs in fifty cities. He promoted football games, banquets and dances, edited the school's monthly magazine, and acted as director of conventions for the American Alumni Council, a national organization of collegiate officers. He was also founder and director of the university's radio station.

In terms of baseball, Stoughton was the organizer and secretary of the Christy Mathewson Memorial Corporation. His association with this organization stemmed from his relation to the former Giant pitcher. Mathewson's wife was the former Jane Stoughton, Al's aunt. For the last two years, he had been in charge of public relations, advertising, printing production, and general publicity for the YMCA. A recognized public speaker, Stoughton had spoken before a wide variety of audiences. As he stated to Hannagan, he "knew how to use the right fork, wear the right tie, and order a meal or a drink—in most any company." More importantly, in terms of his future connection with the anniversary celebration, he had made contacts with baseball people and had a deep affection for the game.[18]

This correspondence initiated the working relationship between two public relations specialists who would become an important part of the centennial celebration. In August, Hannagan contacted Commissioner Landis concerning some promotional ideas for the anniversary—many of which would later be adopted by the Centennial Commission. Hannagan lamented that baseball had probably done less than any other major sport to develop a continuing clientele. Even though he admitted that the game received a great deal of coverage in the sports pages throughout the nation, most of these stories were aimed at the ardent fan who could generally be counted on for attendance. Little, he felt, had been attempted to entice new business, and baseball was missing a chance to increase attendance by revivifying the childhood interest that many people had held for the national pastime. He realized that occasionally a talented personality would emerge as a top gate attraction, but this was an accident of chance and not something that was made to happen. Another drawback was that this act could only play in one city at a time, which limited its marketability. It was Hannagan's plan to attract nationwide attention to the sport by promoting the centennial program in local districts throughout the country.

Realizing that his organization had gained recognition "in the unsettled field of industrial promotions and advice...in these times of quandary," Hannagan pointed out that the majority of people in his company had begun their work in the area of sports and that his group had achieved a continuous and successful interest in advertising a variety of sporting events. Their biggest success involved the Indianapolis 500 race which they had covered since 1919, but they were also responsible for speed boat races, professional football in Detroit, bowling and a number of other major business pursuits throughout the country.

Hannagan then proceeded to lay out an impressive plan to attract national attention to baseball and the centennial. First, he felt that someone familiar with the game and experienced in organization should be selected as the focal leader of the campaign. This person would not only be responsible for baseball's promotion of the Cooperstown celebration but also the entire revival program designed to spread the interest in baseball throughout the nation. Hannagan assured the commissioner that no organization, not even his own, should be put in charge of operations because he thought it would be more cautious and effective to select a single individual for the position. He should be an important enough figure in the minds of the public and organized baseball to make everyone aware of the significance of the venture.

Once the leadership position had been filled, Hannagan suggested that the chief executive should be provided with an organization that would operate with the full cooperation of league officials and other groups that would be added as the promotion expanded. He felt that his own business should be considered for this role and promised to turn them loose on every promotional aspect of the plan including newspapers, radio, newsreels, and motion pictures. He stated that with the injection of a new personality into the picture, baseball could resume its former position in society.

According to the public relations expert, promotion and organization were two different functions and should be handled by different groups. Eventually, of course, the two would have to work together; and they would always present a united front to the public. While Hannagan was stating that no public relations firm should be hired to do organization work, he was also implying that current major league officials had small expectations from a typical publicity service and did not realize the thoroughness of a modern, sophisticated business in this field. In addition to advertising, it was also involved in merchandising the product in every aspect. The emphasis was on creative thinking to develop interest and marketable items associated with the new fascination.

Hannagan proposed a detailed plan which emphasized the responsibilities of his organization. The publicity groups should, he felt, create a variety of plans to reach effectively every town in America in rekindling the nation's interest in baseball. He believed that the national publicity for the 100th anniversary should be handled tastefully and yet with a flair of showmanship. In regard to newspapers, Hannagan emphasized large circulation concerning articles, fiction, and picture layouts. In terms of motion pictures, he felt that baseball should encourage the utilization of the biggest producers, greatest stars and the best technical knowledge available. National radio networks could be used to build up the public's interest in the months before the season started. In order to make these programs available to smaller communities, they could produce a series of them on records and thus make superior material available to local stations at an affordable cost. Hannagan realized that it would be economically unfeasible to hire a large group of people to disseminate information through the various levels of baseball. He assumed that organized baseball had competent local representatives to carry out this aspect of the campaign. If in fact this super structure was already in place, it would be a major factor in the success of localized celebrations.

Although Hannagan wanted to lay out the entire campaign to baseball's hierarchy immediately, he did not want to begin the dissemination of material nationally until the end of the football season because the nostalgia for baseball would be at its peak at this time. The announcement of the complete details of the program could wait until the baseball writer's banquet in January in New York City. This would give enough time for every group in the country to contemplate the proposal and make preparations to carry it out during the summer. Hannagan suggested that an enthusiastic speaker from his organization or from baseball attend the annual meetings of groups at all levels of the game in order to create an exciting atmosphere of participation. In this manner, club owners could have a complete understanding of the entire campaign.

A major aspect of Hannagan's proposal was the financial benefits that it would bring. He suggested that his "numerous promotions...would awaken in this country a...profitable interest in baseball." Hannagan emphasized that this was not a one-time affair but rather something that would continue to increase gate receipts on a yearly basis. In order to enhance the fiscal aspects of the summer's campaign, he suggested that the general program focus its attention on the opening celebration in Cooperstown. The anniversary could be further infused during the all-star game and reach a climax with a program in late August that would capture the imagination of baseball fans throughout the country.

The plans laid out by the promoter were dynamic and innovative; but he reminded Landis that they were just a starting point, and he expected a great deal of input from the commissioner and his associates the next time they got together. Concerning his own organization, Hannagan wanted to begin activity immediately, and because of this emphasis he hoped that Landis could expedite the matter and hopefully select his organization to fulfill the role of heading up the entire centennial celebration.[19] The commissioner was obviously impressed with the wide range of Hannagan's proposals. Within two months he scheduled the first meeting of the National Baseball Centennial Commission, and both the original promoter and Al Stoughton were in attendance.

Organized baseball had set their machinery in motion to commemorate the 100th anniversary of the national pastime, but what specific role would Cooperstown play in this grand scheme? Would the committees already formed there be incorporated into the program or would baseball officials ignore the measures they had initiated? Perhaps they felt that the village was simply too small and remote from the world of big business to add any significant aspects to the celebration. Obviously, Cleland and his associates had to be concerned about these matters, but their worries were set aside in December, 1938, when Landis officially extended an invitation to the executive secretary of the museum to join the newly created commission. The commissioner assured him that there were no financial obligations involved and that his acceptance would merely be an expression of his interest and concern for the events to take place in the following summer. Cleland immediately accepted the invitation to join the commission and stated his belief that they would demonstrate to the people of America that baseball was indeed the national game.[20]

Actually, Cleland had been integrated into the program before the official invitation was extended to him. Two weeks before he was contacted by Landis, the secretary made a list of items for Stoughton to consider and offered his assistance. The public relations man had followed through on most of these requests including contacts with two local pitchers—Hal Schumacher of the Giants organization, who was born in Mohawk Valley, and Ken Chase of nearby Oneonta, who played for the Washington Senators. Cleland hoped that both could perform in Cooperstown the following summer. Part of the centennial activities involved the Boy Scouts, and Stoughton had contacted the editor of *Boy Scouts Magazine* in order to find out how many former Scouts were currently in the major leagues. He also worked on details involving college teams who would perform in Cooperstown in May and June.[21] The evasive link between the major leagues and the birthplace of baseball had finally come to fruition and, ironically, a group of promoters previously associated with neither one had helped to provide the connection.

In his original proposal to Landis, Hannagan stressed that the centennial celebration was, as he understood it, a plan that was fostered in the interest of all groups involved in playing baseball. To him, this meant that the minor leagues should not have a role that was secondary to the big leagues. Therefore, they should be incorporated into the program on an equal basis. Evidently Cleland felt the same way because he contacted Lester Bursey and promised to bring two executives from the minors when he visited Cooperstown with Stoughton.[22]

Even though the minor league office was a separate organization from the two major leagues, it governed a group whose history extended almost as far back as the National League. Three minor league circuits were initiated in 1877, a year after the senior league began its operations. In September 1901, a meeting of all minor league presidents was held, and the National Association of Professional Baseball Leagues was formed. The number of leagues that it represented varied, beginning with 15 in 1902 and swelling to 39 by 1914. The depression had reduced their number to 16 by 1931, when Judge William G.

Bramham was elected president of the Association. He instituted a number of reforms designed to provide a solid economic foundation, and his controls produced immediate results. The number of leagues rose to 19 in 1934 and, more dramatically, to 37 in 1938.[23] Obviously, they had reached a point of maturity that had begun to produce attendance records almost every year, and these factors necessitated that they should play a major role in the anniversary year.

Minor league interest in the Cooperstown museum commenced in January, 1938, when J. P. Corbett of the Syracuse Chiefs contacted Cleland and expressed his complete cooperation with the museum project. Being one of the closest minor league cities to Cooperstown, Corbett offered the secretary an open invitation to call on him for assistance at any time.[24] That summer Cleland met with Bramham, Trautman and other members of the Association's executive committee in New York City. At this time the secretary was still in the dark concerning the role of the major leagues in the centennial. Therefore, he had to be experimental in his proposals to the minor league representatives.

Cleland advanced the idea that the minor leagues should participate in the museum. He informed their executives that while the first floor of the building had been set aside for major league baseball, he hoped that the second floor, or at least part of it, could house contributions from the minors and be identified as the "minor league" floor. Still, no one knew exactly what the minor leagues should contribute to the museum although Cleland suggested that the Association might consider sponsoring a library. This idea was later approved at their convention in New Orleans, and they appropriated $5,000 to cover the cost of the venture. The minor league officials also suggested that each of its leagues would present a plaque to signify all of the divisions that were in operation in 1939.[25]

The precise role of the minor leagues in the museum was a difficult matter for Cleland to decide. Stoughton was also aware of this problem, and he contacted the secretary relative to this matter. As he saw it, the Association wanted a small part of the Hall of Fame for their own, and he hoped that the secretary could come up with some ideas for their participation. Cleland was genuinely anxious to cooperate with any group connected with organized baseball, but he was also concerned that the museum should represent a true and dignified picture of baseball history in America. Only on this basis, he felt, could the minor leagues be incorporated into the program. Specifically, Cleland and his associates felt that no part of the museum should be set aside for any particular group without the approval of president Frick. The secretary had conferred with Stephen Clark on this matter, and the museum's benefactor was in complete agreement.[26] This arrangement was significant because it demonstrated the museum official's concern with emphasizing Frick's role and further strengthen the cooperative effort between the forces of Cooperstown and organized baseball that had only recently been developed.

Although the role of the minor leagues was still up in the air as the year came to a close, Stoughton was busy spreading the word of the plans for 1939. As the secretary for the National Baseball Centennial Commission, he was responsible for generating enthusiasm for the centennial at all levels of organized baseball. The first public announcement for the centennial plans was made on December 6th, when he addressed the National Association of Professional

Baseball Leagues in New Orleans. The secretary spoke prophetically about the events for the next year and claimed that the 100th anniversary of baseball would "be one of the greatest birthday parties in history." The plan was for a "grassroots" celebration that would involve communities throughout the nation, thus allowing the average fan a chance to join in the activities. Stoughton also claimed that it would be one of the longest birthday parties in history since the commission planned to keep the festivities going until the World Series began.

The secretary emphasized that the celebration would involve all of baseball and require the complete cooperation of all leagues and every club within them. He informed the Association that the Centennial Commission had been formed to unify the efforts of baseball groups, to act as a clearing house for plans, and to direct the organization and publicity for the coming events. Stoughton then outlined the makeup of the commission's executive committee and recognized Bramham as a prominent member of this group. Their goal was to enlist the cooperation of the major leagues, the National Association, semi-pro circuits, amateurs, colleges, high schools, sand lots and millions of fans throughout the country.

In order to enhance a cooperative atmosphere for all of the diverse groups involved, Stoughton went to great lengths to link the game of baseball with the nation's history. He claimed that a major purpose of the celebration was "to glorify the game that is so much a real part in the growth of our nation in the past 100 years." The century of baseball's development, according to the secretary, paralleled "the growth and greatness of America." The game had contributed both men of character and the ideals of sportsmanship to the national scene. A nationalistic emblem had been designed that would be reproduced on flags, uniforms, letterheads and advertising. It pictured the American flag in the background with four red stripes and three white ones—representing balls and strikes. The logo also contained a batter completing his swing, the numerals "1839-1939" at the top, and the words "baseball centennial" at the bottom. Stoughton felt that the entire effort of the insignia was the link between nationalism and America's pastime. The emblem was the first step in the promotion campaign designed to reach down to the community level. It would be followed by a centennial handbook, still in the production stage, which would outline how local celebrations could be conducted.

The secretary finished his speech with a brief mention of the plans for the dedication of the Hall of Fame in Cooperstown that would take place in June. He assured his audience that it would be "one of the publicity high spots of the year" and that radio and newsreel coverage was already being set up for the event. A major emphasis of the program would be the dramatization of the history of the game, and once again the promoters were emphasizing the theme of national development.[27]

Nine days later, Stoughton made a similar speech to a joint meeting of the major leagues at the Hotel Roosevelt in New York City. In addition to being a preview of future events, it was also a report on what had already taken place. He revealed that Landis had asked nineteen of the country's leading citizens to serve on the National Commission. In addition, the Hannagan organization had made significant strides in terms of promotion by working on magazine articles, movie scripts, and radio coverage. Stoughton assured the gathering that the complete support of the minor leagues had been taken care of by his speech in New Orleans and that they were awaiting orders concerning their participation. He also stated that the Cooperstown committee was cooperating enthusiastically with the Centennial Commission and had complete confidence in its abilities. The secretary hoped that the subject of the anniversary could be kept alive during the hot stove league season after which another keynote speech would be given at the baseball writer's dinner in February. He predicted that the anniversary celebration would result in "a richer understanding of the greatness of the game on the part of young America."[28]

As the year 1938 came to a close, an air of great satisfaction and anticipation rippled through the community of Cooperstown with good reason. A year that began with many doubts and anxieties had finished with resounding confidence. In an editorial on the day before New Years Eve, Littell addressed both the frustrations of the past and the hope of the future. He recognized that 1939 was destined to be one of the most significant years in the history of the village. Unlike other important dates in the past, this one had been anticipated for a long time. Indeed, he opined that "the eyes of the whole nation are upon this little village." The celebration which originally focused on Doubleday Field was now being promoted by organized baseball on a national level. Even though the direct publicity campaign by the major leagues was still more than a month away from being initiated, people throughout the country were well aware of the connection between Cooperstown and the birth of baseball. Baseball's officialdom, also sensitive of this relationship, had decreed that the village was to be the hub of the anniversary observance.

Littell was well aware that the community and the centennial celebration were already being widely recognized throughout the country. He had recently received a number of articles touting the birth and development of baseball which had appeared in the *Christian Science Monitor,* the New York *Herald Tribune,* the Detroit *Free Press* and various papers on the Pacific coast. Littell doubted that the World's Fair, in spite of the millions of dollars spent advertising it, was better known than the centennial and the Hall of Fame. The editor was very specific as to why this situation had developed. In his mind, nobody deserved more credit for this recognition than Alexander Cleland, who had undertaken the task four years ago.

Littell emphasized that Cleland assumed the job initially because he believed in it. Although the record ascribing the honor of the invention of the game had long ago been given to Doubleday by the Mills Commission, little had been done to capitalize on it. In fact, no one in the village even recognized the amazing appeal that came with this historical connection. Even Cleland had no definite concept at the very beginning, but gradually it developed into a national program thanks to his experience, perseverance, and masterful diplomacy. These attributes, coupled with the intrinsic appeal of the hall-museum complex and the generous support of the concerned people of Cooperstown, had resulted in national recognition of the centennial celebration. Littell felt that the success that Cleland had achieved had gone "far beyond the hopes of the most sanguine friends of the project."

The editor also believed that there was a lesson to be learned from Cleland's experience. He recognized that even the most ardent supporters had witnessed many discouragements, delays, and exasperations in the past few years. In spite of the numerous causes for concern, Cleland had never wavered. Littell felt that his success was a direct consequence of his ability, courage, and optimism and that Cooperstown should remember that what made him successful in the past could also achieve the same thing for them in the future. He cautioned the people of the community that they should anticipate changes and misunderstandings in the coming year. However, if they copied the determination of the executive secretary, the village would be rewarded historically, culturally, and economically. As Littell saw it, the year 1939 was not the end in sight but rather the beginning of Cooperstown's history "as the shrine of base ball which will last for a long time."[29]

At this stage of development, it would seem that all systems were interlocked in a united effort to initiate a shrine for baseball's immortals in the village that was by now recognized as the birthplace of the national game. Still another great challenge had to be faced. A controversy had already erupted that would attack the very foundation of Cooperstown's claim to fame in the baseball world. It involved the man behind the game's creation, but who was he? Of course to Cleland and his associates, this was Abner Doubleday, but to others it was a man who had moved to Hawaii almost a century before—Alexander Cartwright.

Alexander Cleland, 1936
Don Cleland; Alexander Cleland Collection, Las Vegas, Nevada

AMERICA PREFERS BASE BALLS TO CANNON BALLS

1st Day Issue Stamp plus Centennial Post Card
Don Cleland; Alexander Cleland Collection, Las Vegas, Nevada

Abner Graves
Denver Post February 2, 1927, Colorado Historical Society

Crowd leaving Doubleday Field June 12, 1939
National Baseball Hall of Fame Library, Cooperstown, NY

Babe Ruth Induction Ceremony, June 12, 1989

Centennial Stamp
National Baseball Hall of Fame Library, Cooperstown, NY

Alexander Cleland (left) Ford Frick (right) December 21, 1936 AP
Don Cleland; Alexander Cleland Collection, Las Vegas, Nevada

Baseball Hall of Fame with Alexander Cleland in foreground Circa 1938
Don Cleland; Alexander Cleland Collection, Las Vegas, Nevada

The Village Club with 1st Hall of Fame display Circa 1987
Don Cleland: Alexander Cleland Collection, Las Vegas, Nevada

Stephen Clark, Sr.
National Baseball Hall of Fame Library, Cooperstown, NY

The Otsego Farmer, (A Cooperstown, NY newspaper).
Courtesy of The New York State Historical Association.

Chapter Seven
Fair or Foul

Unquestionably the supporters of Cooperstown's claim as the birthplace of baseball had faced a myriad of problems since the museum-hall concept had been introduced. Renowned players had been reluctant or unable to supply historical mementos for display. The voting procedure, although it helped to advertise developments in the village, raised considerable criticism among baseball fans throughout the nation. Advertising ideas were slow to develop and attracted a variety of promoters with designs to capitalize on the centennial celebration. Even though the connection with organized baseball had finally come together, it was painfully slow in its development.

All of this activity had been frustrating and yet, at the same time, exciting and eventually rewarding. There was another questionable aspect of developing the village as the cradle of the national pastime that would continue to damage the Hall of Fame's credibility into modern times. It centered around the very nature of the museum and hall complex being located in the isolated upstate New York residence. Was Abner Doubleday really the innovator of baseball or had someone else initiated the game? If it weren't the Civil War hero, then who deserved the credit? More importantly for Cooperstown, if the former resident didn't invent the game, then the invention must have taken place somewhere else and assuredly at some other date. This of course would mean that the baseball shrine should have been located elsewhere and that there was no reason for the game's authorities either to commemorate the 100th anniversary in 1939 or to honor Abner Doubleday.

Early criticism of the findings of the Mills Commission surfaced soon after its report was published. In the first of a series of four articles on baseball for *Collier's* magazine in 1909, Will Irwin described the game before it became a professional occupation. He recognized that in the early years of the country's development, there was no national sport, but even in colonial times young boys began to play crude games of townball which, by the 1830s, had come to be called baseball. He pointed out, however, that the modern game evolved in the next decade and that it was the product of the inventive mind of Alexander Cartwright. Irwin completely denied the assertion that Doubleday invented the name of the game and mentioned that he was at West Point in 1839.[1]

In 1910, Alfred Henry Spink published a book entitled *The National Game* which traced the early developments in the national pastime and outlined the careers of its great performers. As the founder of *The Sporting News* in 1886, he had a deep appreciation for the pioneer days of organized baseball. Although he dropped out of the leadership role in a dispute with his younger brother Charles, Al remained close to the game and the major figures involved. Never

127

shy concerning his opinions, the older Spink blasted the findings of Mills and his associates as "the latest of all the fakes" in trying to determine the originator of the national pastime. Specifically, Spink cited the year 1839 as the weakest link in the Grave's argument. Too bad, he stated, that the Colorado mining engineer hadn't selected a different year "so that his air bubble could not have been pricked so easily." He claimed that records at both the War Department and West Point would expose the Doubleday story as fraudulent.

Instead, he agreed with Irwin that Alexander J. Cartwright, Jr. should be honored as the game's designer. He based his claim on a statement made by Duncan F. Curry, the first president of the Knickerbocker club, in 1877, and corroborated by Charles A. Peverelly, author of the first history of baseball. Curry stated that in 1845 Cartwright came to their playing field with his plans drawn up for a game. Previously, ball games were constructed rather haphazardly, but young Alexander changed all of that. He laid out the diamond shaped field with canvas bags for the bases and an iron plate for home plate. He also arranged stations for various players thus limiting the number of players on a team to nine.[2]

Spink's claims were based on conversations with people who were there at the time, but they were challenged in the next year by A. G. Spalding, who wrote a book titled *America's National Game*. Although he utilized the baseball archives of Henry Chadwick to document his history of the game, he nonetheless readily accepted the findings of the Mills Commission and even published a picture of Doubleday and an historical sketch of his life. Still, he didn't ignore Cartwright and also included a picture of him in the book with gray hair and a long flowing beard. He also praised the Knickerbockers as the first organized team and commended Cartwright as the first man to secure an organization of baseball players. Spalding included a brief history of him that traced his movement from New York to California in 1849 and then to Hawaii in the next year. He also included a statement from his son, Bruce Cartwright, who had written A. G. in 1909 and claimed that his father never lost his interest in the game throughout his life. However, Spalding did not give him credit for inventing the game or any other innovations outside of developing an organization for baseball.[3] Although the different claims by Spink and Spalding could have been viewed as merely a battle of words between the initiators of two competing sports publications, their arguments would not fade away.

The first hint of trouble over the Doubleday story that threatened the Cooperstown development surfaced in June 1935. Newspapermen in upstate New York were beginning to question the village's credibility. In a speech he made in Amersterdam, New York, former Cubs player Johnny Evers wondered what was being celebrated. He felt that the birth of the game meant the beginning of organized baseball or the first league game. The question that he raised was not new to Littell, who had answered similar queries on numerous occasions in the past. Since the information on the centennial and museum were now being released, he had come to ignore these inquiries; but he was afraid that Cleland would be caught off guard should he encounter such statements. Not wanting the executive secretary to become uneasy in the face of questioning, Littell encouraged him to keep up the work he had done to inform the leaders of baseball of the progress being made in Cooperstown. He warned Alexander that similar problems might arise in the future "which had their origin in the past or possibly through the initiative of some newspaper or reporter," but this would not seriously affect the plan of action.

As a newspaper man himself, Littell recognized the power of the press; but evidently he felt that the truth was on his side. Continuing this theme, Cleland believed that since Cooperstown was so generally accepted as the birthplace of the national game, it would simply be a waste of time to pay any attention to Evers' claims.[4] So while the secretary knew from the very beginning of the hall-museum project that doubters existed, he was still convinced that the Doubleday legend was more fact than fiction.

In October the question of Doubleday's authenticity surfaced again when G. E. Staples contacted Cleland. As director of publicity for the St. Louis Cardinals, he had become aware of the museum through Brandt's *National League Bulletin* and felt that the secretary could supply him with some information on the the game's early history. In order to maintain an interest in baseball during the winter, he was planning a series of radio broadcasts on various phases of the game. However, his research efforts concerning baseball's beginnings had produced several differences of opinions among authorities. Even though most of them recognized Doubleday as the game's founder, others pointed out the role of Cartwright. One source stated that Cartwright was one of Doubleday's companions and another felt that it was the former who drew the first diagram of the diamond. Staples wanted to clear up these matters and especially wanted to know how most authentic sources felt about who made the first drawing.

Littell answered these inquiries about a week later at Cleland's request. He confidently stated that Doubleday had drawn the first diamond and that this was the chief reason why the national baseball commission of 1907 had accorded him the honor of inventing the game of baseball rather than just another ball game. As to the relationship between the two men, Littell was unsure. He felt that Cartwright could have been a fellow student in the area of Cooperstown, but further investigation was necessary to prove this point. However, he did cite Spalding's book which said that Cartwright was present when the game was born.

Littell credited the former resident of Hawaii with initiating the first organization of ball players when he formed the Knickerbockers in 1845. He then cited the Mills Commission report as giving hints to a possible connection between the two men. Within the findings was the statement by D. F. Curry that a man named Wadsworth had brought a diagram of a baseball field to the playing area and that this design was quickly adopted. Littell therefore felt that it was Wadsworth and not Cartwright who introduced Doubleday's diamond to the Knickerbockers. However, Spink had quoted Curry as saying that Cartwright did the deed. Added to this confusion was the fact that Mills had never proved the Wadsworth connection. However, Littell stated that the Knickerbockers based their game on the rules drawn up by Doubleday.[5] The statements made by Littell would be the standard reply to questions about Cooperstown's right to renown until future developments brought doubt about Doubleday's role.

Less than two months later, Bruce Cartwright Jr., a grandson of the famous Knickerbocker and prominent citizen of Honolulu, contacted Littell concerning his ancestor's role in developing the national pastime. The editor referred him to Cleland. Cartwright wanted to know if the national museum would be interested in some of his grandfather's artifacts which he was willing to donate. They included photographs of the famous Knickerbocker, his history, a list of his descendents, and some personal belongings such as jewelry and cups that he had received. In order to justify the importance of these items, Bruce stated that his grandfather was the father of organized baseball—something with which Littell would have to agree. However, he added that Alexander had told a number of local people that he organized the first club, drew up the first rules and laid out the first diamond with measurements used by all other clubs. Doubtless, this last statement caught Littell's eye and led him to allow Cleland to deal with this significant matter.

While the younger Cartwright's statements concerning his grandfather's role in setting up the structure of the modern game of baseball caused considerable consternation for the Hall's promoters, Cleland ignored these claims in his response to Hawaii. Instead, he stressed the contribution of artifacts for the museum. The secretary lamented the dearth of information in his efforts to gather memorabilia on the early days of baseball. So far the museum contained only one old photograph, taken from the Spalding collection, showing the Knickerbockers and another team called the Excelsiors that was taken in 1858. Cleland expressed his sincere desire to obtain any photographs or historical materials on the "Father of Organized Baseball." He revealed that the St. Louis Baseball Club had earlier requested information on Cartwright and felt that as the centennial date drew near, others would ask for data on the beginning history of the game. Therefore, any materials on this aspect would be of great value to the museum. He promised to safeguard all materials and see that they would be displayed in an interesting exhibit with Bruce being credited as the donator.[6]

Although the Hall of Fame supporters were familiar with Doubleday's background, they were not so familiar with the life of Alexander Joy Cartwright, Jr. His family was well rooted in colonial America and were offsprings of Captain Edward Cartwright, who had come to the New World in the 1660s. Renowned for his sailing abilities, he moved to Nantucket Island with his wife Elizabeth and their son Nicholas in 1676. Later he remarried and had five sons by his second wife, Ruth, including one named Samuel. (Ironically, another of their children was dubbed Abner Cartwright). Around 1784, Samuel's son Benjamin and his wife, the former Becky Luce, became the parents of Alexander—who would be raised to become a ship's captain, like earlier members of his lineage.

The War of 1812 had left Alexander's island home economically devastated. Because of the growth of New York City as a commercial center, the 32-year-old shipmaster moved there in 1816 to earn a living. Shortly thereafter he married Ester Burlock, and they had seven children, the oldest of which was Alexander Jr. born on April 17, 1820, almost a year following the birth of Abner Doubleday. Throughout his youth the Cartwright family continuously moved to better locations until they were beset with economic hardships in the early stages of a severe crisis which came to be known as the Panic of 1837. In the previous year 16-year-old Alexander took a job as a lowly clerk for a Wall Street merchant. Gradually, he began to rise professionally; and, by the time of his marriage to Eliza Ann Gerrits Van Wie in 1842, he was a teller at the Union Bank. Within six years they had four children, and Alex had gone into business with his brother Alfred when they opened a bookstore on Wall Street in 1845.

In addition to his work, Alexander was involved in fulfilling his civic obligations by participating as a volunteer fireman. He was apparently a member of the Knickerbocker Engine Company until it disbanded in 1843. He may have named his ball club after this organization, for it was a common practice to do such a thing. In September, 1845, Cartwright proposed the organization of the Knickerbocker Base Ball Club, which was the first organized team to play the modern contest. He and his friends had gathered together on various occasions in the past to play ball games that had been passed down to them through the generations. But in the spring of that year he had come to the playing area with a diagram of the field for baseball which also indicated where the players should be stationed. Those who later supported Cartwright for inventing the rules of the game claimed that he was responsible for drawing the first diamond, establishing the idea for throwing to the bases for an out (instead of throwing at the runner) and setting up an inning as being based on three outs. Later he developed the concept of ending the game after nine innings. More importantly, his supporters claimed, he set the distance between the bases at ninety feet.

Even the most ardent advocates of the Doubleday story could not deny that Cartwright's team was involved in the first organized game of modern baseball ever recorded. This significant event took place in Hoboken, New Jersey, on October 6, 1845. About two weeks before the game, Cartwright had drawn up a constitution and by-laws for the new organization. Industrialization had taken over the area that he and his companions had used for games in the past, and he was able to convince fourteen of them to take the ferry across the Hudson River to a place called Elysian Fields. Unfortunately for the Cartwright Knickerbockers, the result was an 11-8 loss with Alexander going 2 for 4. There were only seven men on each side for this initial event, and the first game involving nine players didn't occur until October 17. This is the date cited by most early sources as the first recorded game of baseball. The first match game (a contest involving a completely different team) did not take place until June 19, 1846 when the Knickerbockers were handed a 23-1 thrashing by a team called New York. This time Cartwright served as the umpire.

Baseball was just beginning as an organized sport when the twenty-nine year old Cartwright caught the lure of gold that had recently been discovered in California. He purchased a Conestoga wagon, outfitted it with supplies, and joined a group of adventurers for the long trip west. They left Newark on March 1, 1849, and arrived in San Francisco on August 10th. (Ironically, this would put him in the San Francisco area about the same time as Abner Graves.) Along the 156-day journey, Alexander did more than just travel. Whenever possible he stopped to teach the game to others and thus became the Johnny Appleseed of baseball. According to one source, he taught the new contest to saloon keepers, miners, Indians and settlers in frontier towns and Army posts along the trail to the west coast.

When Alexander arrived in San Francisco, he met his brother Alfred, who had traveled by ship via Cape Horn. Finding that mining was unattractive work, he decided to look into other ventures that might prove to be profitable. On the advice of a friend who had previously resided in Honolulu, he decided to visit the Hawaiian Islands to investigate the possibility of shipping fruits and vegetables back to the mainland. He also planned to visit China and from there sail back to New York, but this venture would never come to pass. Following his arrival in Oahu on August 28, 1849, he never left the island paradise. Surprisingly, his family's traditional occupation of sailing left baseball's pioneer seasick. Eventually he got involved in a general merchandise business and gradually his abilities as an entrepreneur led him into a variety of concerns which culminated in a prestigious firm known as Cartwright and Company, Ltd. As one of the leading citizens of the islands, he was a close friend and financial adviser for traditional Hawaiian rulers from Kamehameha to Queen Liluokalani. On the more philanthropic side, he also became involved in a number of humanitarian concerns including a hospital, library, and fire department—the latter of which he founded in 1850.

In spite of his numerous activities involving personal and public endeavors, Cartwright never lost interest in the game he helped to develop. In 1852 he laid out the first baseball field in Hawaii and later organized teams and instructed people in the game throughout the island community. Not surprisingly, he had come prepared for the task. In his travels across the country, Alexander packed a light ball about four inches in diameter and a small book with the word "Knickerbocker" on the cover which contained the rules of the game and bylaws of the New York club. His major disappointment concerning baseball involved the failure of Spalding to land his club for a visit to Honolulu on their world tour of 1888.

His interest in the Knickerbockers never waned up to his death in 1892 (a year before Doubleday died). In 1865 he wrote to one of the former members, Charles S. Debost. In this letter he mentioned the original ball that was still in his possession and expressed his hope that the first club was still carrying on their activities. However, baseball had gradually become professionalized; and the Knickerbockers, wishing to remain an amateur organization, faded from the scene of the organized sport.[7] Like their originator, they drifted from the memory of most baseball fans and were not resurrected for the benefit of a national audience until the first histories of the game were published. Even then, the exact role of both Cartwright and his team was vague and controversial.

Cartwright and his Knickerbockers received a sudden boost in the public's mind on February 10, 1936, when Will Wedge, a writer for the *New York Sun*, began to cast doubt about the role of Abner Doubleday as the creator of modern baseball. His article, which was inspired by the forthcoming centennial celebration in Cooperstown, revealed that there were no records at West Point which described the circumstances of how the Civil War general invented the game. This he found strange since the academy had seen fit to display a bronze plaque which credited Doubleday as the father of baseball. Even more surprising was the recent research done by Captain M.P. (Pat) Echols who delved into the school's archives and found an obituary written by a classmate and life-long friend of the general. He referred to Doubleday as "a man who did not care for or go into any outdoor sports." As public relations officer for the academy, he found this statement both revealing and disturbing.

Echol's first concern was the date established for baseball's beginning. Maybe 1839 was wrong and perhaps it could have been 1838 or 1840. Further investigation revealed that Doubleday had entered West Point on September 1, 1838, and following his graduation became a breveted second lieutenant in the Third Artillery on July 1, 1842. Thus it would have been impossible for him to have been in Cooperstown in 1839, for it was during his plebe year; and obtaining permission to leave would not have been realistic. However, he could have gone to the village in 1840 on a furlough because by this time he would have been a second class man. In addition he would have taken two years of mathematics by then, including a course in descriptive geometry. Echols felt that this course would have been helpful to Doubleday in terms of visualizing the dimensions of the playing field. His professor, Albert E. Church, was a mathematician of some note, for he had introduced the subject of descriptive geometry into the United States and wrote the first adequate book on the subject in the English language. Wedge believed, however, that this background was not a prerequisite since the overall effect of Doubleday's work was merely an improvement on town ball and one-old-cat which he had played in his youth. This being the case, he may have initiated the game in the summer of 1838. By that time he would have acquired an adequate background in mathematics through his studies in civil engineering at the Cooperstown Classical and Military Academy.

Wedge then recounted the work of the Mills Commission which credited the Civil War general with laying out the field—the bases about fifty feet apart. However, he cited Cartwright as the person who hit on the idea of ninety feet as the perfect distance between the corners of the diamond. He pointed out that the famous Hawaiian resident was a drafting student and therefore had enough background to accomplish this task. Unquestionably, this was the established distance when the Knickerbockers played their first game in 1845. To demonstrate the importance of Cartwright in the eyes of people in baseball, Wedge stated that in 1923 a group of the game's missionaries to Japan stopped in Honolulu. Herb Hunter, a member of the party and a former major leaguer, had laid a floral wreath on Cartwright's grave. For Wedge this was a substantial act because it demonstrated that if the famous Knickerbocker weren't "the parent of the pastime," he "was at least an honored ancestor."

Wedge's article did not shake the convictions of its readers concerning the role of Doubleday in the formation of the national pastime, but it certainly stirred up controversy over the actual date of baseball's beginnings. Cleland and his associates had to be disturbed over his findings at West Point. If, in fact, Doubleday could not have been in the village in 1839, then the date had to be wrong; and this would upset the forthcoming centennial plans. Wedge's article, coupled with the recent inquiries by Bruce Cartwright and G. E. Staples were not enough to deter the Cooperstown promoters, but they were still upsetting.

Actually the piece by Wedge was one of a series of articles published by the New York *Sun*, and another one from the same author appeared the next day. This time Wedge questioned neither the invention nor the year and verified that Doubleday had indeed established the first diamond and the first rules. In fact, he made a rather convincing argument about the reason why the new invention attracted so little attention at the time. Accordingly, Wedge stated that the big event in Cooperstown in 1839 was not the latest innovation in ball games but rather the visit paid to the village in September of that year by the Democratic candidate for the presidency, Martin Van Buren. Due to the economic crisis that came to be associated with his first term in office, the incumbent was campaigning heavily "against the rising Whig tide, headed by William Henry Hanson [sic]."

The name of Doubleday was also tied with this famous occasion in village history. Following his speech, Van Buren was escorted to another location by six men, probably including Abner's father, Ulysses Freeman Doubleday. Following his work as a newspaper editor, the elder Doubleday had served for four years as a Democratic congressman for the state of New York. Records in the village only mentioned the surname, but Wedge was careful not to confuse the father and son. After all, his article of the previous day had stated quite clearly that the twenty-year-old Abner was then enrolled at West Point.

The Wedge articles came at a time when the Baseball Hall of Fame was just gaining national recognition. The results of the first election process had just been revealed, and the controversy which had resulted brought national attention to the hall-museum complex. However, the series that was published by the New York *Sun* gave additional coverage to the village itself. Littell recognized this fact, and in order to inform local residents of their new fame, he reprinted a complete version of the second Wedge article.[8] This one, of course, was less controversial than the original—which had challenged both the year of baseball's origin and the originator of the established ninety feet between the bases.

Not having heard from Bruce Cartwright in more than two months, Cleland wrote to him three days after the article by Wedge appeared in the newspapers. He also enclosed several recent clippings from the newspaper, and these may have included one of the Wedge articles. At any rate, the secretary felt that Bruce would find them interesting. In his response, Cartwright listed the items that he would be willing to donate to the museum. Perhaps the most important of these was a daguerreotype of six people, including Alexander Cartwright, which Bruce's father claimed to have been taken in New York City some time between 1838 and 1849. He wasn't sure if the others were actually Knickerbockers. His other souvenir items were not directly related to baseball and included two receipts from a Knickerbocker banquet which he had loaned to the archives of Hawaii. He also had some printed books and articles on baseball that he was willing to donate and stated that he could write a brief account of his grandfather's life (including his ancestry and descendants) if the museum desired it.

Cleland was truly appreciative of the cooperation afforded him by the current head of the Cartwright clan. While the daguerrotype and the two banquet receipts were recognized as the two most significant items due to their Knickerbocker relevance, the secretary desired the other artifacts as well. Cleland felt that the other objects were also significant because the elder Cartwright had been "so intimately connected with the beginnings of baseball." In addition the secretary encouraged Bruce to submit any piece he could write on his grandfather's life because the museum was increasingly being besieged by newspapers and magazines concerning the stories and data relevant to the early days of baseball. Even the legislature of the state of New York was considering the passage of a bill that would finance a survey on the history of the game and additional information was needed to accomplish this task.[9]

Besides the items previously mentioned, Cartwright also forwarded to the secretary a copy of a book written in 1902 by Seymour R. Church entitled *Base Ball, 1845-1871*. The author was a resident of San Francisco and an acquaintance of grandfather Alexander. The famous Knickerbocker must have met Church while the latter was on a vacation to the islands; the native Californian was only 47 years old when the book was published and thus wasn't born until six years after Cartwright left the mainland. As an agent for Muirkirk pig iron, the author was involved in selling pig iron, crucibles, foundry facings and firebrick dust, but he was also recognized as a great baseball fan and the foremost authority on the game in the west. Previously he had published a manuscript known as *Base Ball Schedule and Memorandum Book* which Charles Spink of *The Sporting News* reviewed as being "interesting and invaluable to the enthusiasts of the game in all sections of the country."

Church's book was subtitled "The History, Statistics and Romance of the American National Game," but it was really a hodgepodge of information including sections on the first rules of the game, alterations that were adopted by the National Association of Base Ball Players in 1861, the method of selecting an area and developing it for the construction of a field to play the game and the duties of each position on a team. Church also included box scores and brief accounts of famous games, vignettes of renowned players (Arthur Cumming, George Wright and Adrian C. Anson) and the not so famous, and a list of professional players in 1871.

The major emphasis of the book was on the development of baseball on the west coast and especially in San Francisco. Indeed, this volume contained a number of halftone pictures (and some in color) of players who had made their mark in California. However, his section on the early history of baseball cited Cartwright as the person who proposed the first regular organization in the spring of 1845. He also recognized the first match game to be held on June 19, 1846, and listed the dates and places when some of the first clubs were organized. Due to the lack of material concerning baseball's early history, Cleland was pleased to receive this donation; and he sent Cartwright a copy of the latest *Spalding Guide*, which contained information on the development of the Hall of Fame. Included in this edition was the method of selecting former greats of the game to the shrine and of specific interest to Cartwright was the mention of a special committee designated to select a group of five for inclusion from the nineteenth century.[10]

Due to the cooperation that Cleland was receiving from the Cartwright family, he had gathered enough memorabilia to display a special exhibit in a single case. He had also informed Ford Frick of the cooperative effort that had taken place between Honolulu and Cooperstown. Both the secretary and the league president were in complete agreement that when the major leagues finally settled on the kinds of people to be included in the Hall of Fame, the illustrious organizer of the Knickerbockers would "be among the first to be represented by a plaque." Cleland promised to send Bruce a photograph of the one that would represent his grandfather's contribution to the national pastime. Although the Cartwrights had to be pleased by this statement, it seems out of character for Cleland to make such a bold promise. Nobody it would seem, not even the famous Knickerbocker, could actually be considered as a guaranteed selection for baseball's shrine from the 19th century.

Shortly thereafter, the museum received a chart from Hawaii which showed the ancestry of Alexander Cartwright. Cleland found it to be extremely interesting and felt that it would be of great value for display during the centennial. In addition, the secretary had also received a photostat of a letter from Bruce's grandfather to Charles S. Deborst and promised to include it in the display. Still, Bruce must have felt that Alexander had not received recognition equivalent to his role in the game's development. In his correspondence to Cleland, he expressed his hope that eventually his famous relative would "receive a little credit for what he did for baseball." The secretary, on the other hand, felt that Bruce didn't realize the degree of recognition that his grandfather had already been accorded. Judging by his conversations with writers and older followers of the game, the elder Cartwright was generally acknowledged "for the tremendous impetus he gave baseball in its infancy."[11]

Perhaps the Cartwright clan felt better about the growing recognition of their famous ancestor when the *Spalding Guide* of 1937 published a piece on the accumulation of artifacts for the "Doubleday Museum." The items received from Hawaii were noted by its author as perhaps the most interesting historical donations made during the previous year. The article went on to quote A. G. Spalding's book concerning Cartwright's role in the development of the Knickerbockers. It also provided its readers with a brief account of his travels to California and Hawaii and his role in spreading the basic foundations of the game during his westward trek.

The forces supporting Doubleday received another surprise in the spring of 1937 when Robert W. Henderson of the New York Public Library published an article in their April *Bulletin* which denied the Mills Commission findings that the game was of modern American origin. He cited a number of ancient references that utilized the term baseball beginning with a 1744 publication by John Newbery of London entitled "A Little Pretty Pocketbook." In addition to containing the first known use of the term in print, it also had the earliest recognized illustration of the game. The first American edition of this book was published by Hugh Gaine in 1762 and, while there were other books that made reference to the playing of baseball in England, Henderson was not out to destroy Abner's reputation. He pointed out that the game had changed as much between 1839 to the present as it had from the old British pastime to the general's invention. In his mind, Doubleday's major contribution was to combine the concepts of a variety of children's ballgames and create a game for adults.[12]

Correspondence between Honolulu and museum officials came to a halt following the donation of materials, but it was resumed about fifteen months later. The major issue at this time was a commemorative stamp which had been proposed by officials in the village in the spring of 1937. John A. Hamilton, manager of the Honolulu Chamber of Commerce, contacted James A. Farley, Postmaster General of the United States, concerning the proposal of a special postage stamp for the centennial celebration that was under consideration. Recognizing the unique role of Alexander Cartwright as the originator of both the first professional team and the baseball diamond, Hamilton wondered whether the federal authorities might agree that a likeness of him would be appropriate for the occasion. The chamber members had also solicited the support of the Cooperstown museum in this matter. In his request to Cleland, Hamilton stressed the group's desire to cooperate with the museum officials to produce a successful anniversary program and offered their assistance in supplying materials concerning Cartwright's background.

So far as Cleveland was concerned, the design of the stamp was a matter to be considered by others. However, he informed Hamilton that Frick had already taken the matter up with Farley and even President Roosevelt. Since the league president was confident that the baseball stamp would be approved, Cleland felt that the Honolulu authorities should forward their request for a Cartwright picture to the major league officials, and he promised to talk with Frick concerning this matter. While the stamp issue would remain unsolved until the anniversary drew nearer, it was yet another reminder to museum officials and baseball authorities that the forces trying to gain recognition for Cartwright were going to remain active.

The issue over what picture should appear on the proposed commemorative stamp was not confined to the Cartwright forces. In June 1938, Frank C. Carpenter, chairman of advertising for the Cooperstown Centennial Committee, wrote president Frick concerning the image. A local stamp club had contacted the chairman about the possibility of adopting the seal being used by the committee on their centennial stationary. It contained an image of a baseball with Doubleday's picture on the left and that of the museum on the right. On the top of the ball were the words "Base Ball Centennial, 1839-1939, Cooperstown, N.Y." and beneath this heading was a picture of the playing area and the label "Doubleday Field." At the bottom was the phrase "Birthplace of Base Ball." Carpenter estimated that these first day covers could be put out at a profit of 6 cents. He understood the economic possibilities because another historic stamp issued a few years before had sold 130,000 covers. He also knew that Frick, a stamp collector himself, understood the dynamics involved. Carpenter felt that, with proper advertising, the local stamp club could dispose of 200,000 first-day covers; and they had offered to turn over all but 5% of the net profits to the local committee. Even if they only sold half of what he expected, the Cooperstown group could realize a net gain of more than $5,000, and this would greatly relieve the local financial problems.[13]

Carpenter's suggestion was both innovative and timely. It came at a period when local forces realized that the major leagues were not willing to spend some of the $100,000 which they had appropriated for the centennial for developing Doubleday Field. In addition, Cleland had recently turned them away from trying to appropriate more money from Stephen Clark, who had already given a considerable sum to the baseball developments in the village. Frick was probably relieved to find the Cooperstown group adopting a rather innovative and yet simple plan to finance the anniversary. Yet he was painfully aware that if their that if their proposal was adopted, it would add more fuel to the fire of the Cartwright dilemma.

As long as the claims of Cartwright's role in baseball's development were confined to personal correspondence, they posed little threat to Cooperstown and Doubleday. However, in January, 1938, an article by Bob Considine appeared in the New York *Daily Mirror* which attracted considerable attention in the village. The author had recently been visited by a Cooperstown resident concerning the progress of the museum and informed him that Bob Ripley in his famous "Believe It Or Not" section had drawn a picture of the famous Knickerbocker and claimed that he and not Doubleday had laid out the first diamond. Evidently this had caused an indignant stir in the village since, as Considine stated, "they don't like people to meddle with folklore, up-State." So Cleland (whom Considine claimed to be a descendant of James Fenimore Cooper) with the aid of a local historical group began to investigate the matter. According to the newswriter, they had received word from the Cartwright family in Hawaii that their famous ancestor had not become interested in baseball until about 1844 and by this time the game was already five years old.[14] Although he may have dispelled any negative claims to the Doubleday story for a while, Considine's arguments would be questioned.

At the same time that the Cartwright supporters were promoting their claims for the originator of the national pastime, the Doubleday scenario received a boost from two major publications—*Time* magazine and *Baseball Magazine*. The first was, or course, more widely read, but the latter would have a significant impact on the nation's baseball audience. Although the *Time* article focused more on the recent developments in the village than Abner Doubleday, they did state that the "world will little note nor long remember what he did at Gettysburg, but it can never forget what he did at Cooperstown." The other publication touted the Civil War general for his invention and cited the Mills Commission as the basis for this historic claim. The piece, written by a well known resort publicity agent named Aloysius Coll, also gave some details about how he came up with his invention. Apparently dissatisfied with existing ball games of the time, Doubleday allegedly drew the first diagram of the baseball diamond on his drawing board. Coll felt that young Abner was capable of devising the game's proportions because he was a disciple of figures, dimensions, and tactics. According to the author, he then transferred this first pattern of the baseball field to a town plot which came to be known as Doubleday Field.[15]

Although this article did a great deal to convince the public of Doubleday's role in the development of the modern game, Coll was obviously playing with the facts. Perhaps his background in advertisement led him to be more creative than the letters of Abner Graves would allow. In spite of these indiscretions, Coll's work, published in a major baseball magazine, helped to bring Cooperstown, Doubleday, and the game's beginning firmly together in the minds of fans throughout the country.

The publicity that Cooperstown had received in connection with Abner Doubleday had led to some confusion concerning his role in baseball's beginnings. Local promoters could point to stories appearing in national publications, but a certain level of doubt remained. A group of high school students from the village visited the general's grave and placed a wreath there, but this was basically a gesture to advertise the centennial. In order to verify their claims, they needed some support from a veritable source. His name was Robert S. Doubleday of Tacoma, Washington. He wrote to Cleland, and the secretary passed the letter onto Littell with a message that the author was a direct descendant of the Civil War general. Later the editor received another correspondence from Abner's alleged nephew and nearest living relative, and he published it in the Cooperstown newspaper.

The letter was just what local promoters needed. Nephew Robert stated that he had recently been the center of considerable attention since he was considered to be the nearest living relative of the late general. He had even received a letter from Frick relating the plans for the centennial celebration and inviting him to take a major part in the festivities. Robert, who had worked as an editor and publisher all of his life, was anxious to return to New York and hoped to meet personally with Littell. More significantly, he related a story concerning his uncle's last visit to his father's house in New York when Robert was still a young boy. The Tacoma resident remembered Abner telling him "the story of the beginnings of baseball." His famous uncle also expressed interest in the fact that Robert was the captain of his baseball team. For Littell, these statements not only served to demonstrate Abner Doubleday's interest in the game, but they also verified the validity of the Mills Commission findings.[16]

Another aspect of the general's story that could help to establish him and the village as part of baseball's beginnings involved the Doubleday baseball. In April, 1938, *Town and Country* magazine ran an article on the museum that was written by a woman named Baird Leonard. While this story was designed to be an account of Doubleday's invention and the developments that followed in the village, it was rife with exaggerations and misconceptions. For example, the author claimed that the dimensions of the baseball diamond had never been altered since the general first drew it. No matter who drew the first diamond, this statement denied, however, that Cartwright set the bases farther apart than they had ever been; also, the pitcher's mound was later moved back from home plate after he laid out his plans. She also claimed that the members of the Mills Commission came to their final conclusion after a thorough weighing of the evidence. In fact, their ultimate decision rested chiefly on the opinions of Graves, Spalding and Mills. In addition she concluded that the discovery of the Doubleday ball had led to the idea of developing the museum when, in fact, Cleland had proposed the museum idea a year before the ball was discovered. Finally, Leonard stated that the person who discovered the ball set the price at five dollars when all other accounts claim that Clark established its worth and not Littell.

Cleland viewed the article with great interest, and he mentioned it in his correspondence with Littell. The editor also found it enjoyable and was especially fascinated with that section concerned with the ball. After all, he was the person who first became aware of its existence and the one who mentioned it to Stephen Clark, who purchased it shortly afterward. Curiously, he later wrote to Cleland that the section in the magazine article concerning the famous spheroid was "better than any of the stories I ever manufactured about it."[17]

Of course, Littell may have meant that he had simply written up the story of the Doubleday ball after its discovery. Therefore he may have made a poor choice of wording his response to the magazine article in a private letter to a friend. However, it is difficult to interpret the word "manufacture" in any way different than the typical dictionary definition of "invent" or "make up." If indeed Littell meant that he invented the story on the Doubleday baseball, this was a damning statement that, had it been nationally recognized, would have destroyed the credibility of the Cooperstown baseball promoters.

A disturbing article appeared in a national publication the very next day after Littell wrote his statement on the Doubleday baseball. A relatively new magazine called *Ken* published an article by Frank G. Menke which totally debunked the holy trinity of Doubleday—1839—Cooperstown. He felt that the Cooperstown celebration was fine except that baseball didn't originate in Cooperstown, nor was the Civil War general its father. These were bold claims and the first question in the minds of many (if they weren't familiar with him already) was who was making these stunning assertions.

The author had started his career as a reporter in 1912 for the International News Service and one of his early job requirements was to write a daily short sports item that would be distributed to newspapers throughout the country. Gradually, as Americans became more fascinated with the world of sports, editors began to demand more stories of this nature. When there wasn't much current news in the sports world, Menke started to work on human interest stories. Gradually, this required him to become familiarized with both modern records and the origin and development of a wide variety of sports. However, the more he learned, the more frustrated he became. He found it difficult to locate reliable records and so he began to compile his own.

In addition to modern records, Menke also had trouble tracing the origin and development of various sports. Trusting that historians were in general agreement on these matters, he never felt obligated in the beginning to read every source on the particular subject. Rather, he would simply choose a book at random and let it serve as his only basis of information. Later, when he decided to augment his knowledge of a sport, he was surprised to find that authorities often contradicted each other. This rather disturbing discovery led him to check out a much wider variety of source material. Over a period of two decades, Menke consulted almost 2000 books concerned with sports and games—some of which had to be translated from foreign languages. Generally he discovered that sports historians would accept the work of pioneer writers and simply add their own information which was impossible to check for accuracy. Through his research, he started to compile a book on sports which attempted to utilize all the information that was available. His goal was to separate fact from fiction so that his final analysis of the development of sports could withstand the scrutiny of future investigations.[18]

Menke's evaluation of the origin of baseball was contained in the *Ken* article. In it he pointed out that the officials of the game had already sanctioned the centennial celebration of Doubleday's discovery for the upstate New York village that would take place the following year. His conclusions, based on the research he had previously conducted, revealed a contradictory story. Accordingly, the game (which he believed evolved from cricket) was first played along the Atlantic seaboard at least thirty-five years before the general's alleged invention. Menke also pointed out that Doubleday (who had been described as a "schoolboy" in the village at that time) was actually a 20 year-old student at the military academy.

The famous sportswriter reserved his most strident criticism for the Mills Commission report. He felt that under close scrutiny the conclusion reached by that group was replete with guesswork and inaccuracies. Rather than crediting Doubleday with the invention of the diamond, he stated that it was first introduced by Cartwright in 1839! Alexander's motivation was to end all arguments concerning the length between bases and to curtail the common practice of infielders kicking the bags away from the runner as he attempted to arrive safely. Although the former Knickerbocker had been cited in the past as the diamond's designer, the year chosen by Menke for this accomplishment was rather surprising.

Perhaps the most curious conclusion in the *Ken* article was the emphasis on cricket as the forerunner of the national pastime. Menke pointed out that a number of baseball's earliest rules were derived from those governing the British game. When America's game was initiated, there were no bases and the pitching motion, shape of the bat, and method of scoring runs were similar to that of cricket. In addition, pioneer baseball, like its alleged predecessor, contained no concept of the stolen base or foul ball. Menke cited other historical aspects connecting the two sports. For example, British colonists brought cricket equipment over with them when they immigrated to the New World; and there was considerable evidence that their game had been played in New York, Philadelphia, and Boston during the colonial period. Lacking enough traditional equipment to spread the practice of the English game, young boys in America began to construct their own. Gradually they altered the rules to fit nuances that developed in the colonies. In order to accommodate the growing interest in the game, more players were added to each side, and at one time this grew to fifteen. As the number of players increased, more bases were added—third base came first and then second.

Gradually the game moved more away from cricket and became its own distinct entity. Still, the major distinction from one area to another was the distance between the bases. Variations in this length resulted in continuous arguments which were finally settled by Cartwright. He also decided that the pitcher's mound should be half of the distance between the bases, and it remained at 45 feet until 1881 when it was expanded to 50 feet.

While the Knickerbocker game was different than cricket, they continued to share some similarities. Teams played until someone scored a set number of runs; bats and balls of both games remained fairly similar. Still, an evolutionary process had taken place, and the rules designed by Cartwright were proof of this. Menke stated that this was consistent with all sports which developed from crude contests into regularly organized games through the ages. Even the Knickerbockers were witness to this process. To further this point, Menke pointed out that not a single rule laid down by Cartwright was still in effect in modern baseball. Since his first efforts to professionalize the sport in 1845, new rules had been added and old ones were either altered or discarded.[19] Those who credited Cartwright with setting the distance between the bases at 90 feet would have disagreed.

Naturally, these accusations were disturbing to the Cooperstown promoters and had to be answered. Nobody was better prepared to do this than Walter Littell. In an editorial for the local newspaper, he began his rebuttal by attacking Menke, the magazine, and all of those who doubted the authenticity of the village's major claim to fame. First, he recognized that this was just the latest of articles which denied the invention of the game by Doubleday. Although there hadn't been many instances of this nature, these occasional claims were, in his mind, proof of the old saying that a little knowledge was a dangerous thing. Littell claimed that he wasn't particularly threatened by these statements because these responses had attracted about as much enthusiasm "as an oration by Hitler in a Jewish synagogue." He also condemned *Ken* magazine as a relatively new publication that would "have to depend upon a very gullible lot of readers for its support."

Although Menke had cited cricket as the forerunner of baseball, Littell pointed out that others had claimed that rounders, town ball and old-cat were the game's antecedent. Even though the authorities in the village felt that young Abner had more than likely played the old-cat version of ball and used it as the basis for the new game, all of these arguments were futile. The real question in his mind was not what activity baseball had evolved from, but rather when, where and by whom was it started. Ball games had been around, the editor claimed, since man developed a prehensile hand, but nobody had played baseball until Doubleday invented it. The fact that the other games mentioned had various features similar to the one devised by the general did not refute the findings of the Mills Commission. The editor furthered his argument by stating that since nothing more substantial than Menke's assertions had surfaced to show that Mills and his associates were in error, then this was the strongest evidence of the validity of their claims. He stuck by his convictions that the general had outlined the diamond-shaped field, marked the corners with bases, and named his invention baseball.

These aspects aside, Littell reserved his strongest criticisms for the article's attack on the game's originator and the date of his invention. For Menke, it was Alexander Cartwright who had drawn up the first diamond in 1839. Here, the editor felt, the noted sports authority had made his biggest error. After all, what was the basis for these rather astounding claims. The Cooperstown resident felt that it was strange that he provided no evidence for these remarks and that no one else had even heard about it. If, in fact, he was in possession of this proof, then he was simply verifying that one of his own assertions (that the game wasn't invented in 1839) was false. After all, Littell stated, laying out the diamond was the chief basis for establishing the origin of baseball.

Having poked holes in both Menke's evolutionary theory and his case for the date of origination, Littell next attacked his claim that Doubleday had not invented the national pastime. He pointed out that by making this statement, Menke had totally ignored all of the evidence that was offered as proof by the Mills Commission. The editor emphasized that this was no light-weight group, for its members were distinguished figures in the world of baseball at that time. The sports writer's most damaging testimony was his discovery that Doubleday was a student at the military academy in 1839 and thus couldn't have been in the village when his alleged invention took place. Although Littell admitted that this revelation was significant, it didn't dispel the fact that the creation was a product of the general's work. The simple explanation was that the memory of the witnesses (actually there was just one) was fogged by old age. The editor then stated quite surprisingly that the actual date of baseball's beginning was

1838 which, of course, made the current year the time for the centennial celebration. Rather flippantly, he cast this error aside as a matter of little importance. He thought that it was more important that Menke prove that Cartwright had initiated the game in 1839. Like Menke, he offered no proof for his date of baseball's origin.

In leveling his attack on the *Ken* article, Littell did not wish to demean the role of the famous Knickerbocker. He felt that Cartwright's place in the game's history was well established, and thus involved his role as the father of organized baseball. The editor admitted that he had indeed drawn up "the first formal diamond" (although he didn't exactly explain what this meant and how it differed from Doubleday's drawing), but he believed that it was based on Doubleday's design. The editor's basis for this statement rested on "the evidence of his associates that he had the general plan and rules of the game from Cooperstown" which were the basis of the Knickerbocker rules. (Here, of course, he was referring to the alleged Wadsworth connection.) He also pointed out that this event had taken place after 1840 and that there was no evidence to prove otherwise. He recognized that Bruce Cartwright had already forwarded original documentation commemorating his grandfather's role in the game and that they contained no proof that was contrary to the Mills Commission report. Finally, Littell cited the statement of Robert S. Doubleday which attested to Abner's knowledge about the beginning of baseball. This final piece of evidence, he felt, made Menke's theories totally insignificant.[20]

Littell had done an excellent job in defending the reputation of both Cooperstown and Doubleday against its most formidable challenge to date. For one thing, he had labeled the evolutionary arguments as irrelevant to the main contention concerning the inventor of the game. He also pointed out that no proof had been unearthed to discredit Abner as the progenitor of the national pastime. The weakest point in his editorial was that concerning the date which, while he admitted was off by a year, was not terribly important. One wonders how he might have felt if someone had discovered that the Declaration of Independence was actually signed in 1775 or that Columbus really landed in the New World in 1491. Still, he had constructed a formidable defense; and, if he claimed to a local audience that the Mills Commission had errored by a year, a national audience would not raise an eyebrow. Littell's editorial, then, was meant to serve a regional purpose. Coming at a time when local promoters were beginning to doubt the support of major league baseball, he was hoping to rally the village people to the cause when the Hall of Fame was being scrutinized by outside critics.

If Littell believed that he had met and conquered his last and most formidable opponent, he was wrong. The defenses were just being set up, and there would be other challengers in the future. Not having heard from the Hall of Fame authorities for some months, John Hamilton contacted Cleland about a month before the *Ken* article was published. He was still curious about how they planned to recognize Alexander Cartwright. Although the secretary hoped to be privy to the major league plans for the forthcoming celebration, the program was still tentative; consequently there was no concrete information for him to pass on to Hawaii. He felt, however, that Hamilton should contact the commissioner.[21]

The Cartwright-Doubleday debate was about to explode. Previously friendly in their correspondence with baseball authorities, Hamilton and Bruce Cartwright began to push for recognition of the famous Knickerbocker with more conviction. This attitude was a direct result of correspondence received by Hamilton following his inquiry to Landis. Evidently, the commissioner responded to the letter from Hawaii with the Doubleday-based story on the beginnings of baseball. After he received a copy of it, Bruce wrote to the manager of the Chamber of Commerce with an attack on the Mills Commission. He pointed out that before their report was made public, Doubleday's name had never been mentioned in connection with the national pastime. He felt that if a new committee were set up to search for the game's originator, in all probability they would not come to the same conclusion.

The current head of the Cartwright clan emphasized that he was simply interested in historical facts and not the deductions or verdicts of any committee. He then listed a number of events that nobody had ever questioned and they began with the organization of the first baseball club by his grandfather in 1845. Bruce boldly stated that Alexander had, in fact, drawn up the rules, laid out the first diamond with bases 90 feet apart and limited the number of players on a side to nine. From these humble beginnings, the modern game began to develop. Bruce recounted his grandfather's trek to the west coast during which he introduced the game to American pioneers. He felt that this action had helped to establish the national appeal of baseball.

Bruce did not confine his remarks to his grandfather's role in the development of the game. He also attacked the Doubleday claim to fame. First he cited that the general had nothing to do with the formation of the Knickerbockers. Even if young Abner did play a game in Cooperstown in 1839 which he called baseball, there were no historical records to show that this was the forerunner of the modern game. Bruce also pointed out that before the findings of the Mills Commission were published, not even Doubleday had mentioned his connection with the national pastime. Given these indisputable facts, with which even Landis would have to agree, Bruce felt that his grandfather should be honored in the anniversary celebration as the father of organized baseball. "Let us be sports and give credit where credit is due" he concluded. Specifically, he felt that if the federal government approved the idea of a commemorative stamp for "the birth of 'Base Ball' and its founders in 1839," then it should contain the likeness of Alexander Joy Cartwright, Jr., which he could provide.

While this response could be viewed as an attack on the Doubleday story, Bruce was careful not to dispel totally the general's role and the plans to celebrate the centennial in 1939. Hamilton continued this theme when he forwarded Cartwright's response to the museum. Although he clearly stated that Bruce remembered "distinctly discussing the subject of baseball and its origin with his grandfather," they had no objection to using Abner's name or picture in connection with the anniversary; they also felt that Cartwright should receive equal billing. Hamilton encouraged Cleland to investigate the matter further so that "the records may be kept straight for the future."[22] The Cartwright forces were matching those of Doubleday stride for stride. The statement that Bruce recalled talks with his grandfather concerning the beginnings of the sport came to light just two months after Robert Doubleday made similar claims about his uncle.

Obviously, major league baseball had to find a standardized answer to subside the rising tide of controversy. By this time the commemorative stamp had become the focal point of the argument, and it seemed that whoever was chosen to have his picture appear on it would be the winner of the debate. Unable to resolve the issue internally, Cleland sought the advice of president Frick. The president felt that in answering any queries of this nature, the Hall of Fame officials should emphasize that the celebration marked the anniversary of a game and not an individual. The centennial was meant to be national in scope, but it was only natural to focus on Cooperstown since the only available records demonstrated that the diamond was first designed there.

In spite of the historical documentation, Frick did not feel that organized baseball should give all of the credit to Abner Doubleday. Obviously, people like Cartwright, Chadwick, and others had played an important part in the development of the game. He assured Cleland that the former Knickerbocker would certainly be included as one of the immortals to be recognized in the museum. His confidence in this important matter was rather surprising since Cartwright wasn't listed in the original group of nineteenth century baseball figures who had been chosen only six months previous.

The question of the stamp, however, was a more delicate matter. The league president avoided any confrontation here by stating that no individual portrait would appear on it. Rather than throwing more fuel on the fire of the existing controversy, he cited for his reason the fact that it was federal government policy that only photographs of former presidents, military leaders, or other people in high government positions should be considered for use on stamps. Frick felt that the ideal solution would be a picture that would be allegorical in nature. Thus, a scene featuring a baseball game being played would more than suffice. Apparently, the league president didn't seem to think that Doubleday, who had been involved in some significant battles in the Civil War, met the government requirements. More than anything else, he was simply trying to defuse a volatile situation.

Cleland took Frick's advice when he replied to Hamilton's letter. He praised the "spirit and the evidence" of the correspondence and stated that he was gratified by the interest of the Hawaiian contingent in the centennial celebration. The secretary felt that a debate over the issue of who started baseball could benefit no one. Rather, he stressed that the museum wanted to recognize not only the beginning of the sport but also "the growth of the game." He continued the theme of Frick that this was a national celebration and not just a Cooperstown one. Cleland also assured Hamilton that in no way did they plan to minimize the significance of anybody connected with the sport's history, especially Cartwright. He recognized the role of the Knickerbocker organizer and asserted that he was deserving of the title father of organized baseball.

Aside from the claim that the village was the site of the game's invention, Cleland pointed out that there were other reasons for Cooperstown to be the logical site and the focal point of the celebration. Here he was referring to the museum building that had been constructed to house a wide variety of artifacts which reflected the position that the game had achieved in the nation's history over the past 100 years. The secretary emphasized the fact that the construction had only recently been completed and had been financed largely by local funds. Certainly the people in Hawaii wouldn't want to disrupt a movement that had resulted from such a total community effort. Cleland adroitly turned the situation around by reiterating Bruce's statement that the Cartwrights give credit where credit is due.

In case he had wounded any local pride in the islands (after all, he was addressing his remarks to the chamber of commerce), the secretary turned his attention to more positive issues affecting the Cartwrights. He pointed out that while certain features for the celebration had already been arranged, general announcements for the 1939 program had yet to be revealed. Given the historical significance and national prominence of the observance, a great deal of planning and study was required before the program could be revealed to the entire country. Even if the plans had already been made public, Cleland was confident that the Cartwright family would be satisfied with the role accorded to their grandfather in baseball's development.

Since he felt that they had a right to advanced information and because their correspondence had forced his hand to a certain extent, the secretary was willing to share some confidential news. The museum officials expected to hold a special Cartwright day as one of the main features of the centennial celebration. During this phase, they hoped to commemorate both the Knickerbocker organization and its founder's role in the game's development. The schedule of the day's events were set up on a grand scale. In addition to unveiling a bronze plaque in his memory for the Hall of Fame, they also planned to produce a pageant delineating his trans-continental journey and featuring his role as baseball's Johnny Appleseed. To demonstrate their conviction, the local boosters had already obtained a covered wagon for the event, and the program chairman had met with the Washington Square Players of New York City to engage them for the performance. Cleland hoped that the entire production would be authentic and dignified.

Concerning the commemorative stamp, Cleland stated that this was a matter for the Post Office Department. However, he pointed out that the standard government policy precluded any possibility of Doubleday or Cartwright being on it. While this may have disappointed the Hawaiian contingent, they had to be pleased with the scenario laid out by the museum secretary. Always sensitive to the feelings of various factions in the centennial plan, Cleland sealed his commitment to the Cartwrights by extending a personal invitation for Bruce to be in attendance and take part in the festivities.[23]

Before they discovered these plans, the Cartwright forces continued to further their claims by forwarding a copy of the log of Alexander's journey to the gold rush. It contained two entries that were significant to his role in baseball. On April 16, 1849, just west of Independence, Missouri, he wrote in his log that "it is comical to see Mountain men and Indians playing the new game." A week later he wrote that the group passed the time by playing baseball and that they were using the same ball "that we used back home." As they had matched the Doubleday people in the past, the supporters of Cartwright could now give witness to their own ancient ball.

The log of Cartwright's journey was a significant piece of information, and the timing of its arrival fit well with the Cartwright day plans. When Cleland received it, he forwarded a copy to Littell, L. G. Bursey, the Cooperstown program chairman, and professor Randolph Somerville, who taught dramatics at New York University. He requested that the teacher use it as the basis for the proposed pageant on Cartwright day. Although his supporters in Hawaii may have felt that it furthered his claim as baseball's originator, Cleland simply viewed it as a significant contribution to the game's history. He also felt that the museum officials should not anticipate any further arguments nor dissension from the islands during the following year's celebration. So confident was the secretary in his conviction, that he asked Littell to relay this message to Clark. Since Hamilton continued to express his willingness to continue his cooperation, Cleland had every reason to feel this way.[24]

At the same time that the museum officials were wooing the Cartwright clan with promises of Hall of Fame induction and a special day during the anniversary celebration, the Cooperstown forces continued their probe into Doubleday's background. In the summer of 1938, Stephen Clark had met with Robert F. Doubleday of Johnstown, New York, who he thought would be able to supply some background information on his famous relative. Later, Robert was able to furnish him with a copy of the general's war record that he obtained from the office of the state's Adjutant General, but this offered no information concerning baseball nor the date of Abner's entry into West Point. Since Robert couldn't find any enlistment records, he contacted his brother Daniel, who was a lieutenant in the Army Air Corps in Dayton, Ohio; and he began correspondence with friends in Washington, D. C. and West Point. Robert informed Clark that he wasn't trying to demean any of the research already done by the Hall of Fame; he was merely trying to get at the facts.

The investigation by the Doubleday brothers simply verified the dates for Abner's stay at the military academy that had already been published two years before in the Wedge article. Robert felt that this confirmed that his famous relative "was attending no other school" at the time of the game's alleged invention. He was also able to establish that Abner had attended a preparatory school known as the Cooperstown Seminary and this information clashed with Abner Graves' testimony that Doubleday was attending Duff's School at the time of the invention. Perhaps there were two names for the same school, but Robert didn't think so. He promised Clark that he would investigate the matter with the State Bureau of Education. Through correspondence with relatives in Kalamazoo, Michigan, Robert was able to confirm that Abner had attended school at Green's Select School in the village, and another source pointed out that he went to school in Auburn, New York. Curiously, he was able to report to Clark that a man named Abner D. Doubleday was born in Otsego County, but no other mention was made of him.[25]

Clark was not about to leave this significant matter up to chance. He received a copy of some information concerning Abner's record during the Civil War from the Bureau of War Records in Albany. He also contacted Mrs. Isabel J. Kelsay of Drexel Hill, Pennsylvania, to investigate the matter further. She traveled to the nation's capitol to conduct the research, but her initial inquiries were not fruitful. The libraries at the War College could not locate the materials that Clark had requested, but they did suggest other places to research these items. She was able to find two letters by Doubleday at the Adjutant-General's office and forwarded one to him. Abner had written a letter to Joel R. Poinsett, then Secretary of War, in May, 1838, in which he expressed his desire to become a cadet at West Point. In it, he also stated he was a resident of Auburn at that time. There was an additional note from his father that Abner had worked for the corps of engineers for the last two summers on several railroads. His father further stated that his son was well instructed in "Arithmetck [sic], Algebra, geometry, trigonomety, mensuration & surveying and well skilled in drawing, for which he has a natural aptitude."

Kelsay also found some books in the Library of Congress, and they confirmed Doubleday as the inventor of the game in 1839. However, her opinion was that it took place at an earlier date. She continued her correspondence with West Point, but this produced little new information. Lt. Col. C. H. Danielson did mention that Abner went to Green's Select School in the village, but a previous book had stated that. She felt that Clark should inspect county histories or local newspapers that might mention the names of students taking part in school activities. She was sure that Doubleday entered the academy in September, 1838. This, coupled with the fact that Abner's father stated that he had worked two seasons (meaning summers) on the railroad, left Kelsay to conclude that the general could not have been in Cooperstown nor invented baseball after 1836.[26] Clark had to be disturbed by this conclusion, but Kelsay evidently forgot or didn't know that Graves said the invention took place in the spring of the year. Young Abner could have laid out the drawing then in 1837 or 1838.

Clark continued his investigation and contacted Alexander C. Flick, director of the Division of Archives and History for the State Education Department in Albany. Flick confirmed the dates of Doubleday's stay at West Point (1838-42) and felt that it was reasonable to believe that he had attended a local military school under the direction of William H. Duff before entering the academy. Although this school, known as the Cooperstown Classical and Military Academy, was not recognized by the state regents, it was not uncommon to have private and unincorporated schools during that time. However, this would mean that any of the school's records would be difficult to locate. Flick also thought that it was highly probably that Abner would patronize the school in 1838 in order to prepare for his entry into West Point that September. Evidently Duff had set up other schools in 1837-38, and so he must have opened his school in Cooperstown sometime in the 1838-39 term. It was very likely then that Abner was one of his students during this time.[27]

If the majority of the forces behind the 1939 centennial were concerned about the accusation against the Doubleday story, Frick was not apparently among them. After Cleland informed him that Menke had sent his article to Honolulu, the league president expressed little concern about the matter. He felt that it was only natural for some people to take sides in opposition during a controversy, but this dissension, he felt, would have no effect on the celebration plans.

There was good reason for Frick to be so casual. About a month after expressing these opinions, Cartwright became a member of the Hall of Fame. Ironically, he gained membership on the same day as Henry Chadwick—the very person who had initiated the controversy that led to the Mills Commission.

An important point in this selection process concerned who had picked these two famous figures from 19th century baseball. It was clear that the highest executives of the major and minor leagues were chiefly responsible for selecting the first five "builders of baseball" in 1937. When five others were chosen from the early era in 1939, the commissioner and the two league presidents were responsible. Perhaps the same committee who made the first selections were also responsible for choosing Chadwick and Cartwright, but there was no actual vote that was ever made public.[28]

When the news of Cartwright's inclusion in the Hall of Fame was announced in New York, it was stated rather matter-of-factly. For the Honolulu papers it was more of an admission than an election. They felt that the inclusion of the famous Hawaiian was "tantamount to full recognition that he originated the national pastime as it is played today." Recognizing that there had been "considerable dispute and doubt" concerning the originator of the game, they boldly claimed that Cartwright had designed the first diamond, established ninety feet between the bases and limited the number of players to nine on a side. The board of supervisors of the city had already reacted to a suggestion by the recreation commission to change the name of Makiki baseball park to Alexander Cartwright Park.[29]

Soon after the news of Cartwright's election to the baseball shrine was announced, his grandson contacted Cleland to express his gratitude. Bruce mistakenly believed that a statue of his famous relative was already placed in the museum and requested a photograph of it. He also sent the secretary a copy of the newspaper clipping from Honolulu so the authorities in New York were well aware of the reaction in the islands. Bruce also mentioned a park that had been dedicated to his grandfather and reminisced about the times when he had watched games there with him. On one occasion, he recalled, Alexander drew a circle in the dust and then made a cross through it. While he was doing this, a crowd gathered; and he explained to them how he had devised the "Baseball Square." This statement was strikingly similar to Graves' claim that he saw Doubleday draw a diamond in the dirt.

On receiving this response from the Cartwright family, Cleland informed them that a plaque and not a bust would be placed in the museum. He also told them that during the dedication in 1939 each inductee would receive a scroll to acknowledge his election. Since the National Baseball Centennial Commission had not yet set up plans for the centennial, he could not inform them when Cartwright day would take place; but this information would be revealed by the beginning of the year. Unfortunately, neither Bruce nor his wife would be able to attend the ceremony, but he promised that his son William and his spouse would be able to make it if the major leagues would be able to pay their way. Bruce also desired a duplicate plaque, if possible, to be installed in the newly dedicated Cartwright Park; and he forwarded a photograph of a daguerrotype of his grandfather so that it could be used in constructing the Hall of Fame plaque. Cleland was quite pleased with the friendly correspondence from the Cartwright family, and he let them know that he was willing to cooperate with them to the greatest extent possible.[30]

The correspondence with the Cartwrights had gone well, and the museum officials had to feel that they had conquered their most controversial obstacle for national recognition. Ironically, the main source of opposition to the Doubleday story now came from the general's family. Once again, Robert F. Doubleday wrote to Cooperstown, this time to Littell. Since his last meeting with the editor, he had been contacted on two different occasions by Robert S. Doubleday of Tacoma. In neither of these communications was the New York resident able to gain any detailed information or dates which led him to the opinion that Robert S. "can not be considered a relative of Major General Abner Doubleday, now or ever." He went on to explain that although Robert S. had the same last name, he had no knowledge of the family history and possessed no war memorabilia that might be of interest to the museum. If, in fact, he was "a true relative," Robert R. stated, then he failed "to consider it worthy enough to mention." The 80 year-old Tacoma resident was not able to come up with a single fact that could prove his link to the family. Robert F. did not know whether to regard him as a "mystic" or simply ignore him. This decision he would leave up to the authorities in Cooperstown.[31]

This correspondence had to be disappointing for the museum officials. Previously, they had managed to match the Cartwright supporters in trying to prove that their man had invented baseball. Both Bruce Cartwright and Robert S. Doubleday claimed that they remembered a time in their youth when their famous relative had mentioned the beginnings of baseball, and the latter's correspondence was even published in the paper. If Robert S. wasn't really a relative, they had not only lost an important link to Doubleday's baseball past, but they might also suffer some embarrassment in the process.

The Hall of Fame officials received a final piece of correspondence concerning a Doubleday relative before 1938 came to a close. Helen E. Campbell, Social Service Director of the Beekman Street Hospital in New York City, contacted Cleland in November concerning a housekeeper at that institution with the same surname. She claimed that her husband was possibly a nephew of the Civil War general, and she had a book that was written about his exploits during the conflict. Campbell felt that she would have some interesting stories and encouraged the secretary to make an appointment with her.[32] Perhaps this was just an invitation to another blind alley, but it would be reassuring to the museum and major league baseball to have more substantial proof of Doubleday's connection with the national pastime.

Still, the museum officials had done a creditable job of thwarting claims that were counter to their theory that Doubleday had invented the game in Cooperstown. The only real dent in the armor involved the year of the invention, but little attention was being paid to this discrepancy at this time. Although Wedge, Menke, and Bruce Cartwright had somewhat tarnished his claim to fame, Abner's name was becoming firmly attached in the minds of fans throughout the country with the birth of baseball. Myth or reality, the fact of the matter was that most Americans associated the village and the general with the place where man invented the country's most recognized sport.

As the centennial year dawned, the biggest challenge seemed to be organizing and carrying out the celebration. This was no minor task because all of the various aspects of initiating the museum and Hall of Fame were about to coalesce.

Time was running short, and Cleland and his associates would be under a great deal of pressure until the events of the anniversary summer were completed. Advertisement, memorabilia, selection, induction and the committees of Cooperstown and the major leagues had to be addressed. Oh yes, there was still Alexander Joy Cartwright, Jr.

Chapter Eight
Hot Stove League

The year 1939 was more than just another baseball season; it was the year of celebration. Baseball fans around the country were by now well aware of its significance. The national pastime was 100 years old and they were ready to join in the festivities. Major league baseball officials also viewed the new year with great anticipation for they were about to reveal a list of activities that would commemorate the event. After years of dwindling attendance associated with the depression, a grand promotional scheme awaited exploitation. But nowhere was there more excitement than in the small village of Cooperstown. Preparation for the centennial season had been developing for the past half decade and now the wheels that had been set in motion by its baseball promoters were beginning to pick up momentum. Soon the efforts of Cleland, Littell, Clark and others were going to culminate in a most dramatic fashion. Before, there was no rush; there seemed to be more then enough time to prepare for the festivities. Now, anticipation reigned supreme, and there was much to be accomplished before the season started.

Activities in the village were inaugurated with the annual Chamber of Commerce dinner at the Cooper Inn on the 5th of January. One of the featured speakers for the event was Al Stoughton, secretary of the National Baseball Centennial Commission. Also in attendance at the festive event were Mayor Lettis, George Trautman, president of the American Association and chairman of the executive committee of the National Association, Judge W. G. Bramham, the minor league president, and of course Alexander Cleland. The fact that the junior leagues were better represented at the dinner than the majors may have been a disappointment to the locals, but not even this could dull the excitement. After all, the dinner was designed to commemorate the centennial, and Stoughton had some long-awaited information from the officials of baseball.

Having already addressed gatherings of the major and minor leagues in the previous month, the commission's secretary was well prepared to speak to the local community. He told the gathering that he considered his invitation to speak a matter of duty since the group with which he was affiliated actually represented, in a large way, the home of baseball. His first concern was to report all progress for the anniversary that had been made on a national level. Realizing that the Cooperstown establishment had been virtually shunned by baseball's officialdom over the past year, he tried to soothe any pain they had suffered in the process. He acknowledged that, typically, people in the promotion and publicity business encouraged any print space they could receive. However, Stoughton believed that the present situation was unique because the plans called for concentrating the publicity for the period after another month had passed.

Rather than spreading stories thin and presenting them half done, he hoped to launch a publicity campaign that was well thought out and therefore more effective. He encouraged local officials to share in the quiet ground work that had to be organized.

The major event that would kick off the publicity was the annual dinner of the Baseball Writer's Association to be held on the fifth of February. Stoughton told his audience that this gala would initiate the national promotion for the centennial plans. He stated that the members of the National Commission and its executive committee would be announced at that time. However, as insiders to the coming program, he planned to share some of this information with the dinner guests. Heading up the major league committee was Commissioner Landis; and it also included Frick, Harridge, Bramham, Trautman, L. C. McEvoy (the head of radio for the American League), Leslie O'Connor (treasurer of the commission) and Stoughton. The National Baseball Centennial Commission would act as a clearing house for future plans and would also serve as the directing force behind organization and publicity for the centennial year. The secretary made a special mention that Cooperstown would be represented on the commission. Basically he felt that the executive committee's job was to build the skeleton plans while the real flesh and blood would be added later by the major and minor leagues, semi-pros, amateurs, schools, sand lots and fans throughout the country.

Stoughton told his audience that the major purpose of the centennial was to glorify the sport that had such a tremendous impact on the nation. The development of the national pastime paralleled "the growth and greatness of America;" and thus the centennial would recognize "the greatest genuinely American game that this democracy has produced." In the process of its development, baseball had contributed both "men and the ideals of sportsmanship" to the national scene. Continuing the theme of patriotism, the commission's secretary explained the symbolism of the emblem that had been adopted for the 100th anniversary. This logo would be reproduced and distributed throughout the country, thereby helping to unify the nation in the baseball celebration.

Having described the significance of future events in national terms, Stoughton came to the issue that was of greatest concern to his audience—what did all of this mean for Cooperstown. First, it meant that everything about the village would be more widely known than ever before. As the advertisement for the anniversary spread around the country, people throughout America would associate Cooperstown with the birth of baseball. The central focus of the summer of celebration would be known as "the Cavalcade of Baseball" which would take place on June 12th. On that date the stars of major league baseball would gather in the village to dedicate the museum and the Hall of Fame. In order to demonstrate the national significance of this event, he revealed that it would be filmed by every newsreel and carried over all of the major radio networks. Finally, the secretary recognized the formidable efforts that had already taken place in the village and congratulated the various committees and their chairmen for a job well done.[1] This was an important statement for the people who had waited so long for support from baseball's officials. They had to realize at this point that their dreams were going to come true on a major scale.

If the speech by Stoughton to the chamber of commerce hadn't satisfied everyone in the village, an article by Ford Frick concerning the centennial year appeared in the newspapers around the country a few days later. The National League president focused his attention on the past rather than the future. He recognized that the story of baseball's first century was a glamorous one, but he felt that Doubleday's discovery was the most significant aspect of all. Young Abner had "brought order and meaning" to the playgrounds of Cooperstown and helped "the local youngsters get more enjoyment out of their play." He had founded a tradition which spread from the village to all corners of the nation. Frick felt that this achievement "had a scope and an influence much greater than perhaps anybody yet realizes." For him, the celebration of 1939 sought "to crystallize this century of achievement." Through the efforts of many people over the past century, the game had gained national prominence. He believed that, at the present time, "more people than ever before are aware of and impressed by the loftiness of baseball traditions and of how deep are the roots of the game in our national life."

Turning his attention to the future, Frick realized that, even though the national pastime had witnessed a century of amazing development, it was only the beginning of the story. It had started as a boy's game, it was developed along that line, and he believed that a century in the future "youth will still be its breath of life, its fountain of strength." In addition to being a game for America's youth, he felt that it had helped to develop traditional values that had served the country well. For Frick, it was "a game of square-shooting competition, honest play, clean and above any possible suspicion of double-dealing." The next century of development would certainly continue along these lines. The centennial, then, was the opportunity not only to view baseball retrospectively but also to contemplate its future.[2] As a former sports writer, Frick had done well inaugurating the 100th anniversary of the national pastime. Cooperstown and all of America had to be excited about the celebration to follow.

With the centennial year officially opened in Cooperstown and throughout the nation, events for the future began to unfold. The Penn Athletic Club formally accepted an invitation to play the Philadelphia Athletics in the village on a day to be known as "Connie Mack Day." The venerable owner of the club had already been elected to the Hall of Fame in the first round of selections for the "builders of baseball" in 1937. He expressed great pleasure in the match and was happy to have the opportunity "to play baseball at the game's birthplace." He felt that the celebration of the 100th anniversary was "one of the greatest things that game had provided and those in back of the project should be commended." While no definite date had been established for the game, Lester Bursey of the local program committee stated that the people of the village were anxious to honor "the grandest and oldest figure in baseball today."[3]

Philadelphia again helped to usher in the anniversary year when the Athletics previewed the new American League film, "First Century of Baseball." Although it had already been shown during the winter meetings, this was the first time it was viewed by the general public. The occasion for the viewing was the club's annual banquet held at the Bellevue-Stratford with almost 300 people in attendance. Included in the audience was president Harridge of the American League and Lewis Albert Fonseca, former major leaguer and producer of the film. It would continue to be shown on a number of occasions during the off-season and John A. Quinn, an American League umpire, traveled with the film to introduce and explain it. Harridge felt that this event marked the real opening of the centennial celebration and he stated that Philadelphia was the correct place to initiate the anniversary year since so much baseball history had taken place there.[4]

The long awaited plans for the celebration of baseball's 100th birthday were finally released to the public on January 17th. Accordingly, the dedication of the Hall of Fame and museum would feature the official induction of all the members who had been elected to the shrine. Eight of the modern-day players would be in attendance in addition to representatives from all of the major league clubs and minor league organizations. Only Christy Mathewson and Willie Keeler, both of whom died in the previous decade, would be absent from the original inductees. Part of the "Cavalcade of Baseball" involved the unveiling of the plaques for the first members.

While this date would be the central focus of the celebration, the anniversary would actually get under way in early May with a number of events to take place at Doubleday Field. In order to recognize the first intercollegiate baseball game between Amherst and Williams in 1859, a game between these two schools would be one of the special exhibitions. Each of the forty minor leagues would also send two players to the village for two all-star games in July. In addition to these activities, an official centennial insignia had been adopted that was designed by Major Bennett, a young artist from New York. It had been chosen from hundreds of other samples that had been submitted and would be used by all groups throughout the nation who chose to participate in the anniversary. Centennial stamps would also be distributed, but their design had not yet been determined.

At the same time, the official members of the National Baseball Centennial Commission were announced and they included people from a variety of backgrounds who were avid baseball fans. Commissioner Landis had already been selected as chairman of the executive committee. The group included a number of military leaders, and others who followed the game. Most of these men had been part of the original list drawn up when the commission was first being organized, and others would be added before the summer. In addition to setting up its membership, Steve Hannagan had established an $18,000 budget for the commission to cover its operating expenses.

Soon after the initial group of members was announced, others were added. The most renowned of the latest entries was 78-year-old General John J. Pershing who had led American troops in World War I. During the war, Pershing attributed the early success of American soldiers to their participation in sports (including baseball) at home.[5] Four others had also accepted an invitation to join the commission including J. G. Taylor Spink, editor of *The Sporting News*, Claude J. Peck, president of the Inter-Collegiate Athletic Association, and Professor William B. Owens of Stanford University (president of the National Collegiate Athletic Association). In addition, Charles J. Doyle of the Pittsburgh *Sun-Telegraph* was chosen to replace Paul Shannon, President of the Baseball Writers Association, who had tragically drowned in Florida.

Further endorsement for the centennial came from the National League officials during their annual meeting in New York City, February 7th. They expressed their complete cooperation with the anniversary program and decided that June 11th would be an open date on the schedule for the convenience of those who planned to participate in the Cooperstown celebration. An official centennial poster was displayed for the gathering. It contained the figure of Uncle Sam swinging the bat with an American flag in the background. The league officials also announced that all of the baseball uniforms manufactured for 1939 would bear the symbol of the centennial insignia.[6]

About a week later, the plans for the program at Cooperstown preceding the cavalcade were made public. Generally these were college games which were scheduled to begin on May 6th when the academies of Manlius and Albany played each other. Six other contests were scheduled throughout the following month, highlighted by the one between Williams and Amherst on May 13th. Another significant and appropriate game would be played on May 30th between Colgate and Army, Doubleday's alma mater. Three special days were also set aside in addition to the cavalcade, and they included the one previously mentioned for Connie Mack. Also, May 27th was designated as Christy Mathewson day. His wife planned to attend the festivities for the Hall of Famer who had died, and the bust of the pitcher was to be unveiled. Not to be forgotten by the celebrants, Abner Doubleday would have a day of recognition to be coordinated with the Army baseball game.

In addition to the college games, other special events were added to the summer schedule. Les Bursey attended a Boy Scout council meeting in nearby Oneonta for the purpose of working them into the program. He arranged for a "Camporee" for the first weekend in June that would coincide with the last college game. Accordingly, about 1000 scouts would "invade the village," but Bursey pointed out that they would pitch their own tents and arrange for their own meals.[7]

Although the centennial year was becoming more prominent in the eyes of many Americans, other activities associated with it were being planned. Representative James A. Shanley, a Democrat from Connecticut, asked Congress to initiate a national baseball day to commemorate the anniversary. Alluding to the troubling events taking place in Europe, he contended that the game had saved the country from the "excess prevalent among nations abroad" and therefore deserved an honored place on the calendar. His bill authorized President Roosevelt to proclaim June 12th a baseball holiday during which flags would be displayed on public buildings. Shanley felt that "baseball best exhibits the American ideal of true sportsmanship, has contributed most to the development of the American temperament and has been the nation's safety valve." For the past century it had been the country's "pastime and passion," and in the process it "brought despair to Mudville—joy to Middletown." The entire country should "rejoice and thank God for a game that for 100 years has built Americanism." The theme of baseball and nationalism would be reiterated throughout the centennial season, but for Shanley it was more than just playing politics because the game was part of his family tradition. Previously he played centerfield for Yale, and his father had been regarded as one of New England's best shortstops.

Even his grandfather had displayed his talents as a pitcher during the Civil War era.[8]

While all of this activity was capturing the imagination for the American public, it was business as usual for Alexander Cleland. The only difference was that now he was being pulled by two different forces at the same time. Naturally, activities in the village were picking up and required a great deal of attention. Major Lettis made him aware of the dynamics of various developments such as the improvement to the field and the construction of the stands which were progressing rapidly. In addition, the centennial organization in Cooperstown was trying to sell financial certificates to raise $15,000 for expenses which was not meeting with previous expectations. The mayor had also heard from a Mr. Feldman of the National Broadcasting Company, who was planning to put on a one-hour show in conjunction with the centennial. There were also complaints from locals that things were progressing too slowly, that advertising was improperly handled, and that opportunities for raising money had been missed. At the same time, Stoughton sent word to the secretary that he had cancelled a request of a moviemaker to be hired for filming the dedication day. It didn't make any sense to waste money in this direction, he felt, since every newsreel in the nation would be there.[9]

Now that baseball fans throughout the country had been made aware of the centennial, both Cleland and Stoughton hoped to continue the nation's interest through newspaper articles and promotional schemes. Their plans received an outside boost from Sid Mercer, who wrote a series of thirteen articles for the New York *Journal and American* on the history of the game. Naturally, the first of these was concerned with the game's origin; and Mercer stated unequivocally that there was "little doubt...that Cooperstown, N.Y., is where the seed was planted in 1839 by Abner Doubleday, a schoolboy with a flair for organization." He went on the claim that Abner was about to enter West Point when he laid out the first diamond with bases 90 feet apart. The author also cited the work of the Mills Commission and the connection with Abner Graves. Although his next article credited Cartwright with organizing the Knickerbockers, he stated that the first professional team benefited from a diagram of the playing field that was brought to them by one of the team members in 1845.[10]

Even though they were being assisted by Mercer in the print media, Hannagan's public relations firm began to line up programs and sponsors for future broadcasts. Their major focus was the dedication day and they hoped that each of the major networks would do a half or full hour show for the Cavalcade of Baseball. There were many broadcasts scheduled before the celebration commenced, including an NBC show preceding the baseball writers' dinner and a number of others during spring training. They also hoped that programs currently on the air could give special plugs for the centennial and that perhaps a baseball quiz show could be set up. Hannagan's group planned to contact sponsors currently involved in baseball broadcasts who might be interested in serving a similar function for events in Cooperstown or for spring training broadcasts. Finally, they hoped to do a series of thirteen programs, similar to Mercer's articles, that would be broadcasted once a week beginning in April.

Evidently Hannagan wasn't satisfied with Stoughton's work at this point; and he asked two of his other employees, Larry Smits and Murry Martin, to review what his new worker was doing for the centennial promotion. He was especially concerned with shows that would be coordinated with opening day, the Cooperstown Cavalcade, the All-Star game, and the first game of the World Series. He wanted them all to be lined up in advance rather than wait for the last minute. In addition, Hannagan felt that they had not developed enough written material to be distributed to major and minor league clubs.

Later, Martin came up with some suggestions on this line that he passed on to his boss. He felt that essay contests could be conducted under the guidance of local baseball management. Titles for these essays could be distributed to schools, boy scouts, and campfire girls, and the winners would receive season tickets to the movie theaters. They also considered writing special sermons concerning the worth of baseball in terms of fair play and sportsmanship that could be distributed to churches around the country. Martin felt that this could "result in some helpful propaganda from the pulpit."

Martin was also concerned with logistics involved in transporting special guests to the village for the cavalcade. He asked Stoughton to get confirmations from the various inductees to make sure that they would be in attendance on June 12th. He was also curious about how they would travel to the remote village in upstate New York and wanted to make sure that this aspect was well organized. He needed the same kind of information concerning the sixteen major league players who would be chosen to represent their teams in a pseudo all-star game in the village. Martin also wanted to know what managers or major personalities might show up for the celebration. This information could be used on radio and newsreel shows as the promoters built up national interest for the big day.[11]

The Hannagan firm continued to develop the promotion of the Hall of Fame dedication, but they received some competition from the people who were trying to advertise the New York World's Fair. Stuart Cameron of the Miami Beach News Service was contacted by Christy Walsh, who served as Director of Sports for the fair. Walsh hoped to set up a display of major sports trophies for the event in New York City and wanted some suggestions. Cameron made a list of items for his consideration and hinted that since it was baseball's 100th birthday, he might want to think about a special place devoted to trophies from the national pastime. Perhaps a famous suit, glove or ball would be appropriate or why not Babe Ruth's renowned $80,000 contract.

When Stoughton found out about this suggestion, he demurred. Previously, Cleland and his counterparts felt that the fair would be good advertisement for the centennial, but this spirit of cooperation did not carry over to its official promoters. Stoughton preferred a low profile for baseball at the fair. Landis and Frick agreed with him that Walsh was operating a show that was in competition with the celebration in Cooperstown. Besides, Cleland had faced a great deal of difficulty when it came to gathering memorabilia for display in the museum; and there was not enough left over for the world's fair. The commission's secretary added that "as long as we are both working the same side of the street, Gimbel's is not going to advertise Macy's."[12]

Others sought to capitalize on the centennial celebration. S. Allen, sales manager of the Ever Ready Label Corporation, found out about the Hall of Fame through Hannagan's office after he was contracted to print up labels to publicize the 100th anniversary. It occurred to him that the Cooperstown museum could receive further advertisement through the production of poster stamp illustrations of the players to be inducted. If some national organization would be interested in them as items to be sold as curios, then everyone concerned could profit nicely. Allen felt that the matter should be discussed by himself, Stoughton, Cleland, and Frank Carpenter of the village committee so that other angles (perhaps pictures of the museum) could be developed.

A similar request was proposed by Hugh Poe of Pittsburgh, Pennsylvania, who wanted to paint portraits from photographs of each of the inductees. Poe had previously done this kind of work for the Culver Military Academy in Indiana in 1925 and offered the name of the school's superintendent as a reference. He did not realize that his plan conflicted with the scheme of the plaques which were to be installed in the museum. Therefore, his proposal was rejected by Cleland, who though that it might override the general theme of the building.[13]

Actually, the secretary had more significant matters to attend to; and perhaps the one that most appealed to him was the fact that more artifacts were being donated to the museum. In spite of the variety of items already received, there was nothing from baseball's most formidable personality, Babe Ruth. If the visitors to the building couldn't observe some memorabilia from the game's greatest star, they surely would have been disappointed. Oddly, the gifts didn't come directly from the home-run king, who was typically indifferent to the anniversary and his responsibilities to it. Instead, a collector from Louisville, Kentucky, Ward A. Hillerich, donated some of Ruth's former equipment. One was a bat made by Hillerich and Bradsby which contained the slugger's autograph and twenty-eight notches around the trademark representing the number of home runs he hit with it before it broke at the handle. Other relics of the Babe included his favorite and well worn mitt and a pair of his running shoes.

Although the other items received by Cleland didn't have the same popular appeal, they were, nonetheless, significant. Clermont G. Tennant of Cooperstown convinced the New York State Department of Archives and History to donate to the museum a copy of the book entitled *Major-General Abner Doubleday and Brevet Major-General John C. Robinson in the Civil War*. Since it was a very rare volume, the museum officials were pleased to acquire it. The most significant part was a biographical sketch and portrait of the general. The book, published in 1918 by the state, also contained a reprinting of the monument to Doubleday on the Gettysburg battlefield. Jesse A. Morrill of Fulton, Kentucky, donated a silver ball with the name of Arthur Cummings engraved on it. Recognized as the inventor of the curve, he had also pitched the local team to victory in 1866; and they were awarded the ball at that time.

As progress was being made on all fronts, the construction of seats at Doubleday Field kept pace. Although the project commenced the previous fall, the work got under way in earnest in mid-February. By this time, thirty-four men from the Works Progress Administration were on the job; and plans for additional help were being considered. Due to time restraints, the WPA could not provide all of the labor for field construction. So, Harry A. LaDuke, project foreman, had arranged to hire men from the local relief roles. As previously planned, the old grandstands from the county fairgrounds had been taken down, and the steel had already been transferred to the field for the new grandstand construction. W. Carter Burnett, a local engineer, had drawn up the plans for a 700 seat facility; and the construction crew had completed its concrete foundation. They were just about to start the cutting, erecting and combining of the steelwork. Some of the bleachers were already erected and linked with the grandstand; the seating capacity would be over 10,000. Since there was two feet of snow on the ground, the work on the field was delayed. However, the infield sod had been laid the previous fall and a mixture of sand, clay, and peat moss was ready to be placed on the baselines and other bare spots on the infield.[14] Henry Fabian would have been proud of the progress that had been made.

Advertisement, which had been so important to the total development of the centennial project, continued to expand as the baseball season drew near. A radio program called the "Cavalcade of Baseball" was broadcast on the Blue Network of the National Broadcasting System on March 19th. It was a full hour program which detailed the highlights of the game from its inception to the present. Hollywood was lending a hand to promotion again with Warner Brothers planning a feature film commemorating the centennial. Much of the story was to be built around Connie Mack, and producer Bryan Foy had already conferred with Frick and Heydler concerning the project. He planned to use a number of former major league players and location scenes would be shot in Cooperstown.[15]

Of course the print media was still the centennial's best source of promotion, and it had expanded to embrace a wide variety of publications. In January, the cover of *Hardware Age* contained an advertisement for the Louisville Slugger company; and the lead article was devoted to the anniversary and highlighted by the national insignia in the center. Another magazine called *Photo* carried a seven-page article on baseball's first century replete with pictures and references concerning Cooperstown. Newspapers, such as the Albany *Times-Union* and the Springfield Massachusetts *Union*, ran series of articles and cartoons on the game's history. *Buick Magazine* also produced a brief article on the early history of baseball and the plans for the celebration in Cooperstown. The *Christian Science Monitor* published an article on baseball's 100th anniversary that came out at the beginning of the season. The *American League Red Book* for 1939, a baseball compilation for writers and club officials only, was dedicated to the Writers' Association and the Hall of Fame. It also contained a list of landmark dates in baseball's development including the statement that Cartwright had established the distance between the bases at ninety feet.[16] There still seemed to be some confusion concerning the originator of this magical distance, but most sources were leaning toward the former Knickerbocker.

Hannagan's associates had already addressed the problem of transporting baseball's stars and officials to the remote location in upstate New York. This was also an important matter for fans. Nelson Greene, editor of the Fort Plain, New York *Standard*, addressed this issue in an article for local consumption. He also forwarded it to Cleland and sent it to the radio networks for their broadcasts. It was mainly concerned with air transportation since few people knew what was available in this area. Greene pointed out that the airport at Fort Plain was the closest to Cooperstown; but others were also located in Syracuse, Oneonta, Utica, Schenectady, Albany, and Troy. In addition American Airlines was considering a special taxi service from Syracuse to Fort Plain with a bus connection to the village.[17] Nothing was being spared in order to accommodate travelers who wished to attend the centennial.

While the various details were being worked out, the question of minor league involvement also had to be resolved. In November, 1938, Stoughton had contacted Cleland on this matter and revealed that the minors desired "some small part of the Hall of Fame which they can call their own." He thought that the museum secretary could make some suggestions concerning their proper inclusion in the new building on the second floor or perhaps in a separate room. Cleland decided that this decision should be made by the officials of the major leagues and so he contacted Frick. He explained to the league president that although the museum officials were anxious to cooperate with all groups from organized baseball, their representation had to be dignified and present a true picture of the game's history. They felt that no part of the building should be given to the minors or any other group in baseball without Frick's endorsement. Cleland had also conferred with Clark on this matter, and his boss was in complete agreement.

Most of the members of Cooperstown Centennial Committee agreed that the minors should be represented in the Hall of Fame. The only problem was how this could be done properly. Judge Bramham and George Trautman visited Cooperstown on this matter, and their meeting with Stoughton and museum officials resulted in some concrete suggestions. First, Cleland and his associates earnestly felt that their organization should take part in the centennial celebration. The minor league officials desired two days of participation, and the secretary felt that July or August would be the best time since this was the period that most of the tourists visited the village. In addition to participating in the summer activities, Bramham supported the idea that the minors should sponsor a historical library within the museum, and this innovative idea met with the hearty approval of the Cooperstown committee.

Stoughton was working behind the scenes on this situation and, in a conversation he had with Frick, the league president gave his approval to minor league representation in the Hall of Fame. Cleland had the authority to invite them to erect an exhibit, but it had to meet with Frick's approval. Since Hannagan had already shown his skill as an innovator, the secretary turned to his firm for some suggestions. Stoughton told his boss that Trautman would probably approve the idea of the minors erecting a statue of Doubleday or perhaps an entrance gateway to Doubleday Field so long as the name of each league was placed on it. While these plans were still up in the air, the dates for the minor league program were established. Accordingly, their activities would take place on July 10th and 11th (the days preceding the all-star game) and it would be known as National Association days. The plan was for each league in the association to send two players to play on those days. At this time the minors would dedicate whatever type of memorial they had decided to put up.

Another suggestion for minor league involvement came from C. O. Brown, who told Stoughton that they should make a series of thirteen radio transcriptions to be given to every club (even the majors) so that they could use them for local broadcasts. These recordings would "stress civic interests, character building, how to play baseball," and each would be introduced by various baseball officials. These broadcasts would also contain the story of the centennial, and Brown planned to line up well known ball players to speak on the various aspects of the game. Later, Bramham sent a message to all league and club presidents that they could purchase centennial emblem stickers and electros to print their own stickers or other materials. This would allow them to advertise the celebration and perhaps make some profit from it.[18]

By early February, 1939, Cleland and Trautman finally came up with some concrete plans for minor league involvement. First, the secretary set aside space on the second floor of the museum for plaques. One would carry the names of all league teams while others would represent past presidents or men who had been instrumental in setting up the leagues. The American Association president had previously agreed that no players would be represented in the Hall of Fame. Evidently, the idea to include them did not meet with standards set by Cleland that the representation should meet high qualifications. Secondly, the secretary and his associates strongly endorsed the proposal for a historical library. Cleland wanted to start it on the second floor of the museum; and, if more room was needed later on, the entire floor could be used for library purposes. He offered Trautman his complete cooperation in this matter and felt that this would be one of the museum's most significant features. Finally, both men agreed that July 9th would be the best time for the minor league game; the executive committee of the National Association would be responsible for choosing the players and handling the ceremonies for that day. Trautman also felt that the plaques for the minors should be unveiled on this day. Realizing that it would take some time to decide on the make-up of the plaques and the collecting of materials for the library, he decided to implement both of these projects immediately.[19]

As part of the promotional plan to spread the centennial activities throughout the nation, the National Baseball Centennial Commission wrote up a manuscript that would serve as a guide for local communities who wanted to join in the celebration. Stoughton submitted this piece to a number of sources for inspection so they could check it for errors before it went to the printer. Bramham was extremely disappointed when he received his copy because it made no reference to the formation or existence of the National Association of Professional Baseball Leagues, even though it currently represented 275 cities and towns throughout the United States and Canada. He felt that this was "somewhat akin to writing a history of the United States and leaving Washington and Lincoln out of it." The manuscript included information on sandlotters, schools, and the majors while leaving out that branch of the sport that involved the most employees, patrons, and investments.[20]

Despite the oversight, the minor leagues began to organize their forces in preparation for their big day in Cooperstown. L. H. Addington, director of publicity for the National Association, sent a note to sports editors throughout the country to affirm their participation in the Cooperstown celebration. In addition to pointing out their role in the museum, he also stressed the unique all-star game that would involve players from each of the leagues and asked that they advise him if they planned to attend. Judge Bramham began to coordinate the leagues that were scattered throughout the country. His message, which was distributed to league presidents, asked for each leading official to accompany the players who would represent their division and make the trip to the village on July 9th. He also asked them to urge club officials to attend.

Bramham also addressed the manner in which the various leagues would choose a representative to send to Cooperstown. National Association officials desired that the participants be of the highest caliber, but they allowed the individual divisions the option of selecting those representatives. In order to avoid the possible confusion that might be caused by a haphazard selection process, Bramham and his associates made up a list of player assignments to assure that there were enough players for each position. For example, the American Association would furnish a first-baseman with the uniform number 15; and the International League would provide a catcher who was assigned the number 9. This process was continued so that each league provided a player with a different number to fill a certain position. Every player would furnish his own playing equipment, and some of the leagues indicated that they would make up a special uniform for the occasion that would carry the name of the league rather than that of the town. In this case, the Association requested that they use the centennial colors of red, white, and blue.

Bramham also listed a tentative schedule for minor league day in Cooperstown which featured the dedication ceremonies at the Hall of Fame in the morning, followed by the minor's game at Doubleday Field in the afternoon. After the game, the Cooperstown officials had set up a special train that would take all of the participants to New York. Here they could visit the World's Fair or see the sights of the city. On July 11th, the major league all-star game would be held at Yankee Stadium for those who wanted to attend. Since train travel between New York and Cooperstown had been suspended for many years, the scheduling for the special train required commitments from those who wished to utilize it. Bramham pointed out that it would be available to all members of the National Association and their friends and asked that those who wished to use it make reservations in advance. In order to get a firm commitment from each of the leagues, he stated that centennial celebrations were obviously rare occurrences, and he urged "proper observance and participation by all representatives of the Association."[21]

As chairman of the Association's executive committee in charge of minor league participation, George Trautman contacted Cleland on another idea involving colleges throughout the nation. He felt that the secretary might consider another plague in the museum to represent higher education's role in the development of the national pastime. Trautman urged him to contact Philip O. Badger, graduate manager of athletics at New York University and member of the executive committee of the National Collegiate Athletic Association, on this matter. This suggestion interested Cleland because of the role that colleges would play in the centennial celebration, and he felt that such a plaque would create a great deal of interest among the fans. He had already planned to make a trip to the university to meet with professor Somerville, who was working on the pageant for Cartwright day. Thus, it would be convenient for him to contact Badger. Following his meeting with the NCAA executives, professor Badger expressed their support for a plague that would be "symbolic of the interest of the colleges in our National Sport." The executive committee voted to finance the project and asked Cleland to make some suggestion concerning its make-up.[22]

Since Cooperstown was planning a re-enactment of baseball as it was played in the nineteenth century, a similar idea was designed for the minor league celebration. Harry E. Smunsy of Fostoria, Ohio, contacted Elmer M. Daily, President of the Middle Atlantic League, concerning this matter about a month before the season started. Smunsy was employed by the John B. Rogers Production Company which specialized in civic celebrations and pageant spectacles, and they hoped to put on a program for minor league cities and towns that would demonstrate how the game was first played and how it evolved later on. The Rogers company had the backing of the National Baseball Centennial Commission and planned to use prominent local people in their production. Their management service provided costumes, uniforms, and promotion for the production which was supposed to last about a half hour and would precede a regularly scheduled game. The company assured the various leagues that they would not only be participating in the centennial celebration, but their cooperation would also result in greater attendance and increased box office returns.[23]

In addition to minor league participation, the National Baseball Centennial Commission also focused its attention on the National Amateur Baseball Federation. Stoughton sent a message to this organization for their annual meeting in Birmingham, Alabama. In it he stressed the fact that the 100th anniversary celebration was not being confined to any particular league or section of the country. Instead, the entire country should take part in it. The commission's secretary emphasized the role that baseball had played in the nation's development and stated that the game had helped to develop fair play, sportsmanship and aggressiveness. Focusing on the increasingly dangerous war developments taking place in Europe, Stoughton regretted that the "Old world is resounding with the clank of arms and the rattle of guns." By comparison, the talk in America was concerned with baseball; and he felt that the game would prepare young Americans "for the battles of life—whatever they may be."

Stoughton pointed out that during the coming baseball season, fans throughout the country would be made aware of the centennial celebration through newspapers, radio, newsreels, and a feature length Hollywood film. The nationwide publicity was designed to encourage everyone in the country to participate in the anniversary, and he hoped the Amateur Federation would take part in the festivities. The secretary emphasized that the men who sacrificed their time and effort to teach the game to America's youth did so because they believed "in the lessons of citizenship and clean living that baseball teaches." He invited them to join in the celebration by conducting activities in their home towns. In order to accomplish this task, the National Commission had prepared a handbook entitled "Play Ball America" which was designed to aid local communities who wanted to take part in the anniversary. It would be distributed without charge to teams, American Legion posts, Chambers of Commerce, and other agencies. Every member of the Amateur Federation who attended the annual meeting was given one. Stoughton hoped that in this manner the anniversary program would reach into every village, town, and city in America.

Another group that the National Commission hoped to reach in order to spread their message across the nation was the National Semi-Pro Congress or sandlotters. Even before the season commenced, this organization had prepared a number of activities to commemorate baseball's birthday. On May 7th, a total of 12,500 sandlot games were scheduled to start simultaneously around the country in a mass demonstration to recognize the national pastime. The main feature of the day would be an all-star game in Wichita, Kansas, which was the home of the Semi-Pro Congress. According to the organization's president, Ray Dumont, this would initiate the official semi-pro baseball week which would contain a number of unusual and novel contests around the country. The all-star game would involve two teams—one composed of youngsters under 18 and another of men over 50. This meeting would help to symbolize that all ages would be represented in the sandlot ranks. George Sisler, Hall of Famer and high commissioner of the semi-pros, was scheduled to toss out the first ball, which would be the signal for the other games to start.

Other activities were also set up for the semi-pro recognition of baseball's 100th birthday. In the nation's capitol, Representative John Huston of Kansas headed a special committee designed to observe the beginning of the national semi-pro week. A unique game between two Civilian Conservation Corps clubs was scheduled to take place in Washington. Another special game involving the Buford, Georgia, Bona-Allens was set up for that city. This reigning national sandlot championship team would play a leading southern squad and, following the game, they would be awarded the 1938 trophy.[24]

With all of the success that accompanied the 100th anniversary in the preseason, there was still a source of controversy concerning the Cartwrights. Of course, the Cooperstown supporters had taken some action to ease any ill feelings that might have developed in Hawaii by setting up Cartwright day. Les Bursey, of the program committee, attempted to develop this theme by suggesting to Cleland that a team from the islands be sent to the village. The team he had in mind was one sponsored by Doris Duke Cromwell, a famous philanthropists. She had used her influence and money to develop athletics in Hawaii, and Bursey thought that she might have a team from there touring the mainland during the spring. He felt that they would be a natural for the Cartwright celebration and asked the secretary to work on this angle. If some people in the village felt threatened by the contingent supporting the former Knickerbocker, Bursey wasn't one of them. His suggestion to enhance Cartwright day demonstrated the confidence that many people in Cooperstown must have had in the Doubleday story.

More important than Cartwright's role in the celebration was his election to the Hall of Fame. The Spalding *Guide* for 1939 made special mention of the artifacts that the museum had received form Hawaii. The annual baseball book also listed the nineteen selections for induction into the hall and displayed pictures of the seven "Builders of Baseball." Cartwright headed up the group and was recognized as the unquestioned "Father of Organized Baseball."[25] Oddly, one name was missing from the list of seven men who had been recognized for their role in developing the game from its beginnings—Abner Doubleday.

Perhaps this lack of recognition inspired Clark Griffith, president of the Washington Senators, to suggest some kind of ceremony to acknowledge the general during the centennial year. On the forty-sixth anniversary of Doubleday's death, Griffith visited his grave in Arlington National Cemetery. (Evidently, there was some question as to his actual burial site, but Robert F. Doubleday looked into the matter and determined that it took place in Arlington). Following his pilgrimage, the famous club owner suggested that baseball leaders make a similar journey during the summer's celebration. Later he wrote Mayor Lettis concerning a program of this nature, and the Cooperstown authorities were in complete agreement. Since they had invited the Cartwrights to attend the ceremony for their famous ancestor, Littell felt that the Doubleday family should also be extended an invitation for any event to recognize the general. Apparently he had received word that Robert F. was rounding up the family for a summer reunion. This gathering would play right into Griffith's plans. Of this group, Thomas Doubleday, a former resident of Cooperstown, was considered to be Abner's nearest living relative, and his presence in any event was vital to its success.[26]

Following the recognition extended to the founder of the Knickerbockers by organized baseball and the museum officials, the correspondence between Honolulu and Cooperstown had grown friendlier. In January, 1939, John Hamilton contacted Cleland about the plans for the centennial. Almost three months had passed since their last letters, and he wanted to know what new developments were taking place concerning national interest in the celebration and programs that would be sponsored throughout the country. Hamilton's interest stemmed from the fact that a celebration was being planned for the island community and any information that museum officials could pass along would be of great assistance to the local chamber of commerce. Cleland immediately forwarded two baseball calendars for Hamilton and Bruce Cartwright so that they could witness the type of publicity that was being used commercially on the mainland. He made special note of a large colored print of Elysian Fields in Hoboken that it contained. He also stated that the National Centennial Commission would soon make their first statement concerning the celebration, and he promised to forward it to Hawaii as soon as their plans were released.[27]

Criticism against proclaiming Doubleday, Cooperstown, and 1839 as the person, place, and time connected with the discovery of the national pastime was no longer coming from the Cartwright clan. Once again the center of the controversy was the noted sports authority, Frank G. Menke. Previously his complaints had appeared in a magazine article that was not recognized for its national reputation. Therefore, its impact was somewhat limited. Also, almost a year had passed since the *Ken* piece had been published, and museum officials hoped that its disturbing claims had either been forgotten or simply overwhelmed by the publicity surrounding the centennial celebration. In February, 1939, however, a book by Menke entitled *Encyclopedia of Sports* was published. In it he attacked the Doubleday claim to inventing baseball.

Menke stated that "the present ruling powers in the sport had been misled relative to its origin and its development." Specifically they had cited the wrong date, the wrong place, and the wrong man for the beginning of the national pastime. The mistake was not theirs, however, for they had simply taken as accurate the report of the Mills Commission. He referred to Mills as "a doddering old man" and stated that the commission's report was self-contradictory and illogical. While he continued to cite cricket as the forerunner of the national pastime and to claim that the game had been played by a number of locals long before 1839, he changed his opinion about the date of Cartwright's discovery. Menke now believed that the famous Knickerbocker had drawn up the baseball diamond "in 1845 or early 1846." He believed that Cartwright and his associates wrote up the first set of rules during the winter of 1845-46 and that they were utilized for the first time the following June in Hoboken. He also attacked Cooperstown's claim to fame by denying that there was any conclusive evidence that the game had been played in the village as early as 1839.

According to Menke there were two major sources of error that had led to the false conclusions of the Mills report and its acceptance by baseball fans throughout the country. One was major league officials who willingly adopted the Mills thesis without checking for inaccuracies. Even a cursory glance at an encyclopedia of the time would have revealed that it gave credit to the Knickerbockers. The other was A. G. Spalding, who felt that the game had originated before the renowned New York team played it. Although the Mills Commission's word was eventually accepted in most baseball circles, Spalding's claims had been contradicted by his numerous detractors. With his reputation as a baseball historian on the line, A. G. felt that it was necessary to push the group to finish its work. After all, a few years had passed since the question had first come up, and nobody on the commission except Mills had actually put any effort into researching the project.

Menke reprinted the Mills report in his book, and then he began to find fault with it. First, he pointed out that Doubleday was hardly a "schoolboy" in 1839 and he wasn't an "embryo West Pointer" either, since this statement implied that he would be a cadet in the future. Actually, he had already commenced his studies at the academy in the previous year. Menke also noted that Doubleday did not abolish the practice of "plugging" or hitting a runner with a ball, for he felt that it was not outlawed until 1848 when the Knickerbockers revised the rules. Mills had also credited the general with drawing the first diagram of the field and writing the first rules of the game. However, Menke accurately reported that no copy of these significant creations was ever unearthed.

For the sports historian, the most incredible aspect of the Mills report was that even though its creator had known Doubleday intimately for 25 years, he never realized that the general had any connection with the national pastime until 14 years after his death. In fact, the commission's findings were the only basis for connecting him with the sport because his name never appeared anywhere as a ballplayer. The only reason that Mills and his associates cited Doubleday as the game's progenitor was a "circumstantial statement made by a reputable gentleman" to Spalding. Of course, Menke was referring to Abner Graves; but he never mentioned his name. He also claimed that A. G. had never acknowledged that Graves made any such statement. Indeed, Spalding did not mention the retired mining engineer from Denver in his book, *America's National Game.*

In his famous account of baseball history, the former sporting goods magnate felt that it would be an act of disloyalty to question the findings of the commission. However, he found nothing unethical in reproducing data that demonstrated that the game had existed years before the time fixed by their report. Oddly, the very person who was directly responsible for establishing baseball's immaculate conception through the Mills committee was the same author who developed the evolutionary theory in his account of the game's history. Spalding cited a number of authorities who claimed that they had played baseball long before Doubleday's alleged invention, and they included Oliver Wendell Holmes and two former Knickerbockers—Colonel James Lee and Charles DeBost. The fact that A. G. was contradicting himself, however, did not shake the conviction of baseball fans that Doubleday had invented the national pastime.

Menke emphasized that baseball had become extremely popular long before Doubleday's death, and he wondered why the general had not published an article on his involvement in its development. After all, he had written a number of pieces on miscellaneous subjects during his lifetime. Nobody had connected him with baseball in any way before the Mills Commission report, and its decision was based on the word of a man "who remains forever unknown." (Evidently, Menke didn't realize who Graves was, probably because Spalding didn't mention his name and the sports historian never had any other access to information about him). Since Mills and Doubleday belonged to the same military organization, Menke believed "without a doubt" that they had met "hundreds of times through a quarter of a century" and "discussed the increasing popularity of baseball." However, when the investigating commission convened, Mills admitted that he had no knowledge of the general's role in baseball's beginnings. Even Henry Chadwick, who had written more about the game than any man of his time, had never mentioned Doubleday in his writings. Menke also pointed out that in thirty years of researching the history of the game, Spalding never uncovered any connection with Doubleday.

Disregarding the findings of the Mills Commission, Menke traced the evolution of baseball—which he said came from cricket. He mentioned some of the early rules that became fairly common but stressed that there was still a lack of uniformity. As the game grew more popular in the 1820s and 1830s in places like New York, Brooklyn, Boston, Philadelphia, and "some of the cities of inland New York State," teams from these regions began to interchange ideas and "adopt the best features of the sport as it was developing elsewhere."

From this point on, Menke stressed the role of Alexander Cartwright. When he and his fellow Knickerbockers had met on September 13, 1845, Cartwright lamented the fact that the game had been played under haphazard regulations for too many years. He proposed that the rules and the field should be standardized. Menke then went on to demonstrate that it was Cartwright who fixed the position of the players, established 90 feet as the distance between the bases, limited teams to nine players on each side, and sketched the first "baseball square." The sports historian then listed the rules that he had drawn up and included a diagram of the field and positions. He also traced Cartwright's movement to Hawaii and pointed out that his grandson, Bruce, had pleaded with baseball officials to give more recognition of Alexander's role. However, the major leagues had already appropriated $100,000 for recognizing the 100th anniversary and Cooperstown had constructed the museum.[28] With this kind of commitment, it was too late to back down.

Once again, Menke had attacked some sacred notions and institutions. As might be expected, others would soon find fault with his conclusions. The first announcement of Menke's findings appeared in an article by Bob Considine in the New York *Daily Mirror*. Actually, the author did not disagree with anything Menke wrote and referred to him as "the great sports historian." However, Considine felt that his book would be a surprise to baseball moguls who were preparing to honor Doubleday in Cooperstown. He called Menke's conclusions an "embarrassing revelation" and added that the author was "pretty indignant about the whole thing." Considine went on to cite the book's attack on the Mills Commission, whose report was "full of contradictions" and couldn't stand up to a test of logic. He also stated Menke's belief that it was Cartwright who really deserved the credit.[29] Although Considine's article didn't agree with the sports historian's accusations, he made no argument against it. Appearing in a major New York newspaper, his article must have made residents of the nation's most populated city and state quite uncomfortable, not to mention its effect in baseball circles.

The Menke book was also noted by baseball's bible, *The Sporting News*. They acknowledged that it was published just before the centennial celebration took place and claimed that it "completely upsets the base on which the anniversary rests." So far as they were concerned, Menke should be classified as "the leading iconoclast of the century." However, *The Sporting News* admitted that through his thorough research the sports historian had "discovered many myths growing out of the unsupported statements by unidentified authorities for which no kind of proof has yet been found." Still, they recognize that the information he came up with in regard to baseball would cause considerable problems for the National Baseball Centennial Commission and might force their staff "to dig deeper into the dim past for refutation."

The Sporting News went on to describe Menke's thesis and his conclusions about Cartwright's role in the game's development. They stated that even if sports fans disagreed with his assertions, they provided an interesting argument and shed some light on the origin and growth of the national pastime and other sports as well. The weekly magazine also helped to advertise the *Encyclopedia of Sports* by stating the 5,000 copies of the book had been printed and that 4,000 of those would be given to sports editors and executives of various sports organizations who were responsible for supplying information. The rest would be sold to libraries, athletic officials, recreation supervisors, and other specialists on the area of sports.[30] If baseball fans throughout the country had not been aware of the Cartwright-Doubleday controversy before, they had to know by now. No doubt some of them were questioning the legitimacy of the centennial celebration and Cooperstown's role in the origin of baseball. Perhaps some of the people connected with the village's celebration felt the same way.

Obviously, this kind of attitude worked against the efforts of Hannagan's advertising company, who were putting forth their best work to promote the 100th anniversary. About the time that Menke's book came out, they were focusing their attention on spring training facilities. The first baseball stories of the season were being written up and they wanted to utilize local sports writers to promote the celebration for fans throughout the country who were hungry for the first news coming out of the training sites. They employed Stuart Cameron of the Miami Beach News Service to visit training camps in an attempt to increase the interest of baseball writers in the forthcoming centennial. The Hannagan firm hoped that he could encourage them to mention it whenever possible in the stories that originated from Florida. In effect, Cameron was to act as a goodwill ambassador for the anniversary.

Realizing that reporters throughout the south would be asking questions about the observance in Cooperstown, the Hannagan firm drew up a list of typical questions that Cameron might have to deal with and also supplied answers that he might use. They included queries about the plans being made for the centennial, what forms of media would be used to advertise the events, and why the Hannagan firm, instead of some unemployed baseball writer, was given the job by the major leagues to publicize the events of the summer. Included in this list was another question concerning the argument raised by Frank Menke about the wrong place, time, and man for baseball's beginnings. The answer supplied by Hannagan's company stressed that Cooperstown, 1939, and Doubleday had been accepted as the official answer for more than three decades. They told Cameron to stress that the Mills Commission "didn't pull Doubleday's name out of a hat" and that baseball's authorities were satisfied with the proof of his inventions.[31]

In spite of these precautions to avoid further embarrassment over the controversy, the issue surfaced again in the New York *Journal*. An article in that paper pointed to two sources of evidence which disputed the claims of the Mills Commission. One was a recently discovered manuscript, previously written by A. G. Spalding, which set the date of baseball's beginning at 1845. This 2000 word article was essentially written to show the role of the Army and Navy in spreading the game around the country. On two different occasions, A. G. mentioned this date as the start of baseball. It contained no mention of 1839 or Cooperstown. Another source cited was, of course, Menke's book. The article basically laid out his arguments against the claims of major league officials on the initiation of the national pastime. The author felt that all evidence went against Cooperstown, but nothing would change since organized baseball had already spent a considerable sum on the centennial in the village and would stick with the Mills report "whether it was fact or fiction." The writer agreed with this decision, claiming that it was the symbol that was important and not the name or date. To him, no matter who invented the game, it was "something really worth celebrating."[32]

Menke's book also had an impact in Cooperstown. The local paper reported that the Little Falls *Times* was upset about it. They claimed that its author belonged to "the class that would belittle Washington, Lincoln and other men who have played their part in American history." The paper felt that Menke would fade from attention when his real purpose was known. In addition, Walter Littell wrote Cleland that the secretary had done an important job in lining up organized baseball and college groups before the book was published. Evidently he felt that its publication would not destroy the summer celebration for, as he stated, "Menke's poison will pass." The local newspaper editor believed that they had already taken care of any potential problems concerning the Cartwrights with "negotiations (that) were made some time ago and on this account it is very important that you and the New York and Cooperstown authorities make sure that Cartwright Day is a real success."[33] This statement made the day for honoring the famous Knickerbocker seem more like a cover-up than a celebration.

The controversy over the originator of the national pastime had almost vanished with Cartwright's election to the Hall of Fame. Just about the time when the question over Cooperstown's right to house the museum had passed, the famous sports historian resurrected the debate. For the officials of baseball and the Hall of Fame, his timing couldn't have been worse. At the same time that his book came out, the nation became aware that a new stamp would be issued to coincide with baseball's alleged 100th anniversary.

The formal announcement of the issuance of the stamp took place on February 5th at the sixteenth annual dinner of the New York Chapter of the Baseball Writers Association. In attendance at the dinner in the Hotel Commodore were over 1,100 members and their guests, including some of the leading figures in organized baseball. Postmaster General James A. Farley announced to the gathering that the special stamp commemorating the centennial of the game would be issued during the June celebration and placed on sale in Cooperstown with an official first-day cover. Naturally this statement brought a great deal of satisfaction to the centennial supporters in the village. Farley added to their excitement by stating that, so far as he knew, this was "the first stamp ever issued in commemoration of a sport." He felt sure that the stamp would meet with approval of baseball writers, fans throughout the country, and especially children—for whom the game served as "a tremendous influence for good sportsmanship and good citizenship." Concerning the picture on the stamp, Farley explained that, while it was impossible to use the likeness of a living person, his department was open to suggestions. Personally the head of the postal system favored a picture of the immortal Christy Mathewson either alone or combined with some of the game's great stars. As the only deceased modern player among those chosen for induction to the Hall of Fame, he would have been a popular choice.

Since the writer's dinner had been set up to inaugurate formally the centennial year on the part of major league baseball, it was held in a festive atmosphere with Doubleday and Cooperstown given prominent places. A number of speakers that evening made reference to the general and the village, but the official recognition of Cooperstown as the center of the national celebration came from Mayor Theodore R. Lettis. As a special quest of honor, the mayor occupied a seat at the speaker's dais where he was seated between Charles J. Doyle, president of the Writer's Association, and Ford Frick. During the evening, the mayor was toasted by Sid Mercer, who had previously written a series of articles on baseball history. Lettis expressed his appreciation and invited everyone to come to the village during the summer to enjoy the anniversary celebration.

Also in attendance at the dinner was Grover Whalen, president of the New York World's Fair. During the evening, he asked the mayor if the village was trying to steal his show. Whalen was assured by Lettis that the people of Cooperstown wanted nothing but cooperation with the big city officials. The fair's president went on to emphasize that sports would be given a significant place in their celebration and that a special recognition would be accorded to the baseball centennial. Previously in harmony with each other, the two major events for the state of New York had their differences; but this was neither the time or place to mention it.

Before the serious part of the dinner program had started, a group called the "Illiterary Guild" amused the crowd with a production entitled "The Press Box Revels." One of the features was a three-man skit called "Looking Backward or Doubleday's Dilemma." The men in the short comical drama played the general, Cartwright, and a fortune teller. At one point Abner told the former Knickerbocker that although he was glad that the game was catching on in Cooperstown, he was not really concerned about whether it would last. While they were talking, a swami appeared and told them how it would develop in the future. Doubleday was horrified when he learned that the innocent game which he had invented would move thousands of people to eat hot dogs. He lamented that the citizens of the country would want to eat dogs—hot or cold. Cartwright shuddered when he learned that in a reference to Landis, there would be a czar of baseball. He thought that this was un-American and Doubleday felt that it sounded like Russia. The swami informed them that there was no longer a czar in the U.S.S.R. and that baseball would have the only one in the world. There was only one way to prevent this dilemma. Doubleday declared "they will not point the finger of scorn at me a hundred years from now. No, Mr. Cartwright, I will not invent the game."[34]

Following the formal announcement that the stamp would be issued, its design soon became the center of controversy. Suggestions for the picture that it should contain varied from one source to another. Some suggested former major league stars (especially Mathewson) while others supported the idea of having no individual's picture. *The Sporting News* felt that inasmuch as Doubleday had established the game in its present form a century ago, it was appropriate that his picture should be on the stamp. Doubleday was their choice because he was a figure of national importance and he would not create any animosity among the immortals who had already been enshrined in the Hall of Fame. A number of fans concurred, but the debate continued.

In order to arrive at some popular conclusions, various polls were conducted to solve this dilemma. A Mutual Radio Network Show, hosted by John B. Kennedy and broadcasted in New York City on station WOR, held a weekly straw vote of its listeners to decide the design of the centennial stamp. Some of the leading vote getters in this poll were Doubleday, Mathewson and John J. McGraw. In addition to announcing the latest results of their survey, the show's host interviewed a number of guests concerning their opinion. Stan Lomax, well known sports commentator, chose former Dodger manager Wilbert Robinson while Bill Sterms, nationally known football broadcaster, favored Eddie Grant, a former Giant who died a hero's death in World War I. The radio program also polled sports editors on this matter, and they overwhelmingly favored Mathewson with Doubleday and McGraw in second and third place. Radio editors, however, gave the general the edge over Babe Ruth and Mathewson. Curiously, Cartwright attracted no votes in any of these polls. Evidently, the Doubleday story had already attracted national attention and displacing it was virtually impossible.

Speaking on the Mutual Network, Farley stated that every suggestion from the fans would be given serious consideration, but in the final analysis the selection would "typify the heritage of American youth." The Postmaster General also expressed his satisfaction as to how well the idea of the stamp was received. His enthusiasm had increased when he noted how many people had listened to the radio show and voted for their favorite choice. His only regret was that the regulations called for some person who was not living, and this eliminate many of the fan's selections.

The final decision on the commemorative stamp was announced just prior to the start of the 1939 baseball season. Rather than focusing on a single individual, Farley avoided all controversy by selecting a scene portraying youngsters playing ball. At this time the Post Office Department was still considering a picture of the Hall of Fame, but authorities were evidently aware of the debate concerning the authenticity of Cooperstown. Some people in the department believed that the first game may have been played in Hawaii.[35] The confusion over this issue and the lack of support of Cartwright demonstrated that the factual word on the famous Knickerbocker still had not gotten around.

It shouldn't be surprising that Cartwright hadn't surpassed Doubleday in the minds of most Americans. Even the leader of the country touted the former military officer. President Franklin D. Roosevelt had sent a message that was read to the dinner guests at the annual Baseball Writer's dinner. In it, the President stated that Americans should be grateful to Abner Doubleday for he never could have realized the boon that he was giving the country by devising baseball. Although the rules of the game had changed since it was first formulated, Roosevelt noted that it "remains today the great American sport." The president also pointed out that while the general was a distinguished soldier in both the Mexican and Civil Wars, his role in baseball demonstrated "that peace has her victories no less renown than war."[36]

As the start of the baseball season drew near, the excitement over the centennial celebration was reaching a peak in Cooperstown. Littell wrote an editorial to recognize the efforts that had already been put forth and to sum up the meaning of the future events for the village. He felt that "probably no other event of its kind ever was planned that so readily gripped the thought and imagination of the whole country." Littell stated that "many celebrations, like the World's Fair, had to be built up by force while the baseball anniversary was simply everybody's celebration." Although he recognized the remarkable efforts of the Hannagan organization and others, the editor felt that no publicity organization could have created such intense interest; rather, it had developed quite naturally.

Littell then turned his attention to three questions. What did the centennial mean to Cooperstown, baseball, and the nation? Concerning the village, he admitted that many people might conclude that it simply meant a volume of free and favorable publicity that could only have been purchased at an extreme cost. Still, the citizens of Cooperstown had invested a large amount of money and, as was true in any similar situation, it was only natural for them to expect some return in tourist dollars during the centennial. This was outside money which would certainly benefit the entire region immediately, and Littell predicted that the village would continue to profit when the next century of baseball was celebrated. Since this financial harvest was occurring at a time of fiscal crisis for Cooperstown as well as the entire nation, he believed that it would "drive the hounds of depression form our doors and keep them away." Moreover, he stressed that these assets would not go away nor would they be affected by "walk-out and sit-down strikes."

Next, the editor turned his attention to the centennial's impact on baseball. He felt that the anniversary would "give the national game the greatest stimulation it has received since the Civil War." Littell reasoned that the impact would be dynamic because millions of fans and players throughout the country would observe and participate in the activities. This would give the game "a new glamour and a new standing in the eyes of the general public." Baseball would "assume the role of an American tradition" and enter upon "a new era of popularity."

Finally, he addressed the meaning of the anniversary for the country. Littell believed that it would "stimulate interest in history and in sportsmanship" which would be "a healthful influence upon the national morale in a day when the outlook in many directions is depressing." He ended his editorial by quoting Dean Carl Wittke of Oberlin College who had recently addressed the impact of baseball on the American public. Wittke noted that it was a game for everybody for the "sons of immigrants from eastern Europe have risen to fame and fortune on the diamond as rapidly as the native born." Recognizing the famous thesis of the historian Fredrick Jackson Turner, he remarked that the sport had been a kind of "substitute for pioneer days" by furnishing "an outlet for Americans; a new safety valve after the era of free lands had come to an end." The dean stressed how other nations, especially Italy and Nazi Germany, did not have this outlet. He was thankful that the United States did, for he preferred "Old Diz to Il Duce" and "would rather shout my lungs out to an umpire than in heiling to Hitler."[37]

Once again Littell had managed to put the significance of the future events into a clear focus. Certainly there were financial benefits to be had for professional baseball and Cooperstown's businessmen, but the impact of the centennial went far beyond these implications. There was historical significance to be gleaned from the anniversary. Fans could now appreciate the sport's implications in the country's past and project its impact on the nation's future. With the approach of the Second World War, Americans could be thankful for the role of sports in their country's history. That other nations were denied this outlet was soon to be painfully obvious. The new baseball season, with its accompanying anniversary, was then a time not only of celebration but also one of reflection.

Chapter Nine
Season in the Sun

At long last, baseball's 100th anniversary had arrived. Five years of planning by Alexander Cleland, Stephen Clark, and Ford Frick was about to culminate in a season-long celebration. Of course, others had done their share—including the Hannagan firm, Walter Littell, the National Baseball Centennial Commission, and the various committees in Cooperstown. What had started out as a simple idea of a museum and a place of honor for the great performers in the national pastime was about to blossom into a nation-wide recognition of the first century of baseball.

The long awaited centennial baseball season was scheduled to open on April 18th, but inclement weather forced the cancellation of many of the opening day ceremonies. Most notable was the annual inauguration in the nation's capitol, where President Roosevelt had planned to throw out the ball to initiate the elaborately planned pre-game activities. Unfortunately the Senator's contest with the Yankees was postponed, but Abner Doubleday was not forgotten. During the morning the New York club, along with their manager Joe McCarthy, joined forces with owner Clark C. Griffith and his Washington players in a pilgrimage to Arlington National Cemetery. Here they attended a memorial service at the grave of the Civil War general. Both leaders of the teams paid special tribute to the man who allegedly conceived the game of baseball and placed wreaths at the base of his tombstone.[1] Their participation should not have been surprising since McCarthy had already been elected to the Hall of Fame and Griffith had aided Cleland in his early search for memorabilia.

The following day, Roosevelt wrote to the museum to recognize the efforts that had been put forth in Cooperstown. He expressed his belief that it was "most fitting that the history of our perennially popular sport should be immortalized...where the game originated and where the first diamond was devised a hundred years ago." The president felt that baseball was not only the national sport "but also the symbol of America as the melting pot" since baseball players "embrace all nations and national origins." Obviously the president was recognizing how the sons of European immigrants had developed into outstanding players, but he was ignoring the fact that those of African descent were still excluded. The news of Roosevelt's letter was greeted with great pleasure in the village after William Beattie announced its arrival. The correspondence was framed and placed on a wall in the museum so that every visitor could read it. Not only were the museum officials excited by the recognition afforded by the president, but so were the rulers of baseball. After all, it was an unqualified endorsement of the centennial, the game, and the recognition of Cooperstown as the cradle of the national pastime.[2]

Following the inauguration of the anniversary by major league baseball, centennial activities in the village were also initiated. About two weeks after the season started, final preparations were being made for the opening events in Cooperstown. Since Doubleday was the major figure to be honored, it was fitting that the first game, scheduled on May 6th, should involve two of the state of New York's outstanding military schools—Manlius and the Albany Academy. In addition to their baseball teams, both institutions would also provide marching battalions and their entire student bodies as an audience. Shortly before the opening day ceremonies, officials from both schools met with the Cooperstown centennial committee regarding arrangements for the initial events and various details of the program. In expectation of a large crowd for the opening ceremonies, the WPA had finished the construction of a new steel grandstands and bleachers to accommodate 10,000 people at Doubleday Field.

Other activities were also being set up for future events during the centennial summer. Accordingly, American Legion Day was designated for July 15th and promised to be one of the feature attractions of the 100th anniversary. A statewide participation of Legionaries was to be sponsored by Clark F. Simmons, who headed the local post in the village. A number of distinguished Legionaries had already agreed to serve on an honorary committee to govern the local program including Governor Herbert H. Lehman and F. H. LaGuardia, the mayor of New York City. There would be a five-inning baseball game between two teams designated as the Old-Timers of Connecticut and New York state.

As the opening day approached, other developments began to take shape. One of the more unique involved a world amateur championship scheduled to take place from August 12th through the 27th at Tropical Stadium in Havana, Cuba. Sponsors of this tournament had already extended invitations to thirty nations who belonged to the International Federation of Amateur Baseball. This was of special interest to Cooperstown because players representing the United States would be selected in the village during a series of games set up by the U.S. Amateur Baseball Congress at Doubleday Field. During these trials, some 225 players from around the country would participate.

Another idea for the festivities was suggested by *The Sporting News*, whose editors thought that the Cooperstown committee should install a plaque bearing the name of James L. (Deacon) White and make a special invitation for him to attend the ceremonies. Since the former major leaguer was born in 1847, the newspaper reasoned that he was probably the oldest living player and nearly as old as the game itself. The baseball publication felt that the Aurora, Illinois, resident was entitled to this honor because he typified the spirit of baseball's first century. In spite of a distinguished 23 year career, White was never invited to the June 12th celebration. He died about a month after the dedication and some people felt that his exclusion from Cooperstown hastened his death.

The Sporting News wasn't alone in their suggestion for recognition of those who had made substantial contributions to the national pastime. Shortly after the season commenced, Erwin L. Glenke, secretary of the Kiwanis Club in nearby Ilion, contacted Mayor Spraker concerning the early efforts to develop Doubleday Field. A small group of men from his hometown had initiated the concept with a fund-raising drive in 1917; and two of them, Patrick Fitzpatrick and George White, were still alive. F. C. Carpenter, chairman of the Cooperstown advertising committee, told Glenke that while he and others in the village appreciated the efforts of these pioneers, they felt that Doubleday should be recognized before anyone else. Carpenter believed that a monument to the general should be erected at the entrance to the field and hoped that funding for this project could be initiated. He thought that if the people of Ilion wanted to contribute to the summer's activities, they might want to join in the parade for Cartwright day.

Not to be denied of some involvement, one resident of Ilion, Arlie Cole, loaned a copy of *DeWitt's Baseball Umpire's Guide* to the museum. The book was published in 1875, and the editor was none other than Henry Chadwick, the former sportswriter. It is doubtful that many people at this time realized his role in the developments that led to Cooperstown being recognized as the birth place of baseball, but his book was an important display item. It contained a vast amount of information and was in an excellent state of preservation.

While the centennial activities were being planned, articles for the anniversary were on the rise. Baseball had quite naturally become a major topic of interest throughout the country, and the print media was jumping on the bandwagon. Since the game had become a favorite topic in 1939, stories concerning it began to appear in news columns, sports comments, editorial pages, magazines and other periodicals. These included an article in the *Christian Science Monitor* which contained illustrations of Doubleday Field before it was remodeled, the National Baseball Museum, the Doubleday baseball, and the general himself. In addition, weekly newspapers around the state published a variety of editorials promoting the Cooperstown celebration. The thirtieth edition of the *Baseball Blue Book*, the administrative publication of organized baseball, had a picture of Doubleday on its front cover. It also contained a brief history of the game and a list of events that had been planned for the summer. A news release from the Mohawk Valley Towns Association, which was designed to attract tourists into upstate New York, contained a number of references concerning the centennial. Perhaps their greatest assistance was a description of how to take the best routes into the village for summer travelers. Similarly, the Glen Falls Insurance Company published a 1939 baseball calendar complete with a major league schedule, a list of events in Cooperstown, and brief sketches of those who had already been elected to the Hall of Fame.[3]

As the opening of events in Cooperstown drew near, the Hannagan firm was busy with a variety of activities. He personally contacted baseball clubs at the start of the season in order to determine what plans they had firmed up concerning the observance of the centennial. He hoped that they would relay this information to the Centennial Commission so that it could be publicized nationally. The Commission also endorsed a baseball centennial car emblem that could easily be attached to a license plate and sold small quantities of them to major and minor league presidents and club owners.

Al Stoughton came up with other ideas designed to increase the involvement of high school seniors in the anniversary. One involved a contest for boys who would recite "Casey at the Bat," and the youth would gave the best rendition would be awarded a season pass. Another included an essay contest for boys and girls on the subject of "the contributions of baseball to the spirit of American sportsmanship." Evidently the minor leagues were disappointed in their lack of involvement in the program, and Stoughton felt this concept should be directed to them in order to keep the interest of Judge Bramham. Hannagan encouraged the minor league president to adopt the plan and distribute the details of it to various club presidents. He felt that both contests had excellent publicity possibilities and at the same time they could help teach lessons in democracy.

Stoughton also assigned C. O. Brown the task of contacting officials of the minor leagues concerning the involvement of high school ball players in the centennial activities. He had originally discussed this concept at the National Association's annual meeting in New Orleans. At this time, many states had no high school tournament, and the Hannagan agency hoped that enough professional teams would be willing to sponsor one for schools in their surrounding area. They felt that the cost would not be prohibitive and that it would require very little work for clubs willing to participate. They also hoped that the plan would get more high school officials to think about baseball as an interscholastic sport.[4] Obviously, the idea was designed to fulfill the dream of making the centennial a national observance.

From the very beginning of their involvement in baseball's 100th anniversary, the Hannagan publicity firm had promised nation-wide participation in the celebration. In order to fulfill this promise, members of the organization were assigned the task of writing up brochures to increase community involvement. One of these was a small booklet entitled "Play Ball America," and its major theme emphasized how various cities could celebrate the game's birthday. Published by the National Baseball Centennial Commission and highlighted with the centennial seal in red, white, and blue on the front, it contained a concise plan for local participation.

The first part of the pamphlet had messages emphasizing the theme of the benefits of the national pastime for American society that were written by some of the commission's members. According to the publication, local communities could emulate activities in major league cities by staging their own centennial shows with the assistance of their leading citizens. The brochure contained an organizational diagram for local centennial committees that included executive, publicity, programs, entertainment, finance, decoration, tournaments, and clinics. The commission also hoped that each city would file a final report of its activities so that the Centennial Commission could determine the success of their campaign.

With respect to local organizing, the pamphlet suggested that each mayor should call a meeting of the town's leading citizens to discuss participation. They were supposed to emphasize that communities throughout the nation were going to be involved in the anniversary and that for those areas who decided to join in the activities, the economic benefits would be substantial. The Centennial Commission included a suggested address in the package with their pamphlet to be read to local committees. It stressed the role of baseball in the nation's development and encouraged members of the community to give their complete support to the local celebration.

The brochure continued with information concerning the personnel and function of each committee, publicity material that was available, instructions for staging special activities, and tournament plans. The Commission encouraged the purchase of their new centennial poster containing a picture of Uncle Sam swinging a bat and instructions for local printers to insert home game schedules on them. A special concern of the pamphlet was a simplified list of procedures for conducting high school invitational tournaments, amateur contests, special baseball days, clinics, and junior baseball schools. It also made some suggestions as to how colleges and universities could participate in the centennial activities. Rounding out this publication was a brief history of baseball over the last century and information on the museum and the Hall of Fame. A special postcard addressed to the National Commission was also included in the packet with a checklist of items that each community could order which contained information on publicity and tournament plans.[5]

One of the pamphlets that could be ordered to publicize local activities was entitled "Suggested Material for a Public Address by a Civic Leader." It was written up with blank spaces inserted at appropriate spots where local speakers could insert the name of their town, state, or team. The speech recognized that 1939 was baseball's centennial and that the local community planned to join in the celebration. It emphasized the role of the national pastime in the business, social, and economic life of the town. Accordingly, it announced that baseball was "a part of our business as surely as our shops and stores and offices." After all, each community's team served as an excellent form of advertisement for the town; a winning team helped to stimulate excitement and local business activity by bringing in visitors to see it perform. The speech stressed that business and baseball were inseparable in the creation and fostering of goodwill and trade.

Another emphasis of the speech concerned the impact of baseball on the social life of local communities. By participating in regular or make-up games, every youth was developing principles of fair play and sportsmanship that would aid him throughout his life. Every young baseball player learned "to play clean and fair at the top of their form," and in the process they discovered the thrill of doing things correctly and gaining the recognition of their peers. According to the speech, baseball built men of character who would learn how to cooperate in mass activities. As these youths performed at higher levels of the game, they would take further steps "along the road to the rocky realities of life itself." The speech concluded with the idea that baseball had become so second nature to Americans as the national pastime that many people tended to overlook its benefits. However, the Centennial Commission stressed that it should not be taken for granted during its 100th anniversary and that each city in the country should join in the celebration.[6]

Realizing that audiences in larger cities could best be reached via radio broadcasts, the Commission's package also included a "Suggested Radio Speech for a Baseball Player." Designed to be read by a local star player, this speech paid further tribute to the game and the professionals who played it. Accordingly, baseball was proclaimed to be a profession as honorable as medicine, law or journalism. This statement may have lowered some people's opinion of the national pastime. The player who read the speech would also state that he "never met a disreputable character" involved in the game! He would further claim that it was impossible to "spend your nights burning the old candle at both ends and go out on the field the next day and deliver the goods."[7] Some of the game's more notorious carousers and their friends must have smiled at these contentions.

A final speech for the local promotion of the baseball centennial was entitled "Baseball—America's National Game." Specifically designed to enhance community participation, the speech typically stressed nationalism and the benefits of the national pastime. Again, the emphasis focused on the possibilities of world war and concluded that Americans should be thankful that the dangerous talk was being conducted across the oceans while their countrymen were talking baseball. This speech stressed that there was perhaps never a better time to be cognizant of the importance of the game in American life. The speaker would claim that while the "Old World is resounding with the clank of arms and the rattle of guns," in this country "far from the smoke and horror of war," Americans would be listening for the "crack of a hard hit line drive." Baseball had helped to develop a national personality that emphasized a sense of humor, and perhaps this could carry the nation through the difficult times ahead.[8]

Besides the pre-written speeches designed to publicize the centennial and local participation, the Centennial Commission also made available plans for various kinds of tournaments, schools, and clinics. One was concerned with the method of professional organizations to conduct a high school baseball or amateur baseball day. Basically, this was an outline prepared for professional baseball teams to stimulate interest for the sport in their area. Initially, local high school principals would name two teams who would play a game following a regular league contest. Local team authorities would then contact the head of the state high school athletic association to explain that they would assist in furthering the support of the sport at the high school level. Hopefully this would increase interest and attendance for high school baseball games. The brochure also laid out three alternative plans to finance the entire operation and possibly make a profit for purchase of equipment. Finally, it provided information necessary for the publicizing the event. The Centennial Commission stressed that this amateur or high school day should be advertised as recognition of the baseball centennial and the part that these kinds of teams had played in the history of the game. They also urged that the mayor, superintendent of schools, and any former ball players who happened to live in the community be invited to the contest.[9]

In order to utilize the centennial as a method of promoting the interest of youngsters in the national pastime, the Centennial Commission included a pamphlet for extended junior baseball schools. They felt that this program would not only contribute to a better brand of play, but it would also stimulate more of them to get involved in the sport. Although this program was not necessarily designed to produce professional ball players, it would stress fundamentals that would start them in the right direction. Since these types of schools had come into vogue over the last five years, the commission felt they could lay down certain ground rules for local authorities to follow. Consequently, they recommended that classes should be held weekly for about two months. They would be restricted to a maximum of 30 boys, none of whom should be over the age of 17. The rest of the pamphlet described how to obtain the use of fields, train instructors, conduct registration, and arrange the lesson plans. At the end of the instruction period, boys would be rewarded with certificates and a special day at a professional league game. Oddly, the Commission's publication concluded with the statement that baseball was a "sufficiently violent activity to be satisfying to the boy."[10]

Another concept initiated by the Commission to increase local participation in the 100th anniversary was public baseball clinics. As was true of the baseball schools, this was another project that had already been initiated in various parts of the country by professional baseball clubs. Specifically, the clinics were designed to teach rules and strategies to the novice fan. The best time to conduct them was in the pre-season; and, since they were generally conducted by players, managers and coaches, they tended to develop a desirable relationship between them and the local fans that would last throughout the season. The clinics were designed to last about two hours with approximately half of the time spent on rules and techniques and the rest on answering questions. A special emphasis of this activity was its impact on female fans. In fact, this was the only Commission publication that encouraged women to participate. It stated that "in this day and age it applies to millions of her," and they felt that it was beneficial to stage at least one ladies' night. During that evening, the clinic director could provide a brief outline of the game's history that would be designed to be appealing to women. The pamphlet also described how to publicize the clinic and suggested various topics that it could address.[11]

The final publication from the Centennial Commission that could be ordered by local communities involved the method to conduct invitational baseball tournaments. This brochure was specifically designed to promote community interest in the national pastime during the anniversary year. It addressed a variety of questions that local promoters might face in setting up this competition. This pamphlet contained a rather detailed outline that dealt with such specifics as entry blanks, balls, umpires and help in maintaining the facilities during tournament play. They were encouraged to seek cooperation from high school officials and local media sources and to remind these people that all of this was being done to recognize the baseball centennial. The Commission warned the local authorities that they shouldn't budget too much for prizes and awards. A sum of thirty dollars, they felt, should cover this aspect. The brochure had some rather elaborate details for scheduling the tournament, and it encouraged local promoters to contact the National Amateur Baseball Federation or the American Baseball Congress to work out any specific problems they might encounter. Both of these had helped to develop baseball programs in rural areas, small towns, and metropolitan regions in the past.[12]

All of these brochures were designed to insure that the celebration of baseball's first century was truly a national event. Cooperstown was still the central focus of activities, but he Commission felt it was an American celebration because, after all, the game was the national pastime. The Hannagan agency made sure that a major part of their budget was spent on printing up the various pamphlets and mailing them out to interested communities. Before the museum was dedicated, the firm mailed them out to 30,000 Legion posts and junior teams, 3000 high school coaches, 5000 amateur teams, 48 state WPA recreation directors, 500 college coaches, 400 minor league teams, all major league franchises and every member of the commission.[13] Baseball's hierarchy had to be pleased with their effort because it fulfilled a promise that they had made during the inception of the National Baseball Centennial Commission.

Not to be outdone, the Cooperstown Centennial Committee produced a brochure of its own. Published by the Cherry Valley Turnpike Association, it was designed to encourage summer travelers to utilize U.S. route 20 across the central part of the state. At the same time, tourists could take in the sights between Buffalo and Albany—including the village, which was located just south of the route. The pamphlet was replete with photographs of special sites along the road including historic buildings and scenic lakes. The highway itself was historically significant because it had been originated in 1799 and was complete twelve years later. In addition, it was a pragmatic route because it was the shortest and most logical path across the state of New York and allowed travelers the convenience of escaping city congestion. While the brochure contained a great deal of information on numerous sites for tourists to visit, the major emphasis was on the Hall of Fame and the World's Fair. In addition to a picture of the museum, the brochure also contained the addresses of Beattie in the village and Cleland in the city.[14]

With all of the preparations out of the way, Cooperstown was ready for the first big day of the centennial summer. The day before the opening ceremonies, Walter Littell published his typically timely editorial on the forthcoming festivities. According to the local editor, it was a unique celebration which was important to both the village and organized baseball. Part of its significance lay in the fact that it was the first centennial of any sport ever observed in America. During the ceremonies the sport's Hall of Fame, the only exclusive baseball museum, would be dedicated, and the first American postage stamp designed to commemorate a sport would be issued.

Littell recognized that Cooperstown and organized baseball had invested large sums of money, intelligence, and energy into the observance. Naturally, there were high expectations from both sources that there would be an immediate return on their investment. But even if these financial rewards exceeded the hopes of the planners, there were greater awards to garner. For the game's organization, the most important aspect was the exaltation of a contest that was worthy of its recognition as a truly American sport and one that was more widely recognized than any other in the country. Cooperstown had already established a reputation as a literary and historical center long before its ties with baseball were recognized. The lasting reward for its investment in the celebration would be its new claim to fame as the home of the shrine of a competitive sport and a mecca for a new cult of travelers from around the country and throughout the world. Littell felt that baseball was deserving of the recognition being accorded it during the 100th anniversary because it had produced true sportsmen who should be honored "while names such as Doubleday and Cartwright are being exalted.[15]

The national spotlight was focused on Cooperstown when the opening ceremonies took place on May 6th. The plans for the event went off almost like clockwork, and a large crowd estimated to number between 3,500 and 4000 people attended the gala event. The only delay involved a breakdown of an Albany bus which necessitated a fleet of automobiles escorted by two state policemen to bring the occupants into the village. Shortly thereafter, cadets from Manlius and Albany led the parade to the former Phinney lot which had been turned into a professional baseball diamond. Cooperstown was decked out in holiday attire, and the festive atmosphere was enhanced by perfect weather conditions.

After the crowd had gathered at Doubleday Field, Mayor John Boyd Thatcher of Albany gave the principal address. He warmly praised the citizens of the village for their efforts in arranging the celebration. Accordingly, he felt that they had "erected a shrine which honors not only a man but a national game." The mayor went on to contrast conditions in America with those abroad. Thinking of the armed camps of Europe, he was saddened that their youths would be constantly burdened by the militaristic atmosphere. As they prepared their minds and bodies for the awful tragedies of war, they would have little time for the joy, fraternity, and intermingling that could be experienced in the wholesome pastime that was being celebrated. Thatcher thought that it was significant that Doubleday was being honored "not for his bravery as a warrior, but because he pioneered a new and fuller opportunity for life's enjoyment." He declared that if he could offer one solution to the current ills of the world he would "send the dictators and their armies to a baseball training camp to learn something about the American way of life."

Another important figure at the opening ceremonies was Lester W. Herzog, also of Albany, who served as the New York state WPA administrator. He formally turned Doubleday Field over to the village and presented a plaque that was placed on the rear wall of the grandstand near the main entrance. It was inscribed with the following quotation: "Doubleday Field, Birthplace of Baseball— Reconstructed by Works Progress Administration and Village of Cooperstown. 1938-1939." Herzog had been involved in numerous dedications previously from small community works to a major project in Buffalo costing two million dollars, but none had the significance nor the beauty of the one in Cooperstown. He stated that he was proud "to be associated with a government which provided catcher's masks rather than cannonballs for boys." He dedicated the project to the men who had worked on its construction and pointed out they had labored until 4 o'clock that morning to see it to completion. Since the organization that he represented had been criticized throughout the depression as a group that had put forth very little effort, he claimed that their dedication on the Doubleday Field project was proof enough that WPA men wanted to work.

Following Mayor Spraker's acceptance of the field and the plaque, Congressman Bert Lord of nearby Afton presented the museum with the first baseball used by the Washington Senators on opening day. It was autographed by Vice President John N. Garner and the owner of the club, Clark Griffith; and Beattie was in attendance to accept the gift. Lord also mentioned that he had been fortunate enough to have taken part in the dedication of General Doubleday's statue on the Gettysburg battlefield. Following this presentation, a representative of a baseball club in Ballston Spa (Doubleday's birthplace) announced that there would be a special celebration honoring the inventor of the game in the latter part of June and he invited everyone to attend. After the opening ceremonies were completed, the first game on the refurbished diamond took place. While the representatives from Albany had played a major role in the day's activities, they had to be somewhat disappointed that their team lost the abbreviated contest, 9-2.[16]

While these significant events were taking place in the village, other developments were unfolding. Just before the opening day ceremonies, the last six members of the Hall of Fame were added to the list of inductees. All of them were from the pre-1900 era and included Spalding, Radbourne, Anson, Cummings, Ewing, and Comiskey. They had been selected by Landis, Harridge, and Frick—who had worked in coordination with baseball writers throughout the country. In addition, Lester Bursey completed arrangements for the Giants and the Yankees to play games in the village during the month of August. Negotiations with other major league teams were also being arranged.[17]

This wasn't the first time that Cooperstown had served as a source of ball players. Long recognized as the cradle of the game, it was also a place where a number of major leaguers had once played. In a sports column for the Utica Press, writer Jack Kelly quoted George White, a veteran ball player from Ilion, concerning former players from the village. White had pitched there for four summers between 1893 and 1897 and was well aware of other professionals who had done the same. He listed fourteen ball players who made the jump from Cooperstown to the big leagues, the most famous of which was Jack Chesbro— who went on to win 41 games with the 1904 Yankees and would later be elected into the Hall of Fame. According to White, Chesbro developed his famous spitball and change of pace when he pitched in the village in 1895 after he hurt his arm in the Virginia League earlier that season.[18]

The scheduled events for the month of May continued with a game between Amherst and Williams colleges on the 16th. These schools had been credited with playing the first inter-collegiate contest on record on July 1, 1859, and over the years they continued their rivalry by playing 153 games; one had ended in a tie, and the two New England colleges split their remaining ones. The original game was conducted in Pittsfield, Massachusetts, and lasted 26 innings before Amherst won by a score of 73 to 32. At the time a team had to score 65 runs before it could claim a victory. Earned run averages must have been astronomical. Before the historic game took place, Amherst issued a challenge to its opponent, but Williams refused to play until its rival agreed to a chess match which would take place at the same time. Each team supplied its own ball for the contest, and both of them were still on display at Amherst. The 1939 game resulted in another Amherst victory, but this time the score (6-2) was more comparable with modern contests.[19]

The Cooperstown activities continued on May 27th with a combination music festival and baseball game. Musical try-outs were held that morning, followed by a contest between Union College of Schenectady and Rensselaer Polytechnic Institute of Troy. Following the game, a musical program began which included numbers from an orchestra, mixed chorus, and a band. It was held at Doubleday Field with the audience seated in the grandstands and special lighting set up for the occasion. On the same day, another important event occurred when a bust of Christy Mathewson was unveiled at the Hall of Fame. As previously planned, his widow along with the wife of John McGraw were to be present at the ceremony, but Mrs. McGraw was unable to attend. Following this ceremony, another game was played between Christy's alma mater, Bucknell University, and St. Lawrence.

This program was dubbed Christy Mathewson day by the local committee. Mrs. Mathewson made a brief speech recognizing the accomplishments of her husband, and she was followed by three other speakers including L. Francis Lybarger, alumni secretary from Bucknell. The bronze bust, designed by sculptress Gertrude Boyle Kanno, occupied a prominent place in the museum next to the artifacts that Cleland had already received from the Mathewson family. It had been lost following Kanno's death, but the museum officials were finally able to track it down.

While these events were taking place in the village, another Doubleday Field was being dedicated at the United States Military Academy at West Point. Bridagier-General Jay L. Benedict, superintendent of the school, issued the special orders for the Army baseball field to be named in honor of the game's inventor and his name was surmounted on the scoreboard.

Of course, Cooperstown had not forgotten the general; and a special day for him took place on Memorial Day. These events, which preceded the Army-Colgate game, were initiated with ceremonies at the museum when officials unveiled a portrait of Doubleday. This was followed by a similar act involving a plaque at the field entrance. Harris L. Cooke, chairman of the local entertainment committee, acted as the master of ceremonies, and Robert F. Doubleday made a special response for the occasion. The Doubleday family held a reunion in the village to be coordinated with the tribute to their famous relative.[20]

It was important to his supporters in Cooperstown that a contingent of his family be present at the ceremonies. Since Abner had a distinguished career in the military, Lieutenant Daniel G. Doubleday, a 1929 graduate of West Point, was requested to attend ceremonies in the village as a representative of the army. The War Department had designated Daniel as its official representative during the Cavalcade of Baseball. Actually, he was part of the Army Air Corps at Wright Field in Dayton, Ohio, and planned to fly into the nearest airport to Cooperstown. Nelson Greene, chairman of the Fort Plain, New York, Aviation Committee, wrote to him concerning the utilization of their airport with ground transportation to the village from that point.

Daniel was the brother of Robert F. Doubleday of Johnstown and a nephew of William H. Doubleday, Jr. of Cooperstown. Robert was the real authority of Doubleday family history, and he lent the museum two of the family's relics for display that had once belonged to William Harvey Doubleday, his grandfather. They included a tuba and a diary that William kept during his service in the war. William Harvey (1834-1921) was a native of the village and a second cousin of the now famous Abner.

There were other members of the Doubleday family who planned to be in attendance during the centennial celebration and especially on June 12th. They included Mr. and Mrs. William H. Doubleday of the village, Miss Laura Doubleday of nearby Fly Creek, Mrs. Margaret M. Doubleday-Gordon and Thomas P. Doubleday of Long Island, Miss Ann C. Dakin of Cooperstown, Mr. and Mrs. Archibald G. Doubleday and Mr. and Mrs. Robert F. Doubleday of Johnstown, and Mr. and Mrs. Arch N. Doubleday and their son Lawrence of Cobleskill. Another large group was expected from Scarsdale and New York City including George Doubleday, president of Ingersoll-Rand Company, and Frank and Russell Doubleday of the Doubleday, Doran Publishing Company.

A number of other relatives from Binghamton, New York, and Kalamazoo, Michigan also planned to be in attendance.

Twenty-four family members made it to the village for the Memorial Day activities. Major R. Ernest DuPuy represented the Military Academy in the ceremonies where Abner's portrait and plaque were unveiled. Following his dedication speech at the museum, Robert F. Doubleday made a response on behalf of the family. He stated that his famous relative would have preferred that the celebration be quiet and dignified and that the silently directed pageant did "more for the memory of Abner Doubleday and his virtues than any of his spokesmen could ever accomplish by the written or spoken word." Robert continued that Abner was "the victim of two colossal misunderstandings through his century—baseball and Gettysburg." He pointed out that while Abner founded the national game quietly, "he has been publicly and rather caustically castigated for not having said and done more about it." While his famous relative was responsible for the national game, he didn't feel that it was "worth while to put in his claim to immortality as the father of baseball." Rather, Abner "preferred to rest his fame on his military record," if indeed he was concerned about fame at all. Robert assured his audience that the general had "left a subtle heritage of confidence to those of his name" and that his relatives were bequeathed the type of characteristics that they would want to emulate and celebrate.

Robert concluded his remarks on his famous relative by praising the efforts of the Cooperstown Centennial Commission. He pointed out that Abner's "grave might have remained just another soldier's last abode at Arlington" if it hadn't been for the effort of the commission. Following his speech, a procession was formed at the museum's doorway headed up by the local band, and they made their way to the Doubleday Field entrance where the bronze plaque was unveiled. It was a gift from William G. Mennen, who had sponsored the nationwide radio election in which Doubleday had been selected as baseball's most outstanding figure during the first century of its existence.[21]

This concluded the first month of activities commemorating the 100th anniversary of the national pastime, and the success of these events was recognized by Walter Littell in an editorial. He noted that part of the reason for the early accomplishments was the weather which had been unusually pleasant, but he also realized that the people of the community deserved a great deal of credit. As he succinctly stated, "no community the size of Cooperstown has entertained more persons of distinction or been the center of interest of a larger section of the educational world in the same space of time as has Cooperstown during the month of May."[22]

In spite of this initial success, this was no time for the village officials to rest on their laurels. A number of last-minute preparations were taking place including the arrangement of a three-inning ball game involving stars from both leagues during the Cavalcade of Baseball on June 12th. Since no major league games were on the schedule for that special day, each of the sixteen teams promised to send two players each for the contest at Doubleday Field. Another special game that was scheduled at this time involved members of semi-pro baseball. Raymond Dumont, president of their national organization, announced that a unique contest had been set up for August 10th in which the rules that were in effect when the game was invented would be utilized. Participation in the game, which would be held in Wichita, Kansas, during the league's annual tournament, required all players to grow either side whiskers or mustaches in order to be eligible. They were also supposed to wear uniforms that were popular during the early days of the game.

A week before the Cavalcade of Baseball was scheduled to take place, the Cooperstown Centennial Committee held a special meeting in order to firm up some final details for the main event. Some of the long-time participants in the committee were there including Theodore Lettis, Frank Carpenter, and William Beattie; Cleland, who had already arrived in the village, was also in attendance. As most of the preparations had already been planned, the meeting focused on minor concerns such as padlocking the gate to the field to keep the public out while last minute affairs were attended to. At first they planned to charge admission to the field activities for parade participants, but this action seemed to be out of character with the festive mood, and the motion was rescinded. Cleland thought that a special invitation should be sent to Henry Fabian to attend the ceremonies, and the committee also agreed to pay his way in return for the work that he had done on the grounds.[23]

In addition to finalizing these late affairs, the question of the picture on the commemorative stamp was also resolved. On May 17th, Cleland had contacted Lettis on this matter and revealed that it would not contain the picture of any special player—including Cartwright or Doubleday. Instead, the stamp would emphasize the role of sand lotters in the game's development. Although the secretary admitted that those forces supporting the centennial had made no endorsement concerning the picture, they were pleased with the selection of sand lotters who, he felt, truly represented all of baseball. It was also a rather generic choice that avoided any questions about the originator of the game.

Now that the decision had been made by the federal government as to what picture should be used on the commemorative stamp, the postmaster general's office began to lay the groundwork for advertising its issuance. Ramsey L. Black, the Third Assistant Postmaster General, contacted a number of minor league presidents concerning their support for publicizing the stamp throughout their region. In order to accomplish this task, he sent them a small supply of photographs of the model for the stamp that could be reproduced for newspapers. He also included copies of the official announcement pertaining to the first-day sale of the centennial stamp which would take place in Cooperstown on June 12th. Accordingly, the postmaster in the village was authorized to affix the stamp to covers that would be mailed out on that date. These first-day covers would be very valuable souvenirs for baseball fans and stamp collectors, and Black hoped that they would stimulate an appreciation of the national pastime among America's youth.

In his letter to the league presidents, Black laid out the plan whereby one could obtain a first-day cover. Since the Cooperstown post office would be the only one having the privilege of handling the stamp on the first day, collectors were required to send a self-addressed envelope to the village. In order to encourage the interest of youngsters in this project, Black laid out a plan that would also be implemented by some of the major league teams. Local newspapers would carry a picture of the stamp, and young baseball fans would be encouraged to write an essay on the appropriateness of its design in terms of the baseball centennial. Everyone who decided to participate would be allowed to enter their local parks without charge by submitting their essays at the gate. In addition, the Post Office Department made special arrangements with all of their offices to accept single self-addressed envelopes and three cents from youngsters and to forward them to Cooperstown in order for them to obtain the first-day postmark.

A picture of the stamp was released to the public shortly before the Cavalcade of Baseball took place in the village. The central focus was a rectangular picture of youths playing a game of baseball supposedly as it was conducted in the early days. It showed a pitcher taking his wind-up with a batter poised to swing at the forthcoming ball. Players from both sides were shown in what appeared to be a typical game situation. To complement the scene, the picture also contained a house, barn, schoolhouse, and a church. At the bottom was a narrow white panel with the phrase "Centennial of Baseball" in dark letters, and below that was a wider dark panel with the inscription "United States Postage" in white. It also contained an upright panel with a dark background on the left and a superimposed image of the catcher's mask in the center and crossed bats behind it. Between the ends of the bat were the dates "1839" on the top and "1939" on the bottom.

The picture on the stamp satisfied numerous baseball afficionados, but some of its historical inaccuracies did not go unnoticed. In a letter to *The Sporting News*, one fan complained that the federal government had misrepresented baseball veterans. He pointed out that in the picture all of the players were wearing gloves, but historically nobody wore them in the early days of the game. In addition the stamp showed the catcher with a big mitt in a position directly behind the plate. However, the catcher who first put on a glove was considered to be a "sissy" and rather than "taking them off the bat," he usually positioned himself far behind the plate in order to catch the ball on first bounce. Another mistake in the picture concerned the pitcher, who was depicted as being in the middle of his windup with the ball held near his head. The writer recognized that this was an error because in the old days the pitcher didn't throw the ball; rather, he tossed it underhanded on a level with his knees. Finally, the umpire was pictured as standing behind the pitcher when he should not have been stationed on the playing field. The writer could only conclude that Postmaster Farley was as fundamental as William Jennings Bryan in denying the evolution of baseball.[24]

While the issuance of the commemorative stamp signified to many fans that the federal government had sanctioned Cooperstown as the cradle of the game, arguments over Doubleday's claim to fame persisted. Shortly after the season commenced, A. M. Sakolski of New York City wrote a letter to the sports editor of the *Times* newspaper that was critical of his conclusion that Doubleday had originated the game in the upstate village. His statements were based on a thorough investigation of the matter that he conducted a few years before. He claimed that there was no historical evidence to support the Doubleday theory and pointed out that he was actually a plebe at West Point in 1839. Sakolski had searched the records of Otsego County and found that the only reference to the general concerned his Civil War exploits. He lamented that the members of the Mills Commission had accepted a myth without furnishing any supportive evidence.

In opposition to this disclaimer was an article by Edwin C. Hill that appeared in the New York *Journal and American* two days later. The author concluded that the game didn't evolve but rather grew from the invention of Doubleday. Oddly, though, he noted that diligent research in the archives at West Point had produced a statement from one of his professors that young Abner showed little interest in any outdoor sport. Hill added that in all of his writing following retirement in 1873, the general made only a casual mention that he had introduced baseball among Northern troops. He also stated that contrary to the academy's opinion, Doubleday was an excellent catcher. (The origin of these references is unknown and may be exaggerations by the newspaper writer). Hill furthered his contention that the Mills Commission was correct in their choice because they had "sleuthed every available clue and ran down every known story about him."

There was not much new in these statements. Others had drawn similar conclusions in the past, but with the celebration drawing near, more opinions were being expressed than at any other time. When Sakolski stated his contentions concerning the Doubleday myth, the *Times* had followed his letter with a rather weak statement that merely reiterated the findings of the Mills Commission as published in Spalding's book. The newspaper was taken to task on this issue by the noted authority on baseball's beginnings, Robert W. Henderson. He questioned whether anyone should accept the verdict of the committee as the final word on the origin of baseball. Thirty years had passed since their report was first published and during that time, he concluded, a great deal of additional evidence had been presented which completely exploded the Doubleday myth. While Henderson didn't deny that Abner may have played the game in his youth, he also stated that hundreds of other boys throughout the country had done the same long before he did. He was especially upset that the *Times* had cited Spalding as the major source of information on the subject since his more recent research had superseded this earlier work. Henderson specifically cited his most recent publication entitled "Baseball and Rounders" which first appeared in the *Bulletin of the New York Public Library* in April.

While his attack on the Doubleday myth was clearly stated in this article, Henderson was not chastising the people of Cooperstown whom he felt had acted in good faith by erecting the baseball museum. In no way was he insinuating that the building should be moved to another location. On the contrary, he believed that it should remain in the village. However, now that he had incontrovertibly proved that their claims were erroneous, Henderson felt that "it would be unfortunate if they should seek to perpetuate an error"; rather, they should simply admit the truth.

Sakolski's letter drew further response from the *Times'* readers. One man from Long Island was puzzled as to what Doubleday was doing in Cooperstown in 1839 when he should have been at West Point. If Abner had actually introduced the game in the village, then it must have happened in 1840 when he was on furlough. Another man from Brooklyn felt that the Post Office Department may have issued the stamp too early if indeed they wanted to commemorate baseball's 100th anniversary. He pointed out that the Knickerbockers were first organized in 1845 and that the first set of uniform rules was adopted in 1857. He considered the latter date as the most significant since the adoption of a uniform set of rules signified the beginning of the modern game.

Because of these criticisms and especially since one of them had come from an authoritative source, the *Times* took a different stand on the issue. They admitted that while their whole sports department, the Postmaster General, and the Mills Commission had all acted in good faith by accepting the Doubleday story, they appeared "to have struck out." Henderson had exploded the myth in his article "in no uncertain fashion." The newspaper admitted that while he had attacked "a firmly established American legend, his interesting and well-documented study carries undeniable authority." They felt that the baseball museum's curators would serve the truth by setting aside a place for his work.[25]

Not to be forgotten in the rush to promote Doubleday as the founder of the national pastime, the Cooperstown Centennial Committee had also made some arrangements to honor Alexander Cartwright. Lester Bursey contacted Cleland on this matter shortly after the start of the baseball season. Evidently Randolph Summerville had not kept in touch with either man concerning the production he was supposed to stage for Cartwright day and Bursey, as chairman of the program committee, was concerned that he and the secretary might have to become playwrights. As a matter of fact, very little publicity was given to this event and even by late May it was not included in a list of important occasions to be held in the village. Naturally, June 12th was the big day of the summer since it would involve the dedication ceremonies and the enshrinement of the game's biggest stars. Cartwright was simply being relegated to a rather minor rule by comparison.

Actually, the people of Cooperstown didn't have any control over the plans for the Cavalcade of Baseball since this event was entirely in the hands of Landis, Frick, and Harridge. Erwin Glenke found this out when he tried to encourage the local centennial committee to include some residents of nearby Ilion in the June 12th celebration. F. C. Carpenter of the advertising committee explained this situation to Glenke, but he felt that they could take a prominent role in the Cartwright day celebration which was scheduled for later in the summer. Carpenter explained the significance of the former Knickerbocker and revealed that a plaque to his memory had already been placed in the Hall of Fame. In addition he stated that a duplicate would be unveiled in Honolulu at the same time as the one in the village. The committee chairman had already been in contact with the National Broadcasting Company concerning the possibility of a two-way hook up on the radio between the islands and the village during Cartwright day. Bruce Cartwright was scheduled to be the principal speaker at the Hawaii dedication which would be attended by civic leaders and leading athletic figures.[26]

As the June 12th dedication approached, officials of Cooperstown and major league baseball hoped that the controversy over the originator of the game had faded away. However the day before the Cavalcade, articles appeared in newspapers in the nation's two largest cities which disputed the foundation on which the museum was built. One, written by Irv Kupcinet for the Chicago *Times*, praised the work of Chadwick and Cartwright and claimed that the latter had far more to do with formulating the national pastime than Doubleday. He recognized that Chadwick initiated his own profession as the first sports writer for the New

York *Mercury* and was a leading authority of the game during the 19th century. He cited Cartwright as the person who developed the diamond-shaped infield and the rules of the game, but Kupcinet claimed that the sports writer worked in conjunction with him and was mostly responsible for these innovations. No one else had made this claim previously.

Another article, written by Ralph E. Renaud for the New York *Times*, made stinging attack on the Doubleday myth. The author was not surprised by the strong debate that had emerged concerning the baseball centennial because baseball and arguments seemed to go hand in hand. The controversy, as he saw it, began with the assertion that the game was just a century old. It was this statement that had caused "a militant minority" to establish a case of facts against the celebration and attacked the orthodox version concerning Doubleday. Renaud noted that in the Menke article the ruling powers of baseball had cited the wrong place, time, and person concerned with the initiation of the national pastime. He also reviewed the arguments of Henderson as another sports research specialist who attacked the holy trinity behind the June 12th event and claimed that Abner had done practically nothing for the game. Finally, he recognized that Postmaster General Farley had sidestepped the issue by omitting the general's picture from the commemorative stamp.

Typically, Renaud pointed out that the general had written nothing about the game in his memoirs, that the Knickerbockers had long been recognized as the first professional team before the report of the Mills Commission and that Cartwright had been regarded by some historians as the originator of the modern game. However, he added that some of the early experts thought that it came from rounders while others cited old-cat as the game from which baseball developed. He also listed a number of references from people who played the game long before Doubleday's alleged invention and various publications dating back to 1744 which indicated that an early version of the game existed in England. Finally, he noted that the first American book on baseball appeared in 1835 and thus the general could have investigated a widely circulated book of sports that contained the game's rules, the name, the layout of the diamond and the arrangement for an inning. He ended his article by stating that now that the Japanese had learned the game form Americans, perhaps in another century they would claim that a major general from their army should be hailed as the inventor.

An editorial column in the New York *Sun* also blasted the centennial celebration by stating that it simply furthered the "assimilation of a convenient, popular and harmless legend." While the writer contended that historians could easily demonstrate that baseball was played long before 1839 and that its rules were actually taken from other games, this would all be in vain. Since the national pastime was an established American institution, the writer felt that it required a firmly established legend. This was why the American public would embrace such an "innocuous conspiracy."[27]

On the lighter side, a visitor from Canada made a suggestion concerning the originator of the game. Intrigued by the baseball centennial, he had traveled from Montreal to New York City and viewed the game in several big league parks. He made special note of the number of baseball players with Italian and German names in the big leagues. This led him to the comic conclusion that the national pastime could have been developed in one of these European countries. Given the tension that they had been creating throughout the world, many readers may not have viewed his comments very humorously.

Undaunted by this wave of criticism, the Cooperstown supporters continued with their last-minute preparations. The National Broadcasting Company announced that the dedication ceremony would be heard throughout the nation over the Blue Network with host Bill Stern, one of the most widely known sports commentators in the nation. Later in the evening, he would also broadcast his regular sports program from Beattie's office in the museum, and he would probably focus on the high spots of the Cavalcade. Al Stoughton arrived in the village three days before the main event to announce that the time for the dedication had been changed. Originally set at noon, it had to be moved back fifteen minutes owing to a conflict with a speech to be given by President Roosevelt from West Point.[28]

Details for the events of June 12th were announced three days before the ceremony. Secretary Stoughton released a complete program of activities including a list of speakers at the dedication, the names of the major league stars and umpires who would participate in an all-star type game, and some details on the enactment of two old-times games. The first of these latter two involved local high schoolers who would dress in costumes of 1839 to play town ball while the latter employed the services of soldiers from Fort Jay, New York, in an 1850s style contest. The military men would wear handlebar moustaches, side burns and uniforms reminiscent of the Knickerbockers and the Excelsiors. A crowd of 10,000 to 12,000 spectators was expected for the momentous occasion, and those who could not attend would be able to hear it on the radio or see it in newsreels during the following week.

The modern-day players were scheduled to close out the baseball action for the dedication day, but it was not an all-star game as the term is formerly understood. Managers Hans Wagner, coach of the Pirates, and Eddie Collins, business manager of the Red Sox, would simply choose up sides as young boys and girls had always done. Other living immortals would act as coaches and substitutions would be made freely. National League players selected for the special occasion included Bill Terry, Mel Ott, Carl Hubbell, Dizzy Dean, Paul Waner, Joe Medwick and Ernie Lombardi—all of whom would later be elected to the Hall of Fame. The American League was slower to choose its representatives, but they also included an array of stars such as future Hall of Famers Lefty Grove, Charlie Gehringer and Hank Greenberg.

In total, thirty-six major leaguers would participate; but only sixteen from the American League would be there. Even though the Yankees were recognized as baseball's dominant team, having won the last of three World Series and on their way to another championship, only two representatives of the New York team (George Selkirk and second-string catcher Arndt Jorgens, who would have no official at bats that year) would show up in Cooperstown. Naturally, this must have disappointed some of the locals and fans throughout the region since the club was popular, nearby, and loaded with recognized stars such as Joe DiMaggio, Joe Gordon, Tommy Henrich, Bill Dickey, Lefty Gomez and Red Ruffing. In order to augment this rather skimpy delegation from the junior circuit, league president William Harridge asked Yankee manager Joe McCarthy to take a brief vacation from his team in order that he could travel to the village. He stated to the New York skipper that even though the National League would outnumber them at the anniversary exercises, they would have the only manager who ever won three consecutive world championships. General manager Ed Barrow agreed to this idea after some deliberation because he didn't feel that the Bronx Bombers could be "greatly damaged by exposure to the Browns for three days." Harridge also explained the dearth of American League representatives by pointing out that most of their teams would be playing in the west while the senior circuit was scheduled for the east.[29]

Even though General Doubleday had already had a special day in the village, the Cavalcade served to focus further attention on the man recognized for his baseball innovation. Pictures of him were prominently displayed in store windows along Main Street. Anyone who spoke of politics, world affairs, the stock market or anything not associated with the national pastime was viewed with skepticism. Although Doubleday had no children, a flock of his relatives was expected for the big celebration. Besides the 24 family members who attended the special events on Memorial Day, new additions from Binghamton and Kalamazoo would swell the family turnout to at least 35. William Doubleday, Jr., a second cousin, was the only relative from Cooperstown proper, but another second cousin from nearby Fly Creek, an elderly spinster named Laura Doubleday, planned to attend the festivities even though she wasn't particularly interested in baseball.[30]

As the big day drew near, a large response to the celebration began to be received by the museum officials, and some of it came from foreign lands. Arturo Vives Sanchez, president of the Mexican Baseball League, extended his congratulations to America and baseball players throughout the world in his official message. W. Conee Archer of Aquathuna, Newfoundland, acknowledged that he had received a centennial souvenir and was forwarding two homemade balls to curator Beattie. Evidently, Archer had been sent another publication from the National Baseball Centennial Commission that contained information on Doubleday Field, the museum, the Hall of Fame, the invention of baseball, and a complete list of events for the summer. This brochure was distributed across the nation and around the world and was published three different times with each edition containing more information on the scheduled events for the summer as they developed. (The first only made a mention of Cartwright Day while later versions contained the actual date (August 26) of the ceremony.) Evidence of their wide distribution came from the *Japan Advertiser* of Tokyo in which virtually the entire summer program was announced.

Of course, the 100th anniversary also received nationwide publication. The sports section of the Boston *Traveler* contained a half page story on the village by Arthur Siegel, who had actually traveled there to get his material. Robert Winfield of the New York *Times* wrote a major feature for the Sunday edition which reflected a plethora of activities taking place in Cooperstown in preparation for the major event of the summer. Local promoters had set up markers in the shape of giant baseballs along the various routes to the village, and they were flooded with requests for hotel rooms and tickets for the celebration at Doubleday Field. In order to accommodate the visitors, every available facility, even in distant towns, had been organized.

Perhaps the busiest place was the post office, which had been flooded with mail from stamp collectors. The Chicago *Tribune* pointed out that in spite of this national attention, the character of the people of Cooperstown remained unchanged. Although activities were flourishing in the village, only eight full-time people were working on the program. Still, twenty-five part-time employees were hard at work in the local post office where a total of 150,000 orders for the stamp had already arrived and the requests were continuing to come in at the rate of 20,000 per day.[31]

The Cavalcade of Baseball was a major national event, but it would have been diminished without the appearance of the eleven living inductees. Scattered throughout the country and engaged in a variety of endeavors, the former diamond greats responded to their invitations by letter and telegram. George Sisler answered from St. Louis, where he was assisting in the operation of semi-pro activities, and Cy Young wrote from his farm in Ohio. Tris Speaker, currently in the radio business, answered from Cleveland, Hans Wagner replied from his Pirate coaching box, and Connie Mack gave his affirmation from his office at the Philadelphia Athletics headquarters. Another current baseball official was Eddie Collins, who answered from the Red Sox office where he served as business manager. Walter Johnson farmed in Maryland and also served as an announcer on a radio station in the nation's capitol, and he confirmed his arrival in Cooperstown. Grover Alexander, engaged in show business, was discovered in New York, and Babe Ruth was located on a golf course in the same city. Ty Cobb, affluent from wise investments, responded form his estate at Menlo Park, California, that while it was a long distance across the country, he wouldn't miss the celebration.

The only problem in locating the former baseball greats involved Napoleon Lajoie, who was the final player to answer. Baseball authorities scoured the country for his whereabouts and even employed the personal columns in the New York newspapers to find him. The search for Lajoie caused considerable worry for the National Baseball Centennial Commission. When the newspapers in Cleveland picked up on the ads from New York, they promptly forwarded the information concerning his location. Although he had spent the winter in Florida, the former second baseman had returned to his home in Mentor, Ohio. He was discovered in his backyard, sitting in the sun and reading the sports section and he readily agreed to attend the ceremony.[32]

During the week before the Cavalcade, *The Sporting News* ran an article that cited the events that had already taken place in the village and recognized the significance of the June 12th celebration. Even though they appreciated the effort that was being put forth to make the anniversary a success, the baseball bible felt that the real tribute to the game was "being paid daily by the thousands of youths throughout the land" who were meeting on baseball diamonds to "carry on the spirit of competition which inspired Doubleday" and "made fair play and honest rivalry an outlet for the energies of youth." They felt that it was significant that Abner had gone on to win honors on the battlefield while his game allowed the country's youth to conduct its battles on the diamond. With the treat of war circling the globe, it was "comforting to know that Americans are using no other weapon than a ball and a bat" and that conscription wasn't necessary to get youths involved. While the headlines in the sports section carried terms like "bombard," "bury," or "slaughter," nobody was diving for a bomb shelter because everyone knew that this represented the harmless way that Americans let off steam. So the country wasn't merely celebrating the centennial "but also the birth of a democratic institution...in which the only outbreak is one of runs." The village of Cooperstown, therefore, represented a cavalcade "dedicated to the cause of the greatest peace-producing factor in the world—BASEBALL."[33]

When the big day of celebration finally arrived, Cooperstown was ready and teeming with excitement. The well-laid plans of the Centennial Committee and local group went off like clockwork. Even mother nature cooperated with a cloudless day. Ever since James Fenimore Cooper's father founded the village, it had lived a quiet existence that was disturbed slightly by tourists who came to enjoy the sights and comfort of the summers in upstate New York. But June 12th brought a change to all of that. No one was sleeping when the first train in at least five years roared up the Susquehanna Valley along the abandoned spur of the Delaware and Hudson Railroad. Because of this special passenger train, workers in the village had to chop down weeds that had grown two feet high between the rails.

Of course, it wasn't just the train that attracted attention for it contained baseball players (modern and ancient), big league officials, sports writers and photographers—most of whom had never seen the place where Abner Doubleday weaved his magic. Hundreds of local residents and visitors were at the train station to greet the arrival of a host of celebrities who had left the Grand Central Terminal in New York City late Sunday night. A local youngster snapped a picture of the ten-car baseball special and commented to a Chicago reporter that he had never before seen a train in the village. It was a rare day for everyone involved.

Many of the dignitaries went unrecognized by the crowd, and this was especially true of the non-players; but when the moonfaced Babe Ruth appeared, the crowd responded immediately. Among the scouts, writers, announcers, cameramen, owners, officials, umpires, and players, there was a feeling of amazement as they viewed the cradle of the game for the first time. Almost everyone who has ever visited Cooperstown has shared in the pleasant surprise of its beauty. Still, the moment was not without its share of levity. Stage comedian and baseball fan Joe Cook held up an official American League baseball and quipped that it was "the only souvenir not autographed by Babe Ruth." Joining in the frivolity, Carl Hubbell stated with a smile "so this is where all of the grief started."

The first stop for the baseball dignitaries was the spacious and picturesque Cooper Inn which captivated its guests with its authentic colonial design. During the late breakfast, baseball conversations filled the air as old friends got together for the first time in years. Lajoie announced that he had "never had such fun meeting my old opponents." John D. Tener, former National League president and ex-governor of Pennsylvania, summed up the feelings of many when he stated that "nobody except outstanding players should be voted into this Hall of Fame while he is living."

The baseball banter continued, and the scene resembled festivities that were generally associated with the World Series. Hubbell expressed some concern about going to the museum and added jokingly that "they might want to keep my left arm up there." Someone suggested that the Hall of Fame needed a third baseman and that Pie Traynor should pose for a bust. He noted that "they better get me now while I look like something." Hans Wagner picked up one of the black souvenir bats awarded to the immortals and dared Grover Alexander to pitch to him. He added that "every time you grab one of these things, you still think you can hit." Frank Graham, a columnist from New York, observed the Doubleday baseball with its split seams and quipped that it looked "like the Yankees have been playing with it."

Following the meal at the Cooper Inn, the ball players and other guests began to stroll along Main Street before the main festivities took place. Each of them wore a souvenir flannel baseball cap which looked rather amusing on some the dignitaries, but it was a symbol of a very special day. Fans could meet baseball's most famous players as they mingled with the crowd and swapped stories with their contemporaries. It was also a field day for the baseball writers who had gathered in the village from around the country. It was fitting that the game's greatest sports scribes should be treated to the gathering of its most famous players.

Naturally, in such a pleasant setting, everyone had a yarn to spin; and the myraid of journalists missed few notable quotes. Alexander explained to the crowd that gathered around him how his unique delivery caused him to form a blister on his middle finger. The tenderness that resulted forced him to take it easy until a callus formed. When this happened, his teammates always went out for a beer celebration because they knew Old Pete was ready to start throwing. Lajoie autographed a book for a young boy and then told him to ask Ty Cobb for the same because he "might as well get the cream of the crop." Tommy Connally, the senior American League umpire, later congratulated Collins, Lajoie, and Speaker on their excellent speeches and added that "your language has improved a lot."

Witnessing that Collins and Lajoie were talking to Charlie Gehringer and Billy Herman, Casey Stengel called a reporter's attention to this gathering and asked "since when did you see four second basemen as good as those fellows collected in one spot." Ed Barrow recalled how he was the first baseball man to discover Wagner when he was trying to stock his recently purchased Patterson club of the Atlantic League with players. Having heard about the young German kid, he traveled to Carnegie, Pennsylvania, only to find him in a field engaged in a rock throwing contest. Wagner, wearing a derby hat with a chicken feather stuck in the band, was quite a sight, but Barrow soon realized he could play any position and immediately signed him for $125 a month. It was a strange start for the future Hall of Famer.

As the noon hour approached, Main Street became overwhelmed with the masses of people who tried to get close enough to their heroes to listen to these interesting accounts. Car traffic came to a standstill and everyone tried to gather as many mementoes as they could —including paperweights, pillows, windshield stickers, postcards and ash trays. However none of these pieces of memorabilia was as significant to the huge throng as the centennial stamp. The Post Office Department had issued a total of 65 million of them, of which one million were sent to Cooperstown. Naturally stamp collectors recognized the significance of the situation and either lined up at the local post office or sent a representative to do the same. It was a good thing that a cancelling machine was sent to the village because Melvin C. Bundy, the local postmaster, later reported that 450,000 pieces of mail were dispatched on that day.[34]

The first major event of the day began just after noon in front of the new museum building with the dedication of the National Baseball Museum and Hall of Fame. A huge crowd gathered in front of the complex, which was located across the street from the post office. A raised stage had been constructed in front of the edifice and the moving picture cameras and radio microphones were in place so that a national audience could enjoy the festivities. Landis, Harridge, Frick, and Bramham were stationed on the platform along with former National League presidents John Heydler, who played a leading role in the early recognition of Cooperstown, and John K. Tener. Charles J. Doyle, scribe for the Pittsburgh *Sun-Telegraph* and president of the Baseball Writers' Association, served as the master of ceremonies. He opened the festivities by announcing that "we gather in reverence to the game's immortals—living and dead" and that Doubleday's invention would be officially honored for the first time.

Following a brief speech by Mayor Spraker, Heydler introduced the white haired commissioner who gave the major dedicatory address. Landis stated that since baseball had spread throughout the country and around the world, it was "fitting that it should have a national museum." More significantly he added that the museum could be located nowhere except at the birthplace of the game. He paid special tribute to the thirteen pioneers and the twelve players who had been nominated to the Hall of Fame, but he felt that they would agree that the museum should be dedicated "to all America, to lovers of good sportsmanship, healthy bodies, clean minds." For the commissioner those were the real principles of the game.

Before the ceremonies had commenced, the local committee had strung red, white, and blue ribbons across the door of the museum. Following the dedication speech, Theodore Lettis, chairman of the local centennial committee, handed a pair of shears to Frick, who cut the red one. He was followed by Harridge and Bramham, who cut the white and blue ribbons; and then chairman Lettis handed a key to the building to Judge Landis. Doyle read the names of the early pioneers who had already been elected for induction—each being separated by the rolling of drums. This was followed by the mention of the two modern-day players who had already passed away—Willie Keeler and Christy Mathewson. Taps were played for both men.

Then came the moment that everyone was waiting for—the introduction of living inductees. The first man who walked through the doors was Connie Mack, the venerable manager and owner of the Philadelphia Athletics. It was fitting that he should be the initial person because he had been active in the game during a good part of its first century. He was handed a miniature plaque and stepped up to the microphone to speak. Typically loquacious as a speaker, Mack was so visibly moved by the occasion that he was only able to utter haltingly that it was one of the most memorable days in his baseball career.

One by one the other inductees were introduced to the crowd and made their way to the speaker's platform. The bowlegged Honus Wagner was the next member of the group to appear. He amused his audience with the comment that he was born two years before the National League was formed in 1876 and was ready to join it as soon as it opened. He also remarked about the peacefulness of Cooperstown and claimed that it reminded him of Sleepy Hollow. He concluded by stating that in his youth he had walked and hitch-hiked fourteen miles to see Mack catch for the Pirates. Tris Speaker was next and simply echoed the words of Mack. He was followed by Lajoie who said that if the fans were having a good a time as he, then they were having the time of their life. Cy Young, oldest of the modern century ball players, repeated some of the remarks of those who preceded him and added that he hoped that a younger generation would follow in their footsteps.

Walter Johnson was the next in line, and he emphasized his pride in being able to merit the election with the greatest players of his era. George Sisler, the youngest of the inductees, made a brief speech in which he admitted that he had skipped his son's graduation from college in order to attend the Cooperstown ceremony. Eddie Collins mentioned that he had experienced a number of big thrills as a major leaguer but none that could compare with this. Demonstrating his respect for the elite group that accompanied him, the great second basemen added that he would have been happy to be a bat boy for them. The large crowd was well aware of the personal problems of Grover Alexander whose battle with the bottle had forced him to eke out an existence as a member of a West Forty-Second Street flea circus. Still, the hushed crowd listened respectfully as Old Pete recognized that while he had had his share of difficulties, he continued to have his dreams. He wondered, for example, how well he could have done with a team like this. Like the others, he felt that this day was "one of the biggest days I've ever had in baseball."

While Johnson and Alexander were the most popular players in the introduction to this point, the highlight was, of course, Babe Ruth. Long recognized from his super-human achievements on the field and his phenomenal indulgences off the diamond, he was the epitome of extremes; and it was a day for the extraordinary. In addition to being the most revered star, he was also the most recognizable. Nobody had to tell the youngsters in the crowd who he was as he walked onto the stage. The only inductee without a necktie, the Bambino was relaxed in both appearance and speech. It was also a personal celebration for the Babe who pitched his first game for the Red Sox almost twenty-five years to the date. He expressed his thanks for being elected and encouraged young boys in the crowd to excel in the sport so that they could experience the thrill of being a member.

Following Ruth's remarks, Landis declared that the Hall of Fame was officially open; but there was one man, and a very important one, who was missing from the group—Ty Cobb. The player who had received more votes than anyone else had traveled across the country, but he was allegedly delayed by sickness in Utica and arrived just as the ceremonies ended. So while the others stayed on the platform to shake hands and sign autographs, he joined in the festivities. Years later, however, Cobb admitted that he failed to show up on time in order to avoid being in the same picture with Landis due to a long running feud with the commissioner. Because of his irascible personality, the former Tiger great had developed few friendships among ball players; but this was a day for remembering the good times and his former foes and fans accorded him with good cheer.

There was about an hour recess in the festivities as the crowd viewed the museum and enjoyed a brief lunch. Some of the players stayed on to sign their names for the fans, and Ruth joked that he never knew so many people didn't have his autograph. This activity was followed by a parade down Main Street from the hall to Doubleday Field where the baseball activities for the day commenced. The parade was enhanced by a number of people who were dressed in the garb of the mid-19th century and soldiers from Fort Jay who sported handle-bar mustaches. A huge crowd, estimated in excess of 10,000 people, jammed the newly constructed stadium; and they were able to purchase anniversary programs which contained a number of articles on the game's history.

The Cavalcade of Baseball was actually three games in one starting with an example of town ball as it was played over a century ago. Dressed in the apparel of the time, local high school boys participated in the contest. They were followed by the soldier teams who represented two of the first professional organizations (the Knickerbockers and the Excelsiors) in a scoreless two inning contest. To complement the period piece, the umpire wore a silk hat, a frock coat, and carried an umbrella. The players also showed him little respect as was the nineteenth century custom.

The final phase of the baseball exhibition involved the choose-up game which included current major leaguers. Wagner and Collins ran their hands up to the end of the bat in a manner that had always been employed by youths in the pre-game selection of sides. Most of the old-timers enhanced the festive atmosphere by wearing their old uniforms and warming up with the modern day athletes. Once again the highlight of the action involved Ruth who came in to pinch hit. As was true of many of the batters that day, he decided to swing at the first pitch and lifted a pop fly ball that was caught by the catcher. Later, someone asked the Babe why the pitcher didn't give him something easy to hit in a meaningless game. Ruth admitted that he did and added with a grin, "but I can't hit the floor with my hat." The game ended after six and a half innings in order to allow the baseball dignitaries time to make train connections, and Cooperstown's big day came to a close.[35]

The celebration of baseball's 100th anniversary drew a strong reaction from sports writers. Frank Graham of the New York *Sun* claimed that the game "never demonstrated quite so clearly before the place it holds in the American scene." Judged by the scene in the village, he felt sure that baseball would continue in prosperity and popularity for the next century. Walter Littell thought that it was "a fitting tribute to the memory of the inventor...and to the game itself, the development of which over the past century is nothing less than a miracle." He claimed that it was not only a tribute to the living Hall of Famers but also "to the memory of those who have heard the final decision of the Divine Umpire." Dan Daniel of the New York *World Telegram* stated that the village had spent a great deal of time in preparation and doubted that "any other town of its size could have done itself so proud."[36]

Evidently the proceedings in Cooperstown had caused quite an attitude change on the part of major leaguers. Previously viewed as an occasion for laughter, many players joked about it in the early season by referring to the pioneers as Abner Doubleplay and Alexander Cartwheel. But on this day, many of them became sentimental about the role of the birthplace of the game. Indeed, a number of the players had traveled to the village at their own expense and they were awed by the surroundings, the event and the greats of the game. This was quite a reversal, for ball players as a whole were not recognized for being nostalgic or big spenders.[37]

Cooperstown's big day had come and gone. The planning of local and major league forces had culminated in a grand and memorable celebration. It had exceeded everyone's expectations and will long be remembered as the village's finest hour. For many people at the time, it may also have appeared to be the end of a plan to recognize the greatest players and developers, the inventor, and the place of origin of the sport. However, this was more of a first pitch than a final out. The legacy of the initial institution to recognize a sport as an intregral part of American society had just commenced.

Chapter Ten
Same Two Teams Tomorrow Night

Although Cooperstown had managed to pull off its biggest effort to date, there were still a myriad of activities scheduled for the rest of the summer. The events of the month of May had given the people of the village time and experience to prepare for the dedication ceremony, and this was one of the reasons why everything went so smoothly. Still, there was work to be done because seventeen special days remained on the calendar. While none of them would match June 12th in their historic significance, they were still important for those involved. Most of them were special games that had been pre-arranged by the local centennial committee, and some included major league teams such as the Yankees, Giants, and Athletics—the latter participating in Connie Mack Day.

Before any of these significant events came about, however, it was time for writers to reflect on what had already happened. Naturally, one of the first complaints to surface involved people who were not being recognized by the Hall of Fame. Westbrook Pegler of the New York *World-Telegram* noted that the large corps of journalists who followed the game on a daily basis were not being considered. He felt that the centennial observance would be incomplete and unsportsman-like without some kind of acknowledgement because the writers had allowed both ball players and owners a financial foundation through their publicity of the sport. They were the ones who had kept the game in the minds of fans during and after the season, and they were directly responsible for making it a national institution.

Pegler went on to cite a number of sports writers he felt were worthy of recognition. Heading up his list were Ring Lardner and Grantland Rice. While they wrote from conflicting points of view, both were known throughout the country for their expertise in the field. These men were universal in their approach, but there were a number of other writers who were generally associated with a particular city or newspaper. Included in this list were Roy Stockton of the St. Louis *Post-Dispatch*, Bill Hanna of the New York *Herald Tribune*, Bill Phelon of Cincinnati, Gary Schumacher of Brooklyn, Harry Salsinger of Detroit, and Charles Dryden, Dan Daniel, and Rud Rennie of New York. All of these men, according to Pegler, helped to "create the history they write and are of the game itself."[1]

Daniel, in an article for *The Sporting News*, picked up on this theme and added his endorsement for the idea. He noted that no one connected with the ceremony had offered any thanks for "the men who made the heroes of the past famous." He also made a short list of those who warranted recognition and stated that they had developed the heroes of the game by making them "dear to the hearts of all followers of the sport." Daniel recognized that while

201

radio was growing as an important medium of the national pastime, "the high drama of baseball will continue to be set down on white paper." He added that Cooperstown was capable of rectifying the injustice by including writers in the Hall of Fame.

Although Daniel realized that the centennial day in Cooperstown was truly unique, he found fault with certain things connected with it. He was disappointed, for example, that many of the big stars of the current group of players did not participate in the all-star contest. He blamed this on the big league managers who held their best players out and simply didn't appreciate the significance of the event. At first he was sorry that the game didn't involve the two leagues in competition, but later he was persuaded that this would have been in conflict with the traditional all star game that was held every year. Besides, the pick-up exhibition proved to be unique and allowed players of both leagues to fraternize on the same side. Nothing like this had ever happened before, and it made this day seem even more special.

Daniel reserved most of his criticism for the Hall of Fame itself. He recognized that the building and the idea of honoring past stars was in good taste, but he lamented the fact that the inclusion of the old time players was proceeding so slowly. He called on the two major leagues to take any steps necessary in order to see that at least twenty additional heroes from the early days of baseball were inducted. In particular, Daniel questioned the omission of Abner Doubleday. If indeed it was a fact that he invented the game, he queried why he wasn't officially elected to the Hall of Fame. He knew that a painting of the general had been unveiled, but he was not listed as one of those who had been elected. The sports writer also felt that the museum was disappointing because of the lack of memorabilia. He blamed this dearth of material on the fact that the concept of this nature was relatively new and that the search for new artifacts was still being conducted.

Finally, Daniel expressed a concern for the future of Cooperstown and the Hall of Fame. Realizing that the village had had its big day of national recognition, he felt that there was some danger that it would simply be forgotten. The problem, as he saw it, was how to keep the village, hall and museum alive and fresh in the minds of all baseball fans—especially the new ones. He felt that the future was in the hands of the major leagues and suggested that the Cavalcade's pickup game might become an annual affair under their direction. If this were unfeasible, he thought that it might be possible to schedule one club from each league to play a game every year in the village. Not only would this tend to continue its recognition, but it would also help to pay the mortgage on the museum. Daniel hoped that the leagues would assist in defraying the expenses of this event and "prevent Cooperstown from slipping back into that somnolence in which it nestled all through the years until 1939." He hoped that something could be done to keep fans mindful of the "shrine to this greatest of all organized sports."

The most thorough coverage of the baseball centennial was, quite naturally, carried in *The Sporting News*, long recognized as the ultimate source of baseball information. Having originally been published just ten years after the formation of the National League, it had served as a continuous and thorough account of the game. In its June 22nd headline, the publication proudly announced that "All U.S. Celebrates Century of Play." The story was replete with photographs of baseball players, the plaques, the interior of the museum, and Abner Doubleday.

A major portion of this issue was devoted to the history of the game—including its early evolution, the organization of the sport, and the development of Cooperstown's role. In one article, Fredrick G. Lieb listed the arguments between Chadwick and Spalding which ultimately led to the Mills Commission report. The major focus of this piece was concerned with the role of Abner Doubleday and how his game was later perfected by Alexander Cartwright. Accordingly, he stated that the former put eleven men on each side, set up the defense as it basically existed in the modern game, and borrowed concepts from cricket and old-cat. However, Lieb was obviously aware that Henderson had done research in this area because he plainly stated young Abner did not invent the baseball diamond.

After laying out the general's claim to the sports' development, Lieb turned his attention to Cartwright's role. He believed that if Doubleday "planted the seed," the famous Knickerbocker gave the game "its first great impetus." The sports writer claimed that it was Alexander who was instrumental in putting together the first club, heading up the initial rules committee, establishing nine players on a side, three outs in an inning, and setting the bases at ninety feet apart. He also ended the long standing rule established in earlier forms of ball games that a runner hit by a thrown ball was out.

Lieb continued his account of the early history of the game by citing the events involving the Knickerbockers. He recognized the significance of Elysian Fields in Hoboken and claimed that it "deserve(d) a shrine secondary only to the Doubleday Field in Cooperstown, as it was baseball's outstanding field in the period before the Civil War." The author recognized June 19, 1846, as the date that the first game was played under the new rules between Cartwright's club and another known as the "New York Nine." He also stated that the second game of record took place on June 3, 1851, engaging the Knickerbockers against another group from the same city known as the Washington Club. Lieb claimed that the first box score of a game, which also involved the Knickerbockers, appeared in the New York *Clipper* on July 16, 1853. While some of this information was updated by further research conducted years later by Cartwright's biographer, this article served to further his recognition and distinguish his role from that of Doubleday.

In another piece for the same special edition of the baseball newspaper, Lieb focused on the developments that had taken place in Cooperstown from the time that the people in the village first took notice of their newly discovered fame. Beginning with the work of Dr. E. L. Pitcher in 1919, he traced the evolution of Doubleday Field and credited former National League president John Heydler as being the major force behind these events. The author also pointed out that there was "one little fly in the ointment" that remained a sensitive issue in the village. This, of course, involved people who continued to speak of the "Doubleday myth." He pointed out that the supporters of Cooperstown firmly believed in the findings of the Mills Commission, especially since it contained so many reputable luminaries in baseball circles. In addition he noted that the New York State Highway Department evidently accepted their findings for they had erected a sign in the village which labeled it as the cradle of the game.

The museum also contained an artifact which allegedly linked the general with the initiation of the game. This was, of course, the Doubleday baseball displayed above an inscription which claimed that he used it at the time baseball was invented.[2]

The articles by Daniel and Lieb served to further the interest in the Hall of Fame shortly after its dedication. On the one hand, Daniel was one of the few people who was critical of the ceremony and the institution. But it was healthy criticism designed to help induct deserving people and maintain the interest of the American public in the new concept of sports recognition. Lieb, on the other hand, helped to clarify, in the minds of baseball fans, the distinction between the roles played by Cartwright and Doubleday in baseball's development. Earlier sources had given the general credit for certain innovations for which he had not been responsible—especially the idea of 90 feet between the bases. Now the most authoritative publication in baseball circles had apparently set the record straight on this matter. In the process, it had also helped to end much of the argument over the originator of the game. The debate didn't die out completely, but at least for many people the claims of the two men's roles did not appear to be overlapping. From this point on, few fans in America could separate Doubleday from the invention of baseball.

Following the dedication day, a number of special events continued to be celebrated in the village. The month of June witnessed intersectional college games involving teams from different areas of the country and a high school game which included the Cooperstown team. During July there was an Independence Day celebration (matching local players in an all-star game), American Legion Day, Fireman's Day (featuring the Mohawk Colored Giants and the Havana Cubans) and Connie Mack Day (during which his team would play the Penn Athletic Club). In addition, there was a week of baseball games conducted by the American Baseball Congress to select amateur baseball players to represent the United States in international championships in Havana during the next month.[3]

Of the games in July, the most significant was Minor League day which was scheduled for the ninth. Having felt slighted by baseball officials in the earlier events in the village, this was a time for the various leagues of the National Association to play out their role in the centennial celebration. Negotiations concerning their involvement in the 100th anniversary had been initiated during the previous summer, but it wasn't until the season started that the date of their formal participation was announced. George Trautman, president of the American Association and chairman of the National Association's executive committee, was in charge of the Minor League day.

The original schedule of events for the day started with a public reception in the morning, followed by a dedication ceremony at the museum. At this time, plaques would be unveiled that were symbolic of the Association's role in the game. Following a luncheon, a minor league all-star game would take place on Doubleday Field, and this would involve a representative from each of the various loops. The Cooperstown planners also hoped that all presidents and other major officials of each division and the Association would be in attendance. Finally, the minors were sponsoring the memorial baseball library in the museum, and they had already started collecting papers, magazines, books and clippings that pertained to the game.[4]

In spite of all of these arrangements, there was still some negative sentiment in the minors before the dedication day concerning their lack of participation in the Cavalcade of Baseball. W. G. Bramham, president-treasurer of the National Association, didn't share in this feeling and extended a free pass to Cleland for all of the minor league parks in the United States and Canada for 1939. Shortly after this, however, he contacted B. G. Johnson, Secretary of Cooperstown Centennial Committee, concerning complaints that he was receiving from minor league officials. Reluctantly, Bramham communicated the predominant feeling throughout the minors that the June 12th celebration in the village was largely being monopolized by the major leagues. Although the Association president didn't concur with this sentiment, he hoped that by passing on this information to the local committee they could take some kind of action to avoid such a feeling. He tried to drive home the point that it was a celebration of baseball's 100th anniversary and therefore involved all aspects of the game—including both the minor and the major leagues.

The quintessential argument of the minors that justified their belief that they should enjoy equal participation in the Cavalcade centered on sheer numbers. It was the feeling of minor league representatives that they were "the very heart of baseball" because they represented franchises in 280 cities throughout Canada and the United States which constituted 41 leagues. This was compared with 16 cities in the two major leagues. In addition, the minors employed some 60,000 people, which far exceeded the number of major league employees. Thus the minors were far ahead of their big league counterparts in terms of money invested, income disbursement, and attendance. It is no wonder, then, that they felt it would be a grave error for them to be omitted from the biggest celebration of the summer, and they even wanted sandlotters and colleges to be included too. Since Bramham expressed his disagreement with this philosophy, he continued to extend his complete cooperation with the centennial committee and promised to be in attendance for the June 12th festivities.

As chairman for the local executive committee, Theodore Lettis contacted Cleland concerning this correspondence, and the museum's secretary immediately laid out a plan designed to ease the hurt feelings on the part of the minors and to deny any implication that major league officials were running the show. Realizing that Bramham's letter represented a serious problem, he felt that it was imperative that no one should know "that there was any connection between Cooperstown and New York." Although the minor league officials had previously met with Cleland, they were evidently unaware of his link with Frick and other major league officials. Wishing to avoid any conflict of interest, the secretary listed some suggestions which Lettis might incorporate in his response to Judge Bramham.

In the first place, Cleland pointed out that the June 12th Cavalcade had originally been set aside to represent the national pastime and that it had been designed to cover everything that had developed in the game over the past century. This included every level of baseball from the sandlotters to the majors. The Cooperstown committee had previously agreed that the big leagues would undertake the entire program for that day while they would simply provide facilities for the dedication and the baseball activities along with bands, costumes, and provisions for dignitaries. The secretary pointed out that he had only recently received a tentative script for the cavalcade and that it emphasized old-time baseball rather than just the current major league variety. He also stressed that the entire Cooperstown program below the minor league level had been under the direction of their centennial committee and they left the major leagues and the National Association to put on their own program, with local assistance, on the day provided.

Cleland felt that it was significant that the commemorative stamp emphasized the role of sandlotters and didn't recognize any major league player or official. This decision seemed to destroy any link between Cooperstown and the big leagues and simply heightened the awareness of the nation's baseball fans in the 100th anniversary. The village, he pointed out, was only interested in the game as a whole and its recognition as the birthplace of the sport. He requested that in his foregoing letter to Bramham, Lettis should make no mention "of any controversy between the Majors, Minor Leagues, or any other individual interested in baseball."[5]

The friction created by not including minor league participation in the June 12th ceremonies caused serious problems concerning their involvement in Minor League Day. Since many officials of the National Association felt slighted at being relocated to a less significant event, their interest in Cooperstown had begun to wane. Perhaps unaware of their feeling of rejection, the National Baseball Centennial Commission contacted officials of the Pennsylvania State Baseball Association concerning other centennial plans. C. O. Brown sent similar letters to club officials and league president Elmer M. Daily that were intended to stir up interest in the centennial. He included two plans that outlined the procedure of setting up local baseball clinics which, he felt, were both inexpensive to initiate and profitable for those willing to participate. Brown also asked that they furnish him with any newspaper clippings after the clinics had been conducted. Some of the minor league officials may have been put off by the fact that the very organization that had excluded them from the Cavalcade was now attempting to exploit their organizations in promoting the centennial. They had to be aware of the painful irony that Brown's letters were dated June 12th.[6]

Even though the minor leagues may have felt excluded by the Cooperstown celebration, the plans for their big day continued to be carried forward by the village committee and National Association officials. As head of the operations, George Trautman faced numerous problems in the preparations of the July 9th event. He contacted the Lannon Manufacturing Company and asked them to provide a dozen baseballs for the game to be played that day. Honored by the proposal, company president G. S. Lannon, Jr. not only forwarded them promptly but also promised to have one bronzed and sent to the museum as a souvenir. Trautman also initiated a call for players from the 41 divisions of the Association, but his request did not produce a uniform acceptance. Since there was no way of enforcing the directive, some divisions simply failed to reply. A number of league presidents cited financial and personal reasons for rejecting his request. Because each league had to pay for sending a representative, it was not inclined to comply—especially if located a great distance from Cooperstown. Others felt that it would be detrimental to the pennant drive of a particular team if it had to lose its star player for any length of time.

As Minor League day approached, the village newspaper chose to emphasize those big-name players who had agreed to participate rather than those who were missing. First on their list was Joe Hauser, a former major leaguer who had gained fame in 1933 by hitting 69 home runs for Minneapolis and setting an International League record with 63 round-trippers for Baltimore in 1930. Wally Schang and Benny Bengough, both former major league catchers, represented the Canadian-American and International loops. Other headliners included Dutch Ruether, a past big league pitcher from the Pacific Coast League, and Bob Smith, who had pitched in the National League and represented the Southern League.

Although many of these players seemed to fulfill the promise of making the minor league game one of the big events of the summer, there were some problems with these selections. While Hauser was considered a major star in the Association's history, he was currently a manager of a Sheboygan semi-pro team. In addition, Schang was Ottawa's manager and Bengough served as Newark's coach. Ruether was able to participate only because he happened to be on a scouting trip. Smith, near the end of his career, made only brief appearances for Chattanooga during the 1939 season. Other representatives included one player who hit only .207 that year and another who was not even active. Perhaps the biggest disappointment came from the lack of representation from 17 leagues, which forced village officials to utilize local talent as fillers.

The Cooperstown Centennial Committee had a number of reasons for scheduling the Minor League day on July 9th. For one thing it was a Sunday, and local officials felt that this would aid attendance figures by attracting visitors from the surrounding territory to witness the unique event. In addition, they had set up another special train to leave the village directly following the game which would arrive in New York City on Sunday night. This would not only allow travelers to have a complete day to visit the world's fair, but they could also attend the major league all-star game at Yankee stadium on Tuesday. While this set up may have appealed to fans, minor league officials were dismayed because many of their seasonal all-star games were occurring about the same time, and one even fell on July 9th. Since Minor League day had not received a great deal of publicity, some people felt that slating it only two days before the big league annual contest actually detracted from it.

In spite of these problems, there were some attractive features about the program. A number of the players who were invited were having great years, including Warren Huffman (who hit .415 for Stauton in the Virginia League). In the previous year Cyril "Butch" Moran led all minor league rookies in hitting. However, although many of the leagues sent legitimate representatives, only two (Johny Hutchings and Joe Callahan) would later make it to the big leagues.

The biggest drawing cards for the event were not so much the players, but the managers, umpires, and special representatives. Mike Kelley, president of the Minneapolis Millers of the American Association, and Spencer Abbott, pilot of the Springfield, Massachusetts, club in the Eastern League, would manage the rival clubs, and both were well recognized figures in the minors. The former had been in baseball for 43 years and the latter for 39 seasons. Four umpires who had collectively served over a century as arbiters were assigned to work the contest. They included William Carpenter (International), Ollie Anderson (Western Association), Harry Johnson (Southern) and Charles Moore (Eastern). Anderson, who officiated from 1905-36 had called over 5000 contests without missing a game. Perhaps the most significant figures in attendance were John H. Farrell of Auburn, New York, and Thomas J. Hickey of Chicago—the only two survivors of the seven men who formed the National Association in 1901. The former previously served as the organization's treasurer and the latter had been the president of the American Association.[7]

Preparations for the July 9th event were laid out in advance beginning with registration at the Cooper Inn. Ceremonies at the museum commenced shortly afterward, and they took place on the second floor which had previously been vacant. The baseball library, which contained over 400 volumes and documents was formally dedicated; and a large inscribed bronze plaque was unveiled. The original plan had called for several of these tablets, and some minor league supporters may have been disappointed that only one was included in the ceremony. The plaque emphasized the seven original founders of the Association who had established the organization for "community participation and recreation and to perpetuate for the game integrity of administration and high standards of excellence in performance." Recognizing the contributions of minor league baseball, the plaque also contained a complete list of the divisions which were part of the Association.

Theodore Lettis served as master of ceremonies for the dedication and, following the invocation by Father Harold J. Martin, president of the Canadian-American League, he introduced Mayor Spraker—who made some introductory remarks. The village leader stated that local committee members had selected the plaque along with Commissioner Landis less than a month before the ceremony with the hope that it would be the symbol of good sportsmanship. He was followed by Judge Bramham, who commented about the role of minor league baseball in teaching the rudiments of the game to future major leaguers. Commissioner Landis was the next speaker, and he stated that the ceremony was designed to recognize the organization that was the very foundation of baseball. Since young players would have their first professional experience at this level, he felt that it was impossible to minimize the importance of the Association in the hierarchy of baseball. Finally, George Trautman, speaking on behalf of the minor league players and members, formally presented the material collection to the museum with the hope that it would become the most complete library in existence.

Following the ceremonies at the museum, the participants were given a tour of the facilities, and luncheons were held for players and club officials. Festivities at Doubleday Field took place in the afternoon. It included a parade with Landis and Kelley, who were seated in an old-fashioned carriage. The latter wore clothing from the pre-Civil War era and it was the most impressive part of the celebration. A special tribute was made to Deacon White, who was considered to be the oldest professional ballplayer before his death during the previous week. Throughout the game that followed, numerous dignitaries were introduced to the audience over the public address system. They included William

Harridge, Landis, Bramham, Trautman, and a number of other minor league officials.

As for the game itself, there were a number of disappointments. For one thing, since the various leagues had to pay their players' way, some of the representatives were not in attendance. Also, the crowd was sparse and officials blamed this on the high price of the tickets. Perhaps because of the lack of fans, this would be the first and last minor league game ever conducted in Cooperstown.[8] This was also a harbinger of things to come because the minor leagues have been almost totally ignored by the Hall of Fame since that time in spite of many complaints.

Regardless of the negatives associated with Minor League day, certain people continued to look at the brighter side. Elmer M. Daily, president of the Mid-Atlantic League, congratulated Trautman on a job well done and recognized the overwhelming nature of assembling a large number of leagues scattered throughout the United States and Canada. L. H. Addington, director of publicity for the National Association, contacted sports editors throughout the nation in order to thank them for their cooperation in making the 100th anniversary a success. Indeed, even though the attendance at Minor League day was sparse, the event was well covered by the press. This publicity did not come cheaply, however, because the minor league organization appropriated five thousand dollars during their annual convention in New Orleans to cover the expense of its participation in the Cooperstown centennial.

Although the National Association made every effort to make their contribution to the museum worthy of the dignity of baseball's new showcase, they were always subject to the approval of the local committee. This included all of the materials that they gathered for the library. Minor league officials also hoped to continue the process of making donations in the future, and they were fully aware that these items had to be acceptable to museum trustees. An example of this control was the very reason why only one plaque was installed for the entire Association membership. Originally, they wanted one for each league to be displayed in the museum, but this idea was abandoned for a variety of reasons. Paramount of the excuses was that the Cooperstown museum committee objected to it. Following this refusal, the minor league officials proposed the single plague concept and it was readily approved.

As chairman of the Association's executive committee, George Trautman made some suggestions to William Beattie concerning the perpetuation of the museum facilites. He felt that it would have a better chance for continued success if its board of trustees officially included representatives of the minor leagues and members of the Baseball Writers Association along with those of the majors. Trautman believed that in this manner the museum could weather its formative years by attracting attention from all aspects of the sport.[9] To his dismay, only half of this suggestion was eventually adopted as minor league stars never received official induction.

As the centennial summer moved into its August phase, the village prepared for another series of games. These contests included two involving a team from Cooperstown, and one of them featured a group from Ballston Spa—Abner Doubleday's birthplace. Three major league games were also scheduled for this month, but only one was actually played. This contest, which attracted a capacity crowd of 12,000 fans, involved the Yankees and their farm club from the International League—the Newark Bears. The Giants contest, which had been set up before the baseball season started, was later cancelled. Another event that took place outside of the village at this time involved the baseball centennial flag raising ceremony at the World's Fair in New York City. Although the National Baseball Centennial Commission had agreed not to promote their involvement in the 100th anniversary, they encouraged Cleland to attend the festivities if at all possible.[10]

About two weeks after the Cavalcade, William Beattie received some visitors at the museum who were specifically interested in the recognition being accorded to Cartwright. Five visitors from Hawaii came to the village to observe the new facilities, including Loui Leong Hop, sports writer for the *Honolulu Chronicle*. The museum's curator quickly gathered together as many members of the centennial committee that he could find so that they could witness a small ceremony in which the five Honolulu representatives hung leis on the Cartwright plaque. The Hawaiian sports writer was evidently impressed that the famous Knickerbocker's plaque had been given an important position of honor in the museum since it was located just to the right of Doubleday's portrait. Beattie extended every courtesy to the visitors, including a luncheon at the Cooper Inn. Cleland informed the Honolulu Chamber of Commerce about the visit, and they responded with an appreciative note.

It's unfortunate that the Hawaiian contingent couldn't have delayed their visit by two months, for they missed the special day for their honored son— Alexander Cartwright. On August 26th, the founder of organized baseball became the focal point of the centennial program. However, Honolulu was not represented, and residents from Fort Plain, New York, took their place instead. (What had started out as the Fort Plain-Cooperstown Community Day was changed on the schedule.) Festivities for the day began with a parade from the museum to the ball park in old-fashioned apparel. The ceremonies that followed included a sketch depicting how the original baseball diamond was first laid out. After this took place, players and participants were given leis and pineapple juice which had been shipped over from the islands. A game between the two New York communities completed the action for the day. It was witnessed by a scant crowd of only 350 people—many of them from the visiting community.[11] Given Cartwright's status in the game's development, it was a meager acknowledgement compared to other centennial festivities that summer.

There was one final day of celebration to honor John Terry McGovern, a well-known member of the Olympic Committee and president of the New York City Baseball Federation. The Labor Day festivities were to be honored by the presence of the distinguished radio commentator Lowell Thomas, but the National Broadcasting Company required him to stay in New York City to cover news accounts coming from Europe about the war. McGovern, then, was the central focus of the day; and he was something of a local hero. About a half century before, at the age of eleven, he arrived in the village as a runaway by jumping off a boxcar. Through the sympathy afforded by local residents, he stayed on to graduate from high school and went on to get a degree from Cornell University. He moved to New York to practice law and vowed that he would try to do the same favor for poor boys in the big city. This promsie was the impetus behind the formation of the baseball organization which grew to 270 clubs with over 6,000 players. McGovern's special day was a fitting climax to the summer's celebration.

The centennial season had proven to be an extremely successfull program for the village and the museum. Of course, the number of tourists that summer had increased dramatically; and some local businesses profited. According to Beattie's calculations, the number of admissions to the museum had climbed to 27,858; only one state, Wyoming, was not represented in the total. As might be expected, New York led the way with over fifteen thousand visitors. Other states with fairly large numbers incuded New Jersey, Pennsylvania, Ohio, Massachusetts, Michigan, Illinois, Connecticut and Texas. It probably surprised museum officials that people from thirty-one foreign countries also visited the shrine. They included a number of European and Latin American countries in addition to visitors from Africa, China, Japan, and India.

As the centennial celebration drew to a close, it was time for reflection; and Littell, once again, tried to give some meaning to the events of the summer. For the taxpayer, the economic benefits were tremendous. The addition of Doubleday Field, which had been financed by local revenue, and the Museum and Hall of Fame, basically supported by the Clark family, would be a major asset for future prosperity. As the editor pointed out, both facilities were "potent attractions to tourists and others who always will come to see the spot where Abner Doubleday laid out the first diamond and enunciated the first rules of the game." Littell had good reason to emphasize the fiscal aspect since people in the area had invested in other projects in the past with little to show in the form of profits. Not only had taxes been raised for field construction, but people of the community had also purchased certificates from the centennial committee the previous spring to finance the entire celebration. He reassured them that they had made a wise investment. For one thing, the utilization of the work relief authority allowed the village to spread the cost over a period of years. In addition, one-third of the certificates had already been paid back; and he felt that the rest would be taken care of in the near future.

Aside from money matters, Littell focused on the social impact of the centennial. For one thing, all had not gone well; but in the process, the local organizers learned to cope with defeat. Even though some aspects were financially rewarding, he admitted that "the income from the various events fluctuated widely." In addition, some of the early plans had not come together. For example, the New York Giants never appeared as scheduled and, due to illness, Connie Mack could not come for his special day. The editor was not discouraged, however, as he felt that it was only natural to have disappointments with "a program of so pretentious a character." Boosterism had evidently not clouded his reasoning powers, and he realized that a lack of management experience had also hurt the local program. Still, Cooperstown had become recognized as the shrine of the national game, "from the President down to the most humble fan." Publicity in magazines, newspapers and film helped to spread this message throughout the country and so did the 75,000 visitors who made their way to the village that summer. Littell felt that the centennial would eventually result in the community being recognized "as an ideal American village and summer resort."[12]

With the conclusion of the events in Cooperstown for the summer of 1939, the celebration of baseball's 100th anniversary came to a close. Of course, this meant that the Centennial Commission would end its operations, but before this occurred, Al Stoughton contacted John Doyle and Cleland concerning their endorsement for his future employment. He was especially interested in editorial work and public relations and hoped that Stephen Clark would be interested in his services. Before he terminated his job, he made a study of all of the correspondence received by the National Baseball Centennial Commission according to geographical distribution. This recapitulation contained some interesting facts about the interest in the baseball anniversary throughout the nation. The leading areas were New York, Illinois, Pennsylvania, Ohio, and Massachusetts (which ranked sixth). Their interest was based on the fact that together they accounted for 12 major league cities. However, this trend was not consistent because five of the remaining top ten states (Minnesota, Indiana, New Jersey, California, and Oklahoma) had no major league teams at all.

The other major league areas (Missouri, Michigan and the District of Columbia) were well down the list, but the statistical analysis revealed that every state in the Union had replied. The fewest letters came from Idaho, Mississippi, New Hampshire, Vermont and Wyoming. The interest in the centennial was not confined to the United States. Foreign countries or possessions heard from included Alaska, Puerto Rico, Virgin Islands, Canada, Mexico, Cuba, Japan and Australia. Correspondence was particularly high during the centennial summer with the number of letters averaging forty per day from April through July.[13] Although the Commission put on a heavy advertising campaign through the Hannagan firm, a great deal of credit has to be given to Alexander Cleland who, with very little experience in the field, had spread the word of the museum, anniversary, and Hall of Fame in their formative years.

In his final act for the Commission, Stoughton provided Doyle with a recapitulation of the year's events in Cooperstown. As the head of the American Sports Publishing Company, Doyle wanted to use the piece in the *Spalding-Reach Official Base Ball Guide* for 1940. The annual baseball magazine contained an editorial comment section, and the leading article was concerned with the centennial celebration. It didn't bear much of a resemblance to the one written by Stoughton, but it contained essentially the same kind of information.

On October 6, the day after Stoughton finished the piece, the National Baseball Centennial Commission officially closed its doors. In the past year, the organization had done a tremendous job advertising the 100th anniversary, coordinating baseball programs throughout the country and making the Cavalcade of Baseball an occasion to be cherished by everyone in attendance and recognized by future fans as well. For many of the people who were involved in promoting the centennial celebration, it was the highlight of their professional lives.

Landis had to be pleased with the work of the Hannagan firm. The centennial celebration was not only a huge success, it was also cost effective. Originally contracted for a $100,000 budget, Hannagan returned $35,000 to the commissioner. Baseball's authorities wouldn't forget his services for 1939. Eleven years later Frick approached him for the purpose of promoting the 75th anniversary of the formation of the National League. This time, however, frugality wasn't emphasized. In a meeting with Commissioner A. B. Chandler, the Hannagan company was awarded a hefty contract calling for a $50,000 fee and a $100,000 expense account. Due to the intense criticism of major league owners concerning the cost of promotion, the contract was cancelled and the jubilee plans were aborted. It was an embarassing situation for both Frick and Chandler.[14]

The Hall of Fame officials had little time to revel in past glories because the final act of the 1939 dedication was really the first act in its future legacy. Beattie was proud to report to Cleland that the paid attendance at the museum had passed the 30,000 mark. By the summer of 1940, Beattie stated that people from every state in the country as well as several foreign countries had toured the baseball museum. Attendance figures dropped off sharply during the war years, but they picked up dramatically during the late 1940s and finally topped the 100,000 mark in 1952. By July, 1987, the Hall of Fame had been viewed by more than seven million visitors.[15]

Of course, the Hall of Fame wouldn't have continued to attract visitors if new players were not inducted. Even though the rules of the institution required 75% of the votes from the Baseball Writers Association and generally required a player to be retired for five years befoe being considered for induction, an exception was made for Lou Gehrig. His consecutive game streak of 2,130 came to an end in the 1939 season as he was tragically struck with a form of paralysis. Stunned by the loss of one of baseball's greatest and most respected players, the writers agreed in December, 1939, by a unanimous vote to suspend the rules and induct the famous Yankee first baseman without an election.

As soon as Cleland found out about Gehrig's induction by acclamation, he contacted Beattie in order to arrange a special ceremony for him in the summer of 1940. He asked the museum director to contact Sid Mercer, the Writers' Association president, to encourage Joe McCarthy to bring the Yankees to Cooperstown for a ball game on the day of Gehrig's enshrinement. Beattie had already contacted Yankee owner E. G. Barrow for the purpose of acquiring Lou's uniform for display in the museum. Beattie also encouraged Barrow to retire Gehrig's number permanently, and he immediately accepted the proposal. The director also hoped that the hall's newest member would be in attendance for his induction ceremony and predicted that a crowd as big as the one for the cavalcade would show up.[16]

The election of Gehrig and the acquisition of his uniform were important steps in the continuance of the Hall of Fame legacy. They were significant in overcoming the fears of some writers and local officials that Cooperstown might slip from the memory of fans throughout the country. Another action designed for the same purpose was the scheduling of a major league game for Doubleday Field during the 1940 season. A game between the Cubs and the Red Sox was set for June 13th, and it represented the first exhibition contest between two major league clubs on the historic site.[17] Not only did this game help to ease the financial burden of the museum and establish a precedent for future tilts, it was an important step in perpetuating the baseball shrine in the minds of fans, players, and major league officials.

With the continued success of the Hall of Fame virtually guaranteed by these actions, the men who were brought together in its development began to move in separate directions. For Walter Littell there was really nowhere to go. A long time resident of the village, he continued to serve the people of the community and the museum. In addition to his work with the Methodist church, the New York State Historical Association, the Farmers' Museum, the local hospital, the Rotary Club and the Scriven Foundation, he also aided the baseball shrine. After its dedication, he was a member of its Board of Directors as well as being secretary of that group. He died in Cooperstown in 1955 at the age of 75.[18]

As editor and president of the local newspaper, he had served his community with pride and distinction. Unfortunately, his role in the development of baseball's shrine went relatively unnoticed. Local residents realized that he had served the museum well, but his recognition was never extended beyond the village. Future articles on the origin of the Hall of Fame often mentioned the discovery of the Doubleday baseball, but most of them didn't cite Littell as the person who brought it to Stephen Clark's attention.

Even though Clark was an important figure in the creation of the Hall of Fame, he preferred to stay in the background after the original idea took hold. Satisfied that Cleland could handle the day-to-day chores in bringing the matter to fruition, he served mostly in an advisory role. Although he was a member of the local centennial committee, Clark was typically low-keyed in his approach. As a leading citizen in the community, however, his opinions were sought after and respected. In addition to subsidizing the museum, the Clark family helped to support the shrine during the lean years of World War II. Typically, however, he stayed out of the spotlight even though he financed the construction of the building and served as president of the Hall of Fame from its dedication until his death in 1960 at the age of 78. By the time of his passing, he was well known as an industrialist, philanthropist and art collector.[19]

More than any of the major figures associated with the beginning of the Hall of Fame, Ford Frick rose to national prominence. He continued as president of the National League until 1951 when he became the third commissioner of baseball—a post he held for fourteen years. Following his retirement from this position, he served as chairman of the board for the Hall of Fame from 1966 to 1969. He died in Bronxville, New York, in 1978 at the age of 83 following a lengthy illness. He was the only one of the four major figures who was eventually (1970) elected into the Hall of Fame. Before he died, Frick reflected on his life in baseball and claimed that his proudest achievement was his role in starting the baseball shrine. "That is my baby," he claimed, "I started it. This was in 1936 when I was president of the National League." He claimed that the hall began with the discovery of the Doubleday baseball and that several years later Clark sent Cleland to meet with him and the secretary suggested an all-star game for the village as part of a one day celebration. However Frick added "Hell, why do that? If you're going to do that, why not start a baseball museum, a Hall of Fame, and have something that will last."[20]

Without question Frick was the major connection between Cleland and Clark and organized baseball. Neither the commissioner nor the American League president ever took interest in the museum project until the centennial year. It was Frick who gave initial endorsement to the project and he continued to support Cooperstown's recognition. However, he can't take credit for all of the developments in the village, and his recollection of dates certainly wasn't accurate. For one thing, the museum was definitely not his idea; it was originated by Cleland in 1934, and his first correspondence with the league president took place in the next year.

While most sources also give Frick credit for the Hall of Fame concept, this act is not without some disclaimer. In a letter to some friends in Brooklyn at the beginning of the 1939 season, Cleland recognized that, in the past, they had "rather smiled when I mentioned the Hall of Fame and the Baseball Museum." Realizing that the great day of its dedication was nearing, Cleland encouraged them to listen to the ceremony on the major radio networks. He added that Doubleday Field had been "entirely reconstructed since I had my idea of the Hall of Fame." This was the only occasion that Cleland ever took credit for the concept. While critics may claim that he may have been merely boasting to some friends in a personal letter, this was not typical of his personality. Generally reserved and unassuming, it was uncharacteristic for him to seek glory, whether he deserved it or not. However, if he did propose the idea to Frick, he never made record of the fact with the exception of this letter.

The possibility that it was Cleland and not Frick who originally proposed the Hall of Fame idea has some merit. When the secretary first heard from the league president in early February of 1935, the correspondence was only concerned with the museum component. In mid-May, Cleland wrote to some radio officials, and this was the first time that the term Hall of Fame appeared in his letters. Frick did not publically use the phrase until August when the official announcement of the shrine took place. It was a common name that sports writers had used for years to signify a stellar performance by a player. Therefore, neither man could be given credit for its inception.

Actually both men may have had some input into the idea. According to Don Cleland of Las Vegas, Nevada, his grandfather was the person who actually originated the plan to recognize the greats of the game through enshrinement. He wanted to include ten players—five from each century. However, Frick was concerned with the possibility that future stars would come along who would surpass the original members. He therefore suggested a perpetual system that would allow them to be included. This was the league president's real contribution; and, together with the secretary's plan, the actual Hall of Fame concept emerged.

The source of Don's information was his grandmother, Alvilda. She was the person who encouraged her husband to keep his papers concerning his work on the project. To her, it was simply his project. His personal files and the collection therefore belonged to the Cleland family. Alvilda was upset that Frick was taking all of the credit and wanted her husband to have his own records on the subject in order to verify his role in the Hall of Fame development.[21]

Cleland continued to serve the Hall of Fame as secretary until his retirement in 1941. Always regarded as a social worker, he had developed a warm working relationship with his boss, Stephen Clark. A man of many talents, Cleland was named the director of the Rivington Health Center in New York in 1938 at the same time that he was serving the Hall of Fame. When he retired he still held the position of director of the Clark House. He continued to receive Hall of Fame yearbooks and was always invited to inductions, but health problems prevented him from attending.

Cleland died in Whippany, New Jersey in 1954 at the age of 77. The former executive secretary was eulogized as a moral and ethical person who treated people with fairness and charity. Not being affiliated with any particular church, he was unencumbered by religious dogma and ritual. Following his cremation, Walter Littell reminded the residents of his contribution to the Hall of Fame in an editorial in the Cooperstown newspaper. Recognizing his significant role in the Hall of Fame's great success, he wrote that "High tribute is due to the memory of Alexander Cleland for his contribution to this program."[22] It was fitting that the man who had worked so closely with Cleland during the formative years of the baseball shrine should pay tribute to his old associate.

While the Baseball Hall of Fame grew in terms of international recognition and came to be known as the foremost museum dedicated to sports figures, it had a more widespread legacy. Even before the dedication ceremony took place, the famous sports writer Grantland Rice suggested that other sports should adopt the concept of a shrine for recognition of greatness. He felt that these kinds of organizations would enhance the background, history, and tradition of various athletic endeavors. Recognizing that the United States was a country that deified sports and its heroes, he thought that these shrines would help the great names of each activity to last forever.[23]

Rice's suggestion was based on two important factors—idealization of America's heroes and the surprising success of the baseball shrine. When the idea of a museum and hall of fame were first proposed, they were based on the first project of its kind—The Hall of Fame for Great Americans. It was dedicated to significant individuals who made major contributions to the establishment and growth of the country. Originally located on the campus of New York University, it was founded by the school's chancellor, Henry Mitchell MacCracken, in 1900. He felt that the institution would "teach youth that leaders in science and scholarship may be as great as military and naval heroes."

The election process for this unique organization began shortly after it was instituted with the public being invited to submit nominations. By May of that year, the University Senate had received over 1000 names and 100 prominent people throughout the country were named as electors. The original list of nominees was confined to 234 people; and, from the group, 29 received the required number of votes for induction. According to the rules of the first hall of fame, new members were added every five years. This process continued until the mid-1970s. In order to be included for enshrinement, a person had to be dead for ten years. Later this was increased to twenty-five.

Unfortunately, the original hall has become a non-functioning organization. The main reason that it fell on hard times was a lack of funding, and this can be blamed on the deterioration of its surroundings. During the 1920s and 1930s the first hall was able to attract as many as 50,000 visitors a year; but with the urban blight in the Bronx area the number of visitors fell to around 10,000 by the 1970s. The colonnade that was built to display busts of those elected is now a part of the Bronx Community College which took over the campus when NYU moved in 1973.

It would seem that with the early success of the first hall of fame, others would have quickly followed. Whether it was Cleland or Frick who first proposed the concept for baseball, both men were assuredly aware of the existence of The Hall of Fame for Great Americans. Long-time residents of New York City in the decade of the twenties, when hero worship was in vogue, both men had to recognize the success of the project even if they never saw it themselves. The genius of the establishment of the baseeball shrine lay in the fact that its originators applied the concept to sports.

Given the rising fame of the national pastime in the early third of the twentieth century, the success of the project should not have been too surprising. However, the application to baseball was visionary at the time. It may have seemed to be a natural idea and one that was bound to be successful, but there was no guarantee. In addition, the Baseball Hall of Fame would not have become nationally renowned without the inclusion of the museum. Nobody could expect over 300,000 people a year to visit a building full of plaques. Baseball, like no other sport, is a game built on memorabilia—either in artifacts or statistics. Cleland's original plan to house special items to be viewed by fans was brilliant in its conception and overwhelmingly successful in its application.

Although the baseball shrine was not the oldest hall of fame, it could lay claim to being the oldest existing one. The original hall has basically become a thing of the past due to lack of funding, which completely dissipated in 1977. However, the baseball one has some competition from the Helms Sports Hall of Fame in Los Angeles, which was founded in 1936. Although the museum in Cooperstown was not officially dedicated until 1939, its first year was really the same as the California organization. Since the baseball shrine has been more successful than its competitor, its impact on American culture has been far more widespread.

The Second World War slowed the process of applying the hall concept to other endeavors, but the growth of this idea exploded in the 1950s when the number of them tripled. Today, halls of fame have been erected to almost every endeavor known to mankind. Sports was the most natural area, and practically every phase of this aspect has been covered. There are halls of fame for auto racing, basketball, bowling, boxing, figure skating, fresh water fishing, college, Canadian and professional football, golf, hockey, horse racing, jockies, lacrosse, skiing, softball, swimming, tennis, track and field, trotters and wrestlers. Many colleges and states have local halls of fame for their athletes who rose to greatness.

Since sports figures are held in such high regard in North America, their deification should not be surprising. However, a wide variety of non-athletic endeavors have also been served by enshrinement. There are halls of fame for agriculture, aviation, circuses, country music, movie stars, cowboys, Indians, police, songwriters, and women. Sometimes the plethora of these establishments borders on the ridiculous. These include institutions for pickle packers, exotic dancers, piano tuners, numismatists and left-handed golfers.[24]

All of these shrines face two major impediments to their success—funding and collecting memorabilia. Since they were based mainly on the Cooperstown design, it shouldn't be surprising that they would share the same problems that Cleland did. The fact that he was able to attract any donations is rather surprising because people weren't used to the concept while the baseball shrine was being formulated. Players either didn't save their artifacts or they were often unwilling to donate them. Credit must be given to Stephen Clark, whose foresight and historic sense led him to give money to the institution when it needed it most. Major league baseball has also helped to ease the financial burden by continuing the practice of a yearly game in Cooperstown.

Although the Baseball Hall of Fame continued to spawn a variety of sister institutions in and out of the area of sports, it has had a more controversial legacy than any other. The dispute over the very nature of its existence in Cooperstown has continued to tarnish the image of the institution down to the present day. Did Abner Doubleday really invent baseball? Was it in Cooperstown? Did it actually take place in 1839? In the minds of most baseball fans, the answer to all three questions remained affirmative long after the hall was dedicated. The persistence of the Doubleday myth has both mystified its detractors and affirmed the conviction of its supporters.

The baseball shrine received some criticism before its dedication took place. The Cartwright family was perhaps the most threatening source; Frank Menke was the most damning. The Hawaii clan was too far removed and not recognized as a source of sports information to attract nation-wide attention. Also, Bruce Cartwright, Jr., the leading advocate of the family's claim, died about three months before the dedication day. Unfortunately for the Hall of Fame supporters, Menke's book continued to be published in subsequent editions. For example, in 1944 an updated version appeared which contained some minor, but nonetheless significant, changes to the original version. For one thing he included the Chadwick article, which had started the whole controversy and led to the formation of the Mills Commission. More importantly, he changed his mind on the evolutionary process. Previously convinced that baseball came from cricket, he now concluded that baseball "was not governed by any definite rules" in its crudest form.

The noted sports historian also made a case against the baseball centennial celebration. He viewed it as a publicity scheme designed to enhance baseball revenues during the depression. He concluded that someone merely stumbled on the long lost Mills report and decided it was the answer to their problem.[25] Although this was a convenient explanation, it denied the fact that Doubleday Field had been worked on as early as 1919. It also failed to recognize the hard work of Cleland and his associates who, while they were certainly interested in a profit, were also interested in promoting the Cooperstown museum for a social purpose.

The nation's interest in the national pastime was put off during the Second World War, but, following its conclusion, baseball captured the attention of fans throughout the country like never before. Tired from years of depression and war, Americans welcomed the opportunity to relax and enjoy their favorite sport. Accompanying this turn of events was a number of publications associated with the game. Many of them focused on the origin of baseball.

Leading the list of publications following the war was a book by Robert W. Henderson entitled *Ball, Bat and Bishop*. The author had already published an article on the origin of baseball before the museum was dedicated, but it was not widely distributed and had only a regional impact. Also, Henderson had more time to investigate the matter and, given his position with the New York Public Library, he was able to peruse a large collection of books, documents, and old periodicals. In the book's introduction, Will Irwin recognized the pioneer effort by Henderson in tracing original sources to document the evolution of baseball. He also pointed out that although Henderson had made a scholarly investigation, the Mills Commission had not. Irwin was well aware of the problems with the Mills report because he was the first person to criticize it in an article in 1909. Others had attacked the Doubleday myth based on observation and common sense, but Henderson's book was a scientific study that demonstrated the fallacy of an accepted story.

Henderson's work did nore than point out the errors of the Mills Commission. He began by tracing the origin of ball games back to the early Egyptians and worked his way up to the early nineteenth century. The author noted that a large number of bat and ball games had become popular at that time in England and France. He made a careful examination of the literature which described the rules of these games and noted how they began to be played in America. Gradually, the name "baseball" became the common term used to describe the contest, but it still lacked formal rules and uniformity. Before it had reached its final conclusion, even the Mills Commission issued a press release in which several correspondents described how they had played similar games long before Doubleday's alleged discovery.

Continuing with his research, Henderson traced the written documentation that was available at the time and noted that a manuscript entitled *The Boy's Own Book*, originally published in England, had also come out in the United States. This publication reprinted the rules of rounders which he felt served as the foundation for baseball. The American imitation, a book by Robin Carver entitled *The Book of Sports* and published in 1834, made one significant change— instead of rounders, the game was called "base or goal ball." Thus it served as the first printing of the rules of a game called baseball in the United States.

Having covered the origin of the rules of the early contest, Henderson turned his attention to the role of the Knickerbockers and the problems with the Doubleday myth. First, he noted the work of Alexander Cartwright as the prime mover in organizing the club that became the foundation of modern baseball. The question that remained was where did the Knickerbockers get the rules to play the game. Henderson pointed out that many people had made a case for the Wadsworth connection to demonstrate a link between Doubleday and the Knickerbockers. He was the man who had allegedly presented a diagram of a field to the New York ball club which they implemented. However, the author felt that the genesis of the team's rules came from the very popular books on boy's games, especially the one by Carver. Therefore, Henderson had laid out a case demonstrating how the game of baseball had evolved from the English game of rounders.

Henderson's final conclusions were concerned with the creation of the Doubleday myth. He demonstrated that a number of people in the United States in the late nineteenth and early twentieth century felt that the national pastime was strictly of American origin—including Albert G. Spalding. He outlined the baseball magnates' arguments with Henry Chadwick which eventually led to the Mills Commission and their famous report. Then Henderson began to explode the Doubleday myth. At first this seemed rather difficult because the vast correspondence that was received by the Mills group was destroyed by fire in 1911. However, Henderson was able to find copies of two letters written by Abner Graves. From these he was able to demonstrate certain inconsistencies between what the former Cooperstown resident actually wrote and what Spalding said he wrote. Specifically, this was in reference to the actual date of Doubleday's alleged discovery, the exact location of the first game, and the diagram that he supposedly made of the diamond. Graves didn't actually say that it was in 1839. He wasn't sure where the first contest took place, and he made no mention of a drawing. According to Henderson, all of these things existed only "in the fertile imagination of Spalding."

Henderson continued his attack on the Doubleday legend by pointing out more weaknesses. He noted that Graves was an old man when he made his claim and that almost seventy years had passed since the alleged incident. In addition, no mention of Doubleday's connection with baseball was made in the general's obituary which appeared in the New York *Times* in 1893. Given all of the inconsistencies behind the establishment of the myth, Henderson listed a number of things that the general didn't do. He stated that Abner did not invent the game, initiate the name, devise the diamond, allocate field positions, limit the number of players to eleven men on a side, initiate the practice of tagging the runner out, nor draw up the rules. He felt that to continue perpetuation of the myth would only serve to discredit an important American war hero and patriot. If baseball really needed a patron saint, he suggested that it should be Alexander Cartwright.

Henderson realized that it was only natural for a community to take advantage of a historical legend in order to promote tourism, but he was highly critical of the centennial celebration—which he labeled heavy exploitation. On the other hand, he commended the Cooperstown taxpayers for their public spirit and recognized that their efforts were undertaken in good faith. After all, the legend of Abner Doubleday had really been thrust upon them. Still, he felt that the people of the village had to make a choice between continuing the legend or accepting historical fact. Since the museum was established with the best of intentions, he saw no reason why it should not be maintained in the village. However, he believed that a major function of any museum was "to teach the truth" and to insist on "the perpetuation of an error" would lead to it becoming "a thing of ridicule."[26]

While Henderson's book was a damning condemnation of the Doubleday myth, it also influenced other baseball literature at the time. In his book *The Story of Baseball*, John Durant noted the research conducted by the librarian over a period of thirty-five years. He acknowledged the author as "the world's authority on ball games" and his book restated many of Henderson's findings. However, Durant felt that it didn't matter who invented the game; the important thing was the museum itself because it was a source of pride for fans throughout the country, and at that time baseball was still the only sport in the country to boast of a national shrine. Rather than condemning Stephen Clark as an exploiter, he recognized his role as a public benefactor.[27]

Disregarding Henderson's research, other authors continued to perpetuate the Doubleday myth. In an article for *Trailways Magazine* that appeared in the same year, Francis Howard made claims that completely ignored previous investigation. Perhaps Henderson's authoritative account inspired further research on the subject by Isable Kelsay, who continued to support the general. In the summer of 1938, the museum officials had requested that she look into Doubleday's background to see whether he could have been in Cooperstown in 1839. Almost a decade later, she produced a short paper in which she took the stand that no "reasonable person" could doubt that Doubleday had "played an important part in the development of modern baseball." She based this conclusion on her contention that the general was from a local family, that he went to a local school as a boy, and that the letters of Abner Graves seemed trustworthy. On this latter point, she emphasized that most of the people and places mentioned in his letters did exist and that therefore "there must be considerable truth in the statements about baseball which have been the subject of so much controversy."

Kelsay added more credence to her argument by stating that one didn't have to deny the evolutionary theory of baseball in order to give credit to Doubleday. She cited the fact that even Abner Graves contended that he made an improvement to town ball—an old game that youths in the area had been playing for some time. She also took exception to the criticisms that Doubleday couldn't have drawn the diamond about the time of the campaign of William H. Harrison for the election of 1840. While her earlier investigation proved that young Abner was in West Point in 1838, there was another factor to consider. Harrison was also a Whig candidate for the executive office in 1836, and Doubleday was sixteen years old at the time.[28] While she correctly noted that this would have made him just the right age, she did not mention that Graves was only two years old at the time.

In spite of Henderson's excellent research, the Doubleday myth had become too firmly entrenched in the minds of baseball fans to be destroyed. If doubters still existed, their skepticism was somewhat offset by the United States Senate. In 1957 Senator Jacob Javits of New York introduced a resolution to give federal recognition to the Baseball Hall of Fame. It stated that whereas millions of Americans had been involved in the sport "since Abner Doubleday conceived the first game of 'town ball' in 1839 in Cooperstown" and that the Hall of Fame had been established "near the site of the first game," Congress should recognize the shrine as a "fitting and valuable institution."[29]

Adding more fuel to the fire was William A. Rockstroh of Springfield, Massachussetts, who made a visit to the Hall of Fame in 1968. His grandmother on his mother's side was Mary Doubleday, the younger sister of Abner. He claimed that according to stories passed down to him from family members, there were certain connections between the Doubledays and baseball. For example, he stated that Abner's younger brother, Stephen, believed that he was the first person to use a homemade glove. Perhaps this was a necessity because he was a catcher as a youth. In addition, Stephen and his cousin Mabel Robinson claimed that they had seen a diagram of a baseball diamond among Abner's papers. Mabel's son said that he had those papers, but after he died the family was unable to find them.[30]

The confusion over Doubleday's role continued the next year while baseball observed another centennial celebration connected with the 100th anniversary of the first professional team—the Cincinnati Red Stockings. Acknowledging this historical event, *The Sporting News* also focused on the hazy beginnings of baseball. They pointed out that historians agreed that the national pastime evolved from British games and that Doubleday had nothing to do with its origin. However, they also recognized that the legend continued to persist and that major league baseball was making no serious attempt to discourage it. The publication felt that even though the myth had served baseball well, it detracted from the role of Alexander Cartwright. Still, they felt that it might well be a good thing that legends die hard because Cooperstown was a scenic spot and typical of villages where the game evolved.

Another article connected with the 1969 celebration appeared later in the summer. It completely ignored recent historical research. The author was Jimmy "The Greek" Snyder. He not only cited Doubleday as the game's founder but also claimed that Elihu Phinney watched the first contest.[31] His distortion of historical facts was rather embarrassing and a harbinger of things to come. Obviously *The Sporting News* editorial was more factual and carried more weight with fans, but even the baseball bible had not called for a repudiation of the myth.

The early critics of the Doubleday myth had emphasized the evolutionary theory of baseball, but they still had to find someone who had formalized the rules that became the foundation of the modern game. The most logical answer was Alexander Cartwright. But who exactly was this man and why were so many people ignoring his accomplishments in favor of Abner Doubleday? In 1969, the first edition of Harold Peterson's book, *The Man Who Invented Baseball*, was published. In part, this manuscript outlined the evolutionary process, but its greatest impact was to give Cartwright the credit that he had been lacking. Unearthing information on the former Knickerbocker that was previously unknown, the longtime *Sports Illustrated* reporter detailed Cartwright's family history, laid out his accomplishment having to do with the national pastime, and followed his path across the country to the Hawaiian Islands. More importantly, Peterson boldly stated that the Civil War general had nothing to do with baseball. As he so aptly phrased it, "Abner Doubleday didn't invent baseball. Baseball invented Abner Doubleday."[32]

Peterson had joined the ranks of Menke and Henderson as the official debunders of the Doubleday legend. The most surprising result of his book is that it had so little impact on the baseball world. He demonstrated that Cartwright's legacy was not based on superficial information nor the word of an obscure observer. Clearly, this man was more than just the father of organized baseball. However, no baseball officials were openly accepting Peterson's conclusions, and the vast majority of Americans continued to link Doubleday's name with the origin of the game.

Another critic of the myth emerged following the publication of Peterson's book. Victor Salvatore took up the cry in an article that came out three years later. His criticisms were far more caustic than his predecessors and were aimed not only at the museum's originator but also the building itself. He claimed that it was "one of the dullest, most unimaginative museums in the country."

His strongest remarks were reserved for Stephen Clark. He felt that Clark "was obsessed with the goal of putting Cooperstown on the map." He knew Clark well because he lived in the village during his youth. However, he didn't seem to have his facts straight as he claimed that the village leader gave "the baseball powers" a blank check to build the hall. In fact, it was the community who constructed it. Continuing his attack on the baseball shrine, he stated that "an historical fraud deserves...a tasteless mausoleum."

Salvatore never let up on the Hall of Fame through the years. As a retired newspaper editor, he utilized his investigative skills to uncover some information on Abner Graves. He pointed out that the retired mining engineer had killed his second wife and spent the last two years of his life in a sanitarium. He also stated that Graves' claim about the person who invented baseball might simply have been a case of mistaken identity. The former editor believed that there existed a cousin of the general who was also named Abner, and he may have been closer to the age of Graves. Salvatore also mentioned the correspondence written by Bruce Cartwright to the baseball officials concerning his grandfather. He claimed that nothing came of his letter because he died a few weeks after writing it.[33] Actually, Bruce's letters to the Hall of Fame were written over a two year period.

These later assertions reached a wider audience as they were broadcast on the CBS Evening News. Because of this, Salvatore became the target of much criticism. A newspaper editor from nearby Oneonta felt that he was being too harsh on the Cooperstown museum. Although he believed that Salvatore had found many holes in the Doubleday story, he felt that Americans "eagerly embrace any number of legends" such as Washington's cherry tree and Ichabod Crane's terrifying ride. The editor believed that Doubleday's alleged connection with baseball was an "uplifting tribute to the essential decency of mankind, and a quite appropriate falsehood to be preaching to youngsters." Another editor essentially agreed with this conclusion and felt that the museum officials "should celebrate the deception of 1905 without clinging to the myth as fact."[34]

The article by Salvatore also attracted the attention of one of Doubleday's relatives—Stephen W. Rockstroh of Port Charlotte, Florida. The retired Air Force colonel did not believe that he got all of the facts correct. Accordingly, he stated that "if he is going to kill a myth, he should do it properly." He went on to reveal how he grew up believing that Abner had invented the game. In 1960 he had begun to gather all materials he could find in order to write an authoritative biography. Through his research, he had discovered three main characteristics of the general. Being primarily a military man, Abner was intensely nationalistic, outspoken, and critical. In addition, the general was very family-oriented; and his relatives, in turn, were very proud of his accomplishments. Finally, he was not very successful in the self-seeking world of internal military politics. Rockstroh stated that his "many accomplishments seem to have been lost over a fruitless controversy over baseball."

Concerning his possible connection with baseball, the colonel pointed out that Abner could very well have been in the village in 1840. During June of that year he was granted a two-month leave from the military academy. Rockstroh assumed that he probably used the time to visit his father in Scipio, New York, and felt that it was inconceivable that he would have bypassed his relatives in

Cooperstown. However, he realized that Doubleday and Graves were not in the same age bracket and felt that the latter's story was clouded by old age. He thought that perhaps the former Denver resident confused the general with his cousin, Abner Demas, who was born in 1829.

Still, Rockstroh didn't admit that his famous relative had nothing to do with the national pastime. Much had been made of the fact that Doubleday had made no mention of baseball in his memoirs. However, the colonel pointed out that his writings also had omitted many other significant events of his life. He made very little mention of his experiences at West Point, his boyhood, his family (including his wife), or his acquaintance with Abraham Lincoln. Rockstroh felt that he "developed a cloudy impression of historical importance." He concluded that Mills, an old friend of Doubleday, saw an opportunity in the Graves' letters to give Abner "the national recognition he so richly deserved." He ended his correspondence with a quote attributed to Civil War historian Bruce Catton who claimed that while "skeptics have spent years trying to prove that the whole story is a myth...by this time baseball is General Doubleday's game and that is that."[35]

The fact remains that there is no reliable evidence to prove that Abner Doubleday invented baseball. The story of his supposed discovery lived only in the mind of an old western miner who made his claim sixty-six years after the fact. In modern times, the creation of the myth would be virtually impossible. The current media forms, with their tendency to expose the skeletons in every famous person's closet, would not allow this to happen. In an earlier and more innocent age, whatever was put in print was generally accepted as truth. Led by A.G. Spalding, the Mills Commission had planted the seed of the legend; the 100th anniversary celebration nurtured it and caused it to flower into fact. Without this significant ceremony and the publicity that accompanied it, many people today might not even recognize the name of baseball's alleged founder. Oddly, a celebration designed to recognize an important historical event had only helped to perpetuate a legend.

Epilogue

The controversy over the inventor of baseball continues into the modern times. The Doubleday-Cartwright debate has led to some friction between the two states which claim to have been the site of the first contest. Although Cooperstown has its plaque proclaiming the village as the cradle of the national pastime, Hoboken, New Jersey, is still touted as the place where the first official game took place. Citizens of that community dedicated a plaque in 1946 to commemorate the 100th anniversary of the Knickerbockers' first match game. Forty years later, Mayor Thomas Vezzetti objected to Governor Mario Cuomo about a proposed piece of legislation that would have allowed the phrase "Birthplace of Baseball" to be imprinted on New York's auto license plate. He cited as evidence the Elysian Field plaque which is located in a field near a Maxwell House coffee plant.[1] Eventually, it became a vanity plate that could be obtained in the Empire state for a fee.

It is easy to understand why the Doubleday doubters would cite Cartwright, Hoboken, and 1845 as the answers to baseball's origin. There are documents to support these claims. But perhaps they give the former Knickerbocker too much credit. Other members of the team shared in the development of the new game and its first organization. In addition, there is still the Chadwick argument. The best evidence does indicate that baseball was just another step in the evolutionary process of stick and ball games and that town ball was its predecessor. Even in modern times the rules are altered, albeit less dramatically. Strike zones have changed, mounds are lowered and certain pitches are outlawed. So evolution continues (as the word implies) and if the changes are too dramatic (like the designated hitter), purists cry foul.

The recent histories of the national pastime concur with Doubleday's critics and extend most of the credit for the game's beginnings to Alexander Cartwright. Donald Honig called the report of the Mills Commission a maker of "instant mythology." David Q. Voight claimed that "seldom in the history of ideas was a myth easier to track down." In an article by Andrew Wolf, the author doubted that "the truth is going to have much effect on the legend of Abner Doubleday" because generations of fans have grown up believing it" and revisionistic historians are not going to change their minds.[2]

Not only have academic writers found fault with Doubleday's alleged connection with the origin of baseball, but so also have a number of people associated with the Hall of Fame. Shortly before his death, Stephen Clark admitted that the evidence against Doubleday was too overwhelming. He declared "Nobody invented baseball...it grew out of town ball and rounders and things of that sort." Long-time Hall of Fame historian Cliff Kachline was quoted as saying that "if you're going to try and prove that Doubleday invented baseball...I have to admit, you're in trouble." Of course, the state of New York constructed a sign in the village proclaiming it to be the birthplace of baseball; but Dr. Louis C. Jones, director of the state historical association in Cooperstown, wouldn't give his endorsement to this claim. He stated rather humorously that the New York Department of Transportation "is the only group that still believe baseball was invented in Cooperstown."[3]

Although the critics continue to knock the Doubleday myth, it has not been abandoned by the Hall of Fame. Bill Guilfoile, public relations director of the institution, states that while the argument rages on, "until proven otherwise, we prefer to think that baseball was invented in Cooperstown." It's obvious why they would want to hold on to the myth, but why do so many baseball fans continue to cling to it? Richard C. Crepeau, writing on the game in the period between the two world wars, gave several reasons for its appeal. First, it gave the national pastime a national origin. Secondly, since it showed that a boy initiated the game, it made an important link between baseball and young people. Also, it made a strong patriotic connection between the game and an important American military hero. Finally, it gave the sport a rural origin as opposed to the urban genesis concerning the role of Alexander Cartwright.[4]

The central figure in the Doubleday story is, of course, Abner Graves. His credibility as a witness remains cloudy. The idea that a man living in the west, far removed from the seedbed of early baseball activity, could be the ultimate source of knowledge on the origin of the game does not seem probable. However, Graves is not unique in this regard. In 1886, *Sporting Life* published an account of a regional version of the game that was played in Canada in 1838. The author was Dr. Adam E. Ford, a former resident of Beachville, Ontario, who had moved to Denver, Colorado, following some accusations of his involvement in an apparent murder.

There are some curious parallels in the lives of Graves and Ford. Both had lived in Denver in the late nineteenth century and had been involved in a murder. Both were born in the 1830s in the eastern part of North America where ball games were quite common. More importantly, each man had a version of how these contests were conducted in his respective country. Their accounts were accepted by both the American and Canadian Baseball Halls of Fame as documentation concerning early ball games.

Recent research on Ford has established him as an accurate witness, and his reminiscences are therefore considered to be valuable. Unlike Graves, he was much closer to events that had transpired. When Ford's account was published, he had been away from Canada for only six years, whereas Graves left Cooperstown six decades before his story was released by the Mills Commission. Ford was seven years old when the Canadian game was played, and Graves was five when Doubleday's invention allegedly took place. Forty-eight years had passed between the contest Ford described and his publication; the similar gap for Graves was sixty-nine years.

More importantly, nobody has been able to determine whether Graves possessed a remarkable memory or an affinity for exaggeration. Given the paucity of information on Graves, one can only speculate. Certainly, Ford was more precise in his account—citing a specific date and location for the contest that he described. Ford was also more of a sports enthusiast; he administered sports clubs and was an active participant in cricket, baseball, curling, and shooting.[5] Apparently, Graves only had expertise in the latter.

Much has been made of the fact that Graves was labeled a lunatic after he killed his wife and spent the last two years of his life in a mental institution. This situation alone has caused the numerous Doubleday critics to cast doubt on Cooperstown's connection. However, the murder of Minnie Graves took place almost twenty years after Abner wrote his first letter to A. G. Spalding. So, Graves' mental health was not really a factor in the Doubleday story. He was obviously intelligent enough to carry on a lively business career into his late eighties. The fact that his first marriage was an apparent failure and that he murdered his second wife do not completely destroy his credibility. After all, Ford used alcohol freely, may have been involved in infidelity, and was interrogated in a sensational murder inquest. None of the these activities cast aspersions on his character in terms of witnessing early baseball-type games.

To evaluate Graves' story, one must determine what kind of person he was Certainly, the former Cooperstown resident was bold and daring. As a teenager, he wasn't frightened by a dangerous sailing venture around South America. Like many other western miners, he was all too familiar with the precarious nature of his occupation. Thus, he must have been a determined man to have stayed in this kind of work for such a long time. As a business man, he was aggressive and hard-working. He was also a man struck with wanderlust, as witnessed by his constant movements from the time he left New York.

Graves was probably hard to get along with. His business failure with his father-in-law could have resulted in some bitterness between him and the Dow family. His first wife left him out of her will and gave most of her wealth to her son, Nelson. This didn't stop Abner from borrowing the money for investment purposes, but he did pay his son back through his will. Given the vast difference in age between Graves and his second wife, he could have been somewhat of a womanizer or at least quite a charmer. Newspaper accounts of her murder indicate that he had quite a temper. He also had one thing in common with Doubleday. Outside of their childhood days, neither man had any apparent involvement with sports of any kind. However, Graves had to have some way of finding out about the Mills Commission or he wouldn't have written to Spalding. Therefore, he must have read the *Guide* of 1905, and this indicates that his interest in baseball or his role in developing its origin carried on long after he left Cooperstown.

Brave, adventurous, strong-willed, industrious, and hot-tempered, Abner Graves was a man whose conviction cannot be denied. Consequently, he was not shy about expressing his opinions. One of them concerned the origin of baseball and he probably voiced it on more than one occasion. A newspaper account of his wife's murder indicated that he was a shortstop in the first baseball game ever played. This story appeared in print almost twenty years after he wrote Spalding. It is safe to assume that since Abner kept on telling the story, he must have stated it to others long before he contacted the Mills Commission. Therefore, it probably wasn't an outright lie; he was simply reminiscing about his youth. This doesn't mean, however, that his memory was accurate. Certainly, he must have believed it since he was always so firm in his convictions. but it should be remembered that in spite of his resolve in this matter, he couldn't name the exact time and place of the first contest.

Why then should one believe that Graves named the right person as the inventor of baseball? If he were correct in citing Doubleday as the creator of a new game, how can we be sure it was akin to the national pastime? After all, he never stated the exact rules of the game nor drew a diagram of the field. As a matter of fact, neither did Doubleday.

Supporters of Doubleday would cite the Wadsworth connection which allegedly took place in 1845. Given the political tensions between Mexico and the United States following the annexation of Texas in that same year, wouldn't Doubleday have been involved in training for an unavoidable conflict? After all, he was fighting in Mexico the very next year. How much time did he have for drawing diagrams of baseball fields. Also, there is absolutely no proof that connects the general with Wadsworth. Even if Wadsworth did bring a sketch of a baseball diamond to the Knickerbocker playing field, no one claimed that he brought a set of rules. The Wadsworth connection is as weak as Graves' story.

Most of the critics have focused their attention on the person who was chosen as baseball's inventor, but many have ignored the time and place associated with the event. The Phinney lot was only one of three locations cited by Graves in his correspondence with Spalding, but it became the hallowed ground of the game's beginnings. After it was officially dedicated as Doubleday Field, the other two locations faded into insignificance. Correspondingly, the mining engineer did not pick a precise date of the discovery and listed three different years as possibilities. It was Spalding who chose the exact year and location that came to be common knowledge among fans of the national pastime. These possible inaccuracies that were published by the Mills Commission did little to lend credibility to the choice of Doubleday as the man who inspired the creation of the game. The possibility that Graves may even have confused Abner with another person of the same surname also clouds the issue. There are simply too many holes in the Graves story to lead one to conclude that Abner Doubleday invented baseball.

There is another problem. Many people feel that the original promoters of the Hall of Fame were simply exploiting the myth for profit. In the process, however, they were demeaning important contributions of some of the people who worked behind the scenes and possibly misrepresenting their purpose. The very idea to create such an institution was a stroke of genius, and many of the people who worked hard to make it come about probably believed that Doubleday invented the game. Why not? Even the President of the United States believed it. Most people still believe it today, and those who don't have benefited from scholarly research that has taken place over the last half century.

Some detractors have focused their criticism on Ford Frick for promoting a legend in order to bolster baseball's sagging economy during the depression years. Part of his job was to take measures of this nature. To ridicule baseball officials for creative entrepreneurship during the 1930s is to forget the degree of economic deprivation that existed in those bleak days. Virtually every industry in America felt the strain of the crisis and baseball was no different. However, the national pastime was slow to falter; it wasn't until 1931 that the economic slump hit ball diamonds across the country. The next two years were the worst. By 1932 baseball owners showed a net loss and the next year only two teams witnessed a profit. The initiation of the Hall of Fame and the centennial celebration weren't the only measures taken to offset these losses. A number of other ideas were proposed to combat business failures such as profit-sharing, inter-league games, reduction of player salaries, inauguration of a yearly All-Star contest and the introduction of night games.[6]

Others would point an accusing finger at the people of Cooperstown (and especially Stephen Clark) for resurrecting the Mills report for the economic gain. Actually, the village residents were slow to capitalize on it. The report first came out in 1908, and nothing was done about it for over a decade. In addition, the first steps to preserve Doubleday Field received more support from outsiders than from those in Cooperstown. More importantly, the man who initiated the shrine wasn't from the village. Even when Cleland first proposed the idea of a museum, he had at least as much social purpose as economic.

It is strange that more criticism was focused on the myth than the Doubleday baseball. The legend was really the byproduct of the Mills Commission and had nothing to do with the people of Cooperstown. The discovery of the ball, however, served to provide a missing link between Doubleday's alleged invention and the creation of the museum. If the ball were really a false creation and had no link to Graves, as Littell once implied, then the critics have a right to complain. Even today, however, the Hall of Fame only claims that it was preserved by Graves' family and that he was a schoolmate of Doubleday. Nobody will state that it was actually used by the general even though it has been labeled the Doubleday baseball. It certainly doesn't fit Graves' description in his correspondence to Spalding concerning the ball Doubleday used. The former Denverite said that the ball they played with was larger than the modern one, but the museum spheroid is undersized by comparison.

The most troubling aspect of the ball is that no one has ever been explicit about its origin. It is well known that the place of discovery was Fly Creek, located near the village, but who were the owners? Did they know that the ball belonged to Graves or were they just selling a counterfeit souvenir. Were they really related to Graves? If they were, why didn't local officials interview them or acquire Graves' trunk in order to search for more display items? According to local sources, a family by the name of Graves did reside in Fly Creek. There is the possibility that Clark and Littell merely assumed that there was a connection between Graves' ball and Doubleday because they took the Mills report as fact. Since the spheroid has become the focal point of the museum and the major physical link with Doubleday, the first Hall of Fame officials might have served accuracy by clearing up the matter.

If an ethical wrong had been committed, it had to be done by someone who realized the falsehood of Doubleday and tried to cover it up from the very beginning. The incident of greatest concern in this regard involved the museum authorities reaction to the correspondence from Bruce Cartwright. Many writers in the past assumed that the complaints from Hawaii ceased after he died. However, this assessment is not accurate. What is true is that the Hall of Fame investigated Doubleday's record at West Point, determined that he couldn't have been in Cooperstown in 1839, and immediately inducted Cartwright into the shrine and established a day for him during the anniversary celebration. Alexander Cartwright's elevation to the shrine was an indication to officials in Hawaii that the museum was finally acquiescing to their claims that the former Knickerbocker was really the game's inventor. It was this perception that led to a cessation of their complaints, and this happened more than a half year before Bruce died.

There are may questions concerning the circumstances surrounding Cartwright's enshrinement. First, who was responsible for his election? While it is possible to determine the membership of the veterans committee for other years in the prededication era, the year 1938 poses a problem. Since Landis, Frick, and Harridge were on the other pre-1900 group of electors, it is safe to assume that they were involved in the former Knickerbocker's election. Certainly Frick spoke with confidence concerning his enshrinement two years before it officially happened. Why not? Cartwright was considered by virtually everyone to be the founder of organized baseball, and Frick exercised a great deal of influence on the election process. But if he was so sure of Alexander's eventual election to the Hall of Fame, why was it delayed for two years?

The other critical issue, then, was the timing involved. It seems more than coincidental that Cartwright's election took place about six weeks after Stephen Clark initiated his investigation of Doubleday's background. During his acquisition of artistic treasures, he exhibited a sincere concern for history. Intelligent and sensitive to historical accuracy, Clark was not the kind of person who would ignore this issue. Without a doubt, he would have never financed the construction of the museum building if he thought the Doubleday story was false. But this investment occurred more than a year before Clark began to look into the general's career. Obviously, the correspondence that the Hall of Fame received from Hawaii was disturbing to him, and the questions it raised had to be dealt with. In many ways, his personal reputation was on the line, and it was necessary for Clark to have some verification of the Mills Commission report. Shortly after the investigation revealed that Doubleday couldn't have been in the village in 1839, Cartwright was elected. From this point on, it is doubtful that many of the officials of major league baseball or the Hall of Fame were totally committed to the Doubleday story. This was a complete turn-around of events. When the idea of a centennial celebration was first developed, virtually everyone involved accepted Abner as the father of the game.

The question remains. Was the action of those who elected Cartwright merely designed to pacify critics at a time when their complaints were both embarrassing and detrimental to the large investment that had been made by Clark and the major leagues? Obviously, the Cartwright backers were standing in the way of the major league plan to celebrate baseball's 100th anniversary. Clark had already made his commitment and (although the Cavalcade of Baseball had yet to be designed) by this time, the game's officials had set aside $100,000 for the occasion and hoped that it would help increase revenues. Neither party could back down now. It would appear that Cartwright's rather convenient election was merely designed to end criticism of the Mills report and destroy any opposition to Doubleday as the inventor of baseball. To do otherwise might have caused a situation that was both historically embarrassing and fiscally disastrous.

In the first half century of its existence, the Baseball Hall of Fame has received condemnation from skeptics who have actually attacked the wrong party. While the critics have focused their attention on Doubleday, Frick, Clark, and the people of Cooperstown, Spalding and Graves have conveniently been let off the hook. They were the ones who initiated the myth. Also, the doubters have failed to realize that if people like Cleland, Clark, and Frick hadn't initiated the shrine, it wouldn't be in existence today. Can you imagine baseball without a Hall of Fame? Unthinkable!

Whatever historical inaccuracies that may lie behind the formation of the Baseball Hall of Fame, it cannot be denied that the institution has well served the people of Cooperstown, the baseball public, and American society. The village has become a vacation mecca and richly deserves its reputation. If baseball weren't invented there, fans prefer to believe the game evolved form a bucolic background. A trip to Cooperstown enhances that dream, and nobody wants to move the shrine to Hoboken. Most importantly, the greatest legacy of the Hall of Fame is that it spawned a tremendous variety of similar institutions to honor people for excellence in their fields of endeavor. By setting up this method of recognition, halls of fame encourage Americans of all walks of life to pursue quality of the highest standards. In a very simple way, these shrines have helped to add to the development of the nation's pride and in turn have helped to create a class of people who pursue excellence in their work.

The fact that the Doubleday story was accepted virtually without question only highlights a national characteristic. Americans love simple answers to complex questions. How else could Joseph McCarthy thrive or Jim Crow become so readily acceptable? In the process of establishing apparent truths, we often create half-truths or un-truths. How much this affects us depends on the consequences of the story. Does it really matter if Washington didn't cut down the cherry tree or if Ruth didn't point to the area where he hit his famous home run? What, then, should we tell our children about Doubleday? If we say he didn't invent baseball, we should also remind them that he was an American military hero and that he never claimed to have started the game. If we say that he did invent baseball, in an age when most kids are growing up too fast, how much harm is created by interjecting some harmless fantasy? If our children buy a baseball card that cites Doubleday as the man who invented the national pastime, we could simply smile in agreement. When their youthful innocence has passed, we could gently suggest that he did not. Yet the story will not die and perhaps that's a good thing. After all, human imperfection is part of the game's romance, and we shouldn't destroy that.

Notes

Chapter One

[1]*The Sporting News*, June 22, 1939.

[2]Robert W. Henderson, *Ball, Bat and Bishop: The Origin of Ball Games* (New York: Rockport Press, Inc. 1947), pp. 168-69; John Durant, *The Story of Baseball* (New York: Hastings House Publisher's, 1947), p. 3.

[3]W. M. Beauchamp, "Iroquois Games," in *The Games of the Americas*, ed. Brian Sutton-Smith (New York: Arno Press, 1976), pp. 272-73; Ralph Birdsall, *The Story of Cooperstown* (Cooperstown, N.Y.: The Arthur H. Crist Co., 1917), pp. 8-13, 44.

[4]Harold Rosenthal, "The Summer Game," *The World and I* (No. 8, 1986), 174.

[5]Harold Seymour, *Baseball: The Early Years* (New York: Oxford University Press, 1989), pp. 7; Birdsall, *The Story of Cooperstown*, pp. 227-28.

[6]David Quentin Voight, *American Baseball: From Gentleman's Sport to the Commissioner System*, Vol. 1 (University Park, Pennsylvania: The Pennsylvania State University Press, 1983) xxvi, p. 8.

[7]Irving A. Leitner, *Baseball: Diamond in the Rough* (New York: Criterion Books, 1972), pp. 21-30.

[8]Peter Levine, A. G. Spalding and the Rise of Baseball (New York: Oxford University Press, 1985), pp. xi-xiv; Voight, *American Baseball, Vol. 1* pp. xxi-xxiii. Voight's introduction is an excellent essay on the leisure revolution in America.

[9]Levine, *A. G. Spalding*, pp. 75-76.

[10]David Q. Voight, "They Shaped the Game: Nine Innovators of Major League Baseball, *Baseball History* 1 (Spring 1986), 6-7; Jack Selzer, *Baseball in the Nineteenth Century: An Overview* (Cooperstown, N. Y., 1986), p. 3; *Spalding's Official Base Ball Guide*, 1909, pp. 7-9; *The Sporting News*, May 21, 1936.

[11]Levine, *A. G. Spalding*, pp. 7-8, 16, 99, 112; *Spalding's Official Base Ball Guide*, 1878, p. 5; *Spalding's Official Base Ball Guide*, 1881, p. 8.

[12]*Spalding's Official Base Ball Guide*, 1903, pp. 2-9.

[13]Durant, *The Story of Baseball*, 2; *The Sporting News*, May 12, 1938; Levine, *A. G. Spalding*, pp. 112-13.

[14]*Spalding's Official Base Ball Guide*, 1905, pp. 3, 9-13; Seymour, *Baseball: The Early Years*, pp. 8-9.

[15]Paul David Shubin, "Cooperstown U. S. A.," *Montreal Expos' Baseball Magazine* 8 (1976); Harry Paxton, "The Myths of Cooperstown," *The Saturday Evening Post*, January 30, 1960; Birdsall, *The Story of Cooperstown*, pp. 230-231; Levine, *A. G. Spalding*, p. 113.

[16]New York *Times*, July 27, 1975.

[17]*Spalding's Official Base Ball Guide*, 1908, pp. 47-48; Levine, *A. G. Spalding*, p. 114.

[18]*Spalding's Official Base Ball Guide*, 1908, pp. 35-49.

[19]Levine, *A. G. Spalding*, pp. 114-15.

[20]*United States Census for 1840 for New York*; Crawford County, Iowa Marriage Records; F. W. Meyers, *History of Crawford County, Iowa*, Vol. 1 (Chicago: The S. J. Clarke Publishing Company, 1911), pp. 440-442, 449, 451; *United States Census for 1900 for Colorado; Denver Post*, June 17, 1924, *Denver Post*, February 2, 1927, *Denver Post*, February 17, 1927; Abner Graves' Will, Denver Probate Court, July 7, 1921; Minnie L. Graves' Will, Denver Probate Court, July 7, 1921; Denver City Directory, Denver Public Library, 1921.

[21]*The Sporting News*, December 12, 1935; Alexander Cleland, *National Baseball Museum and Hall of Fame*, Cooperstown, New York, Alexander Cleland Collection (ACC), 1939.

Chapter Two

[1]Ford C. Frick, *Games, Asterisks and People: Memoirs of a Lucky Fan* (New York: Crown Publishers, Inc., 1973), pp. 78-79.

[2]*The Sporting News*, June 22, 1939.

[3]*The Sporting News*, April 25, 1956; New York *Times*, April 19, 1956.

[4]*Official Program of the Baseball Centennial Celebration*, National Baseball Hall of Fame Library (NBHFL), (Cooperstown, 1939), pp. 14-15; Ken Smith, *Baseball's Hall of Fame* (New York: Grosset & Dunlap, 1980), pp. 41-43; William J. Guilfoile, "Plaque to Commemorate Doubleday Field's Origin," June 27, 1986, NBHFL.

[5]Paxton, "The Myths of Cooperstown", *Saturday Evening Post*: New York *Times*, August 9, 1973; Oneonta *Daily Star*, July 1, 1986; New York *Herald Tribune*, February 27, 1964; Shubin, "Cooperstown U.S.A."; Staunton, Va., *Daily News Leader*, April 27, 1984; Robert Wernick, "The Clark Brothers Sewed Up a Most Eclectic Collection," *Smithsonian Magazine* (April, 1984), 123-129.

[6]New York *Herald Tribune*, July 8, 1954; David Houser, "Treasures Found in Grandmother's House," *Baseball Hobby News* (February 1984), 20; *The Otsego Farmer*, July 16, 1954.

[7]Alexander Cleland to Stephen C. Clark, ACC, May 8, 1934.

[8]Alexander Cleland to Stephen C. Clark, ACC, July 18, 1934; W. B. Day to Alexander S. Cleland, ACC, June 18, 1834; New York *Times*, August 8, 1936; New York *World Telegram*, August 8, 1936.

[9]Stephen C. Clark to Alexander Cleland, ACC, June 25, 1934.

[10]Alexander Cleland to Stephen C. Clark, ACC, Memorandum, N. D.

[11]Alton G. Dunn to Alexander Cleland, ACC, October 18, 1934; Alexander Cleland to Walter Carter, ACC, November 15, 1934; Walter Carter to Alexander Cleland, ACC, November 23, 1934.

[12]Alexander Cleland to Walter Carter, ACC, January 10, 1935; Alexander Cleland to Ford Frick, ACC, January 30, 1935.

[13]Ford Frick to Alexander Cleland, ACC, February 7, 1935.

[14]Alexander Cleland to Walter Carter, ACC, February 13, 1935; Walter F. Carter to Alexander Cleland, ACC, February 14, 1935; Alexander Cleland to Rud Rennie, ACC, February 27, 1935; Alexander Cleland to William Brandt, ACC, March 9, 1935; John Mimoch to Alexander Cleland, ACC, March 15, 1935; William Brandt to Alexander Cleland, ACC, April 6, 1935.

[15]*The Otsego Farmer*, March 1, 1935; *The Otsego Farmer*, April 5, 1935; Walter Littell, Notes on Meting of Doubleday Field Association, AC, April 10, 1935; W. R. Littell to Stephen C. Clark, ACC, April 11, 1935.

[16]*Freeman's Journal*, November 16, 1955.

[17]New York *Times*, April 13, 1980; *The Otsego Farmer*, April 12, 1935; Paxton, *Saturday Evening Post*, January 30, 1960, pp. 62-64.

[18]*The Otsego Farmer*, April 26, 1935.

[19]Alexander Cleland to W. R. Littell, ACC, April 17, 1935.

[20]Alexander Cleland to K. M. Landis, ACC, May 8, 1935; Alexander Cleland to Leslie M. O'Connor, ACC, June 4, 1935; Kenesaw M. Landis to Alexander Cleland, ACC, June 6, 1935.

[21]"Baseball and the Phi Psis Who Live the Game," *The Shield of Phi Kappa Psi* (Summer, 1966) NBHFL, 213-13; New York *Times*, April 10, 1978; *The Sporting News*, April 22, 1978.

[22]*The Sporting News*, February 19, 1977; *The Otsego Farmer*, January 24, 1936.

[23]Alexander Cleland to W. R. Littell, ACC, May 3, 1935; W. R. Littell to Alexander Cleland, ACC, June 7, 1935; Alexander Cleland to Ford Frick, ACC, June 14, 1935; Ford Frick to Alexander Cleland, ACC, June 6, 1935; Smith, *Baseball's Hall of Fame*, p. 46.

[24]*The Glimmerglass*, Cooperstown, New York, August 16, 1935; Alexander Cleland to Walter R. Littell, ACC, August 16, 1935; *The Otsego Farmer*, August 30, 1970; New York *Times*, August 16, 1935.

[25]Alexander Cleland to Walter R. Littell, ACC, October 10, 1935.

[26]W. R. Littell to Alexander Cleland, ACC, February 14, 1936.

Chapter Three

[1]Alexander Cleland to Roy Witmer, ACC, May 13, 1935; Alexander Cleland to William G. Dittinger, ACC, May 22, 1935; Alexander Cleland to K. Fickett, ACC, May 22, 1935.

[2]*The National League Bulletin*, NBHFL, September 1, 1935; Brooklyn *Eagle*, September 8, 1935; New York *Evening Post*, December 24, 1935; New York *World Telegram*, December 24, 1935; New York *Evening Sun*, December 24, 1935; New York *Evening Telegram*, December 26, 1935; New York *Times*, December 24, 1935; New York *Times*, January 1, 1936; David Quentin Voight, *American Baseball: From the Commissioners to Continental Expansion*, Vol. 2 (University Park, Pennsylvania: The Pennsylvania State University Press, 1983), pp. 132, 144; Robert L. Tiemann and Mark Rucker, eds., *Nineteenth Century Stars* (Kansas City: Society for American Baseball Research, 1989), pp. 45, 71, 108.

[3]New York *World Telegram*, December 31, 1935; Philadelphia *Evening Bulletin*, January 2, 1936.

[4]Thomas S. Shibe to William Harridge, ACC, January 13, 1936; Alexander Cleland to Thomas S. Shibe, ACC, January 16, 1936.

[5]*Spalding's Official Base Ball Guide*, 1936, pp. 7-13.

[6]*The Sporting News*, January 23, 1936.

[7]*The Otsego Farmer*, January 24, 1936.

[8]New York *Evening Post*, January 31, 1936; New York *Evening Telegram*, January 31, 1936.

[9]Charles C. Alexander, *Ty Cobb* (New York: Oxford University Press, 1984), 217; New York *Sun*, February 4, 1936; New York *Times*, February 2, 1936. For some excellent short histories of Hall of Fame players see Lowell Reidenbaugh, *Cooperstown: Where Legends Live Forever* (St. Louis: The Sporting News Publishing Company, 1983), pp. 49, 227, 251, 185, 127.

[10]William Brandt to Alexander Cleland, ACC, October 13, 1936; Alexander Cleland to Walter Littell, ACC, October 14, 1936; W. R. Littell to Alexander Cleland, ACC, May 29, 1937.

[11]Ernest Ackerman to Alexander Cleland, ACC, June 22, 1937; Alexander Cleland to W. R. Littell, ACC, November 10, 1937; William Brandt to Alexander Cleland, ACC, April 14, 1938; William Beattie to Alexander Cleland, ACC, February 1, 1940.

[12]New York *American*, January 20, 1937; Joseph L. Reichler, ed., *The Baseball Encyclopedia* (New York: Macmillan Publishing Co., Inc., 1979), pp. 1081-82; Craig Carter, *The Complete Baseball Record Book* (St. Louis: The Sporting News Publishing Co., 1987), p. 10.

[13]New York *Tribune*, January 25, 1937: *The Otsego Farmer*, February 5, 1937.

[14]*The Sporting News*, February 25, 1937.

[15]*The Otsego Farmer*, January 8, 1937; Tom Tilghman to Alexander Cleland, ACC, March 5, 1937; Joseph Jachin to Alexander Cleland, ACC, March 4, 1937.

[16]Horace J. Bradley to Alexander Cleland, ACC, December 29, 1936; Alexander Cleland to Horace J. Bradley, ACC, February 16, 1937; Reichler, ed., *The Baseball Encyclopedia*, p. 1596.

[17]*The Sporting News*, February 13, 1936; *Spalding's Official Base Ball Guide*, 1937, p. 21.

[18]*The Sporting News*, March 18, 1937.

[19]Smith, *Baseball's Hall of Fame*, pp. 47, 53-53; Voight, *American Baseball*, Vol. 1, pp. 23-26; *Spalding's Official Base Ball Guide*, 1938, p. 21; New York *World Telegram*, January 19, 1938; *The Otsego Farmer*, December 10, 1937; New York *Herald Tribune*, January 28, 1938.

[20]Seymour, *The Early Years*, pp. 77, 84; Bill Brandt to Alexander Cleland, ACC, January 5, 1938; *Jersey Journal*, January 1, 1938; *The Sporting News*, January 27, 1938.

[21]*The Otsego Farmer*, January 21, 1938.

[22]Jersey *Journal*, December 31, 1938; Smith, *Baseball's Hall of Fame*, pp. 54-55; New York *Journal & American*, January 25, 1939; *Jersey Observer*, January 25, 1939; New York *Daily News*, January 25, 1939; New York *Post*, January 25, 1939; New York *Herald Tribune*, January 25, 1939; New York *Times*, May 3, 1939. After the centennial celebration, the veterans committee relaxed their vigilance and did not pick another member of the hall until Landis was inducted in 1944 following his death. However in 1945 and 1946, they elected twenty-one ball players.

[23]*The Sporting News*, January 26, 1939.

Chapter Four

[1]For a discussion of the Peale and Barnum museums, see Charles Coleman Sellers, *Charles Wilson Peale* (New York: Charles Scribners Sons, 1969), p. 333 and Neil Harris, *Humbug: The Art of P. T. Barnum* (Chicago: The University of Chicago Press, 1973), pp. 33-37. *The Freeman's Journal*, February 27, 1935.

[2]Alexander Cleland to Jack Ryder, ACC, 1935; Jack Ryder to Alexander Cleland, ACC, March 14, 1935; Irving Wright to Alexander Cleland, ACC, April 19, 1935; Alexander Cleland to Julian Curtiss, ACC, December 14, 1937; J. W. Curtiss to Alexander Cleland, ACC, December 17, 1937.

[3]John T. Doyle to Keith Spalding, ACC, April 10, 1935; Levine, *A. G. Spalding*, pp. 70, 119; Keith Spalding to H. M. Lydenberg, ACC, April 16, 1935; H. M. Lydenberg to Alexander Cleland, ACC, April 22, 1935; H. M. Lydenberg to Alexander Cleland, ACC, May 3, 1935.

[4]*National Base Ball Museum*, ACC, n.d.; New York *Sun*, May 1, 1935; Smith, *Baseball's Hall of Fame*, p. 45.

[5]Alexander Cleland to Ford Frick, ACC, June 4, 1935; Robert W. Creamer, *Babe: The Legend Comes to Life* (New York: Penguin Books, 1974), pp. 384-400.

[6]Thomas S. Shibe to John T. Doyle, ACC, May 3, 1935; Alexander Cleland to Thomas Shibe, ACC, November 15, 1935; Alexander Cleland to Margaret Moore, ACC, February 26, 1936; *The Otsego Farmer*, March 6, 1936; *Spalding's Official Base Ball Guide*, 1937,

pp. 22-23; Alexander Cleland to George A. Reach, ACC, March 13, 1936; Margaret Moore to Alexander Cleland, ACC, August 7, 1936; Alexander Cleland to Margaret H. Moore, ACC, August 28, 1936. Both Reach and Shibe received museum folders at this time. Alexander Cleland to Thomas S. Shibe, ACC, March 10, 1935; Alexander Cleland to George Reach, ACC, March 10, 1935.

[7]Alexander Cleland to Clark Griffith, ACC, June 4, 1935; Clark Griffith to Alexander Cleland, ACC, June 5, 1935; Elizabeth E. King to Alexander Cleland, ACC, June 14, 1935; Alexander Cleland to Elizabeth E. King, ACC, June 19, 1935; Alexander Cleland to Stephen Clark, ACC, June 19, 1935.

[8]Alexander Cleland to Charles Mullen, ACC, August 12, 1935; Roy J. Miller to Arthur (sic) Cleland, ACC, August 19, 1935; Alexander Cleland to Roy J. Miller, ACC, September 10, 1935; B. O. Mussman to Alexander Cleland, ACC, October 15, 1935; Edna E. Voight to Alexander Cleland, ACC, July 15, 1935; Jim Barr to Alexander Cleland, ACC, February, 1937; Amy F. Bahr to Alexander Cleland, ACC, February 16, 1937.

[9]W. H. Dunbar to Alexander Cleland, ACC, June 19, 1935; Reichler, ed., *The Baseball Encyclopedia*, p. 833; Alexander Cleland to Joseph Connor, ACC, August 12, 1935; Joseph F. Connor to Alexander Cleland, ACC, September 21, 1935; Alexander Cleland to George Mulligan, ACC, October 3, 1935. Connor was elected to the Hall of Fame in 1976.

[10]Alexander Cleland to W. R. Littell, ACC, February 4, 1936.

[11]W. H. Dunbar to Alexander Cleland, ACC, June 19, 1935; Dennis Moore to Alexander Cleland, ACC, January 1, 1936; Jay Feldman, "The Rise and Fall of Louis Sockalexis," *The Baseball Research Journal* (1986), 39-42.

[12]Jesse Morrill to Alexander Cleland, ACC, December 18, 1936; Alexander Cleland to Jesse A. Morrill, ACC, May 11, 1937.

[13]*Spalding's Official Base Ball Guide*, 1937, p. 22; Mrs. Peter Elmendorf to Alexander Cleland, ACC, September 10, 1937; William Beattie to Alexander Cleland, ACC, September 16, 1937; Robert Taylor to Stephen Clark, ACC, August 7, 1938; Herman A. Schindler to Alexander Cleland, ACC, May 2, 1938; Alexander Cleland to Rev. K. H. Krenmyre, ACC, August 31, 1938; K. H. Krenmyre to Alexander Cleland, ACC, September 6, 1938.

[14]*Spalding's Official Base Ball Guide*, 1937, p. 23; William Beattie to Alexander Cleland, ACC, September 15, 1938; William Beattie to Alexander Cleland, ACC, December 30, 1938; *The Otsego Farmer*, February 3, 1939; *Spalding's Official Base Ball Guide*, 1939, p. 30; Leonard Baird, "The Shrine of Swat," *Town and Country*, XCIII (April, 1938), 54; Louise Stendel to Alexander Cleland, ACC, September 6, 1938; William Brandt to Alexander Cleland, ACC, December 10, 1938.

[15]William M. Earle to Alexander Cleland, ACC, April 3, 1938; Alexander Cleland to William M. Earle, ACC, May 10, 1938.

[16]New York *Times*, October 13, 1936.

[17]*The Otsego Farmer*, February 3, 1939; E. L. Robinson to William Beattie, ACC, July 26, 1939; Joseph B. Gunson to William Brandt, ACC, April 23, 1939.

[18]Alexander Cleland to Frank Crumit, ACC, October 3, 1935; John A. Hopper to Alexander Cleland, ACC, February 5, 1936; New York *Tribune*, March 2, 1938. A man named Dan Casey did play for the Phillies in 1877 and led the league's pitchers in earned run average. However he was a lifetime .162 hitter with only one career home run. Vidmer's visitor claimed that the expectations people had for him as a hitter came from the fact that his only previous round tripper had won a decisive game against Boston that year. See Reichler, ed., *The Baseball Encyclopedia*, pp. 1626-1627.

[19]Russ Hall to Alexander Cleland, ACC, July 16, 1936; Hubert S. Mumford to Mary Campbell, ACC, July 13, 1936; Hubert S. Mumford to Sarah Johnson, ACC, July 13, 1936; Hubert S. Mumford to Alexander Cleland, ACC, July 28, 1936.

[20]Ford Frick to Alexander Cleland, ACC, March 29, 1939; *The Otsego Farmer*, May 4, 1939; Carl J. Sturgis to Alexander Cleland, ACC, July 20, 1939; William Beattie to Alexander Cleland, ACC, May 29, 1939; *The Otsego Farmer*, July 21, 1939.

[21]Dorothy Putnam to Alexander Cleland, ACC, n.d.; F. H. Russell to Alexander Cleland, ACC, March 21, 1937; Charles W. Mears to Alexander Cleland, ACC, July 15, 1937; Alexander Cleland to Charles W. Mears, ACC, August 12, 1937; W. F. Coyle to Alexander Cleland, ACC, June 13, 1938; Alexander Cleland to W. F. Coyle, ACC, June 25, 1938; Alexander Cleland to William Beattie, ACC, October 25, 1937; *The Otsego Farmer*, April 28, 1939; News Release, ACC, n.d.

[22]E. T. Stevenson to Alexander Cleland, ACC, July 23, 1936; Alexander Cleland to E. T. Stevenson, ACC, August 12, 1936; E. T. Stevenson to Walter R. Littell, ACC, February 5, 1937.

[23]Tom Rees to Alexander Cleland, ACC, February 11, 1937; Tom Rees to Alexander Cleland, ACC, n.d.; W. G. Bannerman to Alexander Cleland, ACC, October 29, 1937; Alexander Cleland to W. G. Bannerman, ACC, November 10, 1937; W. G. Bannerman to Alexander Cleland, ACC, March 2, 1938; Alexander Cleland to W. G. Bannerman, ACC, May 10, 1938; Keith Tucker to Alexander Cleland, ACC, June 19, 1939.

[24]Alexander Cleland to Mrs. Christy Mathewson, ACC, April 15, 1935; E. T. Stevenson to Alexander Cleland, ACC, July 23, 1936; E. T. Stevenson to Walter Littell, ACC, July 29, 1936; Alexander Cleland to E. T. Stevenson, ACC, August 12, 1936; E. T. Stevenson to Alexander Cleland, ACC, August 31, 1936; W. R. Littell to Alexander Cleland, ACC, September 17, 1936; W. R. Littell to Alexander Cleland, ACC, October 16, 1936; W. R. Littell to Alexander Cleland, ACC, October 9, 1936; *Spalding's Official Base Ball Guide*, 1937, p. 22.

[25]Alexander Cleland to Walter Johnson, ACC, February 26, 1936; Alexander Cleland to Edward F. Balinger, ACC, June 6, 1936; Alexander Cleland to Norris O'Neill, ACC, June 6, 1936; Voight, *American Baseball*, Vol. 2, p. 4; Vincent G. Bird to Hubert Mumford, ACC, August 1, 1936.

[26]Alexander Cleland to Babe Ruth, ACC, February 18, 1937; Alexander Cleland to Napoleon Lajoie, ACC, February 18, 1937; Alexander Cleland to Cy Young, ACC, February 18, 1937; Cy Young to Alexander Cleland, ACC, February 28, 1937; Alexander Cleland to Cy Young, ACC, March 5, 1937; Cy Young to Alexander Cleland, ACC, April 4, 1937; Alexander Cleland to Cy Young, ACC, April 13, 1937.

[27]Alexander Cleland to Honus Wagner, ACC, February 18, 1937; J. Honus Wagner to Alexander Cleland, ACC, n.d.; Alexander Cleland to Honus Wagner, ACC, March 5, 1937; Alexander Cleland to Ty Cobb, ACC, June 14, 1937; Alexander Cleland to Walter Johnson, ACC, June 18, 1937.

[28]Alexander Cleland to Edward Bang, ACC, April 8, 1937; Ed. F. Bang to Alexander Cleland, ACC, April 12, 1937; Alexander Cleland to Tris Speaker, ACC, June 18, 1937; John T. Doyle to M. B. Reach, ACC, May 13, 1937; John T. Doyle to John B. Foster, ACC, April 13, 1937; John T. Doyle to Harry Hull, ACC, April 13, 1937.

[29]N. Lajoie to Alexander Cleland, ACC, August 23, 1937; Alexander Cleland to Napoleon Lajoie, ACC, August 27, 1937; William Beattie to Alexander Cleland, ACC, August 28, 1937; There is some confusion over when Lajoie's 3000th hit occurred due to earlier miscalculations. Actually, it took place in a game in Cleveland in late 1914. See J. M. Murphy, "Napoleon Lajoie: Modern Baseball's First Superstar," *The National Pastime* (Spring, 1988), 40. Tris Speaker to Alexander Cleland, ACC, August 30, 1937; *Spalding's Official Base Ball Guide*, 1938, p. 21.

[30]Alexander Cleland to Mrs. Christy Mathewson, ACC, August 30, 1937; Mrs. Christy Mathewson to Alexander Cleland, ACC, September 11, 1937; Alexander Cleland to Mrs. Christy Mathewson, ACC, September 29, 1937; Mrs. Christy Mathewson to Mr. Cleland, ACC, October 6, 1937; Alexander Cleland to Mrs. Christy Mathewson, ACC, October 13, 1937; Alexander Cleland to Mrs. Mathewson, ACC, December 2, 1937.

[31]E. T. Stevenson to Charles Young, ACC, November 4, 1937; Reichler, ed., *The Baseball Encyclopedia*, pp. 1122, 1374-1375, 2011, 2155-2156; Charles Young to Alexander Cleland, ACC, November 6, 1937; E. T. Stevenson to Tony Lazzeri, ACC, November 15, 1937. This was Lazzeri's last game for the Yankees, but not his last World Series. Traded to the Cubs the next year, he served as a utility infielder for the National League champions and had two at bats against his former team mates in the fall classic.

[32]W. R. Littell to Alexander Cleland, ACC, March 5, 1937; Smith, *Baseball's Hall of Fame*, p. 44-46; *The Otsego Farmer*, July 9, 1937; William Beattie to Alexander Cleland, ACC, March 31, 1939.

[33]John F. Clark to Alexander Cleland, ACC, September 21, 1937; *Spalding's Official Base Ball Guide*, 1938, p. 20.

[34]Hubert S. Mumford to Alexander Cleland, ACC, August 11, 1938; Alexander Cleland to Hubert S. Mumford, ACC, August 15, 1938.

[35]Alexander Cleland to E. R. Reilly, ACC, June 2, 1937; Alexander Cleland to E. R. Reilly, ACC, June 12, 1937; Mrs. W. L. Johnston to William Brandt, ACC, May 2, 1939.

[36]Ty Cobb to Alexander Cleland, ACC, August 18, 1938; Alexander Cleland to Ty Cobb, ACC, August 22, 1938; Ty Cobb to Alexander Cleland, ACC, September 24, 1938; Alexander Cleland to Tyrus R. Cobb, ACC, October 31, 1938; Henry P. Edward to Alexander Cleland, ACC, November 3, 1939; Alexander Cleland to Henry P. Edward, ACC, November 19, 1938; Ty Cobb to Alexander Cleland, ACC, April 29, 1939; Alexander Cleland to Tyrus R. Cobb, ACC, May 9, 1939.

Chapter Five

[1]Alexander Cleland to Roy Witmer, ACC, May 13, 1935; Alexander Cleland to William C. Dittinger, ACC, May 22, 1935; Alexander Cleland to K. Frickett, ACC, May 22, 1935.

[2]P. C. Fox to Alexander Cleland, ACC, June 13, 1935; P. C. Fox to Alexander Cleland, ACC, June 19, 1935.

[3]K. R. Thacher to Alexander Cleland, ACC, June 4, 1935; Alexander Cleland to K. R. Thacher, ACC, June 5, 1935.

[4]W. J. Adams to Fiorello H. LaGuardia, ACC, October 3, 1935; Alexander Cleland to Walter Littell, ACC, October 18, 1935.

[5]W. R. Littell to Alexander Cleland, ACC, October 20, 1935.

[6]Neil O'Brien to W. R. Littell, ACC, August 17, 1935; Alexander Cleland to Neil O'Brien, ACC, September 10, 1935.

[7]Alden E. Calkins to Alexander Cleland, ACC, August 31, 1935; Alden E. Calkins to Alexander Cleland, ACC, September 16, 1935.

[8]Alexander Cleland to W. R. Littell, ACC, December 27, 1935.

[9]Alexander Cleland to W. R. Littell, ACC, January 6, 1936; Alexander Cleland to Walter R. Littell, ACC, January 16, 1936; Alexander Cleland to W. R. Littell, ACC, February 4, 1936; Cleland made sure that Clark was aware of the picture of the first five selections by sending it to Mr. Main. See Alexander Cleland to Charles E. Main, ACC, February 4, 1936.

[10]New York, *Sun*, February 13, 1936.

[11]W. R. Littell to Alexander Cleland, ACC, March 5, 1936; Alexander Cleland to W. R. Littell, ACC, March 6, 1936; W. R. Littell to Alexander Cleland, ACC, March 7, 1935; Allan Regan to Alexander Cleland, ACC, March 9, 1936; Alexander Cleland to Bureau of State Publicity, ACC, March 10, 1936.

[12]Frank Graham, "Coming Events Cast Their Shadows," *Base Ball Magazine* (March, 1936), 443-44. Graham reported that doubts about the Doubleday story had led to the formation of the Mills commission when, in fact, the general's name did not surface until their final report was published; *The Otsego Farmer*, March 13, 1936.

[13]*The Otsego Farmer*, March 13, 1936; *Otsego Farmer*, July 1936.

[14]*Spalding's Official Base Ball Guide*, 1936, pp. 7-11, 30-33; Alexander Cleland to W. R. Littell, ACC, April 1, 1936; *The Sporting News*, May 21, 1936.

[15]Alexander Cleland to W. R. Littell, ACC, March 27, 1936; *Hobbies* (July, 1936), pp. 108-9; F. C. Lane to Alexander Cleland, ACC, July 13, 1936.

[16]Allan Regan to Alexander Cleland, ACC, August 28, 1936; Alexander Cleland to W. R. Littell, ACC, September 8, 1936; W. R. Littell to Alexander Cleland, ACC, September 12, 1936.

[17]W. R. Littell to Alexander Cleland, ACC, September 28, 1936.

[18]H. E. Adamovitch to Alexander Cleland, ACC, March 24, 1937; Alexander Cleland to H. E. Adamovitch, ACC, March 25, 1937; H. E. Adamovitch to Alexander Cleland, ACC, March 29, 1937. By this time the Chamber of Commerce stationary contained the heading "Birthplace of Baseball" and "Home of James Fenimore Cooper".

[19]W. R. Littell to Alexander Cleland, ACC, March 26, 1937; Alexander Cleland to W. R. Littell, ACC, April 2, 1937.

[20]William Beattie to Alexander Cleland, ACC, July 23, 1937; William Beattie to Alexander Cleland, ACC, August 25, 1937; L. E. Adams to Alexander Cleland, ACC, October 8, 1937; Carvel Nelson to Baseball Hall of Fame, ACC, August 19, 1937; Alden E. Calkins to Alexander Cleland, ACC, November 22, 1937.

[21]J. Roy Stockton to Bill Brandt, ACC, February 1, 1938; Alexander Cleland to J. Roy Stockton, ACC, February 4, 1938.

[22]Mary Sotos to Alexander Cleland, ACC, February 16, 1938; Alexander Cleland to J. G. Taylor Spink, ACC, February 18, 1938; Spink planned to use a photograph showing the exterior of the museum until Cleland supplied him with new ones. J. G. Spink to Alexander Cleland, ACC, February 13, 1938.

[23]*Time Magazine*, January 31, 1938; *The Otsego Farmer*, February 4, 1938.

[24]Richard Montz to Alexander Cleland, ACC, May 4, 1938; Miss Rusch to Alexander Cleland, ACC, May 4, 1938.

[25]Robert C. McKinley to Alexander Cleland, ACC, September 19, 1938; Alexander Cleland to Robert C. McKinley, ACC, September 27, 1938; Robert C. McKinley to Alexander Cleland, ACC, October 28, 1938; Alexander Cleland to Robert C. McKinley, ACC, November 19, 1938; Robert C. McKinley to Alexander Cleland, ACC, November 28, 1938.

[26]Donald F. Foresman to Alexander Cleland, ACC, April 14, 1938; Irene Bender to Alexander Cleland, ACC, October 13, 1938; Alexander Cleland to Irene Bender, ACC, October 14, 1938.

[27]Fred C. Seely to Alexander Cleland, ACC, February 4, 1938; Fred C. Seely to Alexander Cleland, ACC, March 9, 1938; Alexander Cleland to Clyde S. Becker, ACC, December 9, 1938; Alexander Cleland to William Beattie, ACC, January 2, 1939.

[28]W. R. Littell to Alexander Cleland, ACC, February 11, 1936; Alexander Cleland to N. W. Ayer & Sons, Inc., ACC, February 16, 1938; Alexander Cleland to Walter Littell, ACC, February 26, 1938; Owen C. Becker to Walter Littell, ACC, March 3, 1938; Owen C. Becker to Alexander Cleland, ACC, March 16, 1938; A. E. Lynch to Mr. Cleland, ACC,

March 28, 1938; Alexander Cleland to Owen C. Becker, ACC, April 14, 1938; Owen C. Becker to Alexander Cleland, ACC, April 16, 1938.

²⁹Alexander Cleland to H. Mumford, ACC, August 1, 1938; Hubert S. Mumford to Alexander Cleland, ACC, August 6, 1938; Hubert S. Mumford to Owen C. Becker, ACC, August 6, 1938; In this letter Cleland mentions the old letterhead that Mumford was still using which continued the phrase "The National Baseball Museum and Hall of Fame, Cooperstown, New York." They were in the process of producing a new one designed around the trademark which Littell was supposed to supply. Alexander Cleland to Hubert S. Mumford, ACC, August 8, 1938; B. Gold to Mr. Cleland, ACC, August 10, 1938; A. E. Lynch to Mr. Cleland, ACC, August 16, 1938; Alexander Cleland to A. G. Spalding & Co., ACC, December 2, 1938.

³⁰Alexander Cleland to W. R. Littell, ACC, April 19, 1938; W. R. Littell to Alexander Cleland, ACC, April 20, 1938.

³¹E. H. Leon to Alexander Cleland, ACC, April 8, 1938; Alexander Cleland to E. H. Leon, ACC, April 19, 1938; Alexander Cleland to F. C. Carpenter, ACC, September 7, 1938.

³²*The Sporting News*, December 8, 1938.

³³Alexander Cleland to Theodore Lettis, ACC, August 30, 1938; Alexander Cleland to Theodore Lettis, ACC, September 3, 1938.

³⁴*The Otsego Farmer*, September 23, 1938.

³⁵Alexander Cleland to Dr. Prince Danforth, ACC, November 26, 1938; Prince Danforth to Alexander Cleland, ACC, December 7, 1938.

Chapter Six

¹Alexander Cleland to Bill Brandt, ACC, June 5, 1935; Cleland felt that Abner Doubleday should head the list of inductees since he was the one who originated the game.

²Bill Brandt to Alexander Cleland, ACC, October 28, 1935; Bill Brandt to Alexander Cleland, ACC, November 15, 1935; Bill Brandt to Alexander Cleland, ACC, November 30, 1935; Bill Brandt to Alexander Cleland, ACC, December 3, 1935.

³William E. Brandt to Alexander Cleland, ACC, February 16, 1937; Alexander Cleland to William Brandt, ACC, February 19, 1937.

⁴W. T. Samson Smith to Walter Littell, ACC, October 12, 1937; Stephen C. Clark to Alexander Cleland, ACC, October 15, 1937.

⁵New York *World Telegram*, November 24, 1937. This same article was also published in the *Sporting News*, January 13, 1938.

⁶Alexander Cleland to W. R. Littell, ACC, November 10, 1937; *The Otsego Farmer*, January 1938.

⁷*The Otsego Farmer*, December 10, 1937.

⁸W. R. Littell to Alexander Cleland, ACC, February 26, 1938; Alexander Cleland to Walter Littell, ACC, March 5, 1938.

⁹W. R. Littell to Alexander Cleland, ACC, May 1, 1937; W. R. Littell to Alexander Cleland, ACC, May 18, 1938.

¹⁰*The Otsego Farmer*, June 3, 1938; *The Otsego Farmer*, June 24, 1938.

¹¹*The Otsego Farmer*, July 15, 1938.

¹²*The Otsego Farmer*, July 22, 1938.

¹³Alexander Cleland to Theodore Lettis, ACC, August 30, 1938; Alexander Cleland to Theodore Lettis, ACC, September 3, 1938.

¹⁴*The Sporting News*, December 22, 1938; *The Otsego Farmer*, December 28, 1938.

¹⁵*The Otsego Farmer*, September 23, 1938.

[16]*Minutes of the Organization Meeting of the National Baseball Centennial Commission,* NBHFL, n.d., Cooperstown, New York; Voight, *American Baseball, Vol. 2, the Commissioners to Continental Expansion* (University Park, Pennsylvania, 1938), p. 140; Walter R. Littell to Alexander Cleland, ACC, April 21, 1938; Alexander Cleland to Frank C. Carpenter, ACC, December 1, 1938.

[17]*American Baseball Centennial,* National Baseball Centennial Commission, NBHFL, n.d. There are actually two versions of this charter and although they are similar, there are some rewordings. Essentially they both cover selected areas and both were used in the writing of this section. The original charter also contained the names of the presidents of the American Bar Association, the American Medical Association, and the National Association for the Advancement of Colored People; but for some reason they were dropped from the list. The first design also included an Honorary Education Committee which would have included the president of the National Education Association, various college presidents, directors of the National Youth Administration, and the American Youth Commission and presidents of the Junior NAACP and the Athletic Coaches Association. Information on the March of Time comes from Ephraim Katz, *The Film Encyclopedia* (New York: Putnam Publishing Group, 1979), p. 775. The idea to utilize television as a means of publicity is rather innovative in 1938 since T.V. broadcasting didn't begin in London until 1936 and in the United States until 1941. See Robert A. Rosenbaum, *The New American Desk Encyclopedia* (New York: Signet, 1984), p. 1159.

[18]*The Sporting News,* February 4, 1953; Al Stoughton to Steve Hannagan, NBHFL, May 17, 1938; Information on Stoughton's background comes from a vita sent to Hannagan.

[19]Steve Hannagan to K. M. Landis, August 30, 1938.

[20]Kenesaw M. Landis to Alexander Cleland, ACC, December 10, 1938; Alexander Cleland to Kenesaw M. Landis, ACC, December 12, 1938.

[21]Alexander Cleland to Lester G. Bursey, ACC, December 1, 1938; Alexander Cleland to Al Stoughton, ACC, November 26, 1938.

[22]Alexander Cleland to Lester G. Bursey, ACC, December 31, 1938.

[23]Robert Oboski, *Bush League: A History of Minor League Baseball* (New York: Macmillian, 1975), pp. 4. 16-21.

[24]J. P. Corbett to Alexander Cleland, ACC, January 21, 1938.

[25]George M. Trautman to William Beattie, NBHFL, August 31, 1939.

[26]Al Stoughton to Alexander Cleland, ACC, November 18, 1938. This is the earliest correspondence between the Centennial Commission and the Hall of Fame, but it is evident by the tone of the conversation that the secretaries of the two groups had been in contact before this date. Alexander Cleland to Ford Frick, ACC, December 3, 1938.

[27]Al Stoughton, *Baseball's 100th Birthday,* Address before the National Association of Professional Baseball Leagues, NBHFL, December 6, 1938. Stoughton revealed that the National Commission had been incorporated as Baseball Centennial, Inc.

[28]Al Stoughton, Address to the Joint Meeting of Major Leagues, NBHFL, December 15, 1938.

[29]*The Otsego Farmer,* December 30, 1938.

Chapter Seven

[1]*Collier's,* May 8, 1909.

[2]Lowell Reidenbaugh, *The Sporting News: The First Hundred Years (1886-1986)* (St. Louis, Missouri: The Sporting News Publishing Company, 1985), pp. 6-7; Alfred H. Spink, *The National Game* (St. Louis, Missouri: The National Game Publishing Company, 1910), p. 54.

³Albert G. Spalding, *America's National Game* (New York: American Sports Publishing Company, 1911), pp. 19-26, 51-53.

⁴W. R. Littell to Alexander Cleland, ACC, June 7, 1935; Alexander Cleland to Walter R. Littell, ACC, June 13, 1935; W. R. Littell to Alexander Cleland, ACC, June 15, 1935.

⁵G. E. Staples to Alexander Cleland, ACC, October 11, 1935; W. R. Littell to G. E. Staples, ACC, October 18, 1935.

⁶Bruce Cartwright to Alexander Cleland, ACC, December 4, 1935; Alexander Cleland to Bruce Cartwright, ACC, December 18, 1935.

⁷Harold Peterson, *The Man Who Invented Baseball* (New York: Charles Scribner's Sons, 1973), pp. 91-93, 96-98, 100, 102-105, 57, 52, 1-3, 69-77, 109-113, 171-176.

⁸New York *Sun*, February 13, 1936; New York *Sun*, February 11, 1936; *The Otsego Farmer*, February 21, 1936. Wedge would later serve as the hall's librarian from 1950-51.

⁹Alexander Cleland to Bruce Cartwright, ACC, February 13, 1936; Bruce Cartwright to Alexander Cleland, ACC, February 27, 1936; Alexander Cleland to Bruce Cartwright, ACC, March 10, 1936.

¹⁰Bruce Cartwright to Alexander Cleland, ACC, March 20, 1936; Seymour R. Church, *Base Ball, 1845-1871* (San Francisco: Seymour R. Church, 1902), pp. XIV, 11, 5-6; Alexander Cleland to Bruce Cartwright, ACC, April 3, 1936; *Spalding's Official Base Ball Guide*, 1936, p. 9.

¹¹Alexander Cleland to Bruce Cartwright, ACC, May 29, 1936; Alexander Cleland to Bruce Cartwright, ACC, June 6, 1936; Bruce Cartwright to Alexander Cleland, ACC, June 16, 1936.

¹²*Spalding's Official Base Ball Guide*, 1937, p. 22; New York *Times*, April 24, 1937.

¹³John A. Hamilton to James A. Farley, ACC, September 4, 1937; John A. Hamilton to Alexander Cleland, ACC, September 9, 1937; Alexander Cleland to John A. Hamilton, ACC, September 24, 1937; Frank C. Carpenter to Ford Frick, ACC, June 1, 1938.

¹⁴New York *Daily Mirror*, January 6, 1938.

¹⁵*Time Magazine*, January 31, 1938; *Base Ball Magazine*, February, 1938.

¹⁶New York *Times*, April 11, 1938; Alexander Cleland to W. R. Littell, ACC, March 5, 1938; *The Otsego Farmer*, March 25, 1938. Cleland felt that Abner Doubleday also had a direct descendant in Cooperstown and thought that some local people should research the matter before the centennial.

¹⁷*Town and Country*, April 1938. For an account of the discovery of the ball see Smith, *Baseball's Hall of Fame*, p. 44. Alexander Cleland to W. R. Littell, ACC, April 1938; W. R. Littell to Alexander Cleland, ACC, April 20, 1938.

¹⁸Frank G. Menke, *Encyclopedia of Sports* (Chicago: George G. Renneke, Co., 1939), p. 3-6. The background information on Menke was published in this book a year after the *Ken* magazine article came out. In both publications, he debunks the Doubleday myth.

¹⁹*Ken*, April 21, 1938. The early 1880s was a time of numerous rule changes. Tradition had not yet set in and the various new additions brought the game much closer to the modern version. See Voigt, *American Baseball*, Vol. 1, p. 205.

²⁰*The Otsego Farmer*, April 29, 1938.

²¹John A. Hamilton to Alexander Cleland, ACC, March 18, 1938; Alexander Cleland to John A. Hamilton, ACC, April 19, 1938.

²²Bruce Cartwright to John Hamilton, ACC, May 25, 1938; John A. Hamilton to Alexander Cleland, ACC, May 27, 1938.

²³Ford Frick to Alexander Cleland, ACC, June 14, 1938; Alexander Cleland to John A. Hamilton, ACC, July 23, 1938.

[24]John A. Hamilton to Alexander Cleland, ACC, July 19, 1938; Alexander Cleland to John A. Hamilton, ACC, August 10, 1938; Alexander Cleland to W. R. Littell, ACC, August 10, 1938; John A. Hamilton to Alexander Cleland, ACC, August 24, 1938.

[25]Robert F. Doubleday to Stephen C. Clark, ACC, July 23, 1938; Robert F. Doubleday to Stephen C. Clark, ACC, July 30, 1938; Robert F. Doubleday to Stephen C. Clark, ACC, August 9, 1938. Robert was also able to find out that Abner had been appointed to the academy from the state of New York and that his father, a congressman, was probably instrumental in getting him an appointment. Robert F. Doubleday to Stephen C. Clark, ACC, August 4, 1938.

[26]William A. Saxton to Stephen C. Clark, ACC, July 27, 1938; Isabel Kelsay, ACC, July 30, 1938; Isabel J. Kelsay to Stephen Clark, ACC, August 2, 1938.

[27]Alexander C. Flick to Stephen Clark, ACC, August 2, 1938.

[28]Alexander Cleland to Stephen Clark, ACC, August 1, 1938; Smith *Baseball's Hall of Fame*, pp. 53-54. Smith claims that the same committee made the 19th century selections for 1937 and 1938. For the 1938 selection see New York *Daily Mirror*, September 8, 1938.

[29]Honolulu *Star Bulletin*, September 7, 1938.

[30]Bruce Cartwright to Alexander Cleland, ACC, September 13, 1938; Alexander Cleland to Bruce Cartwright, ACC, September 27, 1938; Bruce Cartwright to John Hamilton, ACC, October 18, 1938; John A. Hamilton to William E. Brandt, ACC, October 29, 1938; Alexander Cleland to John A. Hamilton, ACC, November 19, 1938.

[31]Robert F. Doubleday to Walter R. Littell, ACC, October 31, 1938.

[32]Helen E. Campbell to Alexander Cleland, ACC, November 7, 1938.

Chapter Eight

[1]*The Otsego Farmer*, January 13, 1939; Al Stoughton, Cooperstown Speech, Chamber of Commerce, NBHFL, January 5, 1939.

[2]*The Jersey Journal*, January 10, 1939; New York *Herald Tribune*, January 11, 1939; New York *Times*, January 11, 1939.

[3]*The Otsego Farmer*, January 6, 1939.

[4]*The Sporting News*, January 12, 1939.

[5]*The Otsego Farmer*, January 20, 1939; Steve Hannagan to the newspapers, NBHFL, January 17, 1939; Steve Hannagan to Al Stoughton, NBHFL, January 12, 1939; New York *Sun*, February 2, 1939.

[6]New York *Times*, February 8, 1939.

[7]*The Sporting News*, February 16, 1939; Les G. Bursey to Alexander Cleland, ACC, December 2, 1938.

[8]New York *Sun*, February 3, 1939; New York *Times*, February 3, 1939.

[9]Theodore R. Lettis to Alexander Cleland, ACC, January 28, 1939; Al Stoughton to Alexander Cleland, ACC, February 6, 1939.

[10]New York *Journal and American*, January 30, 1939.

[11]Murry Martin to Hannagan, Larry Smits and Stoughton, NBHFL, n.d.; Steve Hannagan to Larry Smits and Murry Martin, NBHFL, February 16, 1939; Murry Martin to Hannagan, NBHFL, February 20, 1939; Murry Martin to Al Stoughton, NBHFL, February 23, 1939.

[12]Stuart Cameron to Christy Welsh, NBHFL, February 27, 1939; Al Stoughton to Stuart Cameron, NBHFL, March 4, 1939.

[13]S. Allen to Frank C. Carpenter, ACC, March 6, 1939; Hugh M. Poe to William Brandt, ACC, February 13, 1939; Alexander Cleland to Hugh Poe, ACC, February 24, 1939.

[14]*The Otsego Farmer*, February 17, 1939 and January 5, 1940.

[15]*The Otsego Farmer*, March 17, 1939.

[16]*The Otsego Farmer*, February 17, 1939; *Buick Magazine*, March 1939; New York *World Telegram*, February 20, 1939; *Christian Science Monitor*, April 15, 1939.

[17]Nelson Greene to W. R. Littell, ACC, February 25, 1939.

[18]Al Stoughton to Alexander Cleland, ACC, November 18, 1938; Alexander Cleland to Ford Frick, ACC, December 3, 1938; Alexander Cleland to George M. Trautman, ACC, January 26, 1939; Al Stoughton to Steve Hannagan, NBHFL, January 9, 1939; W. G. Bramham to E. M. Daily, NBHFL, January 12, 1939.

[19]Alexander Cleland to George M. Trautman, ACC, February 10, 1939; *The Otsego Farmer*, February 17, 1939; George M. Trautman to Alexander Cleland, ACC, February 21, 1939; *The Otsego Farmer*, March 3, 1939.

[20]W. G. Bramham to Al Stoughton, NBHFL, January 28, 1939.

[21]L. H. Addington to All Sports Editors, NBHFL, n.d.; W. G. Bramham to Minor League Presidents, NBHFL, n.d.

[22]George M. Trautman to Alexander Cleland, ACC, March 1, 1939; Alexander Cleland to George M. Trautman, ACC, March 4, 1939; Philp O. Badger to Alexander Cleland, ACC, n.d.

[23]Harry E. Smunsy to Elmer M. Daily, NBHFL, March 24, 1939.

[24]Al Stoughton to The National Amateur Baseball Federation, NBHFL, February 19, 1939; New York *Sunday News*, March 26, 1939.

[25]Les Bursey to Alexander Cleland, ACC, December 22, 1938; *Spalding's Official Base Ball Guide*, 1939, p. 33.

[26]Passaic *Herald News*, January 25, 1939; William Beattie to Alexander Cleland, ACC, March 15, 1939; W. R. Littell to Alexander Cleland, ACC, February 1, 1939.

[27]John A. Hamilton to Alexander Cleland, ACC, January 30, 1939; Alexander Cleland to John A. Hamilton, ACC, February 1, 1939.

[28]Frank G. Menke, *Encyclopedia of Sports*, pp. 34-46; Spalding, *America's National Game*, pp. 19, 47.

[29]New York *Daily Mirror*, February 18, 1939.

[30]*The Sporting News*, February 23, 1939.

[31]Larry Smits to Stuart Cameron, NBHFL, March 2, 1939.

[32]New York *Journal*, March 10, 1939.

[33]*The Otsego Farmer*, March 17, 1939; Walter Littell to Alexander Cleland, ACC, March 11, 1939.

[34]New York *Herald Tribune*, February 6, 1939; *Otsego Farmer*, February 10, 1939.

[35]*The Sporting News*, February 16, 1939; New York *Times*, February 18, 1939; *The Otsego Farmer*, March 17, 1939; *The Sporting News*, March 23, 1939; New York *Times*, April 9, 1939.

[36]*The Otsego Farmer*, February 10, 1939.

[37]*The Otsego Farmer*, March 24, 1939.

Chapter Nine

[1]New York *Times*, April 18, 1939.

[2]*The Otsego Farmer*, April 28, 1939.

[3]*The Otsego Farmer*, April 28, 1939; Tiemann and Rucker, *Nineteenth Century Stars*, p. 135; F. C. Carpenter to Erwin L. Glenke, ACC, May 5, 1939.

[4]Steve Hannagan Memorandum, NBHFL, April 19, 1939; Herman A. Bloom to Elmer M. Daily, May 4, 1939; Steve Hannagan to Judge W. G. Bramham, NBHFL, n.d.; C. O. Brown to Leo T. Miller, NBHFL, May 6, 1939; C. O. Brown to Walt B. Powell, NBHFL, May 6, 1939.

[5]National Baseball Centennial Commission, "Play Ball America," ACC, 1939.

[6]National Baseball Centennial Commission, "What the Baseball Centennial Means to Our City," ACC, 1939.

[7]National Baseball Centennial Commission, "Why I Play Baseball," ACC, 1939.

[8]National Baseball Centennial Commission, "Baseball— America's National Game," ACC, 1939.

[9]National Baseball Centennial Commission, "How to Conduct a High School Baseball Day or Amateur Baseball Day," ACC, 1939.

[10]National Baseball Centennial Commission, "Extended Junior Baseball Schools," ACC, 1939.

[11]National Baseball Centennial Commission, "Public Baseball Clinic," ACC, 1939.

[12]National Baseball Centennial Commission, "How to Conduct Invitational Baseball Tournaments," ACC, 1939.

[13]Al Stoughton to Steve Hannagan, NBHFL, April 23, 1939; Al Stoughton to Steve Hannagan, NBHFL, June 5, 1939.

[14]The Cooperstown Centennial Committee, "The Cherry Valley Turnpike," ACC, 1939.

[15]*The Otsego Farmer*, May 5, 1939.

[16]Albany *Knickerbocker News*, May 6, 1939; Oneonta *Daily News*, May 8, 1939; *The Otsego Farmer*, May 12, 1939.

[17]New York *Daily Mirror*, May 3, 1939; *The Sporting News*, May 14, 1939.

[18]*Freeman's Journal*, May 24, 1939. Other major leaguers who once played in Cooperstown included Dave Fultz, Bill Lauder, Billy Mills, Bill Duggleby, Ted Lewis, Bill Bernhardt, Al Miner, Cy Seymour, Pete McBride, Leo Fishal, Myron Grimshaw, Arthur Madison, Bill Fox and a man named Gammell.

[19]*The Sporting News*, May 25, 1939.

[20]*The Otsego Farmer*, May 26, 1939; New York *Post*, May 25, 1939; New York *Times*, May 28, 1939; *Glimmerglass*, May 29, 1939.

[21]Nelson Green to Daniel G. Doubleday, ACC, May 5, 1939; *Otsego Farmer*, May 5, 1939; *Glimmerglass*, May 31, 1939.

[22]*Otsego Farmer*, May 2, 1939.

[23]New York *Times*, June 4, 1939; New York *Daily Mirror*, June 4, 1939; Minutes of Cooperstown Baseball Centennial Inc., ACC, June 5, 1939.

[24]Alexander Cleland to Theodore Lettis, ACC, May 17, 1939; Ramsey L. Black to Elmer m. Daily, NBHFL, May 26, 1939; *The Sporting News*, June 1, 1939; *The Sporting News*, August 17, 1939.

[25]New York *Times*, April 29, 1939; New York *Journal and American*, May 1, 1939; New York *Times*, May 6, 1939.

[26]L. G. Bursey to Alexander Cleland, ACC, April 25, 1939; *Jersey Journal*, May 25, 1939; F. C. Carpenter to Erwin L. Glenke, ACC, May 5, 1939; Alexander Cleland to John A. Hamilton, ACC, July 5, 1939; Steve Hannagan, NBHFL, n.d.

[27]Chicago *Times*, June 11, 1939; New York *Times*, June 11, 1939; Henderson, *Ball, Bat and Bishop*, p. 195; New York *Times*, August 26, 1939.

[28]*The Otsego Farmer*, June 9, 1939; *Glimmerglass*, June 10, 1939.

[29]*The Otsego Farmer*, June 9, 1939; *Christian Science Monitor*, June 9, 1939; New York *Journal American*, June 10, 1939. Actually DiMaggio had injured his leg and was unavailable for action.

[30]New York *World Telegram*, June 10, 1939.

[31]*The Otsego Farmer*, June 9, 1939; These two balls were evidently made of seal skin. The centennial publication that received wide distribution was entitled "A Nation's Shrine" and it was put out in two sizes for the convenience of the museum; Chicago *Tribune*,

June 11, 1939; *Glimmerglass*, June 8, 1939. The first cancelled envelope had already been produced by a special cancelling machine that had been brought into the village by George Knorline of the Post Office Department in Washington. Cooperstown Postmaster Melvin C. Bundy addressed the cover to President Roosevelt.

[32]*Glimmerglass*, June 5, 1939; *The Sporting News*, June 8, 1939.

[33]*The Sporting News*, June 8, 1939.

[34]For the best account of the June 12th celebration see Smith, *Baseball's Hall of Fame*, pp. 3-11; *New York Daily News*, June 13, 1939; New York *Times*, June 13, 1939; New York *Sun*, June 13, 1939; Chicago *Daily News*, June 13, 1939.

[35]Smith, *Baseball's Hall of Fame*, p. 12-22; New York *Sun*, June 12, 1939; J. G. Taylor Spink, *Judge Landis and Twenty-Five Years of Baseball* (New York: T. Y. Crowell Co., 1947) p. 241; *The Sporting News*, June 15, 1939; New York *Post*, June 13, 1939; New York *World Telegram*, June 12, 1939; Chicago *Daily Times*, June 13, 1939; For the story on Cobb's late arrival see Alexander, *Ty Cobb*, 1984, p. 218.

[36]New York *Sun*, June 13, 1939; *The Otsego Farmer*, June 16, 1939; New York *World Telegram*, June 13, 1939.

[37]New York *Sun*, June 12, 1939; Jersey *Journal*, June 12, 1939.

Chapter Ten

[1]New York *World Telegram*, June 14, 1939.

[2]*The Sporting News*, June 22, 1939. Evidently the centennial also helped to further historical recognition of important events. Lieb commented that due to Cincinnati's claim to be the home of the first wholly professional club, the city was awarded the site of the baseball winter meetings of 1939.

[3]National Baseball Centennial Commission, "A Nation's Shrine," ACC, 1939; Smith, *Baseball's Hall of Fame*, p. 49.

[4]*The Sporting News*, April 20, 1939.

[5]W. G. Bramham to Alexander Cleland, ACC, May 6, 1939; W. G. Bramham to B. G. Johnson, ACC, May 11, 1939.

[6]C. O. Brown to Elmer Daily, NBHFL, June 12, 1939; C. O. Brown to Charles H. Howe, NBHFL, June 12, 1939; C. O. Brown to J. J. Dunlevy, NBHFL, June 12, 1939; C. O. Brown to Claire Donnelly, NBHFL, June 12, 1939.

[7]G. S. Lannon to George M. Trautman, NBHFL, June 2, 1939; Ed Brooks, "Minor League Classic 'Doubleday vs. Cartwrights' " *Baseball Research Journal* (1981), pp. 87-92; *The Otsego Farmer*, June 30, 1939; Steve Hannagan News Release, NBHFL, July 1939; Jersey *Journal*, July 8, 1939; New York *Herald Tribune*, July 9, 1939; New York *Post*, July 8, 1939. Brooks says the umpires had 123 years of experience while the New Jersey newspaper claimed it was 135 seasons.

[8]*The Otsego Farmer*, July 14, 1939.

[9]Elmer M. Daily to George Trautman, NBHFL, July 14, 1939; L. H. Addington to All sports Editors, NBHFL, 1939; George Trautman to William Beattie, NBHFL, August 31, 1939.

[10]New York *Sun*, August 21, 1939; *The Sporting News*, April 14, 1940; *The Sporting News*, June 6, 1940; National Baseball Centennial Commission, "A Nation's Shrine," ACC, 1939; Al Stoughton to Alexander Cleland, ACC, August 10, 1939.

[11]William Beattie to Alexander Cleland, ACC, June 26, 1939; William Beattie to Alexander Cleland, ACC, June 28, 1939; *The Otsego Farmer*, September 1, 1939.

[12]*The Otsego Farmer*, September 8, 1939.

[13]Al Stoughton to John Doyle, NBHFL, July 28, 1939; Al Stoughton to Alexander Cleland, ACC, September 8, 1939; Al Stoughton to Steve Hannagan, NBHFL, September 12, 1939.

[14]John Doyle to Al Stoughton, NBHFL, September 16, 1939; Al Stoughton to John Doyle, NBHFL, October 5, 1939; *Spalding-Reach Official Base Ball Guide*, 1940, p. 8; New York *World Telegram and Sun*, January 10, 1951; *The Sporting News*, February 4, 1953.

[15]William Beattie to Alexander Cleland, ACC, October 10, 1939; *The Society for American Baseball Research Bulletin*, (July 1987), p. 8; *The Sporting News*, August 15, 1940.

[16]New York *Times*, December 7, 1939; Alexander Cleland to William Beattie, ACC, December 15, 1939; William Beattie to Alexander Cleland, ACC, December 19, 1939.

[17]*The Sporting News*, June 6, 1940.

[18]*Freeman's Journal*, November 16, 1955.

[19]*The Sporting News*, September 28, 1960 and also August 8, 1981.

[20]*The Sporting News*, April 22, 1978 and also February 19, 1977.

[21]Alexander Cleland to Henry C. Yoxall, ACC, April 20, 1939; Like most sources on this subject, Ken Smith gives Frick credit for the Hall of Fame concept. See Smith, *Baseball's Hall of Fame*, p. 46; Interview with Don Cleland, September 25, 1987.

[22]New York *World-Telegram and Sun*, July 8, 1954; New York *Times*, July 8, 1954. The *Times* obituary gives Frick credit for the Hall of Fame idea. Cleland was married twice—first to Hilda Johnson in 1904 and then to Alvilda Johansen in 1922. He had a son, Donald, and a daughter, Margaret, by his first marriage. For more information on Cleland see *The National Cyclopedia of American Biography; Otsego Farmer*, July 16, 1954.

[23]New York *Sun*, February 20, 1939.

[24]Thomas C. Jones, ed., *The Halls of Fame*, (Chicago: J. G. Ferguson Publishing Company, 1977), pp. 5-7, 31-32, 339-342; Leonard McGill, "Has America Gone Hall of Fame Crazy," *Cavalier*, n.d., NBHFL, 59, 63.

[25]*Honolulu Star Bulletin*, March 13, 1939; Frank Menke, *Encyclopedia of Sports*, (New York: A. S. Barnes and Company, 1944), pp. 56-61.

[26]Henderson, *Ball, Bat and Bishop*, pp. xvi-xx, 19-21, 138-196.

[27]John Durant, *The Story of Baseball in Words and Pictures*, (New York: Hastings House, 1947), pp. 3, 60.

[28]*Trailways Magazine*, Winter, 1947, 8-11; Isabel J. Kelsay, "Report on Abner Doubleday," NBHFL, December 6, 1947.

[29]Senate Concurrent Resolution No. 37, 85th Congress, NBHFL, July 3, 1957.

[30] William A. Rockstroh, NBHFL, May 14, 1968. There is no title to this document. Evidently someone in the Hall of Fame interviewed Rockstroh and made notes of the conversation.

[31]*The Sporting News*, April 19, 1969; Las Vegas *Sun*, August 5, 1969. In one of his letters Graves did claim that Phinney may have pitched in one of the early games.

[32]Peterson, *The Man Who Invented Baseball*, p. 7.

[33]*Patent Trader*, NBHFL, May 27, 1972; *American Heritage Magazine*, 1983, pp. 65-67.

[34]Oneonta *Daily Star*, October 17, 1983; *The Daily Press*, NBHFL, May 26, 1983.

[35]Stephen W. Rockstroh to *American Heritage*, NBHFL, June 19, 1983.

Epilogue

[1]Seymour, *Baseball: The Early Years*, p. 18; The Sporting News, May 5, 1986.

[2]Donald Honig, *Baseball America*, (New York: MacMillan Publishing Company, 1985) p. 3; Voight, *American Baseball*, Vol. I, p. 5; USAIR, September, 1985, p. 46.

[3]Paxton, *Saturday Evening Post*, January 30, 1960, p. 64; *Washington Star*, NBHFL, 1977; Kay Harrington, "Cooperstown, Jewel of the Otsego," *New York Alive*, NBHFL, (May/June, 1983), p. 53.

[4]Mike Bass, "Cooperstown, N.Y.—A Day at the Hall of Fame," *Yorshire Sampler*, NBHFL, July 13, 1981; Richard C. Crepeau, *Baseball: America's Diamond Mind*, (Orlando, Florida: University Presses of Florida, 1980), pp. 193-194.

[5]Nancy B. Bouchier and Robert Knight Barney, "A Critical Examination of A Source on Early Ontario Baseball: The Reminiscence of Adam E. Ford," *Journal of Sports History*, (Spring1988), pp. 75-90.

[6]Bill Rabinowitz, "Baseball and the Great Depression," *Baseball History (1989)*, 49-58.

Bibliography

Archival Resources:
Abner Graves' Will, Denver Probate Court, July 7, 1921.
Alexander Cleland Collection. Don Cleland, Las Vegas, Nevada.
Hall of Fame Collection. National Baseball Hall of Fame Library, Cooperstown, New York.
Minnie L. Graves' Will, Denver Probate Court, July 7, 1921.
National Baseball Centennial Commission Collection. National Baseball Hall of Fame Library, Cooperstown, New York.
United States Census for 1840 for New York.
United States Census for 1900 for Colorado.

Personal Communications:
Interview, Don Cleland, Las Vegas, Nevada, September 25, 1987.

Newspapers:
Albany *Knickerbocker News*, 1939.
Brooklyn *Eagle*, 1935.
Chicago *Daily Times*, 1939.
Christian Science Monitor, 1939.
Collier's, 1909.
Daily News Leader, 1984.
Denver Post, 1924, 1927.
Freeman's Journal, 1935, 1939, 1955.
The Glimmerglass, 1935, 1939.
Honolulu *Star Bulletin*, 1938-39.
Jersey *Journal*, 1938-39.
Jersey *Observer*, 1939.
Las Vegas *Sun*, 1969.
New York *American*, 1937.
New York *Daily Mirror*, 1938-39.
New York *Daily News*, 1939.
New York *Evening Post*, 1935-36.
New York *Evening Sun*, 1935.
New York *Evening Telegram*, 1935-36.
New York *Herald Tribune*, 1938-39, 1954, 1964.
New York *Journal*, 1939.
New York *Journal & American*, 1939.
New York *Post*, 1939.
New York *Sun*, 1935-36, 1939, 1954.
New York *Sunday News*, 1939.
New York *Times*, 1935-39.
New York *Tribune*, 1937-38.
New York *World Telegram*, 1935-37, 1939, 1951, 1954.
The Otsego Farmer, 1935-39, 1954, 1970.
Oneonta *Daily News*, 1939.

250   A Legend for the Legendary

Oneonta *Daily Star*, 1983, 1986.
Passaic *Herald News*, 1939.
Philadelphia *Evening Bulletin*, 1936.
Spalding's Official Base Ball Guide, 1878, 1881, 1903, 1905, 1908-09, 1936-39.
The Sporting News, 1935-40, 1953, 1956, 1960, 1969, 1977-78, 1981, 1986.

Books:

Alexander, Charles C. *Ty Cobb*. New York: Oxford University Press, 1984.
Birdsall, Ralph. *The Story of Cooperstown*. Cooperstown: The Arthur H. Crist Co., 1917.
Carter, Craig. *The Complete Baseball Record Book*. St. Louis: The Sporting News Publishing Co., 1987
Church, Seymour R. *Base Ball, 1845-1871*. San Francisco: Seymour R. Church, 1902.
Creamer, Robert W. *Babe: The Legend Come to Life*. New York: Penguin Books, 1974.
Crepeau, Richard C. *Baseball: America's Diamond Mind*. Orlando: University Presses of Florida, 1980.
Durant, John. *The Story of Base Ball in Words and Pictures*. New York: Hastings House, 1947.
Frick, Ford C. *Games, Asterisks and People: Memoirs of a Lucky Fan*. New York: Crown Publishers, Inc., 1973.
Harris, Neil. *Humbug: The Art of P. T. Barnum*. Chicago: The University of Chicago Press, 1973.
Henderson, Robert W. *Ball, Bat and Bishop: The Origin of Ball Games*. New York: Rockport Press, Inc., 1947.
Honig, Donald. *Baseball America*. New York: MacMillian Publishing Company, 1985.
Jones, Thomas C., ed. *The Halls of Fame*. Chicago: J. G. Ferguson Publishing Company, 1977.
Katz, Ephriaim. *The Film Encyclopedia*. New York: Putnam Publishing Group, 1979.
Leitner, Irving A. *Baseball: Diamond in the Rough*. New York: Criterion Books, 1972.
Levine, Peter. *A. G. Spalding and The Rise of Baseball*. New York: Oxford University Press, 1985.
Menke, Frank G. *Encyclopedia of Sports*. Chicago: George G. Renneke Co., 1939.
Menke, Frank. *Encyclopedia of Sports*. New York: A. S. Barnes and Company, 1944.
Meyers, F. W. *History of Crawford County, Iowa*, Vol. 1. Chicago: The S. J. Clarke Publishing Company, 1911.
Obobski, Robert. *Bush League: A History of Minor League Baseball*. New York: MacMillian, 1975.
Peterson, Harold. *The Man Who Invented Baseball*. New York: Charles Scribner's Sons, 1973.
Reichler, Joseph L., ed. *The Baseball Encyclopedia*. New York: MacMillian Publishing Co., Inc., 1979.
Reidenbaugh, Lowell. *Cooperstown: Where Legends Live Forever*. St. Louis: The Sporting News Publishing Company, 1983.
———. *The Sporting News: The First Hundred Year (1886-1986)*. St. Louis: The Sporting News Publishing Company, 1985.
Rosenbaum, Robert A. *The New American Desk Encyclopedia*. New York: Signet, 1984.
Sellers, Charles Coleman. *Charles Wilson Peale*. New York: Charles Scribner's Sons, 1969.

Selzer, Jack. *Baseball in The Nineteenth Century: An Overview*. Cooperstown, 1986.

Seymour, Harold. *Baseball: The Early Years*. New York: Oxford University Press, 1989.

Smith, Ken. *Baseball's Hall of Fame*. New York: Grosset & Dunlap, 1980.

Spalding, Albert G. *America's National Game*. New York: American Sports Publishing Company, 1911.

Spink, Alfred H. *The National Game*. St. Louis: The National Game Publishing Company, 1910.

Tiemann, Robert L. and Rucker, Mark, eds. *Nineteenth Century Stars*. Kansas City: Society for American Baseball Research, 1989.

Voigt, David Quentin. *American Baseball: From Gentleman's Sport to The Commissioner System*. University Park: Pennsylvania State University Press, 1978.

———— *American Baseball: From The Commissioners to Continental Expansion*. University Park: Pennsylvania State University Press, 1983.

Articles:

Bass, Mike. "Cooperstown, N.Y.—A Day at the Hall of Fame." *Yorkshire Sampler*. NBHFL. July 13, 1981.

Baird, Leonard. "The Shrine of Swat." *Town & Country* XC111, April 1938.

"Baseball and the Phi Psis Who Live the Game." *The Shield of Phi Kappa Psi*, NBHFL, Summer, 1966.

Beauchamp, W. M. "Iroquois Games." In *The Games of The Americas*, ed. Brian Sutton-Smith, 272-73. New York: Arno Press, 1976.

Bouchier, Nancy and Robert Knight Barney. "A Critical Examination of A Source on Early Ontario Baseball: The Reminiscence of Adam E. Ford." *Journal of Sports History*, Spring 1988.

Brooks, Ed. "Minor League Classic 'Doubleday vs. Cartwrights'." *Baseball Research Journal*, 1981.

Feldman, Jay. "The Rise and Fall of Louis Sockalexis." *The Baseball Research Journal*, 1986.

Houser, David. "Treasures Found in Grandmother's House." *Baseball Hobby News*, February 1984.

McGill, Leonard. "Has America Gone Hall of Fame Crazy." *Cavalier*, NBHFL, n.d.

Murphy, J. M. "Napoleon Lajoie: Modern Baseball's First Superstar." *The National Pastime*, Spring 1988.

Paxton, Harry. "The Myths of Cooperstown." *The Saturday Evening Post*, January 30, 1960.

Rabinowitz, Bill. "Baseball and The Great Depression." *Baseball History*, 1989.

Rosenthal, Harold. "The Summer Game." *The World and I*, 8, 1966.

Shubin, Paul David. "Cooperstown U.S.A." *Montreal Expos' Baseball Magazine*, 8, 1976.

Voight, David Q. "They Shaped the Game: Nine Innovators of Major League Baseball." *Baseball History*, 1, Spring 1986.

Wernick, Robert. "The Clark Brothers Sewed Up a Most Eclectic Collection." *Smithsonian Magazine*, April 1984.

Index

252